Advance P

Advising Lesbian, (
Queer (

"This text is certain to transform the ....ering on the needs and experiences of LGBTQA college ... Combining a deep focus on theoretical concepts with reflection opportunities and vignettes along the way to make connections to practice, the book is a must-read for advisors as they seek to support LGBTQA students on college campuses."—**Antonio Duran**, *Assistant Professor, Administration of Higher Education, Auburn University*

"Drs. McGill and Joslin created this exciting new resource for department advisors and student affairs staff as well as higher ed faculty and graduate students. Advisors in every area of campus must be aware of issues unique to LGBTQ students and how these issues affect students' ability to persist to graduation. This important work offers LGBTQ historical foundations and holistic ways of providing informed services for LGBTQ students. It invites not only thought and emotion but also action to create an enduring connection that furthers student development."—**Ronni Sanlo**, *Founder, Lavender Graduation*

"This groundbreaking book comes at a time when academic advisors are becoming increasingly aware of the unique challenges that marginalized students face in institutions of higher learning. With specific chapters devoted to the discussion of intersectionality and the practice of advising LGBTQ student athletes, STEM majors, and international students, this book serves as an essential tool to bettering advising practice and ensuring that academic advisors have the competencies and the perspectives needed to be strong advocates for their students. This book contains chapters written by regarded experts in the fields of advising and queer studies and is intentional about centering the voices of LGBTQ+ allies through the various Ally Narratives written throughout. Simply a must-read for anyone involved in the practice and/or research of academic advising."—**Kyler J. Sherman-Wilkins**, *Assistant Professor of Sociology, Missouri State University*

ADVISING LESBIAN, GAY, BISEXUAL,
TRANSGENDER, AND QUEER COLLEGE STUDENTS

Forthcoming Titles from NACADA: The Global Community for Academic Advising

Comprehensive Advisor Training and Development: Practices That Deliver, 3rd Edition

Scholarly Inquiry In Academic Advising, 2nd Edition

Academic Advising Administration: Essential Knowledge and Skills for the 21st Century, 2nd Edition

ADVISING LESBIAN, GAY, BISEXUAL, TRANSGENDER, AND QUEER COLLEGE STUDENTS

Edited by Craig M. McGill and
Jennifer E. Joslin

Foreword by Kristen A. Renn

STERLING, VIRGINIA

Published by Stylus Publishing, LLC.
22883 Quicksilver Drive
Sterling, Virginia 20166-2019

Library of Congress Cataloging-in-Publication Data

Names: McGill, Craig M., editor. | Joslin, Jennifer, editor. | Renn, Kristen A., author of foreword.

Title: Advising lesbian, gay, bisexual, transgender, and queer college students / edited by Craig M. McGill and Jennifer E. Joslin ; foreword by Kristen A. Renn.

Description: First Edition. | Sterling, Virginia : Stylus., [2021] | "NACADA The Global Community of Academic Advising." | Includes bibliographical references and index. | Summary: "In the face of hostile campus cultures, LGBTQA students rely on knowledgeable academic advisors for support, nurturance, and the resources needed to support their persistence. This edited collection offers theoretical understanding of the literature of the field, practical strategies that can be implemented at different institutions, and best practices that helps students, staff, and faculty members understand more deeply the challenges and rewards of working constructively with LGBTQA students"-- Provided by publisher.

Identifiers: LCCN 2021027225 (print) | LCCN 2021027226 (ebook) | ISBN 9781642671766 (Cloth : acid-free paper) | ISBN 9781642671773 (Paperback : acid-free paper) | ISBN 9781642671780 (Llibrary Networkable e-Edition) | ISBN 9781642671797 (Consumer e-Edition)

Subjects: LCSH: Sexual minority college students--Services for--United States. | Counseling in higher education--United States. | Faculty advisors.

Classification: LCC LC2574.6 .A39 2021 (print) | LCC LC2574.6 (ebook) | DDC 378.1/98266--dc23

LC record available at https://lccn.loc.gov/2021027225

LC ebook record available at https://lccn.loc.gov/2021027226

13-digit ISBN: 978-1-64267-176-6 (cloth)
13-digit ISBN: 978-1-64267-177-3 (paperback)
13-digit ISBN: 978-1-64267-178-0 (library networkable e-edition)
13-digit ISBN: 978-1-64267-179-7 (consumer e-edition)

Printed in the United States of America

All first editions printed on acid-free paper
that meets the American National Standards Institute
Z39-48 Standard.

Bulk Purchases
Quantity discounts are available for use in workshops and
for staff development.
Call 1-800-232-0223

First Edition, 2021

We dedicate this book to all the students who fight like hell to be recognized and valued. You work tirelessly to make your campuses safe.

CONTENTS

PART TWO: CAMPUS ISSUES AND ADVISING APPROACHES

    RETENTION NARRATIVES   79
    Jennifer E. Joslin

7   LGBTQA+ STUDENTS AND CAREER ADVISING   89
    Carolyn Meeker, Richard A. Sprott, and Craig M. McGill

    CONVERSATIONS: CAREER ADVISING FOR LGBTQA+
    STUDENTS IN NONLINEAR CAREER PATHS   110
    erin donahoe-rankin and Ashley Glenn

8   LGBTQA+ STUDENTS AND MENTAL HEALTH   118
    kristen a. langellier and Jennifer M. Gess

9   ADVISING LGBTQA+ STUDENTS AT CHRISTIAN-BASED
    INSTITUTIONS   138
    Natalie S. Oliner

10 PROVIDING SUPPORT TO LGBTQA+ STUDENTS WHO
    HAVE EXPERIENCED SEXUAL VIOLENCE AND INTIMATE
    PARTNER VIOLENCE   160
    Ryan Fette and Pat Tetreault

    ALLY NARRATIVE   176
    Janie Valdés

    ALLY NARRATIVE   178
    Cody Harrison

PART THREE: ADVISING LGBTQA+ STUDENT POPULATIONS

My major advisor. Yeah, she was the person who really got me through the hard times when I stopped believing I should be here—like I should be here in college or I should be here on earth, at all. I go to her office and we can talk about my classes, but also she helped me find people in other offices. She can pick up the phone and call someone on campus, then she'll say to me, "Go see this person. You can trust them." So I know that my being [gender] non-binary isn't going to freak them out, or they're not going to misgender me. Because of my advisor, I've got a lot of people here who have my back. And that's made a big difference. Yeah. My advisor. She's the one. (Excerpt from an interview with a transgender college senior)

The academic advising profession has never been more important in higher education. At community colleges, liberal arts colleges, regional comprehensive institutions, and large research universities, thousands of faculty advisors and professional academic advisors have become a critical connection point for success in student learning, development, persistence, transfer, and degree completion. For many students, an advisor not only provides helpful institutional and educational guidance but also thoughtful engagement in conversations about educational and career goals. Specifically, for low-income and first-generation students and those students minoritized by race, gender, or sexual orientation, an advisor can be a cornerstone of support for navigating a higher education system that was not designed with them in mind. For lesbian, gay, bisexual, transgender, queer, and asexual/allies (LGBTQA+) students, academic advisors may be a source of encouragement and identity acceptance, a guide to connections to other campus and community resources, and a person ever in their corner, rooting for their success.

Although obstacles to LGBTQA+ student success are well-documented through campus climate studies (see Greathouse et al., 2018 for a synthesis of several major national studies) and research on LGBTQA+ college students (Mathies et al., 2019), there is also research on LGBTQA+ student thriving (Hill et al., 2020). This research points to the ways students engage with faculty members, administrators, and peers to create successful academic, social, and leadership pathways. In fact, the influence of caring, well-informed instructors, advisors, counselors, and mentors is a detectable theme across the literature. These individuals can bolster a positive campus climate or create a buffer in a less welcoming climate. On a larger scale, they participate as staff members in conversations about campus policies and programs that have the potential to shift the entire institution in the direction of equity for LGBTQA+ and other minoritized students.

As noted in the literature and as is evident in the opening quote from a transgender student in a research interview, on a relational level, academic advisors can be guides for connecting LGBTQA+ students to other supportive individuals across campus. Advisors can do this by knowing someone in financial aid who can talk with students whose parents are threatening to cut off financial support, by identifying staff members in the counseling center who are not only affirming but also knowledgeable about issues transgender students face, and by guiding students to undergraduate research opportunities with faculty members doing LGBTQA+-related projects.

As the chapters in this book reveal, being an ally goes a long way in supporting LGBTQA+ students, as does equipping oneself with knowledge about LGBTQA+ students, their identities, and considerations for their well-being. Additionally, activating allies is a powerful strategy for improving the quality of campus life and academic advising for LGBTQA+ students.

Regardless of institution type (e.g., public, private, for-profit, religiously affiliated) and regional attitudes about LGBTQA+ issues, every academic advisor in higher education serves LGBTQA+ students because LGBTQA+ students are in every major and transfer pathway program. Therefore, every academic advisor has a part to play in their success.

This book provides insight, inspiration, and instruction for this important work. The first section provides background on some concepts that have developed substantially over the past decade and which can feel intimidating to learn on one's own (e.g., queer theory, intersectionality). The fear of getting something wrong holds some potential allies back, but the information thoughtfully distilled in this section—as well as in the ally narratives—creates a solid foundation for working with diverse LGBTQA+ students.

Part Two, "Campus Issues and Advising Approaches" illuminates specific aspects of advising LGBTQA+ students by putting the advising process in discussion with other campus contexts. This section illustrates that academic advisors are key parts of campus-wide networks of support, guidance, and enrichment. It is also made clear in this section that LGBTQA+ students are just like other students; they think about staying or leaving, contemplate careers and what they will do after college, cope with challenges to well-being, and sometimes are survivors of sexual violence and intimate partner violence. Furthermore, Natalie Oliner's chapter (chapter 9) offers insight into advising LGBTQA+ students at religious institutions, offering an important addition to advising literature and to literature on Christian higher education.

Part Three, "Advising LGBTQA+ Student Populations," introduces additional specificity for advising students from sub-populations. Some academic advisors will work in contexts like athletics or STEM departments and these chapters identify issues specific to these areas. However, attention to trans students, international LGBTQA+ students, and queer and trans students of color are valuable to advisors in any campus context.

Part Four, "Creating Inclusive Spaces," features the "big picture" work of academic advisors becoming allies and advocates in an effort to create an LGBTQA-inclusive campus. This balance of student advising with ally and leadership roles for campus transformation highlights the multiple opportunities advisors have to make a difference in the lives of LGBTQA+ students. Academic advisors are positioned to span these roles, and LGBTQA+ students, like the one featured in the opening quote, need their advisors to seize this opportunity to make higher education more inclusive for all students, regardless of gender and sexual orientation identities.

—Kristen A. Renn
Michigan State University

References

Greathouse, M., BrckaLorenz, A., Hoban, M., Hueman Jr., R., Rankin, S. Stolzenberg, E. B. (2018). *Queer-spectrum and trans-spectrum student experiences in American higher education: The analyses of national survey findings.* Tyler Clementi Center, Rutgers University. New Brunswick, NJ. https://tcc-j2made.s3.amazonaws.com/uploads/2018/09/White-Paper-Final.pdf

Hill, R. L., Kilgo, C. A., Shea, H. D., Nguyen, D. J., Lange, A. C., Renn, K. A., & Woodford, M. R. (2020, April 21). How LGBTQ+ students thrive in college. *Journal of Student Affairs Research and Practice.* https://doi.org/10.1080/19496591.2020.1738241

Mathies, N., Coleman, T., McKie, R. M., Woodford, M. R., Courtice, E. L., Travers, R., & Renn, K. A. (2019). The effects of hearing "That's so gay" and "No homo" on academic outcomes for LGB college students. *Journal of LGBT Youth, 16*(3), 255–277. https://doi.org/10.1080/19361653.2019.1571981

ACKNOWLEDGMENTS

We heartily thank the team of LGBTQA+ authors who contributed brilliant chapters to this book; they asked provocative questions and raised significant issues that moved this book forward. This book would just be a great idea without each and every author who worked during the most difficult time in living memory. Their contributions during a time of upheaval and global pandemic are unprecedented. We pray that at the time of publication we are all well and safe.

We acknowledge the support we received from our supervisors and workplaces during the writing and editing of this book. I (Jennifer) thank NACADA and Drury University for your unwavering support. I (Craig) thank Florida International University, the University of South Dakota, and Kansas State University. We both wish to thank NACADA and Stylus for your dedication to writing and publishing in the academic advising field. A big thanks to NACADA's Ashley Thomas, who is extraordinarily hard-working and was the perfect managing editor for us. A special thanks to our chapter reviewers who provided substantive feedback that improved the quality of the chapters.

We joyously acknowledge every fearless LGBTQA+ colleague, friend, and forward-looking ally, who has come before, with, and will come after us (several of whom are authors in this book). We believe in a moral arc that is bent toward justice, and we walk in the footsteps of and beside people who say, "We need to do this thing at once!" and it begins, and we are all better for it.

Craig: I wish to thank my dissertation chair, Tonette S. Rocco, who has shaped me as a scholar and thinker. And my numerous friends and colleagues who challenge my thinking and support my scholarship. To my family, especially my sister (Elizabeth) and four nieces, Addison, Ella, Izzy, and Marissa: I love you more than you will ever know. And to mom and dad: thank you for the best childhood one could dream of and for loving me (and all my gender-defying eccentricities) with all the fervor in the world. I miss you every day.

Jennifer: Thank you to my wife, Kathy J. Davis, who helps me feel loved, capable, safe, and whole. #lastbookever Thank you to my children Melissa, Anthony, and Katherine who inspire me and bring joy to my life every day.

Chapter Reviewers

Amalauna (Amy) Brock	Auburn University
Andrea Osborn	Western Washington University
Caleb Howell	Columbus College of Art & Design
Christopher (Cody) Harrison	DeBusk College of Osteopathic Medicine at Lincoln Memorial University, Knoxville
Janneal Gifford	Valparaiso University
Javier Franco	University of Southern California
Jessica Henault	Kansas State University
Julie Nelson	The University of Iowa
Karen Lederer	University of Massachusetts Amherst
Kasandrea Sereno	University of South Florida
Katherine Walker-Payne	Spalding University
Kelsie Potter	Virginia Commonwealth University
Leonor L. Wangensteen	University of Notre Dame
Lisa Rubin	Kansas State University
Louise Vasher	The Ohio State University
Luca Maurer	Ithaca College
Madison Crist	Indiana University – Purdue University Indianapolis
Mark Nelson	Oklahoma State University
Marsha Miller	Kansas State University
Paula Kerezsi	Independent Scholar
Shannon Shivers	Oregon State University
Tyler Hall	Dalhousie University
Wendy Kay Schindler	Northern Kentucky University
William Smith III	Indiana University–Bloomington

I

INTRODUCTION

Craig M. McGill and Jennifer E. Joslin

One of the first gay undergraduate student organizations to be
officially recognized by a student government was the University of
Iowa's Gay Liberation Front in 1970, formed in the aftermath of the
1969 Stonewall Riots. The 6-day riot at the Stonewall Inn, a bar frequented
by drag queens and trans street hustlers in New York City's Greenwich
Village, followed a tumultuous decade of increasing protests marked by the
Civil Rights Movement and opposition to the Vietnam War (Franke-Ruta,
2013). Unlike Compton's Cafeteria Riot in San Francisco in 1966, which
also involved trans women and drag queens revolting against police harassment and brutality (Silverman & Stryker, 2005), the Stonewall Uprising
made news across the United States and inspired the formation of a new kind
of activist group for gay rights: the NYC Gay Liberation Front (GLF). The
GLF, though short-lived, represented a dramatic break from previous organizations like the Mattachine Society, which advocated for tolerance from
mainstream society (Gosse, 2005). Similar to the NYC GLF, the University
of Iowa group represented a growing reality: College students who identified
as gay were unwilling to remain invisible any longer. They were prepared to
identify as gay and proud in exchange for acknowledgment of a gay student
presence on their college campuses. In the 50 years since Stonewall, colleges
and universities have seen an explosion of lesbian, gay, bisexual, transgender,
queer, and asexual/allies (LGBTQA+) student organizations, and academic
advisors have experienced the joys and challenges of working with this unique
population.

Changes on college and university campuses have echoed changes in
U.S. popular culture, politics, and religion since the 1970s through unprecedented visibility of LGBTQA+ persons and issues. The past 35 years have
been characterized by the major issues taken up by activists and scholars,

1

which include the AIDS epidemic, same-sex marriage debates, and, eventually, marriage equality. Highly charged political issues also contribute to ongoing commentary about gender and sexuality in U.S. culture. The debates over LGBTQA+ people in the military, which began in earnest in the early 1990s, have continued with the involvement of U.S. forces in the Middle East. The same-sex marriage and civil union debates have attracted a great deal of media attention in the United States and are considered controversial and galvanizing issues during election years by advocates on both sides. The debate over ordination of gay and lesbian clergy by several mainstream faith traditions has been in the public eye continuously for over 2 decades. This increased visibility has led to enormous strides for LGBTQA+ persons in some areas of U.S. life.

The LGBTQA+ movement has grown globally and expanded to include greater social and individual human rights goals as society acknowledges LGBTQA+ people and becomes more inclusive of people's sociocultural identities (Hill & Grace, 2009). Worldwide, the Pride Movement has gradually taken many forms, including annual marches and celebrations of LGBTQA+ rights and freedom from oppression (e.g., Pride Month and Pride parades); political and legislative efforts to attain legal rights and protections for LGBTQA+ people equivalent to those of heterosexuals; increased and balanced portrayals of LGBTQA+ persons in news media, arts, and entertainment; and the right to marry same-sex partners (Bronski, 2011).

Although great strides have been made, LGBTQA+ people still face oppression across the globe. The United Nations (UN) secretary-general opined that LGBTQA+ rights protection was "one of the most neglected challenges of our time" (African Commission on Human and Peoples' Rights [ACHPR] et al., 2016). These issues are complicated by international differences around the types of legal jurisdictions regarding homosexuality (Mendos, 2019). While the UN and other international organizations have reported progress in LGBTQA+ rights and protections in some countries in the past few decades, they have also identified persistent areas of concern (ACHPR et al., 2016). There are countries passing progressive laws and making social changes (e.g., Netherlands, Canada, Sweden, New Zealand), countries passing progressive laws but experiencing little social change (e.g., South Africa, Ecuador), countries making social changes but few legal changes (e.g., Eastern European countries), countries with mixed internal legal and social systems and municipalities or states with varyingly progressive laws (e.g., United States, Australia), and countries making few legal changes and little social progress (e.g., Uganda, Saudi Arabia, Pakistan, Russia). None of these situations constitute a "gay heaven" where there is an entirely unproblematic and completely respectful society for sexual minorities, but obviously some are better than others (Eichler & Mizzi, 2013, p. 95).

The tension between these enormous strides and increasing civic restrictions creates a perception of both progress and resistance to progress that can be stressful for LGBTQA+ individuals. In addition, institutional responses to LGBTQA+ students can vary widely by region of the United States and institutional affiliation. While some states may have a restrictive legal climate for LGBTQA+ persons, higher educational institutions (and the college towns they reside in) within that state may have nondiscrimination policies that create a positive climate for LGBTQA+ students, staff members, and faculty members. Institutional affiliation also plays a role in the development of campus policies. Despite living in a state that has a more favorable political climate, an LGBTQA+ student at a school with restrictive policies due to a religious affiliation, for example, may measure campus climate using a very different scale than a student at a different institution in that same state. The visibility of LGBTQA+ persons and issues in the public consciousness, as well as the 38-year history of LGBTQA+ organizations and centers on campuses, demonstrates that Americans are speaking out about LGBTQA+ issues as never before.

However, this sense of visibility is often belied when individual LGBTQA+ students work with advisors. Despite the sense that discussions of LGBTQA+ issues abound, advisors are not always cognizant of LGBTQA+ students in their caseloads and classes. Whether due to fear of discrimination or feeling restricted to the discussion of academic issues (to name two of many possible explanations), LGBTQA+ students may not disclose their identity during advising sessions. Therefore, to support this population, in addition to typical college student issues (e.g., the development of racial identity, spiritual faith formation, the importance of mentoring relationships), as well as major and career development questions, advisors must be aware of issues unique to LGBTQA+ students, including identity development, campus climate, and restrictive or discriminatory policies at the institutional level.

To thrive in college, LGBTQA+ students need support, safety, nurturing, and education. Without such supports, students may experience marginalization, isolation, and invisibility, and they may drop out of college. In the face of hostile campus cultures, LGBTQA+ students should be able to rely on their academic advisors for support, nurturing, and information about safe outlets on campus. As LGBTQA+ students work through their identities and navigate heterosexist environments, advisors can "connect students to the campus and help them feel that someone is looking out for them" (Kuh et al., 2005, p. 214). As the NACADA Core Values make clear, advisors must work with the whole student (NACADA, 2017). A holistic approach requires that advisors engage each student while being mindful of their academic, social, cultural, economic, and individual situations. Programmatic responsibilities include creating a welcoming environment, offering professional development on working with LGBTQA+ students, and offering a safe space for all students in advisors' caseloads. Advisors also face a personal responsibility to respect and meet students where they are. The result of a conscientious and holistic approach to students is the creation of an enduring and rich connection that furthers student development. Taken in this context, advocacy for LGBTQA+ students is not the province of one crusading advisor or administrator but rather the responsibility of all advisors, administrators, and educational professionals who are part of the NACADA community.

Purpose and Audience

There is a dearth of literature on advising LGBTQA+ students. Even since the formation of the previously titled LGBTA Concerns Commission in 1997, only two full-length chapters (Joslin, 2007; Self, 2007) and a handful of short articles in the *NACADA Clearinghouse* and *Academic Advising Today* (Forest, 2006; Lindenberg, 2012; McGill, 2013; Menke et al., 2015; Moorhead, 2005; and Smith, 2006) addressing the advising of LGBTQA+ students have been published by NACADA. Most of these works are over 10 years old. Further, to our knowledge, no empirical work has ever been conducted on LGBTQA+ advisors or on advising LGBTQA+ students. Although important work is being done in related fields (e.g., higher education, student affairs/personnel, gender and queer studies), academic advising is lagging. LGBTQA+ studies is a growing academic field. In the ever-changing political landscape, there is an increasing need to identify diverse student populations and learn to work with them effectively. This edited collection offers essays on a wide variety of advising topics that have never been addressed. In this book, we offer a theoretical understanding of the literature of the field, practical strategies that can be implemented at a variety of different institutions, and a best practice that brings students, staff members, and faculty members into a deeper understanding of the challenges and rewards they confront when working constructively and meaningfully with the LGBTQA+ student population on campus. Specifically, we offer the following:

- to establish theoretical foundations for topics including sexual and gender identity development, the concept of intersectionality, and theoretical lenses such as queer theory as they relate to academic advising;
- to apply sexual and gender identity development, the concept of intersectionality, and theoretical lenses such as queer theory to academic advising;

- to examine critical campus issues and advising approaches impacting LGBTQA+ students (e.g., sexual assault, mental illness, and career advising);
- to explore the intersections of LGBTQA+ identities with other important identity factors (e.g., athletes, international students, students of color, and those majoring in certain academic fields);
- and to offer advisors exercises and resources to (re)consider their own identities and privileges within the framework of allyhood formation.

There are primary and secondary audiences who will find value in this book. The primary audiences for this book include:

- primary-role academic advisors: Whether they are aware or not, academic advisors work with LGBTQA+ students all the time;
- faculty academic advisors: Not only do they share the need for knowledge with primary-role advisors in the advising setting, they can also use this information in the classroom;
- graduate students in higher education, student affairs/personnel, and academic advising roles: This text would be useful in courses dealing with multiculturalism, diversity/inclusion, and especially a graduate course on advising LGBTQA+ students;
- researchers of academic advising and LGBTQA+/queer studies: Every chapter of this book will conclude with implications for both practice and research, providing a launching point for a variety of research topics;
- and LGBTQA+ students: Because this book is about working with LGBTQA+ students, there will be some who are interested in its chapters, particularly those who are studying LGBTQA+, queer, and/or women's and gender studies.

The secondary audiences for this book include:

- other practitioners in higher education settings: since many of the chapters deal with the identity intersections of LGBTQA+ students, this book will be of interest to those working with LGBTQA+ students outside of an advising context;
- and practitioners who work with LGBTQA+ people outside of a higher education setting: Although this book focuses on advising, much of the information will be applicable in other settings.

A note about terminology: In this text, we have encouraged authors to name and claim their use of the ever-shifting landscape of language and terminology as it applies to their chapter and, indeed, to their focus. As you read, you will realize that authors have defined terms such as *heteronormativity* and *cisgender* consistently but not with identical words. The definitions reflect age and generational influences, class, race, identity, expression, background, and familiarity (or lack thereof) with queer theory. In several chapters, authors have staked a claim to new terms and language that will be heard for years to come, including Black and indigenous people of color (BIPOC) and trans (for transgender or trans) individuals.

There has been a long history of how to group and describe people who belong to a sexual or gender minority. In our living memory, there has not been consensus around a term that sufficiently describes all members of such a community. We have navigated the tension between consistency for the reader and having authors use their own chosen acronym. Ultimately, we have adopted LGBTQA+, but recognize certain limitations of the use of any acronym and acknowledge that language and identity will continue to evolve.

Overview of Book

This book is organized across four major parts: Theoretical Foundations, Campus Issues and Advising Approaches, Advising LGBTQA+ Student Populations, and Creating Inclusive Spaces. In addition to the main chapters outlined to follow, we have incorporated voices from the field centered on allyhood development. Allies in the field of academic advising (both straight/cis-identified and queer) reflect on becoming an ally, the obstacles and challenges they have experienced in the past and perhaps currently grapple with, and offer advice to those seeking to deepen their commitment to allyhood.

In Part One, Theoretical Foundations, the authors lay some groundwork regarding theories of sexual and gender identity development (chapter 2), an advisor's role in the coming-out process (chapter 3), queer theory (chapter 4), and intersectionality (chapter 5). Each of these areas undergird the concepts found throughout the rest of the book. In chapter 2, Henault, Thomas, McGill, and Vega briefly review different types of developmental theories for gender and sexual-identity development and suggest ways in which advisors can use these theories to better understand their LGBTQA+ advisees. In chapter 3, Kocet and Valente suggest ways advisors can use these lenses to better understand and support students. In chapter 4, Carlson discusses ways in which queer theory dismantles the status quo while illustrating how it can be fruitfully used to problematize arbitrary structures and categories that limit the human experience. In chapter 5, Schindler and Stevens demonstrate how intersectionality provides a framework for understanding that a person's identities are interconnected and can combine to create a complex system of oppression.

In Part Two the authors illuminate Campus Issues and Advising Approaches. In chapter 6, Joslin reenvisions the completion agenda narrative in terms of the LGBTQA+ student experience in U.S. higher education, asking, "What do academic advisors and advising administrators need to know?" Meeker, Sprott, and McGill explore the career advising needs of LGBTQA+ students in chapter 7. In response to the career advising needs discussed in chapter 7, donahoe-rankin and Glenn provide an in-depth vignette to explore advising LGBTQA+ students in nonlinear career majors. In chapter 8, langellier and Gess describe common mental health concerns exhibited by LGBTQA+ college students, as well as warning signs to enable advisors to detect the ways these concerns present themselves. Suggestions are offered for starting a conversation about counseling, and resources are provided to academic advisors looking to find an LGBTQA+ affirmative, queer-competent counselor in their community. In chapter 9, Oliner describes the challenges for students who attend Christian-based institutions. Fette and Tetreault provide some context in chapter 10 regarding the prevalence of sexual assault and intimate partner violence rates for LGBTQA+ people, impacts of victimization and perpetration on student development and student success, unique aspects of LGBTQA+ students as survivors/victims, and considerations about the role advisors have in working with LGBTQA+ students.

The authors of Part Three, Advising LGBTQA+ Student Populations, discuss some unique challenges experienced by specific sub-groups of LGBTQA+ students. In chapter 11, Menke, McGill, Fletcher, and Pfeiffer describe how a student-athlete's inability to be open about who they are poses serious harm to their emotional and psychological well-being, as well as their athletic performance. In chapter 12, Oliner and McGill illuminate issues LGBTQA+ students encounter within their STEM environments and offer efficient strategies for advising LGBTQA+ students in STEM. In chapter 13, Venable and Inselman outline a vision for working with trans students that rejects a deficit-oriented approach. They identify structural barriers to trans student success and ways advisors and advising administrators can reject harmful tropes and, instead, employ a more nuanced approach. Wangensteen outlines some unique challenges experienced by LGBTQA+ international students and ways advisors can support these students in chapter 14. In chapter 15, Mora and Lucero explore the intersections of gender and sexuality experienced by students who identify as queer and trans students of color QTSOC and address challenges they experience. Following this chapter, we re-present (with permission) Matthews's (2019) article on approaches for advising and supporting Black queer and gender nonconforming students.

The final part of the book, Creating Inclusive Spaces, outlines specific tools for advisors seeking to improve their advising practice. In chapter 16, McGill and Schindler situate theories of ally formation in the context of academic advising and propose a model for academic advisor ally development. Finally, in chapter 17, Self and Oliner outline strategies for campuses and advisors to develop more inclusive campus environments.

References

African Commission on Human and Peoples' Rights, Inter-American Commission on Human Rights, & United Nations. (2016). *Ending violence and other human rights violations based on sexual orientation and gender identity.* Pretoria University Law Press.

Bronski, M. (2011). *A queer history of the United States.* Beacon Press.

Eichler, M. A., & Mizzi, R. C. (2013). Negotiating the confluence: Middle-Eastern, immigrant, sexual-minority men and concerns for learning and identity. *Brock Education: A Journal of Educational Research and Practice, 22*(2), 84–98. https://doi.org/10.26522/BROCKED.V22I2.344

Forest, L. (2006). Advising gay, lesbian, bisexual, and transgender students. *Academic Advising Today, 29*(4). https://www.nacada.ksu.edu/Resources/Academic-Advising-Today/View-Articles/Advising-Gay-Lesbian-Bisexual-and-Transgender-Students.aspx

Franke-Ruta, G. (2013, January 24). An amazing 1969 account of the Stonewall Uprising. *The Atlantic.* https://www.theatlantic.com/politics/archive/2013/01/an-amazing-1969-account-of-the-stonewall-uprising/272467/

Gosse, V. (2005). *The movements of the new left, 1950–1975: A brief history with documents.* Palgrave Macmillan.

Hill, R. J., & Grace, A. P. (2009). Introduction: Queer silence no more—Let's make some noise. In R. J. Hill & A. P. Grace (Eds.), *Adult and higher education in queer contexts: Power, politics, and pedagogy* (pp. 1–10). Discovery Association Publishing House.

Joslin, J. (2007). Working with lesbian, gay, bisexual, transgender, and queer students. In P. Jordan & L. Huff (Eds.), *Advising Special Populations* (Monograph No. 17, pp. 87–95). National Academic Advising Association.

Kuh, G. D., Kinzie, J., Schuh, J. H., & Whitt, E. J. (2005). Never let it rest: Lessons about student success from high-performing colleges and universities. *Change: The Magazine of Higher Learning, 37*(4), 44–51. https://doi.org/10.3200/CHNG.37.4.44-51

Lindenberg, M. J. (2012). *Transgender students: Seven recommendations for academic advisors.* NACADA: The Global Community for Academic Advising. https://www.nacada.ksu.edu/Resources/Clearinghouse/View-Articles/Transgender-Students-Seven-Recommendations-for-Academic-Advisors.aspx

Matthews, M. (2019, June). Approaches for advising and supporting black queer and gender nonconforming students. *Academic Advising Today, 42*(2). https://nacada. ksu.edu/Resources/Academic-Advising-Today/View-Articles/Approaches-for-Advising-and-Supporting-Black-Queer-and-Gender-Nonconforming-Students. aspx

McGill, C. M. (2013). LGBTQA allyhood: Academic advisors reflect. *Academic Advising Today, 36*(4). https://www.nacada.ksu.edu/Resources/Academic-Advising-Today/View-Articles/LGBTQA-Allyhood-Academic-Advisors-Reflect. aspx

Mendos, L. R. (2019, December). Author's preface. In L. R. Mendos (Ed.), *State-sponsored homophobia: Global legislation overview update* (pp. 7–8). International Lesbian, Gay, Bisexual, Trans and Intersex Association. https://ilga. org/downloads/ILGA_World_State_Sponsored_Homophobia_report_global_legislation_overview_update_December_2019.pdf

Menke, D., McGill, C. M., & Fletcher, J. (2015). *Advising lesbian, gay, bisexual, transgender, and queer student athletes*. NACADA: The Global Community for Academic Advising. https://www.nacada.ksu.edu/Resources/Clearinghouse/View-Articles/Advising-Lesbian-Gay-Bisexual-Transgender-and-Queer-Student-Athletes.aspx

Moorhead, C. (2005). *Advising lesbian, gay, bisexual, and transgender students in higher education*. National Academic Advising Association. https://www.nacada.ksu. edu/Resources/Clearinghouse/View-Articles/Advising-Lesbian-Gay-Bisexual-and-Transgender-Students-in-Higher-Education.aspx

NACADA: The Global Community for Academic Advising. (2017). *NACADA academic advising core competencies model*. https://nacada.ksu.edu/Resources/Pillars/CoreCompetencies.aspx

Self, C. (2007). Advising lesbian, gay, bisexual, and transgender first-year students. In M. S. Hunter, B. McCalla-Wriggins, & E. R. White (Eds.), *Academic advising: New insights for teaching and learning in the first year* (pp. 213–221). National Resource Center for the First-Year Experience & Students in Transition.

Silverman, V., & Stryker, S. (Directors). (2005). *Screaming queens: The riot at Compton's cafeteria* [Film]. Frameline.

Smith, B. L. (2006). Working more effectively in advising: Understanding multicultural dimensions of gay, lesbian, bisexual, and transgender identities. *Academic Advising Today, 29*(3). https://www.nacada.ksu.edu/Resources/Academic-Advising-Today/View-Articles/Gay-Lesbian-Bisexual-and-Transgender-GLBT-Issues-in-Advising-Situations.aspx

PART ONE

THEORETICAL FOUNDATIONS

2

GENDER AND SEXUAL
IDENTITY DEVELOPMENT

Jessica L. Henault, Ashley A. Thomas, Craig M. McGill, and Gisela P. Vega

In this chapter, we explore gender and sexual identity development. Gender and sexuality are separate yet related identity development processes. *Gender* has been defined as "socially constructed roles, behaviors, activities, and attributes that a given society considers appropriate for men and women" (World Health Organization, 2014, p. 3). Gender encompasses *gender identity* (i.e., a person's internal sense of their own gender) and *gender expression* (i.e., a person's way of outwardly expressing and performing their sense of gender). A person's gender identity and expression are distinct from their sexual anatomy and sexual orientation, and gender identity and expression are influenced by and understood in terms of a person's culture. Gender is not a fixed process but rather an ongoing experience that changes over one's lifespan (Bussey, 2011). Research demonstrates that most people's sense of gender identity begins forming during childhood and intensifies through adolescence, prior to entering college (Savin-Williams & Diamond, 2000). Students continue to explore their sense of gender identity, roles, categories, and expectations during college.

Early gender identity development models were based on fixed, binary assumptions that asserted that gender identity is connected to biological sex and that a person is either a man or woman. Binary social constructions of gender lead people to assume a person's pronouns (e.g., he/him/his, she/her/hers) or titles (e.g., sir, madam, ma'am) based on their name, physical appearance, and/or gender expression. The prevailing hegemonic assumptions are that (a) gender is assigned at birth, (b) there are only two genders (man or woman), (c) a person's gender matches their genitalia, and (d) there are no deviations from these norms (Patton et al., 2016).

Sexual identity is an umbrella term encompassing sexual behaviors, social affiliations, and emotional attachment preferences (Dillon et al., 2011). *Sexual orientation* is defined as "an often-enduring pattern of emotional, romantic and/or sexual attractions of men to women or women to men (heterosexual), of women to women or men to men (homosexual), or by men or women to both sexes (bisexual)" (American Psychological Association, 2018, para. 1). We acknowledge this as a basic definition of sexual orientation that practitioners and scholars should problematize. In addition to sexual actions, sexual orientation encompasses emotional and romantic thoughts as well as a person's connection to a community of people who may also experience those emotional, romantic, or sexual desires. Importantly, sexual orientation is about sexual *attraction*, not necessarily sexual *behavior* (e.g., a gay man having sex with women in the past *or present* does not mean he identifies as straight or bisexual). Throughout much of history and into the present day, heterosexual is deemed the "default" sexual orientation (Edwards & Brooks, 1999). Sexual minorities, however, are nonheterosexual people who "are denied civil rights, the right to work, and other human rights because of their sexuality and sexual orientation" (Rocco et al., 2009, p. 8).

Identity development theories are used to theorize student developmental processes and help professionals better understand how biological and environmental factors impact students' cognitive, emotional, social, physical, and spiritual development (Bronfenbrenner, 1979, 1993; Renn & Arnold, 2003). Additionally, educators gain a clearer understanding of how these environmental factors impact a student's sense of self and their relationships with others. Utilizing identity development theories "enable[s] student affairs professionals to proactively identify and address student needs, design programs, develop policies, and create healthy college environments that encourage positive growth in students" (Patton et al., 2016, p. 8). Broadly, these theories promote the understanding of issues students face and help educators identify best practices to provide support and guidance. Student affairs professionals have an ethical responsibility to promote students' academic success and to support them along their personal development journeys. Given that each student's needs are influenced by their multiple identities and interactions, it is important that academic advisors and student affairs professionals possess a wide breadth of knowledge about identity development theories (Abes et al., 2007).

Utilizing scholarship as the foundation for advising practice has been promoted throughout the literature (Patton et al., 2016; Troxel, 2019; van den Wijngaard, 2019). To effectively build strategies and maintain confidence in their daily work, advisors must think and practice according to the foundations of a theoretical framework. The connection between theory and practice is termed *praxis*, which involves "the exploration of the rationale behind the *how* of what advisors do" (van den Wijngaard, 2019, p. 5). Referencing the three pillars of the NACADA Research Committee's agenda, Troxel (2019) suggests that utilizing a theoretical foundation for advising practice permits advisors to "advance the role of academic advising in the broader mission of education" (p. 53). Using theory to inform practice is key to the advancement of advisors' professional development and the continued growth of the profession.

To gain a clearer understanding, advisors should view frameworks and theories as potential road maps for designing strategies to deepen their conversations with students. It is important to have strategies readily available to attend to students' needs and aid in their decision-making processes. The advisor must be able to justify their strategies. Using a theoretical framework to guide interventions can help create an understanding of *why* advisors choose to give certain advice, based on the context of the student's situation. In this chapter, we lay the foundations for theorizing gender and sexual identity as development processes, describe types of development theories, and offer implications for advising praxis to assist advisors in moving toward a more theory-based practice.

Evolution of Identity Development Theories

Jones and Stewart (2016) described the evolution of identity development theory through a series of "waves" as introduced by feminist scholars. These waves are grouped under *first wave* (foundational), *second wave* (perspectives), and *third wave* (developmental). The wave structure allows educators to frame conversations and questions regarding the evolution of student identity development theories, making space for more critical perspectives and discussions.

First Wave Theories

The first wave of identity development theory included foundational theories, which were primarily psychological and developmental in nature, falling into categories such as psychosocial, cognitive-structural, person-environment, typology, and maturity. Foundational psychosocial theories had a profound impact on psychological literature in the latter half of the 20th century (Patton et al., 2016). Psychosocial theories have historically been used (and continue to be used) by student affairs professionals as foundational frameworks and that emphasize the importance of holistic student development.

TABLE 2.1
Eight Stages of Psychosocial Development

Stage	Conflict	Age	Resolution
1	Trust versus Mistrust	< 2 years	Hope
2	Autonomy versus Shame	2–4 years	Will
3	Initiative versus Guilt	5–8 years	Purpose
4	Industry versus Guilt	9–12 years	Competence
5	Identity versus Role confusion	12–19 years	Fidelity
6	Intimacy versus Isolation	20–39 years	Love
7	Generativity versus Stagnation	40–59 years	Care
8	Ego identity versus Despair	> 60 years	Wisdom

Source: Erikson, 1959.

Erikson (1959) developed the first psychosocial theory addressing a person's identity development from adolescence through adulthood across eight stages. Table 2.1 summarizes these stages.

Each of the eight stages includes developmental tasks that must be met before progressing to the next stage. When individuals measure their success of self against environmental factors, crises occur (Widick et al., 1978). Given that an individual's response to a crisis may influence how they manage future life conflict, these moments can serve as developmental opportunities. When an individual positively resolves the crisis (in what Erikson terms the *resolution* stage), they gain additional coping tools that support them in future crises. Should an individual fail to reach a resolution, their crisis may deepen or even halt their developmental progress.

The first four stages occur during childhood when children begin learning how to trust their immediate caregivers and explore their environments. Upon reaching school age, children begin to recognize socially acceptable norms by watching their peers. Stage five marks a transition from adolescence into emerging adulthood when young adults begin defining their identity. This crisis of developing a clear sense of self and purpose is known as *identity diffusion*. The work of defining a sense of self in relation to others is a unique task that occurs in the *identity versus role confusion* stage (Erikson, 1959). Building and recognizing healthy relationships, as opposed to harmful relationships, marks stage six (*intimacy versus isolation*). In stage seven (*generativity versus stagnation*), positive relationships continue to develop with others and solidify the individual's sense of self and purpose. The individual develops long-term goals, and their energy is channeled toward productive activities like career advancement and starting a family. Erikson's final stage (*ego integrity versus despair*) occurs during late adulthood as the individual experiences physical and mental changes, while possibly exploring other careers or considering retirement. Weighing life successes, challenges, and regrets may promote either feelings of acceptance and peace or regret for failing to find a clear life purpose.

Another theory included in Jones and Stewart's (2016) first wave of foundational theories is Marcia's (1966) "Development and Validation of Ego-Identity Status," which expands upon Erikson's *role confusion* stage. Young adults begin to question the values and beliefs instilled in them as children and experiment with alternative options (*exploration*). Seeking guidance from individuals they value helps solidify their *commitment* to new values and beliefs. This model also includes four identity statuses occurring in no specific order: *foreclosure, moratorium, achievement, and diffusion.* Movement through the statuses is a fluid and lifelong process that reoccurs as individuals experience future crises. Young adults who follow and rely on authority figures' values and beliefs experience little to no crises (*foreclosure*). Individuals questioning and exploring the values established by authority figures experience the highest level of anxiety while in the *moratorium* status. During the process of *identity achievement*, individuals commit to their new values and beliefs while remaining willing to take additional risks. Those who are unable or unwilling to explore alternatives outside of those prescribed by authority figures enter *diffusion* and subsequently lack the cognitive complexity to understand consequences, which limits their higher consciousness (Marcia, 1989).

While first wave theories had a profound impact on student affairs and advising practices and continue to be used as foundational frameworks today, these theories have been critiqued due to their limitations. Since first wave theories were often developed based on the limited perspectives of "white men from privileged socioeconomic backgrounds" addressing "singular developmental domains" (Jones & Stewart, 2016, p. 19), the theories' applicability to other student populations is limited.

Second Wave Theories

In the continued evolution of identity development theory, the second wave highlighted the unique experiences of students by including aspects of their social identities, including racial, ethnic, and sexual identities. Theorists began to focus on minority populations while also discovering the intricate ways in which a student's identity and campus environment shape their individual development. At the same time, scholars began to draw upon the theories of other disciplines and to recognize the various systems of oppression that affect college students (Jones & Stewart, 2016).

An individual's sexual identity development is an ongoing process that includes awareness and acceptance of their sexual orientation. The expression "coming out of the closet" (or "coming out" for short) describes a process in which an individual discloses their sexual identity to another person (Manning, 2015). This personal journey is different for each individual and is not a one-time event, but a lifetime of navigating degrees of "outness." While various types of sexual identity models explore the development experiences of sexual minority college students, there are three basic tenets that consistently appear across sexual identity development models: *alienation* (i.e., the experience of seeing oneself as different from, and not fitting into, the heteronormative majority), *disclosure/coming out* (i.e., the need to announce oneself as a sexual minority), and *self-acceptance* (i.e., acceptance of a nonheterosexual identity; Bilodeau & Renn, 2005; Henrickson, 2013). These models help explain the cognitive and psychosocial components of identity, the ways identity components are interwoven throughout a person's life, and the identity components' level of salience to a person's overall identity.

Bem (1981) introduced gender schema theory to explain how children learn about gender roles from their cultures. A schema, or "cognitive structure, a network of associations that organizes and guides an individual's perception" (Bem, 1981, p. 335), helps individuals make sense of and interpret information. Social influences impact children's understanding of gender schemas and how they make sense of attitudes and beliefs associated with gender. Children learn to align their behavior to the norms of the "proper" gender. Gender schema theory utilizes both cognitive-development theory and social learning theory to posit that individuals fall into one of four gender categories: *sex-typed* (i.e., gender matches sex assigned at birth), *cross sex-typed* (i.e., gender does not match sex assigned at birth), *androgynous* (i.e., displaying both masculine and feminine gender traits), and *undifferentiated* (i.e., flexible with gender identity; Bem, 1981). The Bem (1974) sex role inventory includes 60 attributes used to place a person under one of the four categories outlined previously. Despite its age and the emerging work on gender-identity development, the Bem sex-role inventory is still widely used.

Stage models (e.g., Cass, 1979; McCarn & Fassinger, 1996; Troiden, 1989), that examine gender and sexual identity development in college students, also emerged in the 1970s. These models present a linear progression with the assumption that an individual works through the identity formation process in an equally linear fashion. Furthermore, these models suggest that people experience *incongruence* when they recognize that their thoughts and feelings differ from those of their peers. The desire to find meaning and peace with their identity motivates an individual's exploration. This exploration may result in the individual becoming overwhelmed with the process, leading to identity foreclosure and the individual limiting their development. To cope, people may attempt to block, deny, or minimize their thoughts and feelings. Influences from the environment may further impact development. For instance, positive and affirming interactions with family, peers, and others may encourage the individual to accept their identity, whereas negative experiences may encourage them to repress and minimize their exploration and expression. Table 2.2 references examples of leading gender and sexual identity development models.

Though popular in the literature, stage models are critiqued for a lack of consideration regarding the ways a multiplicity of identities influences an individual's gender and sexual identity development. White males were historically the primary participants of stage model research, and many stage models fail to consider how diverse populations experience and move through gender and sexual identity development (Patton et al., 2016). "Stage models assume that identity development follows a linear progression and that identity is 'achieved' once an individual reaches the final stage." Instead, gender and sexual identity development are lifetime processes continually (re)constructed throughout one's entire life. However, due to the prevalence of stage models in the literature, these models have been easily understood and applied on university campuses (Bilodeau & Renn, 2005; Sanlo, 2004). Stage models may help practitioners understand how students go about discovering their identities in the context of their experiences and environments, allowing practitioners to assist students in achieving their maximum potential in college and life (Jones & Abes, 2013).

TABLE 2.2
Sexual and Gender Identity Development Stage Models

Stage	Lee (1977)	Cass (1979)	Troiden (1989)
1	Signification	Identity confusion	Sensitization
2	Coming out	Identity comparison	Identity confusion
3	Going public	Identity tolerance	Identity assumption
4		Identity acceptance	Commitment and integration
5		Identity pride	
6		Identity synthesis	

Third Wave Theories

Third wave theories used critical and post-structural frameworks to critique and challenge the norms and values reflected in dominant groups (Jones & Stewart, 2016). With the introduction of queer, feminist, and critical race theories, educators reexamined previously considered notions of identity development theories, placing more attention on the ways power, privilege, and oppression influence students' identity development. This reexamination opened doors for emerging research on gender identity development utilizing social-cognitive perspectives in which gender identity formation is fluid and ongoing. For example, queer theory views individuals' lived experiences as socially constructed; that is, a person's sense of self is influenced and shaped by the society at large (Sullivan, 2003). Queer theory also suggests that environmental and cultural factors influence an individual's perception of their gender identity, their gender identity formation process, and their daily performance of those gendered norms. As a result, people may identify with several different pronouns beyond the male/female dichotomy (see chapter 13).

Diversity perspective models (e.g., Boykin, 1996; Evans & Broido, 2002; McCarn & Fassinger, 1996) examine the ways gender, race, religious affiliations, disabilities, and other identities intersect and influence sexual identity formation. In these models, "no one dimension may be understood singularly; it can be understood only in relation to other dimensions" (Jones & McEwen, 2000, p. 410). Using a multicultural lens supports the integration of a cross-discipline framework because it "creates conditions where multiple truths about identity perceptions are assumed; students bring their own identity-based experiences and stories into the mix to co-construct with peers, advisors, counselors, and instructors new truths, understandings, and perspectives about their sense of self" (Abes et al., 2007, p. 19).

McCarn and Fassinger (1996) studied the sexual identity formation of lesbians and developed a model with phases instead of stages to show the fluid and continuous nature of sexual identity development. The model distinguishes between developing a new sexual identity and redefining a new group membership and meaning. Fassinger (1998) later replicated her original study and found evidence supporting the model's application to sexual identity development for gay men and bisexual individuals. Further research demonstrated the intersections between lesbian identity development and other dimensions of identity. As a result, Abes et al. (2007) proposed "a more complex conceptualization of the model of multiple dimensions of identity that integrate[d] intersecting domains of development" (p. 1). The authors discussed how an individual's self-perception and contextual influences impact their ability to create meaning from their lived experiences (also known as *meaning-making filter*). Creating meaning from everyday experiences allows individuals to live a more intentional life and increases their cognitive understanding of the world around them. Abes et al. (2007) also demonstrated the need to incorporate perspectives addressing the fluidity of gender performance. Interacting with others allows the individual to gain further insight into the ways people perform gender. These meaningful interactions allow the individual to gain a deeper sense of self and the ways in which they consciously or unconsciously choose to perform their own gender.

Having a wide breadth of knowledge about various identity development theories equips advisors to better understand the multiple truths students bring into advising conversations while also elucidating how their identities influence and impact their perception of and relationship with their advisor. Additionally, knowledge of various identity development theories provides advisors with the tools needed to engage in deeper conversations with students and personalizes their advising experience to meet individualized student needs and goals. This further exemplifies the importance for professionals to possess a wide breadth of knowledge about various identity development theories to better address students' development as a whole. Table 2.3 briefly highlights some of the key diversity perspective models that have influenced the field of student identity development theories.

TABLE 2.3
Diversity Perspective Models of Gender and Sexual Identity Development

Phase / Process	D'Augelli (1994)	McCarn-Fassinger (1996)	Lev (2004)
1	Exiting a heterosexual identity	Awareness	Awareness
2	Developing a personal LGB identity status	Explore	Seeking information / Reaching out
3	Developing an LGB social identity	Deepening/ Commitment	Disclosure to significant others
4	Becoming an LGB offspring	Internalization/ Synthesis	Exploration (Identity and self-labeling)
5	Developing an LGB intimacy status		Exploration (Transition issues and possible body modification)
6	Entering an LGB community		Integration

Although diversity perspective models are relatively new to the literature, suggesting further development is needed, authors have critiqued the models' fixed assumptions of various social constructs. Gender and sexual identity development are not homogenous experiences for everyone, and individual experiences are not solely bound to personal identities (Bilodeau & Renn, 2005).

Praxis: The Intersection of Theory and Practice

Familiarity with a variety of theoretical frameworks equips advisors with helpful strategies to understand students' experiences, thoughts, and feelings. Furthermore, advisors can provide recognition, validation, and guidance to assist students in their exploration. In this section, we offer a vignette exploring possible ways advisors could apply identity development theory to better understand their students' experiences.

Vignette

Darius is a 22-year-old first-generation, African American English major enrolled at State University. State University is a large, public 4-year research institution located in a rural area. Jean has acted as Darius's academic advisor since he began at the university, and their work together has resulted in a very positive relationship. During his first semester, Darius enrolled in 15 credit hours, including two English courses, one math course, one general biology course, and one gender and sexuality studies course. Darius was highly dedicated to his academics in the first semester, earning a 3.0 GPA, and he received a small scholarship after entering and winning a writing contest.

During their first meeting following winter break, Jean noticed a change in Darius's behavior. Darius seemed reserved, engaged very little in their conversation, and provided minimal detail about his break. Although he was concerned, Jean assumed Darius was simply readjusting to his academic routine and did not press the matter. Darius then canceled his following meeting with Jean with little notice, saying he was sick. Again, Jean felt this was unusual but understood and rescheduled the meeting for 3 weeks later.

Two days before the rescheduled meeting, Jean was notified by one of Darius's professors that his grade was slipping. The professor noted that Darius seemed distracted during class and turned in an assignment 2 days late. After reflecting on this information and their recent interactions, Jean decided to discuss his observations with Darius during their next meeting. Although Darius did attend the meeting, he was 15 minutes late and seemed upset. Jean told Darius that he had noticed some changes in his behavior and reminded Darius that if there was something he wished to talk about, Jean was there to listen and provide support. Darius shifted in his seat and started tearing up. After a moment of silence, Darius began to share: "The women and gender studies course I took was really interesting. I thought about things I never questioned before." Jean quietly nodded, not wanting to break Darius's thought process. Darius continued, "My favorite assignment was a final portfolio that included some of my assignments throughout the semester. The best part was writing a self-reflection paper on how the course altered my meaning and perceptions of gender and sexuality." He paused before concluding, "It brought up a lot of emotions and weird feelings I was not expecting, but I tried to push them off as nothing."

Darius went on to share that a few of his friends mentioned they were going to a drag show at the local bar over break and invited him along. This made Darius nervous; he had never been to a drag show and was worried about his father finding out because "he was weird about that kind of stuff." With the support and understanding of his friends, Darius decided to go and told his dad he was hanging out with friends. Darius had a blast and mentioned that, at one point, he "tried not to cry because the performances were so beautiful." After the show ended, Darius had the opportunity to talk to a few of the queens and told them how exciting and amazing their performances were. The queens commented that anyone could participate in drag and he should consider trying it. Darius continued to think about this during the rest of his break.

The longer Darius reflected on his experience, the more desire and confusion he felt. These feelings continued to grow once he returned to campus. Darius mentioned his experience and feelings to one of his friends. She was very supportive and let Darius know he was welcome to try her makeup. Darius felt conflicted, but ultimately decided to borrow makeup with his friend's encouragement. In the comfort and solitude of his apartment, he experimented with the makeup. Darius shared with Jean that it "made him feel free and powerful." However, these emotions quickly subsided when he thought about what his dad would say if he found him "playing around with women's makeup."

Darius admitted to having difficulty paying attention in class and that he was experiencing anxiety over his dad finding out about his recent experiences. He also wanted to continue experimenting with makeup but felt shame and confusion about those desires. As tears formed in Darius's eyes, he told Jean, "I am not sure what this means, but I do not 'feel' gay and I also really love wearing guys' clothing and playing sports. I feel embarrassed and like something is off with me." After giving Darius a moment to collect himself, Jean thanked Darius for sharing the information.

Application of Models

"One of the most difficult considerations in translating theories to practice is deciding which theories to use and how to use them in practice" (Patton et al., 2016, p. 58). While there are different models to consider when approaching the implementation of praxis (e.g., Abes, 2009; Reason & Kimball, 2012), the use of several theories in a holistic, integrative approach is recommended (Patton et al., 2016). Through this holistic, integrated approach, gender and sexual identity development should be viewed as an ongoing process rather than a linear process with an "end goal." It is also important to acknowledge the power differentials in advisor-advisee relationships, as advisors possess extensive knowledge of many different developmental theories about which the student may be unaware. Advisors may consider their responsibility to share readings or information with students, allowing students to determine their own identities through theoretical models. Does sharing models and engaging in deep, reflective, narrative-based conversation provide a way to combine identity development theory with a narrative advising approach?

For instance, Jean could look at Darius's experience through the framework of Marcia's (1966) ego identity status model. Darius is questioning the values and beliefs instilled in him by his parents and specifically expressing concerns about how his dad (a close personal relative) will react to his experimentation with makeup. Using Marcia's (1966) model, the advisor might ascertain that Darius is in the *moratorium (crisis/no commitment)* status, which marks the highest level of anxiety and indicates that the crisis is having a significant impact on Darius's academic, personal, and emotional health. Marcia's (1966) framework could help Jean understand that Darius is experiencing a potential identity crisis. Furthermore, this perspective could assist Jean in encouraging Darius's potential exploration of his gender expression by connecting him to resources such as the LGBTQA+ Resource Center, student organizations, and additional women and gender courses like the one he enjoyed.

Advisors must recognize the impact campus environment, demographics, culture, social norms, and institutional policies have on students' development. As illustrated in the vignette, college students who are financially dependent on their families may experience anxiety about the possibility of sharing their identity in fear of being rejected and punished. As diversity perspective models demonstrate, gender identity and gender expression are "on a continuum and [exist] in interaction but not causation with other elements" (Patton et al., 2016, p. 177). Thus, the advisor realizes Darius is potentially exploring a less binary identity that conflicts with how he was raised. Until this point, Darius has been raised in an environment where gender identity was strictly expressed according to socially accepted binary norms, such as playing sports and wearing masculine clothing. Darius is comfortable expressing traditionally masculine traits but also enjoys experimentation with makeup, a traditionally feminine expression of gender.

Using theories or models to identify students' current developmental positions can help advisors assist students in making meaning of their identities. Further understanding of practical techniques based on theory can assist Jean in suggesting possible activities that may help Darius explore his identity development. Jean understands that gender and sexual identity development are continuous, lifelong processes. He also acknowledges that Darius may need different resources should he feel uncomfortable with the ones Jean provided. With this information, Jean is prepared to continue working with Darius, supporting him through the challenges he will experience. Most importantly, Jean recognizes the privilege it is to support Darius through his development, and he looks forward to witnessing Darius's milestones and personal and academic achievements.

Implications for Practice

As advisors help students grow and learn to develop their own ideas, it can be helpful for advisors to initiate conversations with students addressing the purpose and motivation behind certain strategies. In day-to-day advising practice, it may be easy to give students a checklist of to-do items or direct advice on what needs to be done. While this transactional approach to advising may be effective in accomplishing tasks, it does little to help the student grow and develop. Having a conversation with students about *why* they are being guided in a certain direction can help the student develop their own strategies.

Students come to college with a preexisting understanding of gender identity and gender expression (Bussey, 2011). Attending college "has a generally liberalizing—that is, less constricting—effect on students' gender-role attitudes" (Patton et al., 2016, p. 189). Academic advisors can facilitate guided conversations that challenge heterosexual and/or cisgender students to begin identifying the various levels of privilege they may operate with as a result of living in a heteronormative and fix-gendered society. This includes recognizing the prevailing assumption that heterosexuality is the default sexuality, and that only two genders exist. The college culture and climate provide an opportunity to either solidify or challenge students' inherent thoughts, ideas, and expressions of gender as they understand them.

One particularly powerful approach to help students examine and/ or deconstruct their preconceived ideas relating to gender ideas is narrative theory. As Hagen (2018) stated, "Narrative—storytelling—is the most important way we have of creating, maintaining, defining, or changing our identities. It is the most important way we have of communicating that identity to another person" (p. 5). Narrative storytelling can be used by advisors to help students reflect on their past growth and development. Academic advisors can assist students in making sense of their life stories and demonstrate that they oversee the narratives they tell about themselves, supporting students' ability to construct meaning and performances of their gender and sexuality.

Although advisors cannot expect students be comfortable enough to disclose their identities, they can work to understand what is important to the student and how students make meaning of their experiences while encouraging them to consider their identity. This process sets the stage for students to continue exploring their identities and beliefs moving forward. A forward-thinking mentality can also provide the conditions necessary for expanding students' levels of consciousness, helping them work toward achieving self-authorship (Kegan, 1994). For example, an advisor might use this knowledge to discuss the student's major and career path to help the student assess their current major choice. Did the student choose their major career path or extracurricular activities based on who they *thought* they should be? Is that vision changing since they are now exploring other gender expressions? How is the student rewriting their previously held story?

An additional benefit of utilizing narrative theory is the process of the academic advisor coming to understand their own narrative. Recognizing how and why advisors construct their own meaning can be useful, as doing so helps expose implicit biases that impact the conversations advisors have with students. We believe that advisors who encourage and utilize self-reflection discussions and materials like narrative storytelling are more likely to develop deeper connections with students. Research demonstrates that students are more likely to develop skills needed for self-authorship when advisors discuss and explore students' nonacademic experiences (Pizzolato, 2006).

Conclusion

Supporting students on their journey to academic and personal success requires a thorough understanding of how students' identities influence and impact their lives. Familiarity with a broad range of identity development theories can assist the advisor in identifying the student's stage in the development process (psychosocial, gender identity development theories), while also providing guidance for interventions and strategies to be employed (narrative theory). Although the theories and information discussed in this chapter are not exhaustive, they do provide advisors with a foundation to begin considering practice through the lens of a more scholarly approach.

References

Abes, E. S. (2009). Theoretical borderlands: Using multiple theoretical perspectives to challenge inequitable power structures in student development theory. *Journal of College Student Development, 50*(2), 141–156. https://doi.org/10.1353/csd.0.0059

Abes, E. S., Jones, S. R., & McEwen, M. K. (2007). Reconceptualizing the model of multiple dimensions of identity: The role of meaning-making capacity in the construction of multiple identities. *Journal of College Student Development, 48*(1), 1–22. https://doi.org/10.1353/csd.2007.0000

American Psychological Association (2018). *Lesbian, gay, bisexual, transgender.* http://www.apa.org/topics/lgbt/index.aspx

Bem, S. L. (1974). The measurement of psychological androgyny. *Journal of Consulting and Clinical Psychology, 42*(2), 155–162. https://doi.org/10.1037/h0036215

Bem, S. L. (1981). Gender schema theory: A cognitive account of sex typing. *Psychological Review, 88*(4), 354–364. https://doi.org/10.1037/0033-295X.88.4.354

Bilodeau, B., & Renn, K. (2005). Analysis of LGBT identity development models and implications for practice. *New Directions for Student Services, 2005*(111), 25–39. https://doi.org/10.1002/ss.171

Boykin, K. (1996). *One more river to cross: Black and gay in America.* Doubleday.

Bronfenbrenner, U. (1979). The ecology of human development: Experiments by nature and design. Harvard University Press.

Bronfenbrenner, U. (1993). The ecology of cognitive development: Research models and fugitive findings.

Bussey, K. (2011). Gender identity development. In S. J. Schwartz, K. Luyckx, & V. L. Vignoles (Eds.), *Handbook of identity theory and research* (pp. 603–628). Springer.

Cass, V. C. (1979). Homosexual identity formation: A theoretical model. *Journal of Homosexuality, 4*(3), 219–235. https://doi.org/10.1300/J082v04n03_01

D'Augelli, A. R. (1994). Identity development and sexual orientation: Toward a model of lesbian, gay, bisexual development. In E. J. Trickett, R. J. Watts, & D. Birman (Eds.), *Human diversity: Perspectives on people in context* (pp. 312–333). Jossey-Bass.

Dillon, F. R., Worthington, R. L., & Moradi, B. (2011). Sexual identity as a universal process. In S. J. Schwartz, K. Luyckx, & V. L. Vignoles (Eds.), *Handbook of identity theory and research* (pp. 649–670). Springer.

Edwards, K., & Brooks, A. K. (1999). The development of sexual identity. *New Directions for Adult and Continuing Education, 1999*(84), 49–57. https://doi.org/10.1002/ace.8406

Erikson, E. H. (1959). *Identity and the life cycle: Selected papers.* International Universities Press.

Evans, N. J., & Broido, E. M. (2002). The experiences of lesbian and bisexual women in college residence halls: Implications for addressing homophobia and heterosexism. *Journal of Lesbian Studies, 6*(3–4), 29–42. https://doi.org/10.1300/J155v06n03_04

Fassinger, R. E. (1998). Lesbian, gay, and bisexual identity and student development theory. In R. L. Sanlo (Ed.), *Working with lesbian, gay, bisexual, and transgender college students: A handbook for faculty and administrators* (pp. 13–22). Greenwood Press.

Hagen, P. L. (2018). *The power of story: Narrative theory in academic advising* (J. Givans Voller, Ed.). NACADA: The Global Community for Academic Advising.

Henrickson, M. (2013, February 27). *Identity satisfaction in sexual minorities: A queer kind of strength.* Presentation at LGBTTI Wellness and Suicide: What Do We Need to Change?—a one-day symposium hosted in Auckland, New Zealand, by Auckland DHB, Affinity Services, OUTLine NZ, Rainbow Youth and the Mental Health Foundation.

Jones, S. R., & Abes, E. S. (2013). *Identity development of college students: Advancing frameworks for multiple dimensions of identity.* John Wiley & Sons.

Jones, S. R., & McEwen, M. K. (2000). A conceptual model of multiple dimensions of identity. *Journal of College Student Development, 41*(4), 405–414. https://psycnet.apa.org/record/2000-00479-003

Jones, S. R., & Stewart, D. L. (2016). Evolution of student development theory. *New Directions for Student Services, 154*(2016), 17–28. https://doi.org/10.1002/ss.20172

Kegan, R. (1994). *In over our heads: The mental demands of modern life.* Harvard University Press.

Lee, J. A. (1977). Going public: A study in the sociology of homosexual liberation. *Journal of Homosexuality, 3*(1), 49–78. https://doi.org/10.1300/J082v03n01_05

Lev, A. I. (2004). *Transgender emergence: Therapeutic guidelines for working with gender-variant people and their families.* Haworth Clinical Practice Press.

Manning, J. (2015). Communicating sexual identities: A typology of coming out. *Sexuality & Culture: An Interdisciplinary Quarterly, 19,* 122–138. https://doi.org/10.1007/s12119-014-9251-4

Marcia, J. E. (1966). Development and validation of ego-identity status. *Journal of Personality and Social Psychology, 3*(5), 551–558. https://doi.org/10.1037/h0023281

Marcia, J. E. (1989). Identity diffusion differentiated. In M. A. Luszcz & T. Nettelbeck (Eds.), *Psychological development: Perspectives across the life-span* (pp. 289–295). Elsevier.

McCarn, S. R., & Fassinger, R. E. (1996). Revisioning sexual minority identity formation: A new model of lesbian identity and its implications for counseling and research. *The Counseling Psychologist, 24*(3), 508–534. https://doi.org/ 10.1177/0011000096243011

Patton, L. D., Renn, K. A., Guido, F. M., & Quaye, S. J. (2016). *Student development in college: Theory, research, and practice* (3rd ed.). Jossey-Bass.

Pizzolato, J. E. (2006). Complex partnerships: Self-authorship and provocative academic-advising practices. *NACADA Journal, 26*(1), 32–45. https://doi. org/:10.12930/0271-9517-26.1.32

Reason, R. D., & Kimball, E. W. (2012). A new theory-to-practice model for student affairs: Integrating scholarship, context, and reflection. *Journal of Student Affairs Research and Practice, 49*(4), 359–376. https://doi.org/10.1515/ jsarp-2012-6436

Renn, K. A., & Arnold, K. D. (2003). Reconceptualizing research on peer culture. *Journal of Higher Education, 74*, 261–291. https://doi.org/10.1080/00221546.2 003.11780847

Rocco, T. S., Landorf, H., & Delgado, A. (2009). Framing the issue/framing the question: A proposed framework for organizational perspectives on sexual minorities. *Advances in Developing Human Resources, 11*(1), 7–23. https://doi. org/10.1177/1523422308328528

Sanlo, R. (2004). Lesbian, gay, and bisexual college students: Risk, resiliency, and retention. *Journal of College Student Retention: Research, Theory, and Practice, 6*(1), 97–110. https://doi.org/10.2190/FH61-VE7V-HHCX-0PUR

Savin-Williams, R. C., & Diamond, L. M. (2000). Sexual identity trajectories among sexual-minority youths: Gender comparisons. *Archives of Sexual Behavior, 29*(6), 607–627. https://doi.org/10.1023/a:1002058505138

Sullivan, N. (2003). *A critical introduction to queer theory*. New York University Press.

Troiden, R. R. (1989). The formation of homosexual identities. *Journal of Homosexuality, 17*(1–2), 43–74. https://doi.org/10.1300/J082v17n01_02

Troxel, W. G. (2019). Scholarly advising and the scholarship of advising. *NACADA Journal, 39*(2), 52–59. https://doi.org/10.12930/NACADA-19-203

van den Wijngaard, O. (2019). Academic advising: A discipline of praxis. *NACADA Review, 1*, 5–13. https://doi.org/10.12930/NACR-18-1020

Widick, C., Parker, C. A., & Knefelkamp, L. (1978). Erik Erikson and psychosocial development. In L. Knefelkamp, C. Widick, & C. A. Parker (Eds.), *Applying new developmental findings: New Directions for Student Services, 1978*(4), pp. 1–17. Jossey-Bass.

World Health Organization. (2014). *What do we mean by "sex" and "gender"?* https:// www.legal-tools.org/doc/a33dc3/pdf/#:~:text=%22Sex%22%20refers%20 to%20the%20biological,appropriate%20for%20men%20and%20women

3

SUPPORTING LGBTQA+ STUDENTS THROUGH THE COMING-OUT PROCESS

Michael M. Kocet and Aurélio Manuel Valente

Coming out is a process unique to lesbian, gay, bisexual, transgender, queer, and questioning members of the LGBTQA+ community. Students' identities, growth, and development evolve and are influenced by environmental, cultural, and contextual factors during college, which include their affectional and gender identities (Stewart et al., 2015). To best support the growth and development of LGBTQA+ students, academic advisors should become familiar with gender and sexual/affectional identity models while recognizing each model's fluidity (Kocet, 2014; Manning, 2015; Riggle et al., 2014; Zubernis et al., 2011). Advisors must be ready to provide the information and resources LGBTQA+ students need, as the coming-out process can have personal, academic, financial, social, and familial implications. Through their relationships with faculty members, staff members, and administrators, academic advisors can play a central role in helping these students navigate campus obstacles that impede personal and academic success. In this chapter, we will discuss ways advisors can utilize LGBTQA+ identity development theories to inform their work with students who are navigating the coming-out process, specifically considering students' affectional or gender identities. We will also address the challenges LGBTQA+ students sometimes face when coming out, including rejection by family members, friends, and places of worship, as well as financial strains related to rejection by family systems. This chapter will conclude with an overview of the campus and community resources advisors can share with students to provide wraparound support.

While research studies and conceptual articles have examined the role academic advising plays in supporting college students (Burt et al., 2013; Gordon, 2019a; Vianden, 2016), there has been a dearth of research that explores how academic advisors can support the success of LGBTQA+ students. Advisors must understand the issues that pertain to the lived experiences of queer students—as minoritized populations on campus (Garvey et al., 2015; Sanlo, 2005; Stewart et al., 2015). One way advisors can better understand the lived experiences of LGBTQA+ advisees is by having a strong foundation in LGBTQA+ and queer identity models (see chapter 2) and current factors that impact the well-being of sexual and gender minority students. Bilodeau and Renn (2005) presented a thorough and descriptive summary of the key LGBTQA+ identity models that can strengthen service delivery, especially in academic advising settings.

Academic advisors and educators working with college students may have knowledge of some of the traditional and early coming-out identity models (e.g., Cass, 1979; Fassinger & Miller, 1997). In addition to these early familiar models, there exists a growing body of emerging models that can help advisors better understand LGBTQA+ identities. Chapter 2 of this book further elaborates on these identity models. These emerging models help integrate unique identity markers into a more holistic understanding of the various environmental, intersectional factors that impact the lives of LGBTQA+ students (Few-Demo et al., 2016). Cass (1979) developed one of the first coming-out models, which involves six stages:

1. Identity confusion: growing awareness of internal feelings related to affectional or gender variance.
2. Identity comparison: increase in self-awareness as an LGBTQA+ person.
3. Identity tolerance: acknowledgment and tentativeness related to having an LGBTQA+ identity.
4. Identity acceptance: embracing and accepting of internal affectional or gender variant identity.
5. Identity pride: coming out to others and engaging with other members of the LGBTQA+ community.
6. Identity synthesis: integration of sexual/gender identity into other aspects of self.

Fassinger and Miller's (1997) model focused on awareness of affectional or gender identity, the sense of feeling different, exploration, deepening commitment toward an LGBTQA+ identity, and an internalization/synthesis stage. One of the emerging identity models, the integrative empowerment model (IEM; Matthews & Salazar, 2012), examines an individual's coming-out process in relation to the environmental factors the student is facing. The IEM explores the internal and external factors that contribute to a person's coming out, but the model also aids advisors in identifying intervention strategies that may provide students with the optimal services they need during their coming-out journey (Kocet, 2014). The IEM identifies five internal factors that impact the coming-out process: stages of sexual identity formation, internalized homoprejudice, self-esteem and self-acceptance issues, and mental health behaviors. The six external factors of IEM include family environment, school or peer environment, access to an LGBTQA+ support network, race/culture, religion, and previous counseling experience. Internal and external factors will be addressed in the vignettes later in this chapter.

Advisors should be familiar with the stages involved in the coming-out process. Whether someone is gay, bisexual, trans, lesbian, queer, questioning, or identifies with another marker, coming out is a fluid and ongoing process with multiple benchmarks rather than a single episodic experience; it is a series of moments where individuals make intentional decisions to disclose their sexual/affectional and/or gender identity to others in their lives—in personal and professional contexts (Manning, 2015; Zubernis et al., 2011). However, students may be "outed" by others, which removes a student's agency to choose with whom and when they disclose their identity. Other times, acquaintances, friends, or family members may disclose the student's identity without their knowledge or consent. This outing can contribute to anxiety, depression, and stressors that need to be mitigated through academic and psychological support along with the student's emotional regulation (Kocet, 2014). To effectively advise LGBTQA+ students, academic advisors can include LGBTQA+-specific programming in their professional development sessions in order to understand the impact coming out has on students' abilities to focus on their academic and personal goals. This chapter will address some strategies advisors can integrate into their professional toolbox to help students during the coming-out process.

Supporting Out Students Who Lost Their Support Systems

While research supports the notion that coming out generally has a positive psychological effect on the individual, when working with an LGBTQA+ student, the goal may not always be to encourage a person to come out to everyone in their lives (Matthews & Salazar, 2012). It is important to support students in identifying safe individuals in their academic and personal lives they can come out to—in their own way and in their own time. There are times students may approach their academic advisor because they have lost someone in their support system (e.g., a parent, partner, friend, or coworker) as a result of coming out and they are seeking that support from their advisor. While LGBTQA+ individuals have their unique coming-out process, so too do friends and family members have their own type of coming-out process in which they acknowledge having an LGBTQA+ child, sibling, roommate, or friend. Advisors working with newly out students can help students be mindful of the coming-out process their family members and friends may also be going through and how to navigate those transitions. Advisors can play a significant role in a student's life by offering support and serving as an emotional and psychological buffer or by using relationship management (Vianden, 2016).

In relationship management, advisors form collaborative partnerships with the faculty of students facing significant stressors related to being newly out. These partnerships seek to create a new normal with full integration of a student's sexual or gender identity. The stressors experienced by LGBTQA+ students can be categorized as minority stress (Alessi & Hartman, 2018; Holman, 2018; Parra & Hastings, 2018), a term that acknowledges the high levels of stress experienced by individuals or groups from minority populations. While minority stress has traditionally been researched in the context of persons of color, LGBTQA+ individuals can also exhibit physical, emotional, psychological, career, and financial challenges while managing minority stress (Alessi & Hartman, 2018; Chaudoir et al., 2017; Frost et al., 2019; Mereish & Poteat, 2015; Meyer 2003; Michaels et al., 2015). Academic advisors can alleviate some of these stressors by helping students identify healthy coping strategies to manage and reduce sexual minority stress. Advisors should also be mindful that students may experience a type of grieving process if they are rejected by family members, friends, places of worship, or other central figures, meaning the student must mourn the loss of a part of their self and their relationship with others. It is critical for advisors to help normalize this grieving process for students and to refer them to mental health services when possible. Additionally, LGBTQA+ students may also be managing minority stress if they are experiencing microaggressions or other acts of prejudice and discrimination on campus. An astute advisor can mitigate this stress by recognizing how stress related to cultural identity can impact the well-being of their advisees.

Linley et al. (2016) identified ways faculty members can support LGBTQA+ students both in formal and informal contexts. These recommendations, while originally intended for university faculty members, can easily be adopted by primary-role academic advisors. First, students need to feel supported in formal academic and nonacademic settings. Students need to see advisors confront and challenge homophobic, biphobic, and transphobic language, comments, and jokes made by other students or faculty or staff members. Academic advisors should use terminology that is affirming and inclusive, reflecting the language and terms students use to identify themselves. For example, not all students may identify as gay or lesbian; some may choose a more fluid designation, such as queer, or some trans or gender nonconforming students may identify using mixed or variant pronouns, such as he/him and they/them. Advisors should use students' chosen names and pronouns, providing a model for other staff and faculty members. Advisors should remain up-to-date on the social and political issues impacting the LGBTQA+ community.

Advisors should also find ways to support LGBTQA+ students as they navigate challenges within their academic majors. For example, some trans students may be in academic majors that are dominated by cisgender males, and faculty members may be unsure of how to create a welcoming environment for trans or gender nonconforming (GNC) students. In fact, faculty members may even show biased behavior toward GNC students (see chapter 12 for a discussion of cismale-dominated STEM environments). In such instances, an advisor can act as an advocate for students by working to educate faculty members and administrators on LGBTQA+ issues, ensuring they receive appropriate professional development on how to mentor and provide a safe educational atmosphere for all students in their major (Reicherzer et al., 2014; Vianden, 2016). LGBTQA+ students also feel supported when their advisor—along with faculty members—assists with issues affecting their personal well-being in addition to academic issues (Burt et al., 2013). Advisors should be mindful that it may be challenging for students to disclose deep personal struggles they are facing during a 15-minute academic advising appointment. Advisors need to create a space where students have the time and ability to raise sensitive subjects without feeling rushed or minimized during advising appointments. Advisors are encouraged to view students holistically by demonstrating unconditional positive regard for LGBTQA+ students. Advisors can achieve this by employing active listening skills and asking open-ended, probing questions that elicit reflective responses and can help students navigate the discrimination, microaggressions, and bigotry they may be facing on and off campus (Linley et al., 2016).

Many campuses today offer some form of Safe Zone professional development for faculty and staff members on campus to better understand LGBTQA+ issues. Advisors should attend such sessions whenever possible and actively seek out workshops, seminars, and classes that further their professional understanding of gender and affectional minority topics. Advisors who display rainbow stickers, flags, LGBTQA+ books, magazines, and images in their offices and common spaces send implicit messages to students and to the broader campus community that their environments are inclusive and safe.

Advising LGBTQA+ Students Struggling Financially

For traditional college students who live with family, the coming-out process includes fears about family rejection that are compounded by worries about the financial implications of coming out. While families are becoming increasingly supportive of individuals' decisions to come out, 68% of LGBTQA+ homeless youth (ages 16–25) experience family rejection, and more than half (54%) experience abuse in their family (Durso & Gates, 2012). These statistics are just as applicable to LGBTQA+ college students. LGBTQA+ students are at much greater risk of basic needs insecurity than heterosexual students, with bisexual and gender nonbinary students at the highest risk (Goldrick-Rab et al., 2018). Another study found that 44% of heterosexual respondents reported housing insecurities, compared to 53% of homosexual and bisexual respondents, 57% of transgender respondents, and 59% nonbinary and third-gender students (Baker-Smith et al., 2020).

The data are compelling, and the imperative is clear: LGBTQA+ students need academic advisors who are familiar with social services that provide on- and off-campus resources to address financial, food, and housing insecurities. By leveraging financial aid and institutional resources, along with utilizing institutional foundations to access scholarships supporting LGBTQA+ students, academic advisors have historically unprecedented resources to support LGBTQA+ students struggling financially.

While financial aid processes are often perceived as rigid and uncompromising, there are options for LGBTQA+ students who might experience abrupt changes in their expected family contribution (EFC) as a result of family rejection; options can include receiving a waiver from a financial aid administrator for unusual circumstances. Unusual circumstances may merit a dependency override, which is subject to a case-by-case review by and the professional judgment of the college financial aid administrator. These circumstances include an abusive family environment (e.g., court protection from abuse orders against the parents), abandonment by the parents, or the incarceration, hospitalization, or institutionalization of both parents. Academic advisors are encouraged to establish a strong and collaborative relationship with financial aid administrators at their institution.

#RealCollege Initiatives

Without sufficient access to food and a safe place to sleep, college students struggle to learn, and LGBTQA+ students are at much greater risk of basic needs insecurity than heterosexual students. #RealCollege is a national movement created by the Hope Center for College, Community, and Justice. Focused on the struggles, triumphs, and realities of what it means to be in college today, #RealCollege seeks to change the landscape of higher education so all students receive the support needed to complete their studies. As a result of this movement, more than 600 colleges and universities have established food pantries (College & University Food Bank Alliance, 2020). Moreover, many institutions, such as the Advocacy and Resource Center at Amarillo College (Magan & Scmalz, 2019) and the Human Services Center at Oregon State University (Day, 2020), are expanding on-campus services beyond food pantries to consider other aspects of student life. Academic advisors should be aware of campus efforts and participant-as-advocate programs such as the GSU4U Ambassador Program (Governors State University, 2020).

Emergency fund programs are another #RealCollege initiative increasingly being adopted by colleges. In a recent study, Kruger et al. (2016) surveyed 523 colleges and found that 82% have offered emergency aid programs for 3 or more years. Emergency programs take several forms, the five most common of which include emergency loans (67%), unrestricted grants (54%), restricted grants and campus vouchers (47% each), and food pantries (45%; Kruger et al., 2016). Increasingly, emergency aid programs are a viable option for LGBTQA+ students struggling financially.

Campus and Foundation Scholarships

Many schools offer institutional funding opportunities specifically for their LGBTQA+ students. A growing number of institutional scholarships are designated for LGBTQA+ student by the donor's intent. One such example is the Barney Frank Equality Scholarship (Bridgewater State University, 2020). Additionally, many private foundations and community-based organizations offer scholarships, such as those found in the Campus Pride National LGBTQA+ Scholarship Database. Academic advisors should be familiar with the voluminous resources online to help their LGBTQA+ advisees navigate scholarship opportunities. Additionally, campus-based writing centers often assist students writing essays required for campus and foundation scholarships. The following chapter vignettes reflect important considerations for advisors when working with LGBTQA+ students.

Vignette 1: The Case of Kyle

Kyle is a 20-year-old junior majoring in mechanical engineering. Kyle goes to Paul, his academic advisor, mid-Fall semester to talk about some issues that are contributing to his stress and anxiety. Paul has been Kyle's advisor since he was a first-year student, so he has known him for almost 2 years and has built a strong rapport with Kyle. Kyle shares with Paul that he has been dating a guy on campus named Sebastian. Sebastian is a sophomore and lives in the same residence hall as Kyle, which is where they met earlier that year. Sebastian openly identifies as queer, but Kyle isn't sure how he identifies himself. He isn't sure if he likes women or not, and he hasn't dated a girl since his senior year of high school. During a recent trip home, Kyle's parents discovered an affectionate text message Kyle received from Sebastian. They confronted Kyle about his relationship with Sebastian. Kyle grew up in a religious and politically conservative family. Kyle did not directly come out to his parents and said the text message was just a joke from a college friend.

Kyle reports to Paul that his parents did not handle seeing the text message well. They told him, "If you don't find Jesus again and repent away from this perverted, liberal lifestyle, then we are no longer supporting you financially and you will no longer reside in this house." Kyle is stressed because he is worried that he will have to quit school if his parents find out about his relationship with Sebastian. Kyle also indicates that he and Sebastian have been arguing lately because Kyle is not out among their friends. Kyle is not comfortable holding his boyfriend's hand out in public. Sebastian came out in high school, and his family and friends accepted him unconditionally. Kyle and Sebastian are at different stages of their respective coming-out processes. Kyle shares with Paul that he has not come out to his peers or his professors in his major because he often hears them making homophobic comments in class. Kyle says the field of mechanical engineering is male-dominated and not very open-minded. He seeks Paul's guidance on what to do.

When providing support to Kyle, Paul needs to be mindful that it could potentially be harmful to encourage Kyle to come out before he is ready. Knowing Kyle's parents didn't respond well to Sebastian's text message, coming out could result in significant financial struggles for Kyle, which could result in him having to drop out of college if his parents cut him off. In this case, Kyle's advisor should reaffirm that his coming-out process is unique to him and that no one should coerce Kyle to come out prematurely. Paul should normalize that identity markers such as gay, bisexual, and queer are fluid and that Kyle is not required to adhere to rigid labels even if his boyfriend is at a different stage of his coming-out process. It may also be useful for Paul to consult with Cass's (1979) identity model to determine the identity development stages Kyle and Sebastian are in and how that may be impacting their romantic relationship. Paul should provide Kyle with financial aid options that can support him in the event Kyle chooses to come out and his parents cut off their financial support. Paul can offer to set up a confidential meeting between Kyle and a financial aid staff member that is experienced with the unique and sensitive issues related to being out and LGBTQA+ on campus. Turning to the IEM for guidance may also help Paul while advising Kyle.

The internal factors from the IEM Kyle may be grappling with are his internalized homoprejudice and struggle with self-acceptance. Additionally, some of the external factors of IEM—such as family environment, school or peer environment, and his family's religion—are impacting how Kyle is managing his own affectional identity.

Vignette Reflection Questions

1. What considerations should Kyle's advisor take into account when providing support to Kyle?
2. What stages in the sexual/affectional identity models are Kyle and his boyfriend Sebastian in? How does being in two different developmental stages impact their romantic relationship?
3. What financial resources should his advisor look into for Kyle, especially if he loses financial support from his parents for coming out?

Issues and Challenges Faced by Newly Out Students

Once students come out and have disclosed their identities to family members, friends, roommates, faculty members, and campus professionals, LGBTQA+ students still experience many of the same academic and career decisions other students face. Using an intersectional lens, advisors must take into account the extra burdens sexual or gender minorities face in their academic and career development process. Career-advising frameworks, such as those identified by Gordon (2019a), can be useful but should be applied with LGBTQA+ identity models in order to shape student success (see chapter 7). Gordon (2019a) identified a 3-I Process that begins with an exploration stage of career planning, moves into a crystallization stage in which students make progress towards a career or occupational choice, and ends with a choice stage in which a commitment to a career path is forged. However, it is imperative advisors are mindful that LGBTQA+ students cannot begin career planning if systemic barriers negatively impede their wellness and success. If students do not feel safe on campus as a sexual or gender minority student, they will not be able to engage in career decision-making or selecting an appropriate major or minor. Academic advisors must utilize a developmental advising approach when working with these students and help them get beyond the notion that academic advisors are there only for course scheduling and registration queries (Gordon, 2019b). Once an LGBTQA+ student declares a major and is maintaining academic success in their grades and performance, advisors can play a key role in helping students consider whether or not to come out to prospective employers during job interviews and how to ask potential employers about same-sex partner benefits or nondiscrimination policies (Manera & Frank, 2014; Manning, 2015).

Advisors should continue to support students, especially those facing social, academic, or familial challenges from disclosing their affectional or gender identities. Taking a strengths-based perspective, an advisor can help newly out students identify what is going well and develop coping strategies for dealing with relationships that may have soured after the student shared their LGBTQA+ identity. Advisors can also help LGBTQA+ students with the stress, anxiety, and depression related to potential rejection by family members and friends, asserting that any negative reactions and nonacceptance may only be temporary. Family members, friends, and roommates may need time to adjust to the student's newly out identity and to integrate this information into their perception of the person they have previously known and cared for.

Vignette 2: Queer Student of Color

Marwan is a 19-year-old African American male who is a second-year student on campus. Marwan grew up in an urban city surrounded by a strong African-American community. Marwan and his family have been active members in the Black church since he was a baby. Marwan sang in the youth choir and faithfully attended services every Wednesday evening and all day Sunday until he left for college. In college, Marwan is actively involved in the Black Student Union and a gospel choir. Over the past few months, Marwan has struggled with his sexual orientation. It is something he has kept hidden since he was 10 years old. Marwan had one experience with a young boy in his neighborhood when he was 12, but they never talked about it after the experience and nobody ever found out. For many years, Marwan stifled his thoughts and feelings about his same-gender attraction.

A month ago, Marwan came across a flyer posted in the student center promoting a guest speaker who was giving a talk entitled: "Coming Full Circle: Black, Same-Gender-Loving Men and the Black Church." Marwan decided to attend and sat in the back. While listening to the speaker, he related to what he was hearing. Although Marwan wasn't sure if he was "gay," he did connect with the term "same-gender-loving men," which resonated with his life experience. After attending the talk on campus, Marwan discovered books in the library that dealt with the intersections of being Black and gay. The more he read, the more he realized that he was not attracted to women at all. He was exclusively physically and emotionally attracted to men. Marwan knew that, given his upbringing, he would not be accepted by his home church community. Marwan recently disclosed his identity to another Black male in the gospel choir who is gay but not out in the choir. A week later, Marwan decided to stop inside the LGBTQA+ Pride Center on campus. When he walked in, he noticed that all the students were white—even the director was a white woman. The students in the Pride Center welcomed him and asked him if he had any questions. Marwan lied, telling them he had a paper due for a class and just wanted to take a few brochures.

Over the following weeks, Marwan felt conflicted. He feels at home in the Black Student Union organization and knows the importance of having a comfortable place where he can be around other students of color. However, he often overhears homophobic and transphobic comments made by some students of color and he doesn't feel safe disclosing his same-gender feelings. At the same time, Marwan does want to spend more time inside the LGBTQA+ Pride Center to help him learn more about what is means to be gay, but he does not feel supported as a queer student of color.

Marwan has an appointment with his academic advisor, Mariana—a Latina who he has known for a year. Marwan noticed that Mariana attended the lecture on same-gender-loving men, so he is hoping that she is open to him sharing his struggles.

As an ally for LGBTQA+ students, Mariana might work on deepening her professional rapport with Marwan by discussing the lecture on same-gender-loving men. She could also provide Marwan with additional resources and reading material he could use to reflect and that might help him discover more about his identity. Additionally, Marwan may believe he is the only queer student of color on campus. Mariana might recommend he meet some of the other queer students of color (QSOC) on campus so he can experience a sense of significance and connection with others who share his racial identity and affectional orientation.

Vignette Reflection Questions

1. How might Marwan's intersecting identities—as an African American and same-gender-loving man—impact his academic, interpersonal, and professional development on campus?
2. What steps can Marwan's advisor take to ensure Marwan feels a stronger sense of significance and support as a queer student of color?

Vignette 3: Supporting a Trans Student

Blake is a senior majoring in business and has been active in the LGBTQA+ student organization, Q'nnections. Blake has come out as a trans man (FtM), but he identified as a cisgender lesbian when he first arrived at the university. During his senior year, Blake has been wearing baggier clothes that make him feel more masculine and using different pronouns to identify himself. He publicly identifies as Blake. Blake has made the decision to transition, including taking testosterone and having top surgery. Before the Spring semester begins, Blake files paperwork with the university to have his name changed on his student ID and school rosters from Brianna to Blake.

In his Fall semester, Blake had Professor Fielding in Economics I and has him again for Economics II in the Spring. When Blake shows up to the first day of Economics II, his instructor looks confused when he goes through the class roster. He asks Blake if he is really Brianna. Blake doesn't know how to respond to Professor Fielding's questions, especially in front of the other students. Most of the students in Blake's class know about his transition and are supportive. However, as the Spring semester progresses, Professor Fielding continues to misgender Blake and refers to him as Brianna and with female pronouns. Blake is reluctant to attend Professor Fielding's class, so his grades and performance in the class are slipping. He doesn't know what to do. Blake makes an appointment with Karen, his academic advisor, for guidance.

It is important for Karen to ensure she is using Blake's correct pronouns. If she knows Professor Fielding, it may be helpful to schedule a meeting on Blake's behalf with the professor to talk about trans college students and the importance of using students' chosen names and pronouns. Karen can also offer to host a professional development session for faculty members on LGBTQA+ issues in the College of Business and work with the administration to provide resources on trans issues to faculty members. Karen should encourage Blake to explore the impact his transition is having on his emotional, mental, and physical well-being. Karen can also encourage Blake to reach out to other upper-class trans students in Q'nnections to see how they manage transphobic comments and microaggressions on campus.

Vignette Reflection Questions

1. How does Professor Fielding's lack of knowledge about trans college students and his interactions with Blake impact Blake's academic and personal life?
2. What role can Karen take to support Blake's transition and to help Professor Fielding understand the impact of his biased conduct?
3. What additional campus and community resources addressing trans students can Karen call upon to help Blake?

Resources for LGBTQA+ Students

Miller (2012) stated, "Advisors teach students how to make the most of their college experience" (p. 1). Understanding that LGBTQA+ students are among the diverse student populations being advised at a university is central to effective advising. To effectively advise LGBTQA+ students, advisors—regardless of their sexual orientations—must understand LGBTQA+ identity development and the full scope of resources necessary to support LGBTQA+ advisees, both on and off campus. Discussed in the following sections are the three most common resources for LGBTQA+ students.

LGBTQA+ Resource Centers

A primary resource for LGBTQA+ students is LGBTQA+ resource centers, which may take the form of an institutionally-sponsored campus center or a community-sponsored center. LGBTQA+ resource centers are administrative offices that provide resources and support for gender nonconforming and queer students. These centers can be invaluable in creating safe and affirming environments. While centers were initially incorporated into variety of different organizational structures, most are now self-standing or part of a women's or gender resource center. Unfortunately, too few colleges have dedicated LGBTQA+ student centers—about 150 such centers exist across the 2,000 colleges and universities in the United States (Fine, 2012). Whether on or off campus, resource centers provide powerful assets to LGBTQA+ students. Increasingly, many community-based centers now include medical services, which can be a particular benefit to trans students (Hoffshire & Campbell, 2019).

Counseling Centers

At institutions without LGBTQA+ Resource Centers, counseling centers often serve as an alternative resource. The professional ethics and clinical experience required for clinical mental health counselors allows them to serve LGBTQA+ students. Not only do counseling centers provide individualized student support, they often coordinate support groups and host Safe Zone workshops.

Network of LGBTQA+ Faculty and Staff Members

Mentors are a powerful resource for LGBTQA+ students who are coming out to themselves and others. It is important for advisors to be aware of faculty and staff members who can serve as mentors (Burt et al., 2013). It can be particularly helpful to pair a sexual and/or gender minority student with mentors who share their intersectional identities. Human resources and alumni departments often sponsor LGBTQA+ affinity groups, and members from those groups are eager to engage with students and serve as mentors.

Conclusion

Academic advisors are often the first point of contact for students accessing support and resources on campus (Ottenritter, 2012; Zamani-Gallaher & Choudhuri, 2016). The field of academic advising needs to engage in further research and exploration of ways the field can offer more formal support to LGBTQA+ students. For institutions to retain sexual and/or gender minority students, intentional interventions must be systematically created for supporting students in their individual coming-out journeys.

References

Alessi, E. J., & Hartman, E. (2018). Incorporating minority stress theory into clinical practice with sexual-minority populations. In M. P. Dentato (Ed.), *Social work practice with the LGBTQ community: The intersection of history, health, mental health, and policy factors* (pp. 249–265). Oxford University Press.

Baker-Smith, C., Coca, V., Goldrick-Rab, S., Looker, E., Richardson, B. & Williams, T. (2020). *#RealCollege 2020: Five years of evidence on basic needs insecurity*. The Hope Center for College, Community, and Justice. https://hope4college.com/wp-content/uploads/2020/02/2019_RealCollege_Survey_Report.pdf

Bilodeau, B. L., & Renn, K. A. (2005). Analysis of LGBT identity development models and implications for practice. *New Directions for Student Services, 2005*(111), 25–39. https://doi.org/10.1002/ss.171

Bridgewater State University (2020). *Our opportunities*. https://bridgew.academic-works.com/opportunities/5232

Burt, T. D., Young-Jones, A. D., Yadon, C. A., & Carr, M. T. (2013). The advisor and instructor as a dynamic duo: Academic motivation and basic psychological needs. *NACADA Journal, 33*(2), 44–54. https://doi.org/10.12930/NACADA-13-006

Cass, V. C. (1979). Homosexual identity formation: a theoretical model. *Journal of Homosexuality, 4*(3), 219–233. https://doi.org/10.1300/J082v04n03_01

Chaudoir, S. R., Wang, K., & Pachankis, J. E. (2017). What reduces sexual minority stress? A review of the intervention "toolkit." *Journal of Social Issues, 73*(3), 586–617. https://doi.org/10.1111/josi.12233

College & University Food Bank Alliance (2020, May 25). *About us*. https://www.cufba.org/about-us/

Day, J. (2020, March 6). Aiming to meet students' basic needs. *Corvallis Gazette-Times*. https://www.gazettetimes.com/news/local/aiming-to-meet-students-basic-needs/article_c3e45385-29ca-5c50-9faa-007ac5aba7d9.html

Durso, L. E., & Gates, G. J. (2012). *Serving our youth: Findings from a national survey of service providers working with lesbian, gay, bisexual, and transgender youth who are homeless or at risk of becoming homeless.* The Williams Institute with True Colors Fund and The Palette Fund. https://escholarship.org/uc/item/80x75033

Fassinger, R. E., & Miller, B. A. (1997). Validation of an inclusive model of sexual minority identity formation on a sample of gay men. *Journal of Homosexuality, 32*(2), 53–79. https://doi.org/10.1300/J082v32n02_04

Few-Demo, A. L., Humble, A. M., Curran, M. A., & Lloyd, S. A. (2016). Queer theory, intersectionality, and LGBT-parent families: Transformative critical pedagogy in family theory. *Journal of Family Theory & Review, 8*(1), 74–94. https://doi.org/10.1111/jftr.12127

Fine, L.E. (2012). The context of creating space: Assessing the likelihood of college LGBT center presence. *Journal of College Student Development, 53*(2), 285–299. https://doi.org/10.1353/csd.2012.0017.

Frost, D. M., Fine, M., Torre, M. E., & Cabana, A. (2019). Minority stress, activism, and health in the context of economic precarity: Results from a national participatory action survey lesbian, gay, bisexual, transgender, queer, and gender non-conforming youth. *American Journal of Community Psychology, 63*(3–4), 511–526. https://doi.org/10.1002/ajcp.12326

Garvey, J. C., Taylor, J. L., & Rankin, S. (2015). An examination of campus climate for LGBTQ community college students. *Community College Journal of Research and Practice, 39*(6), 527–541. https://doi.org/10.1080/10668926.2013.861374

Goldrick-Rab, S., Richardson, J., Schneider, J., Hernandez, A., & Cady, C. (2018). *Still hungry and homeless in college.* Wisconsin Hope Lab. https://hope4college.com/wp-content/uploads/2018/09/Wisconsin-HOPE-Lab-Still-Hungry-and-Homeless.pdf

Gordon, V. N. (2019a). The 3-I process: A career-advising framework. *NACADA Journal, 39*(2), 64–71. (Reprinted from *NACADA Journal, 14*(2), 1994, 72–76). https://doi.org/10.12930/NACADA-19-202

Gordon, V. N. (2019b). Developmental advising: The elusive ideal. *NACADA Journal, 39*(2), 72–76. (Reprinted from Career advising: *An academic advisor's guide*, pp. 45–65, by V. N. Gordon, 2006, John Wiley & Sons.) https://doi.org/10.12930/NACADA-19-201

Governors State University. (2020, March 14). *GSSU4U student assistance.* https://www.govst.edu/gsu4u/

Hoffshire, M., & Campbell, E. (2019). Examining the advisor experience of student-run LGBTQ+ organizations within community colleges. *New Directions for Community Colleges, 2019*(188), 55–66. https://doi.org/10.1002/cc.20378

Holman, E. G. (2018). Theoretical extensions of minority stress theory for sexual minority individuals in the workplace: A cross-contextual understanding of minority stress processes. *Journal of Family Theory & Review, 10*(1), 165–180. https://doi.org/10.1111/jftr.12246

Kocet, M. M. (Ed.). (2014). *Counseling gay men, adolescents, and boys: A strengths-based guide for helping professionals and educators.* Routledge.

Kruger, K., Parnell, A., & Wesaw, A. (2016). *Landscape analysis of emergency aid programs*. National Association of Student Personnel Administrators (NASPA). https://www.naspa.org/images/uploads/main/ Emergency_Aid_Report.pdf

Linley, J. L., Nguyen, D., Brazelton, G. B., Becker, B., Renn, K., & Woodford, M. (2016). Faculty as sources of support for LGBTQ college students. *College Teaching, 64*(2), 55–63. http://doi.org/10.1080/87567555.2015.1078275

Magan, K., & Scmalz, J. (2019, April 3). A culture of caring. *The Chronicle of Higher Education.* https://www.chronicle.com/article/a-culture-of-caring

Manera, J. J., & Frank D. A. (2014). Coming out and identity development needs in gay men, adolescents, and boys. In M. M. Kocet (Ed.), *Counseling gay men, adolescents, and boys: A strengths-based guide for helping professionals and educators* (pp. 3–23). Routledge.

Manning, J. (2015). Communicating sexual identities: A typology of coming out. *Sexuality & Culture, 19*, 122–138. https://doi.org/10.1007/s12119-014-9251-4

Matthews, C. H., & Salazar, C. F. (2012). An integrative, empowerment model for helping lesbian, gay, and bisexual youth negotiate the coming-out process. *Journal of LGBT Issues in Counseling, 6*(2), 96–117. https://doi.org/10.1080/15538 605.2012.678176

Mereish, E. H., & Poteat, V. P. (2015). A relational model of sexual minority mental and physical health: The negative effects of shame on relationships, loneliness, and health. *Journal of Counseling Psychology, 62*(3), 425–437. https://doi.org/ 10.1037/cou0000088

Meyer, I. H. (2003). Prejudice, social stress, and mental health in lesbian, gay, and bisexual populations: Conceptual issues and research evidence. *Psychological Bulletin, 129*(5), 674–697. https://doi.org/10.1037/0033-2909.129.5.674

Michaels, M. S., Parent, M. C., & Torrey, C. L. (2015). A minority stress model for suicidal ideation in gay men. *Suicide and Life-Threatening Behavior, 46*(1), 23–34. https://doi.org/10.1111/sltb.12169

Miller, M. A. (2012, November 5). *Structuring our conversations: Shifting to four dimensional advising models.* http://www.nacada.ksu.edu/Resources/Clearinghouse/View-Articles/Structuring-Our-Conversations-Shifting-to-Four-Dimensional-Advising-Models.aspx

Ottenritter, N. (2012). Crafting a caring and inclusive environment for LGBTQ community college students, faculty, and staff. *Community College Journal of Research and Practice, 36*(7), 531–538. https://doi.org/10.1080/10668926.2012.664094

Parra, L. A., & Hastings, P. D. (2018). Integrating the neurobiology of minority stress with an intersectionality framework for LGBTQ-Latinx populations. *New Directions for Child and Adolescent Development, 161*, 91–108.

Pollitt, A. M., Muraco, J. A., Grossman, A. H., & Russell, S. T. (2017). Disclosure stress, social support, and depressive symptoms among cisgender bisexual youth. *Journal of Marriage and Family, 79*(5), 1278–1294. https://doi.org/10.1111/ jomf.12418

Reicherzer, S., Garland-Forshee, A. S., & Patton, J. (2014). Counseling in the periphery of queer discourse: Transgender children, adolescents, women, and men. In M. M. Kocet (Ed.), *Counseling gay men, adolescents, and boys: A strengths-based guide for helping professionals and educators* (pp. 178–194). Routledge.

Riggle, E. D. B., Gonzalez, K. A., Rostosky, S. S., & Black, W. W. (2014). Cultivating positive LGBTQA identities: An intervention study with college students. *Journal of LGBT Issues in Counseling, 8*(3), 264–281. https://doi.org/10.1080/15538605.2014.933468

Salfas, B., Rendine, H. J., & Parsons, J. T. (2019). What is the role of the community? Examining minority stress processes among gay and bisexual men. *Stigma and Health, 4*(3), 300–309. https://doi.org/10.1037/sah0000143

Sanlo, R. L. (Ed.). (2005). Gender identity and sexual orientation: Research, policy, and personal perspectives [Special issue]. *New Directions for Student Services, 2005*(111).

Stewart, D.-L., Renn, K. A., & Brazelton, G. B. (2015). Gender and sexual diversity in U.S. higher education: Contexts and opportunities for LGBTQ college students [Special issue]. *New Directions for Student Services, 2015*(152).

Vianden, J. (2016). Ties that bind: Academic advisors as agents of student relationship management. *NACADA Journal, 36*(1), 19–29. https://doi.org/10.12930/NACADA-15-026a

Zamani-Gallaher, E. M., & Choudhuri, D. D. (2016). Tracing LGBTQ community college students' experiences. *New Directions for Community Colleges, 2016*(174), 47–63.

Zubernis, L., Snyder, M., & McCoy, V. A. (2011). Counseling lesbian and gay college students through the lens of Cass's and Chickering's developmental models. *Journal of LGBT Issues in Counseling, 5*(2), 122–150. https://doi.org/10.1080/15538605.2011.578506

4

QUEER THEORY AND
ACADEMIC ADVISING

Christy Carlson

I am a cis, White, queer woman whose background in English Literature and, more specifically, in literary theory (deconstruction, feminist poststructuralism, queer theory), has helped inform my worldview and, more recently, my approach to academic advising. Inspired by advising scholarship coming out of the humanities and by the call for proposals at the 2011 Region 5 NACADA conference with the theme, "Beyond Normal: Expanding Your Advising Potential," I found connections between my past engagement with queer theory and my present role as an academic advisor (linked, in part, by an episode of Buffy the Vampire Slayer *titled "Normal Again"). This chapter conceptualizes an advising approach inspired by queer theory.*

"While colleges and universities have generated much of the existing queer theory literature, they have remained substantially untouched by the queer [theory] agenda" by resisting "the queering of higher education itself" (Renn, 2010, p. 132). The difference between studying *queer identities* and *queering higher education institutions* hinges on the distinction between queer as a *noun* and queer as a *verb*. Queering higher education involves applying queer theory to a broad array of issues in higher education. In the context of this chapter, queering involves examining and questioning the ways identities are produced, policed, and naturalized within the everyday practices of our colleges and universities. The goal of this process is to "open up . . . possibilities" that are unintelligible or are yet to come (Butler, 1999, p. viii). This chapter builds on the work of others (e.g., Abes, 2019; Abes & Kasch, 2007; Denton, 2016, 2019; Fraser & Lamble, 2014) who have answered Renn's (2010) call for queer theory-based scholarship that examines higher education institutions in ways reaching beyond LGBTQA+-specific topics and identities. I begin with a brief overview of the terms *queer* and *queer theory* before outlining Butler's theory of performativity. Finally, I propose several ways of applying Butler's theory to the practice of academic advising.

Framing Queer Theory

The term *queer* has been and continues to be used in multiple, conflicting ways: as an epithet used to shame those who are perceived as abnormal, particularly in relation to sexuality (Butler, 1993); as an identity category that functions as an "umbrella term for nonconforming genders and various sexualities, ones that did not easily submit to categorization" (Butler, as cited in Ahmed, 2016, p. 490); and as a term that critiques identity categories and the very notion of categorization (Butler, 1993, 1999, 2004). Each of these conceptualizations of queer appropriates previous iterations of the term. Queer, as an umbrella term, reclaims the epithet, redefining queer as a shared identity seeking recognition and rights; queer as a critique of identity categories reframes these categories as constructed, marginalizing, and exclusionary (Butler, as cited in Ahmed, 2016).

In this chapter, I use the term *queer* to signal a critique of identity categories. From this perspective, queer challenges notions of unity, coherence, and stability that have traditionally been associated with identity. As Sedgwick (1993) noted, etymologically "[t]he word 'queer' itself means *across*" (p. xii). Queer is an "open mesh of possibilities, gaps, overlaps, dissonances, resonances, lapses and excesses of meaning when the constituent elements of anyone's [identity] . . . are made (or *can't be* made) to signify monolithically" (p. 8). In other words, queer, as it is deployed in queer theory, does not refer to an identity (a noun) and is not a descriptive term. Rather, queer is a verb that signals a *disruption* of identity that is often understood as natural or fixed.

Queer's "definitional indeterminacy," or its inability to be defined and its critique of processes of definition, makes the task of defining the field of queer theory similarly challenging (Jagose, 1996, p. 1). Queer theory is not a coherent body of work (Hall, 2003). Moreover, it has no proper subject (Eng et al., 2005); as Halperin (1995) argued "[t]*here is nothing in particular to which* [the term queer] *necessarily refers*" (p. 62). Queer, as it is taken up in queer theory, does not refer to any particular subject, and it is better understood as a set of practices that disrupt the naturalization and stabilization of identities. Indeed, as the next section of this chapter discusses in more detail, identity, as perceived through a queer theory perspective, is illusory. What we consider reality is a reality *effect* rather than something real (i.e., natural, essential, coherent; Butler, 1993, 1999, 2004).

Additionally, because queer is oriented to the future, it is a category that is always necessarily in the process of *becoming* rather than *being* (Halberstam, 2005; Muñoz, 2009). Viewed through a queer theory perspective, identity categories are open and contestable, "never fully owned but always and only redeployed, twisted, queered from a prior usage" (Butler, 1993, p. 228). As a result, queer theory does not escape its own queering. Critiques of queer theory's exclusions—its privileging of some identities and marginalization of others—have resulted in a wide range of redeployments or reiterations that take the term in new directions. Indeed, the incompleteness of queer means it is always open to challenge. A few of the many iterations of queer theory include queer(s) of color critique (Ferguson, 2003), "quare" theory (Johnson, 2001), queer disability studies/crip theory (McRuer, 2006), queer indigenous studies (Driskill et al., 2011), and queer diasporas (Eng, 2003; Puar, 2005).

While queer theory is not a theory of identity and does not center a queer subject, it is nevertheless a theory and critique of identity *construction*, a set of practices which queer theory is both critical of and complicit with. Queer theory's relation to identity is, in this sense, deconstructive. While acknowledging that we cannot escape identity categories, queer theory puts identity "under erasure" (Spivak, 1976, p. xiv). It acknowledges the concept is "inaccurate" but also "necessary" (Spivak, 1976, p. xiv). Typographically, putting a term under erasure entails "writ[ing] a word, cross[ing] it out, and print[ing] both the word and deletion" (Spivak, 1976, p. xiv). Conceptually, this act conveys that we are using "the only available language while not subscribing to its premises" (Spivak, 1976, p. xviii). For queer theory, the aim is not to create a better, more inclusive identity category because categories, by definition, marginalize and exclude. Instead, the aim is to denaturalize and destabilize identity categories and practices of categorization by focusing on and challenging mechanisms of normalization (Warner, 1999).

Butler's Theory of Performativity

In this section, I outline certain aspects of Butler's theory of performativity in order to lay the groundwork for the final section of this chapter— applications to advising. While Butler's work is closely identified with queer theory, this field, as I mentioned previously, is not a singular entity. I am not making a claim for Butler's work as representative of queer theory, nor do I provide a comprehensive overview of Butler's work as a whole. I frame my discussion of an advising approach informed by queer theory through Butler's theory of performativity as means for providing a helpful lens through which to view certain aspects of advising practice.

Butler provided a perspective on marginalization and oppression that focused on the ways identities (or subjects) are produced, policed, and naturalized. For Butler (1993, 1999, 2004), a girl is not a preexisting subject who behaves in certain ways because of who she naturally is. Instead, she is brought into existence as a girl through the performance of idealized norms of girlhood. The forcible assignment of gender—"the naming of the 'girl'" as such—initiates a process that compels the girl to regulate her behavior (Butler, 1993, p. 232). In order to be recognizable as a girl, she is required to repeat preexisting norms including "bodily gestures, movements, and styles" (Butler, 1999, p. 179). The continual, forced citation of norms through the embodiment and enactment of an idealized concept of girl produces the gendered subject as "an effect of this performance" (Butler, 2004, p. 218).

The notion of an internal "gender core" (Butler, 1999, p. 173), an essence of gender "behind the expressions of gender" (Butler, 1999, p. 33), is an illusion produced by "the very 'expressions' that are said to be its results" (Butler, 1999, p. 33). There is no preexisting girl who chooses to enact gender norms; instead, the repetition of preexisting norms retroactively produces the girl. Over time, the repetition of gender norms "congeal[s] to produce the appearance of . . . a natural sort of being" (Butler, 1999, pp. 43–44) which conceals the mechanisms that produce the subject. As a result, the regulatory and disciplinary nature of norms remains obscured and unquestioned (Butler, 1993, 1999). These norms remain at the same time "violently policed" and "taken for granted" (Butler, 1999, p. xix).

The performative construction of the subject is a relational process. The naming of the girl is also the establishment of a boundary whereby *girl* is defined in its difference from *boy*. Further, the construction of binary categories (man/woman, masculinity/femininity) works to regulate and consolidate each term within "the obligatory frame of reproductive heterosexuality" (Butler, 1999, p. 173). Compulsory heterosexuality requires the coherence of sex, gender, and sexuality such that "man" aligns with "masculinity" and with desiring women, while "woman" aligns with "femininity" and with desiring men (Butler, 1999). When these categories do not align, for example, when a man is perceived as not masculine enough, as outside the norm of ideal masculinity, the naturalness and stability of these norms is put into question (Butler, 2004).

Foreclosing and erasing what is not legible within the bounds of these categories shores up their coherence (Butler, 1993). Those who "do not appear properly gendered" are refused social recognition and figured as impossible subjects (Butler, 1993, p. 8). In this way, the production of human subjects also produces "the less 'human,' the inhuman, the humanly unthinkable" (Butler, 1993, p. 8). Expelled from the category of "human," these subjects "haunt" the borders of this category "with the persistent possibility of their disruption" (Butler, 1993, p. 8). If a person threatens norms of binary gender by appearing to do gender differently, policing ensues in an attempt to make that subject illegible: "to question its possibility, to render it unreal and impossible in the face of its appearance to the contrary" (Butler, 2004, p. 35). The categorization of some individuals as impossible subjects reinforces the boundaries of and naturalizes identity categories.

Gender normativity, in this way, impacts people's lives. The production and reproduction of gender norms "has consequences for how gender presentations are criminalized and pathologized, how subjects who cross gender risk internment and imprisonment, [and] why violence against . . . [trans] subjects is not recognized as violence" (Butler, 2004, p. 30). When we do not conform to gender norms, which is to say, when we do not behave in the ways we are "supposed" to behave as men or women, "it is unclear whether our genders are real or ever can be regarded as such," and it is unclear "whether our lives are valuable, or can be made to be" (Butler, 2004, p. 206). For Butler (2004), if we are not recognizable within the social norms that organize our lives, "then we are not possible beings; we have been foreclosed from possibility" (p. 31). Butler's (2004) critique of normativity aimed to "open up the possibility of different modes of living" (p. 4) and to extend legitimacy to "bodies that have been regarded as false, unreal, and unintelligible" (Butler, 1999, p. xxiii). This requires, among other things, that we "cease legislating for all lives what is livable only for some" (Butler, 2004, p. 8).

While Butler is most often associated with the concept of gender performativity, she has also written about the regulation and production of other normative categories, including race. In conversation with Yancy, Butler discussed the ways performing Whiteness perpetuates relations of dominance between White and Black people (Yancy & Butler, 2015). Norms that communicate that "[B]lack lives do not matter" are produced and reinforced by performative acts, "daily practices, modes of address, through the organization of schools, work, prison, law and media" (Yancy & Butler, 2015, para. 23).

Butler argued that Whiteness is produced as the norm by defining *Blackness* "as a deviation from the human or even as a threat to the human, or as something not quite human" (Yancy & Butler, 2015, para. 20). As a result, "it becomes increasingly easy for [W]hite people to accept the destruction of [B]lack lives as status quo, since those lives do not fit the norm of human life" (Yancy & Butler, 2015, para. 20). As Butler (Yancy & Butler, 2015) explained, maintaining norms results in full subjecthood being denied to some and lives thus being devalued, discarded, and destroyed. What is at stake in "the universal formulation, 'all lives matter'" is that it "miss[es] the fact that [B]lack people have not yet been included in the idea of 'all lives'" (Yancy & Butler, 2015, para. 18). Ultimately, it is by interrogating the category of human, where human equates to White people, and redeploying this category such that Black people are intelligible as human, that change becomes possible (Yancy & Butler, 2015).

Butler's theory of performativity emphasized the ways people are constrained and compelled to repeat and embody norms, but, paradoxically, the repetitive nature of this process means the subject "cannot be wholly defined or fixed" (Butler, 1993, p. 10); rather, the subject is always in a state of becoming, of possibly exceeding the norm (Butler, 2004). In other words, the subject "never quite inhabits the ideal" they are trying to replicate (Butler, 1993, p. 231). The reiterative nature of subject formation opens up "gaps and fissures" (Butler, 1993, p. 10) and, in so doing, reveals norms as "nonnatural and nonnecessary" (Butler, 2004, p. 218). Exaggerated efforts to fix and naturalize norms—for example, by demanding subjects work harder to approximate them—belies the fact that they are "continually haunted by their own inefficacy" (Butler, 1993, p. 237). The repetition that fails has the potential to reveal the norm's built-in instabilities (Butler, 1993).

In reconceptualizing gender (and other normative identity categories) as an effect, Butler (1999) introduced agency into a field in which agency has been "foreclosed by positions that take identity categories as foundational and fixed" (p. 187). While it may appear that the names we are called (e.g., girl) fix us, calling us these names "may also produce an unexpected and enabling response," a repetition that initiates change (Butler, 1997, p. 2). Critique, or an interrogation of the mechanisms by which norms are produced and naturalized, is also a way in which these norms become legible and denaturalized (Butler, 2004). This interrogation might involve noticing and drawing attention to ways in which norms are deemed real or not real and ways certain performances render categorization challenging (Butler, 2004). By being attentive to the discontinuities between normative ideals and attempts to approximate these ideals, we can open transformative possibilities of "becoming otherwise" (Butler, 2004, p. 217). As Butler (1993, 1999) argued, agency is paradoxically enabled by the constructedness of identity.

Applications to Advising

I propose that an advising approach informed by Butler's theory focuses on challenging norms and normativity. It interrogates and denaturalizes identity categories, revealing ways these categories constrain, exclude, and marginalize. In other words, this advising approach addresses identity only insofar as it puts identity categories into question. Rather than centering marginalized identities, this approach challenges the practices that produce marginalization in the first place (Butler, 1993, 1999, 2004). For this reason, the applications to advising I will discuss in this chapter do not involve strategies to increase inclusion and representation in the name of LGBTQA+ (or other) identities. For the same reason, this is not an approach for advising students who identify as LGBTQA+. While some who identify as LGBTQA+ or as other marginalized identities may find this approach helpful, precisely because it challenges and destabilizes identity categories, others may find it unhelpful for the same reasons. As Butler noted, some who are marginalized on the basis of identity may want and require stable, binary identity categories in order to live a livable life (as cited in Ahmed, 2016).

Most broadly, this approach addresses the exclusion and marginalization of students in the context of higher education by questioning the normative mechanisms that subjectify and constrain students, making some lives more intelligible and thus more livable while obscuring and excluding other, non-normative possibilities. That is, this approach unpacks the ways our student-centered practices reproduce and naturalize idealized norms and, in so doing, cause injury to the very students we seek to help. Ultimately, this approach asks how challenging or denaturalizing normative categories may open new possibilities.

A Butlerian approach to addressing the ways categories marginalize and exclude differs in certain ways from other approaches. Many scholars (e.g., Harper & Quaye, 2015; Kuh & Love, 2000; Museus, 2014; Rendón et al., 2000) have critiqued the ways normative identity categories circulating within institutions of higher education marginalize students by obscuring differences. Kuh and Love (2000) argued that Tinto's theory of student departure uses a singular notion of culture and, as a result, does not "account for experiences of members of different groups" (p. 199) or differences within subgroups of these groups. Smit (2012) posited that students "who come from academic disadvantage" . . . [do not all] experience the same difficulties in higher education" (p. 377). Similarly, Jack (as cited in Hough, 2017) explained that low-income college students bring with them significantly different amounts of cultural and academic capital.

In different ways, these scholars all called for a more nuanced and differentiated approach to understanding students' experiences and needs. From a Butlerian perspective, however, addressing the exclusionary nature of normative categories by recognizing differences within these categories does not challenge the system of categorization. Indeed, by drawing attention to, studying, and targeting increasingly specific identity categories, we reinforce and naturalize the very processes we seek to challenge. A Butlerian approach would examine the *productive* nature of these normative categories; it would denaturalize the practices of categorization that produce the very identities they ostensibly describe.

On an institutional level, a Butlerian approach could begin by identifying and interrogating normative categories we use to specify and regulate students. More pointedly, this approach could reveal how categories that appear natural and coherent are produced and unstable. Some examples of naturalized categories within higher education include high achieving/low achieving (often reframed by students as smart/not smart), engaged/not engaged, first-generation/not-first-generation, and at-risk/not-at-risk. A few additional binary categories that circulate regularly in advising conversations are best/worst majors and easy/hard courses. In the remaining part of this section, I provide a few examples of how a Butlerian approach could address the reproduction and denaturalization of these categories.

From a Butlerian perspective, *smart* is not an essential identity. It is not a *being*; it is a *doing*. Smart students are not naturally smart; they *perform* smartness and, as a result, are intelligible as smart. This is not to say there is no biological basis for intelligence; rather, that the biological is always already cultural. We cannot know intelligence outside of normative, culturally based ways of understanding. Using a Butlerian approach, intelligence is not a trait but rather the product of a relationship between practices and categories. Smart is a constructed, unstable category always on the verge of failure. When we subjectify individuals as *smart*, we naturalize this category. Further, the construction of the category *smart*, by definition, also constructs the category *not smart* and establishes a hierarchy.

In the end, this process of categorization has the potential to cause injury to students, not just by constraining their behavior by calling them into being as normative subjects, but also by marginalizing and excluding those who do not sufficiently approximate the idealized norm. When "smart" students fail, the essential nature of the category is called into question. But instead of recognizing the constructed, nonnatural nature of this category, these students may conclude that they are, in essence, not smart—the categories are sound, and the students were just mis-categorized—thus shoring up and naturalizing the boundary between these categories.

Similarly, when we attempt to help students who are "not yet" smart "become smarter" by teaching them how to achieve the norm of smartness, we leave these normative categories unquestioned and, in so doing, leave intact the hierarchy that privileges some and marginalizes others (Dweck, 2015). In teaching students how to become intelligible as smart, we are just redrawing the boundary line, adjusting who is inside and who is outside of the category. As a result, we reinforce and naturalize the smart/not smart divide. Advisors could help students understand the constructed nature of this category by asking: "What does smart look like in this discipline or that course? What does this perspective exclude? To what ends are these things excluded?" Advisors could also ask students to interpret this category: "What does smart mean? Could smart mean other things? Are there other ways of understanding a student's academic performance?"

One of the most commonly cited categories in higher education—the at-risk student—is naturalized through the creation of programs, policies, workshops, and committees, all of which aim to support and retain at-risk students. *At-risk* is not, however, a natural or preexisting identity; it does not describe attributes of individuals. Rather, this identity is produced through mechanisms that name and subjectify certain students as at-risk. Further, the construction of the *at-risk* category simultaneously and necessarily constructs the category *not-at-risk*. The programs we create to help at-risk students become less-at-risk or even not-at-risk simultaneously reinforce the boundaries between these categories and naturalize them.

It is not my intention to suggest these programs are not helpful; indeed, I believe they are helpful and perhaps even necessary. However, I want to consider the possibility that these efforts also cause harm to the very students we are ostensibly helping. Deficit models of student support locate the problem in the student rather than the higher education institution, which leaves unchallenged the obstacles to student success created by dominant norms of higher education (Smit, 2012). When we admit students conditionally and/or place them on probation or conditional probation, we are naming them in injurious ways and constraining their behavior as students. By producing and naturalizing the category *at-risk*, we are communicating that these students are lesser than those who are not-at-risk; we are telling them they are not fully students or, perhaps, not real students. This reality effect suggests that not only do these students pose a problem for our institutions—insofar as they are made to represent our retention problem—but also that these students *are* problems.

Although I am arguing that our categorization and subjectification of students as at-risk is injurious to these students, I am not advocating for us to abandon our efforts to support these students. Instead, I am calling for us to be vigilant about attending to and questioning the ways in which the framing of our help causes harm. This vigilance includes interrogating and denaturalizing the categories we construct and the boundaries we police. In addition, as we study, track, and regulate at-risk students, we need to continually question these processes in order to unpack what we are taking for granted and what these processes are obscuring. As advisors, we can ask what counts as at-risk and why. What remains invisible when we focus on the category *at-risk*? Where are the gaps and discontinuities within the categories *at-risk* and *not-at-risk*, and where is there overlap? Are there ways we could think about our students outside the categories of at-risk/not-at-risk?

One way of responding to the exclusionary nature of categorization would be to advocate for a more holistic approach, one that addresses the needs of the "whole student" (Grites, 2013, p. 5). A Butlerian approach would, however, conceptualize the whole student as a construct, a reality effect that produces an illusion of a natural, coherent, stable, and whole subject. I would argue that we need to go beyond approaches that more fully recognize and thus naturalize students' identities. We also need to recognize the instability and necessary incompleteness of the subject (Butler, 1993) and consider whether we can support students without categorizing and thus subjectifying them in this way.

Advisors are also subjectified, compelled to approximate norms in our advising practice. Our students call us experts; they position us as those who have the answers and, as a result, they ask us to perform expertness. Further, given that the category of *expert* is constructed through its differentiation from the category of *nonexpert*, we often unwittingly produce our students as such and compel them to act in accordance with norms of this category. We ask them to perform nonexpertness and thus reinforce and naturalize the hierarchy implicit in the advisor/advisee binary. A Butlerian approach would challenge the advisor/advisee binary, examine how these normative categories constrain both advisor and advisee, and ask how these categories could be performed differently. How can we repeat the norms of these categories in ways that open other possibilities? The stakes of challenging this binary are significant insofar as this hierarchy impacts our ability to support students who are questioning normative ideas about various topics that are commonly discussed within advising contexts, such as choosing/changing majors, course selection, the purpose of higher education, and "the logic of the curriculum" (Lowenstein, 2005).

When students ask for our expert advice on how to achieve various norms or how to find normative educational options, we have an opportunity to help them find ways to approximate these norms and/or to help them question them. If students inquire about the "best" major or the "easiest" elective, we can help them consider what is brought into view and what is obscured or taken for granted by these questions. An approach that draws on Butler's theory does not encourage students to achieve a different set of norms (Butler, 1999). Rather, this approach asks students who have been compelled to approximate certain idealized norms to denaturalize these norms and thereby create openings for unforeseen possibilities.

Whether we are talking with students who are struggling to choose a major, seeking a sense of purpose in their education, or questioning their forcibly assigned gender or sexuality, we can help them notice what does or does not align and what is or is not visible from a normative perspective. We can help them examine the ways they are being produced and policed as subjects and encourage them to recognize that ideas, beliefs, and identities that they have taken for granted or assumed were natural, essential, and thus fixed may be open to change. For Butler, the process of repeating norms is never complete; we never fully achieve these norms. The effect of gender, or any other identity we are perceived as embodying, is both retroactive and informed by an unknown future (Butler, 1999, 2003, 2004). If students conceptualize their identities as *doing*, not *being*, they may recognize the possibility that these identities could be done differently, which may in turn enable them to live more livable lives.

How do we open new possibilities in our advising practice? How do we help students make decisions within an uncertain, unstable, unknowable world where we cannot predict the future and where most answers to advising questions begin with "it depends"? A Butlerian approach to advising would help students understand their identities as performative, teach them to think critically about the normativity of their education (inside and outside of higher education institutions), and help them remain open to possibilities that are not intelligible in the present. On an institutional level, advisors can challenge the ways our policies, programs, and practices constrain and subjectify, marginalize and exclude, by constructing, reinforcing, and cloaking normative categories. We can ask what is and is not legible from the vantage point of these categories and remain open to the possibility that the built-in inevitability of failure to achieve norms can open a different future.

Questions for Advisors to Consider

- What are some examples of language we use in an advising context that produce reality effects? How could we render visible the processes that produce these effects?
- How do our categories affect our interpretation of students' behaviors and academic performances? What does the arbitrary nature of the boundaries between categories obscure?
- What strategies could advisors use to help students denaturalize idealized, marginalizing norms, including educational norms? What

are some examples of how students are challenging these norms by inhabiting them differently?

- How can we make fewer marginalizing, exclusionary assumptions regarding who students are, what they are capable of, and what they need?
- What are some strategies that can help us "rethink the possible" (Butler, 1999, p. xx)? What are some questions advisors could ask that might open different ways of thinking about common advising topics such as educational goals?

References

Abes, E. S. (2019). Crip theory: Dismantling ableism in student development theory. In E. S. Abes, S. R. Jones, & D.-L. Stewart (Eds.), *Rethinking college student development theory using critical frameworks* (pp. 64–72). Stylus.

Abes, E. S., & Kasch, D. (2007). Using queer theory to explore lesbian college students' multiple dimensions of identity. *Journal of College Student Development, 48*(6), 619–636. https://doi.org/10.1353/csd.2007.0069

Ahmed, S. (2016). Interview with Judith Butler. *Sexualities, 19*(4), 482–492. https://doi.org/10.1177/1363460716629607

Butler, J. (1993). *Bodies that matter: On the discursive limits of "sex."* Routledge.

Butler, J. (1997). *Excitable speech: A politics of the performative.* Routledge.

Butler, J. (1999). *Gender trouble: Feminism and the subversion of identity.* Routledge.

Butler, J. (2004). *Undoing gender.* Routledge.

Denton, J. M. (2016). Critical and poststructural perspectives on sexual identity development. *New Directions for Student Services, 2016*(154), 57–69. https://doi.org/10.1002/ss.20175

Denton, J. M. (2019). Queer theory: Deconstructing social and gender identity, norms, and developmental assumptions. In E. S. Abes, S. R. Jones, & D.-L. Stewart (Eds.), *Rethinking college student development theory using critical frameworks* (pp. 55–63). Stylus.

Driskill, Q.-L., Finley, C., Gilley, B. J., & Morgensen, S. L. (Eds.). (2011). *Queer indigenous studies: Critical interventions in theory, politics, and literature.* University of Arizona Press.

Dweck, C. (2015). Carol Dweck revisits the 'growth mindset.' *Education Week, 35*(5), 20–24. https://www.edweek.org/ew/articles/2015/09/23/carol-dweck-revisits-the-growth-mindset.html (Originally published as Growth Mindset, Revisited).

Eng, D. L. (2003). Transnational adoption and queer diasporas. *Social Text, 21*(3), 1–37. https://doi.org/10.1215/01642472-21-3_76-1

Eng, D. L., Halberstam, J., & Muñoz, J. E. (2005). Introduction: What's queer about queer studies now? *Social Text 23*(3-4[84–85]), 1–17. https://read.dukeupress.edu/social-text/article-pdf/23/3-4 (84-85)/1/513589/st84-85-01_intro.pdf

Ferguson, R. A. (2003). *Aberrations in black: Toward a queer of color critique.* University of Minnesota Press.

Fraser, J., & Lamble, S. (2014). Queer desires and critical pedagogies in higher education: Reflections on the transformative potential of non-normative learning desires in the classroom. *Journal of Feminist Scholarship, 7*(7), 61–77. https://digitalcommons.uri.edu/cgi/viewcontent.cgi?article=1115&context=jfs

Grites, T. J. (2013). Developmental academic advising: A 40-year context. *NACADA Journal 33*(1), 5–15. https://doi.org/10.12930/NACADA-13-123

Halberstam, J. (2005). *In a queer time and place: Transgender bodies, subcultural lives.* New York University Press.

Hall, D. E. (2003). *Queer theories.* Palgrave Macmillan.

Halperin, D. M. (1995). *Saint Foucault: Towards a gay hagiography.* Oxford University Press.

Harper, S. R., & Quaye, S. J. (Eds.). (2015). *Student engagement in higher education: Theoretical perspectives and practical approaches for diverse populations* (2nd ed.). Routledge.

Hough, L. (2017, Summer). Poor, but privileged. *Harvard Ed. Magazine.* https://www.gse.harvard.edu/news/ed/17/05/poor-privileged

Jagose, A. (1996). *Queer theory: An introduction.* New York University Press.

Johnson, E. P. (2001). "Quare" studies, or (almost) everything I know about queer studies I learned from my grandmother. *Text and Performance Quarterly 21*(1), 1–25. https://doi.org/10.1080/10462930128119

Kuh, G. D., & Love, P. G. (2000). A cultural perspective on student departure. In J. M. Braxton (Ed.), *Reworking the student departure puzzle* (pp. 196–212). Vanderbilt University Press.

Lowenstein, M. (2005). If advising is teaching, what do advisors teach? *NACADA Journal 25*(2), 65–73. https://doi.org/10.12930/0271-9517-25.2.65

McRuer, R. (2006). *Crip theory: Cultural signs of queerness and disability.* New York University Press.

Muñoz, J. E. (2009). *Cruising utopia: The then and there of queer futurity.* New York University Press.

Museus, S. D. (2014). The culturally engaging campus environments (CECE) model: A new theory of success among racially diverse college student populations. In M. B. Paulsen (Ed.), *Higher education: Handbook of theory and research* (Vol. 29, pp. 189–227). Springer.

Puar, J. K. (2005). Queer times, queer assemblages. *Social Text, 23*(3-4[84–85]), 121–139. https://doi.org/10.1215/01642472-23-3-4_84-85-121

Rendón, L. I., Jalomo, R. E., & Nora, A. (2000). Theoretical considerations in the study of minority student retention in higher education. In J. M. Braxton (Ed.), *Reworking the departure puzzle* (pp. 127–156). Vanderbilt University Press.

Renn, K. A. (2010). LGBT and queer research in higher education: The state and status of the field. *Educational Researcher, 39(2)*, 132–141. https://doi.org/10.3102/0013189X10362579

Sedgwick, E. K. (1993). *Tendencies.* Duke University Press.

Smit, R. (2012). Towards a clearer understanding of student disadvantage in higher education: Problematising deficit thinking. *Higher Education Research & Development, 31*(3), 369–380. https://doi.org/10.1080/07294360.2011.634383

Spivak, G. C. (1976). Translator's preface. In J. Derrida, *Of grammatology* (G. C. Spivak, Trans; pp. ix–lxxxvii). Johns Hopkins University Press. (Original work published 1967)

Warner, M. (1999). *The trouble with normal: Sex, politics, and the ethics of queer life.* The Free Press.

Yancy, G., & Butler, J. (2015, January 12). What's wrong with 'all lives matter'? *The New York Times.* https://opinionator.blogs.nytimes.com/2015/01/12/whats-wrong-with-all-lives-matter/

5

INTERSECTIONALITY AND ACADEMIC ADVISING

Wendy Kay Schindler and Sarah E. Stevens

Intersectionality is a critical analysis of the ways multiple oppressed identities interact, leading to a compound web of marginalization (Crenshaw, 1989; Nash, 2008). The interconnectedness of social identities is more complex than a simple summation implies (Goodman, 2014). When we advise LGBTQA+ students, an intersectional framework helps us understand their identities and locate their place within complex systems of oppression. Narrowly focusing on only one identity—such as their sexuality or gender identity—can cause us to overlook situations where multiple identities intersect and increase marginalization. In addition, a discussion of interlocking oppressions can help us interrogate our own role in maintaining the power structures of the academy and deepen our connection to dismantling structural inequity. Therefore, in this chapter, we explore intersectionality and its applications when working with students. We hope this material undergirds subsequent chapters and your thinking on issues affecting LGBTQA+ students.

Before we launch into our discussion of intersectionality, we want to first acknowledge our own authorial identities. Wendy Kay Schindler is a white, cisgender woman who identifies as bisexual/queer (the language of her self-identification is ever evolving), which is an aspect of her identity that is often erased because she is married to a man. She is an able-bodied brain tumor survivor; a fat, middle-class, middle-aged, secular humanist (raised evangelical Christian) who is child-free by choice; and an English-speaking U.S.-born citizen by way of St. Louis, Missouri (and several other states). Sarah E. Stevens is a cisgender, white, middle-class, bisexual, atheist, mostly able-bodied (with hidden PTSD) woman. She is care partner to a husband with advanced Young Onset Parkinson's and a mother of three. Our discussions of identity are informed by our knowledge of privilege and oppression in the United States. We both acknowledge that our words and experiences arise from these multiple identities in ways we try to interrogate and in ways we may not notice.

A note about language: Throughout this chapter, we will capitalize Black to highlight its central function as an identity characteristic and to redress social and historical subordination of Black peoples. We do not capitalize the word white because the concept of whiteness as a monolithic source of identity is closely aligned with white supremacy. When we discuss whiteness, we urge readers to focus on privilege and structural racism. When we address the cultural identity of people who identify as white, we recommend looking at specific countries or regions of family origin or connection.

Origin and History of Intersectionality

The framework of intersectionality arises from Black feminist thought, and we must understand these origins before applying intersectional theory to our work with LGBTQA+ students. In 1989, Kimberlé Crenshaw coined the term *intersectionality* to describe the oppression of Black women who are impacted by both sexism and racism. Crenshaw's work harkened back to Audre Lorde's (1983) essay "There Is No Hierarchy of Oppressions." Lorde (1983) discussed her experiences as a "Black, lesbian, feminist" woman (para. 1). Lorde's (1983) multiple identities were misunderstood by groups that focus narrowly on one issue like racism, heterosexism, or sexism: "Within the lesbian community I am Black, and within the Black community I am a lesbian" (para. 5). Neither community enabled her to claim her multiple identities and fight against systemic oppression. Lorde (1983) concluded, "There is no hierarchy of oppression. . . . And I cannot afford to choose between the fronts upon which I must battle these forces of discrimination" (paras. 5–6). Lorde's (1983) short essay illuminates the crux of intersectional identity. We do not embody only one facet of our identity at any moment in time; we inhabit multiple identities simultaneously. When we interact with people and systems, we bring our multiple identities with us in ways that compound and complicate the oppression we face.

In 1989, Kimberlé Crenshaw first used the term *intersectionality* to highlight the problematic "tendency to treat race and gender as mutually exclusive categories of experience and analysis" (p. 139). Crenshaw (1989) noted that, without a true intersectional approach, we tend to view "subordination as disadvantage occurring along a single categorical axis" (p. 140). A single-axis focus limits and erases the experiences of Black women and therefore limits understanding of their oppression. This oversimplified view of oppression results in a focus on the most privileged individuals in a category—those individuals stand in for the "universal" subject, while people whose oppression encompasses multiple categories are otherized and ignored. In other words, when we investigate issues of discrimination or oppression, we tend to focus on one specific category of identity and implicitly prioritize the privileged individuals within that category. For instance, when investigating issues of race, we assume maleness; when investigating issues of gender, we assume whiteness (Crenshaw, 1989). When we look at racism, we look at Black men and, when we look at issues of sexism, we look at white women. Crenshaw (1989) demonstrated how Black women are therefore ignored in both feminist theory and antiracist politics. She specifically examined Black women in the legal system and shows how "because Black females' claims are seen as hybrid, they cannot represent those who may have 'pure' claims of sex discrimination" (p. 145) or racial discrimination.

The oppression experienced by Black women is compounded due to the interconnection of race and gender, which affects their relationship to the power structure. Patricia Hill Collins (2000), whose work focuses on the intersections of race, gender, class, sexuality, and nationality, approached power "as an intangible entity that circulates within a particular matrix of domination and to which individuals stand in varying relationships" (p. 274). This matrix of domination is another way to describe the complex systems of oppression experienced by people with multiple marginalized identities, who may encounter oppression based on race *and* class *and*—in the case of LGBTQA+ students—sexual orientation and/or gender identity. Collins applied "the knowledge gained at intersecting oppressions of race, class, and gender" (pp. 8–9) to critique the role of systems in maintaining inequity. She specifically calls out white feminism for excluding issues of race, thereby falling short of real change to power structures (Collins, 2000). She reminded us that "empowerment also requires transforming unjust social institutions that African-Americans encounter from one generation to the next" (Collins, 2000, p. 273).

As academic advisors, we must therefore recognize that "unjust social institutions" include our educational system and, indeed, our individual colleges and universities, which have perpetuated oppression, engaged in gatekeeping, and defined knowledge in ways that marginalize particular voices and experiences. When we advise LGBTQA+ students, a focus on intersectionality can help us identify students facing multiple sites of oppression, so we do not generalize from a monolithic view of LGBTQA+ identity. We should ask ourselves: Which LGBTQA+ students don't fit neatly into our existing structures? Which LGBTQA+ students experience gatekeeping within their own communities? Whose voices are heard and what experiences do we ignore because they don't match our single-axis understanding?

Framing Intersectionality

Even as a pioneer in conceiving intersectionality, Collins (2015) conceded the concept is often misconstrued and its definition fraught with dilemma. General consensus of the term acknowledges individual identities such as "race, class, gender, sexuality, ethnicity, nation, ability, and age operate not as unitary, mutually exclusive entities, but as reciprocally constructing phenomena that in turn shape complex social inequalities" (Collins, 2015, p. 2). However, in the work of scholars and practitioners, the concept of intersectionality manifests in radically different, often incorrect ways (Collins, 2015). Intersectionality becomes conflated with diversity and is misused in a feel-good way to talk about how everyone has multifaceted identities, instead of as a specific tool to unpack multiple layers of oppression.

Higher education and academic advising are not immune to this predicament. Diversity has become ubiquitous as a core institutional value in academia (Beighley et al., 2014), but real contemplation of structural oppression is often overlooked. Many colleges and universities have created cultural centers and affinity groups, allowing students to find others who identify in similar ways. Unfortunately, these groups can turn into silos with monolithic views of identity (Anders & DeVita, 2014) and may shut out students who would otherwise be welcome in the group. For example, Black gay men can experience homophobia in Black student centers and racism in LGBTQA+ student centers (Strayhorn, 2013). Shifting to a sole focus on diversity only considers individual identity differences and does not create justice for all students. With such a trend toward institutional diversity, it is no wonder intersectionality is often misconstrued to refer merely to the multiple categories of identity inhabited by all individuals without considering systems of oppression (Craven, 2019).

However, we must acknowledge "individuals are not simply a sum of their identities" (Goodman, 2014, p. 100). To simplify the tenets of intersectionality in this way appropriates and erases the work of Black women scholars who created the theory. Moreover, doing so ignores the domination and oppression of certain social identities (Morgan, 1996; Nash 2008). For example, a white man has both a racial and gender identity, but neither of these identities are oppressed. Therefore, his case would not be a good application of intersectionality. Even if he were from a lower socioeconomic background, that would be a single axis of oppression. Now, if he were also a member of an LGBTQA+ identity group and had a disability, we could use intersectionality to examine his complex experience of marginalization due to the matrix of oppression created by his identities.

Systems of Domination and Oppression

All categories of identity exist on an axis, with one end of the continuum representing maximum privilege and the other embodying extreme oppression (Morgan, 1996). We can map an individual's multiple identities on axes representing various categories, thereby examining their personal identity matrix and the juxtaposition of privilege and oppression they may experience. For instance, when examining the identity category of race, whiteness is privileged, while people of color are oppressed. In the category of gender identity, cisgender people are privileged, while transgender people are oppressed. Each individual exists at different points on different axes and experiences different elements of privilege and oppression because of their social group memberships. Intersectionality asserts that all systems of oppression are part of one overarching structure of domination (Collins, 2000). Constructs like race, class, gender, sexuality, ability, religion, and age are all part of one interlocking system of oppression and domination—that is, "there is no hierarchy of oppression" (Lorde, 1983, para. 5).

Privilege is unearned access to power—be it social or political. Those with privilege have the power to dominate through institutionalized systems (Morgan, 1996). Domination forces people to replace their individual and cultural ways of knowing with the dominant group's ways of knowing (Collins, 2000). Marginalized people are pressured to dismiss the empowerment they may have gained from personal experiences and buy into the very systemic structure that oppresses their group. The power of dominant groups is then maintained through interlocking social institutions that reproduce oppression and refuse to acknowledge connections among marginalized groups by focusing on a single axis of oppression. Bureaucracy, surveillance, and discipline are key strategies to maintain power relationships (Foucault, 1977). These strategies permit the dominant group to justify and reinforce their power (Collins, 2000). Further, when dominant groups suppress the knowledge created by an oppressed group, it becomes easier and easier for dominant groups to maintain power. Without access to knowledge created by their group, the oppressed group seems to willingly participate in their own exploitation (Scott, 1985). However, "oppressed people resist by identifying themselves as subjects [as opposed to objects], by defining their reality, shaping their new identity, naming their history, [and] telling their story" (hooks, 1989, p. 43).

As members of the academy and individual institutions of higher education, academic advisors must continually interrogate our role in maintaining the dominant power structure. How can we use our advising work to dismantle the tools of oppression in lieu of shoring up its foundations? We must navigate the academy—and support our students in their navigations—without buying into the power structure it represents. One way advisors can challenge the power structure of the academy is by advocating for students of identity groups that are unduly impacted by university policies and procedures.

Standpoint Theory

Dorothy Smith's (1974) standpoint theory adds a helpful layer to intersectionality by reminding us that what we know is affected by our social identities and "standpoints." Standpoint theory provides a framework with which to analyze the ways systems of power affect knowledge production (Harding, 2004). The tenets of standpoint theory can be summed up by three main points: (a) there is no objective knowledge, (b) no two people have the same exact view, and (c) one must not take their personal standpoint for granted but rather examine it (Drew et al., 2015; Stevens et al., 2016). Perhaps more importantly, those in marginalized groups are necessarily more aware of oppression than those in nonmarginalized groups. Systems of oppression are more visible to those being oppressed. Therefore, any discussion of intersectionality and associated social justice issues should be centered on those who experience the deepest oppression. As authors, Wendy and Sarah are highly aware that, as white, middle-class, highly educated women, our voices should not overwhelm those experiencing more oppression.

We need to remember that some aspects of identity can be fluid as opposed to static. Where a person falls on each axis of identity can be inherent at birth or acquired and may change over time. Our advisees gain increasing educational privilege throughout college, but they may face severe oppression based on their other identities. Additionally, some aspects of identity are not readily apparent to an outsider and therefore a person may be afforded the privileges of the dominant group. On the flip side, the erasure of invisible identities can also lead to further oppression. A cisgender, bisexual woman who marries a cisgender man may inadvertently receive privilege from heterosexism, but she may feel invalidated while maintaining her queer identity internally.

Ultimately, we should not make assumptions about our students' identities and their standpoints within the world. Communication and dialogue are key to learning how a student identifies and how those identities intersect within their college experience. It is easy to get frustrated when it seems like students are refusing help, but advisors need to dig deeper. For example, some students experiencing depression or anxiety may come from a background where mental illness was stigmatized. They may need many discussions before accepting counseling and accommodations that could enable their success. Further, we can use our knowledge of student identities to challenge deficit-based frameworks causing inequity within our institutions (Fujimoto & Luna, 2014).

Application to Advising LGBTQA+ Students

Intersectionality is not just a buzzword, but a framework that undergirds all advising work with LGBTQA+ students and subsequent chapters within this book. All individuals inhabit multiple identities and LGBTQA+ students are no different; however, we can easily fall into the trap of labeling advisees based on just one of their social identities. This is certainly a simpler way to view the world, but focusing on a single axis of identity does a serious disservice to our students. Students are more than their LGBTQA+ identities. As we strive to advise holistically by learning more about how each student identifies, we must pay attention to how identifying as LGBTQA+ interacts with other areas of marginalization for students. Doing so requires actively listening to what a student is telling us and asking questions for a deeper understanding of the student's experience. For example, if a student confides she is worried about coming out as a lesbian to her parents, it would do no justice to solely focus on her sexual orientation. Keeping an intersectional framework in mind would compel us to learn more about the situation. Perhaps the student is Muslim and there are cultural or religious factors at play, but we will not know unless we are prepared to have an open dialogue with the student.

Our advisees may be experiencing even more oppression than we realize due to the intersections of their marginalized identities. For example, transgender and gender nonconforming students of color experience extremely high levels of harassment (Rankin et al., 2010). Additionally, campus programs and services that cater to a single axis of identity may be marginalizing students who would otherwise feel welcome. For example, a Black student may experience homophobia in a Black student organization and racism in a LGBTQA+ student organization (Consortium of Higher Education LGBT Resource Professionals, 2016; Strayhorn, 2013). For this reason, academic advisors must continually listen to our students' experiences and seek knowledge about intersectional trends.

Less than 15% of U.S. institutions of higher education have an employee whose role is at least 50% focused on serving "queer-spectrum and trans-spectrum" students (Greathouse et al., 2018, p. 3). On many campuses, such services are lumped into the work of a general multicultural center that may not have specific competence in LGBTQA+ issues *or* intersectional identities. As a corollary, campuses that *do* have a center focusing on the LGBTQA+ population may not ensure that the center prioritizes students' other marginalized identities, including race, class, ability status, and so on. A recent white paper released by the Rutgers Tyler Clementi Center, "Queer-Spectrum and Trans-Spectrum Student Experiences in American Higher Education," analyzes national findings of major surveys from 2016–2017, but fails to mention how intersections among LGBTQA+ identities and other marginalized identities might impact students (Greathouse et al., 2018). Too often, our work is siloed in this fashion.

The Consortium of Higher Education LGBT Resource Professionals (2016) released "Recommendations for Supporting Trans and Queer Students of Color" to address the "lack of awareness around race/racism/whiteness in LGBTQ+ spaces, as well as a lack of awareness around sexual orientation, gender identity, and gender expression . . . in multicultural center spaces" (p. 1). They remind us that, in order to support queer and trans students of color, we must work to dismantle white supremacy as well as working for LGBTQA+ liberation. As advisors, we need to remember not all such work can happen within multicultural or queer resource centers. Advisors, too, are responsible for shaping our campus climate and must reach across campus to collaborate on student support.

Before we can truly work toward ending marginalization for our LGBTQA+ advisees, we must acknowledge our own position within society. To become aware of our individual participation within hierarchies of power, we must strive for honesty in self-reflection about our social group memberships. Those who find themselves mostly to be members of dominant groups are not at fault for the privilege they have been afforded (Harro, 2000); however, there *is* fault in failing to recognize our power and our contributions to an oppressive society. We must ask ourselves where we may lack knowledge or experience. The reflection activity at the end of this chapter is constructed to help advisors think through our own identities and potential areas of intersectional oppression. Using reflection to identify gaps within our worldview gives us a starting point for learning new information. For example, if a white, middle-class advisor discovers the privilege they have been afforded has distorted their view on the intersections of race and class, they can seek out resources to better recognize the oppression of others.

In addition to this internal reflection about our identities, we must consider how students "read" our identities. Despite our best intentions, the impact we have on student success is ultimately what counts in our work as academic advisors. Do students see the marginalized categories we might inhabit? Or do they perceive us as privileged members of the academy who are unlikely to understand their intersectional struggles? Advisors with hidden marginalized identities may want to consider strategically revealing their experiences in order to demonstrate their allied identity. All advisors should think about how they can show in words and actions that students with multiple oppressed identities can count on their support. No matter how our other identities situate us in society—dominant or oppressed—our position as academic advisors automatically grants us some power not possessed by our advisees. We should use our position to dismantle the structure of power at our institutions. All colleges and universities must contend with the challenges associated with persistence and graduation of marginalized students. As Fujimoto and Luna (2014) asserted, "the widespread failure to educate these students is a failure of the educational system as a whole and not individual students" (2014, p. 256). Due to our close work with advisees and our access to students, we are in a unique position to work across identities and interrogate the matrix of oppression in higher education.

Advisors who have experienced marginalization have a unique standpoint from which to recognize certain types of oppression, but we must still work to learn about the oppression of other groups. Pursuit of this knowledge is our responsibility. We cannot ask marginalized people to undertake the labor of educating us; we must actively seek to further our understanding of all identities. We hope the chapters in this book—and the works cited within—serve as a step toward understanding LGBTQA+ identities and encourage learning about multiple intersectional identities.

Reflection Activity

Following is a list of social identity groups. Use this list as a reference for answering the following questions. When finished, use your answers to identify potential gaps in your knowledge then seek out resources and information to fill those gaps. As it can be difficult to locate gaps in our own knowledge and experience, consider discussing the activity with a trusted friend or colleague who will bring a critical eye and honest opinion to your discoveries.

- Gender Identity
- Sex Assigned at Birth
- Sexual Orientation
- Race
- Ethnicity
- Ability Status
- Age/Generation
- Country of Origin
- Native Language
- Religious Beliefs
- Marital Status
- Parental Status
- Economic Status
- Level of Education
- Mental Health Status

1. How do you identify in terms of each group listed previously?
2. Which of your individual identities are marginalized? Which are dominant?
3. When did you first become aware of these identities?
4. Has the way in which you identify changed over time?
5. Which of these identities are most salient to your everyday life?
6. How do your identities combine to further your oppression (or strengthen your privilege)?
7. Why have you chosen to use certain language over other choices? (E.g., *bisexual* versus *pansexual* versus *queer* or *African American* versus *Black* versus *person of color.*)
8. How do you behave around members in your same social groups? How do you behave around members of different social groups?
9. Would others identify you in the same ways you identify yourself?
10. How will you use this information to fight systems of oppression in your institution and become a better advocate for your advisees? What concrete actions will you take?

References

Anders, A. D., & DeVita, J. M. (2014). Intersectionality: A legacy from critical legal studies. In D. Mitchell, Jr., C. Y. Simmons, & L. A. Greyerbiehl (Eds.), *Intersectionality & higher education: Theory, research, & praxis* (pp. 31–44). Peter Lang.

Beighley, C. S., Simmons, C., & West, E. (2014). Beyond identity politics: Equipping students to create systemic change. In D. Mitchell, Jr., C. Y. Simmons, & L. A. Greyerbiehl (Eds.), *Intersectionality & higher education: Theory, research, & praxis* (pp. 269–280). Peter Lang.

Collins, P. H. (2000). *Black feminist thought: Knowledge, consciousness, and the politics of empowerment* (2nd ed.). Routledge.

Collins, P. H. (2015). Intersectionality's definitional dilemmas. *Annual Review of Sociology, 41*, 1–20. https://doi.org/10.1146/annurev-soc-073014-112142

Consortium of Higher Education LGBT Resource Professionals (2016, April). *Recommendations for supporting trans and queer students of color.* LGBT Campus. https://lgbtcampus.memberclicks.net/assets/tqsoc%20support%202016.pdf

Craven, S. (2019). Intersectionality and identity: Critical considerations in teaching introduction to women's and gender studies. *Frontiers: A Journal of Women Studies, 40*(1), 200–228. https://doi.org/10.5250/fronjwomestud.40.1.0200

Crenshaw, K. (1989). Demarginalizing the intersection of race and sex: A black feminist critique of antidiscrimination doctrine, feminist theory and antiracist politics. *University of Chicago Legal Forum, 1989*(1), 139–167. http://chicagounbound.uchicago.edu/uclf/vol1989/iss1/8

Drew, C., McGill, C. M., Schindler, W. K., Stevens, S. E. (2015, October 5). *Intersectionality and advising: There is no hierarchy of student identity* [Conference presentation]. NACADA: The Global Community for Advising Annual Conference, Las Vegas, NV, United States.

Foucault, M. (1977). *Discipline and punish: The birth of the prison*. (A. Sheridan, Trans.). Pantheon Books. (Original work published 1975)

Fujimoto, M.O., & Luna, M. U. (2014). Theory to practice: Problematizing student affairs work through intersectionality. In D. Mitchell, Jr., C. Y. Simmons, & L. A. Greyerbiehl (Eds.), *Intersectionality & higher education: Theory, research, & praxis* (pp. 249–258). Peter Lang.

Goodman, D. J. (2014). The tapestry model: Exploring social identities, privilege, and oppression from an intersectional perspective. In D. Mitchell, Jr., C. Y. Simmons, & L. A. Greyerbiehl (Eds.), *Intersectionality & higher education: Theory, research, & praxis* (pp. 99–108). Peter Lang.

Greathouse, M., BrckaLorenz, A., Hoban, M., Huesman Jr., R., Rankin, S., & Bara Stolzenberg, E. (2018). *Queer-spectrum and trans-spectrum student experiences in American higher education: The analyses of national survey findings* [White paper]. Rutgers Tyler Clementi Center. https://tcc-j2made.s3.amazonaws.com/uploads/2018/09/White-Paper-Final.pdf

Harding, S. (Ed.). (2004). Introduction: Standpoint theory as a site of political, philosophical, and scientific debate. In *The feminist standpoint theory reader: Intellectual and political controversies* (pp. 1–16). Routledge.

Harro, B. (2000). The cycle of socialization. In M. Adams, W. J. Blumenfeld, R. Castañeda, H. W. Hackman, M. L. Peters, & X. Zúñiga (Eds.), *Readings for diversity and social justice: An anthology on racism, antisemitism, sexism, heterosexism, ableism, and classism* (pp. 15–21). Routledge.

hooks, b. (1989). *Talking back: Thinking feminist, thinking black*. South End Press.

Lorde, A. (1983). There is no hierarchy of oppressions. *Bulletin: Homophobia and Education*. Council on Interracial Books for Children.

Morgan, K. P. (1996). Describing the emperor's new clothes: Three myths of education (in)-equity. In A. Diller, B. Houston, K. P. Morgan, & M. Ayim (Eds.), *The gender question in education: Theory, pedagogy, and politics* (pp. 105–122). Westview Press.

Nash, J. C. (2008). Re-thinking intersectionality. *Feminist Review, 89*(1), pp. 1–15. https://doi.org/10.1057/fr.2008.4

Rankin, S., Weber, G., Blumenfeld, W. J., & Frazer, S. (2010). *2010 state of higher education for lesbian, gay, bisexual & transgender people*. Campus Pride.

Scott, J. C. (1985). *Weapons of the weak: Everyday forms of peasant resistance*. Yale University Press.

Smith, D. E. (1974). Women's perspective as a radical critique of sociology. *Sociological Inquiry, 44*(1), 7–13. https://doi.org/10.1111/j.1475-682X.1974.tb00718.x

Stevens, S. E., Drew, C., & McGill, C. M. (2016, April 13). *Intersectionality: Understanding our students' multifaceted identities* [Webinar]. In NACADA Webinar Series. https://nacada.ksu.edu/Events/Web-Events.aspx

Strayhorn, T. L. (2013). And their own received them not: Black gay male undergraduates' experiences with white racism, black homophobia. *Counterpoints, 383*, 105–119. https://www.jstor.org/stable/42981251

Ally Narrative

Ashley A. Thomas

In full disclosure, when I think about my journey in becoming (or attempting to become) an ally for LGBTQA+ people, it is difficult for me to fully consider myself an ally. The term *ally* makes me think of someone who actively searches for ways to fight and end oppression. Morally and ethically, I internally and fully disagree with oppression of any person or group. However, I am continually learning the ways my privilege as a white, cisgender, heterosexual, middle-to-upper-class woman both elevates my position and contributes to the oppression of others. In Jackson and Hardiman's (1982) model (summarized in Broido, 2000), I likely fall into the passive resistance stage. In this stage, a dominant agent (myself) will likely feel overwhelmed by the thought of resisting oppression and only do so in comfortable situations. Why do I feel this way? Why would I not speak out against all oppression of LGBTQA+ people? The truth is that I am not overly confident in my knowledge, and I am not internally comfortable with actively seeking out and opening myself up for the possibility of conflict. My lack of confidence comes from inadequate experience and education in LGBTQA+ studies.

Growing up in a small town in southeast Kansas, I had little exposure to others who were different from me. If there were people in my high school class who identified outside of cisgender/heterosexual, our high school was likely not an environment that supported that disclosure. Additionally, I was raised in a household with very traditional and conservative gender roles. My father was a farmer and the sole income provider for our family. He worked long hours and, although he was present when he could be, he was often in the fields during any activities my sister and I attended. My mother was a stay-at-home mom and was highly involved in our lives and activities. She undertook the majority of the household's cooking, cleaning, and caretaking. We were actively involved in 4-H for most of our young lives, and my mother was the main facilitator of these activities.

Some of the gender norms present in my childhood home have transferred to my relationship dynamics with my husband and children. While I do have a successful, outside-of-the-home professional career (and thus differ from my mother in this respect), I am the primary caregiver of our children. I also facilitate and perform the majority of daily household-related tasks such as childcare, meal preparation, and housekeeping. This is largely due to our lifestyle, as my husband works very long hours in his own career, but the gender norms I was taught at a young age perpetuate in our household.

Through my professional career, I have had the opportunity to work with both students and colleagues who identify differently from myself. These connections have been incredibly eye-opening, challenging the assumptions under which I was raised that one's gender (male/female) and sexuality (heterosexual) were binary and "assigned" at birth. My experience falls directly in line with the following: "People from privileged groups are routinely denied information and opportunities to understand their role in an unjust social system as well as honest feedback from people in oppressed groups" (Torres et al., 2003, p. 25). I grew up in a community that was limited in diversity, and I had very little exposure to those who differed from me in terms of gender and sexual identity. Given the lack of diversity in my community, I did not have the opportunity to receive critical feedback to identify my own privilege and consider how that privilege could be oppressive to others. Through both my education and my professional career, I have worked with diverse individuals and continue to do so. Identifying and acknowledging these biases and privileges have forced me to see and think about the challenges others face. I continue to build my knowledge by reading and learning from those in the LGBTQA+ community.

The biggest challenges I have faced have been combatting the binary constructs I was taught from birth. For example, I have learned to be very cognizant of the language I use, particularly in reference to LGBTQA+ people. I often use the term *guys* even when referring to a group of all women. From my upbringing, the saying "hey guys" was synonymous with "hello." However, this terminology often misgenders individuals and is offensive and oppressive to some in the trans community. Additionally, it has been a challenge to overcome the tendency to refer to individuals as "he" or "she" based on their outward appearance, a behavior I learned from the binary classification system. I am working tirelessly to continually change my internal vocabulary to be more inclusive of all individuals by using the term *they*. Since I was taught a very binary-focused vocabulary from the time I started elementary school, this has also been a significant experience in my journey.

As I think forward to the future, one challenge I anticipate for myself is teaching my children about diverse perspectives in gender and sexual identities. Although we are fortunate to live in a more diverse community than the one in which I was raised, we still reside in a smaller town in the Midwest.

My husband and I will need to continue to teach our children that differences should be embraced and that they need to learn about others' experiences. My biggest piece of advice for allies would be the same advice I need to hear myself: continue to learn! Continue to keep an open mind to those who are different from you. Understand and acknowledge that your knowledge has gaps and you are going to make mistakes. Acknowledge those mistakes, apologize for them, and learn from them. These sometimes painful yet necessary learning opportunities have helped me continue to grow as an individual.

References

Broido, E. (2000). Ways of being an ally to lesbian, gay and bisexual students. In V. Wall & N. J. Evans (Eds.), *Toward acceptance: Sexual orientation issues on campus.* (pp. 345–369). University Press of America.

Torres, V., Howard-Hamilton, M. F., & Cooper, D. L. (2003). Identity development of diverse populations: Implications for teaching and administration in higher education. *ASHE-ERIC Higher Education Report* (Vol. 29, no. 6). John Wiley & Sons.

Ally Narrative

Heather Doyle

If I think back, I have always considered myself an ally . . . which, as I reflect on it now, is problematic in itself. I saw allyship as a title an individual owned as opposed to something that requires constant reflection and action. However, when I began to engage in social justice research and theory, which led me to critically reflect on what being an ally really entails, I recognized that allyship is much more than having a title bestowed upon you. Through this reflection, research, and the labor of those in my life, I realized that being an ally is so much more than having good intentions, and I began to recognize the tremendous privilege I possess as a white, cisgender, heterosexual woman. Although I already believed in equal rights and was often vocal of my beliefs regarding social justice and equity in conversations and through social media, once I began to examine critical theories and understand the intricacies of privilege, I discovered how much I didn't know and may never fully know. I also learned that, even as an ally, I commit harms. Moreover, it is not up to any person or group to bestow upon me the title of ally or recognize my allyship. Although allyship must be active, it must also be active without recognition. I have grown to wonder if allies should even claim such a title, as allyship requires the ally to decenter themselves and use their privilege to center others' experiences and voices.

Being an ally isn't easy, but neither is being on the receiving end of constant microaggressions, racism, and/or homo/transphobia. I don't believe an ally is something people are; I believe it is something people need to continually strive to be. Allyship is a constant and reoccurring process, not something a person can shelve and take out when convenient. As allies, we must live this process every day, question every assumption we have, and view the world with a critical lens. At a recent conference, I spent most of my time with individuals who identify with at least one historically marginalized identity. For a very short period of time, I saw the constant remarks, misgendering statements, and microaggressions they experience. It was exhausting even as a bystander to witness these constant microinvalidations and the impact they have on an individual's very being. I take this experience and every experience I see or read about and keep them at the forefront because I want to do better. The more aware I am, the less likely I am to commit these harms.

My advice for other allies? Recognize that you are going to do harms. You are going to make mistakes, and you need to consider how you will work through these mistakes and provide reparations. It is important to decenter your own feelings in the process. Always question and critically examine your own biases and preconceptions . . . because they exist. If you believe they do not, you need to take a closer look.

PART TWO

CAMPUS ISSUES AND
ADVISING APPROACHES

6

LGBTQA+ STUDENTS AND COMPLETION AND RETENTION NARRATIVES

Jennifer E. Joslin

"We are at a critical moment for a reexamination of how to center queer and trans students' experiences in the retention narrative."
(Garvey, 2019, p. 432)

L GBTQA+ college and university students face numerous challenges in their journey to 2- and 4-year degrees. The authors cited in this chapter point to personal, interpersonal, sociopolitical, economic, cultural, structural, and institutional factors that act as barriers to progression and graduation. Faculty members and full-time academic advisors should be aware of these barriers. To understand the challenges that LGBTQA+ students face, advisors should be attuned to the external and internal university initiatives that can positively affect the general student body as a whole, but can also divert resources and attention away from LGBTQA+ student success. Gains for LGBTQA+ students can take years of relentless activism. In comparison, state-sponsored completion initiatives come with legislative backing, ad campaigns, and grant-funded conference travel. LGBTQA+ faculty members and staff balance their personal identities and professional roles, which makes it possible for them to advocate for LGBTQA+ students. However, these faculty and staff members participate in national or campus initiatives that do not directly address LGBTQA+-specific student issues. This balancing act is a dilemma that I, and I suspect other authors cited in this chapter, have experienced firsthand. There are many narratives present when LGBTQA+ academic advisors, who are LGBTQA+ allies and advocates, are at work.

The First Narrative: National Completion and Retention

One of the dominant narratives in U.S. higher education during the last 15 years has been the college completion narrative. The focus on timely college completion—which is not restricted to the United States but has had its largest impact there—has been funded and advanced by philanthropic foundations while heavily influencing federal and state policy (Joslin, 2018; White, 2015). In the United States, this narrative focuses on addressing the structural, procedural, and institutional barriers to student persistence, progression, and graduation (Joslin, 2018).

The completion conversation focuses on improving graduation rates for college students at 2- and 4-year institutions. National data shows poor graduation rates for students at 2-year institutions (where fewer than 20% of students graduate within 3 years) and at 4-year institutions. (As of 2009, only 60% of students graduated within 6 years; National Center for Education Statistics, 2017.) As poor graduation rates have resulted in scrutiny of higher education, state and federal legislatures have become increasingly involved in addressing higher education's perceived shortcomings. National philanthropies, foundations, and think tanks have also begun to focus on higher education issues, leading to a marked increase in grant opportunities for higher education associations, businesses, and technology vendors. These grant-driven initiatives include: monitoring credit completion in the first year (e.g., Complete College America's Momentum Pathways and 15 to Finish), providing access to career planning and development assessments prior to matriculation (e.g., Strada Education Network's Pathways with Purpose and Complete College America's Purpose-Driven Education), and providing access to sophisticated technology tools to monitor student performance and advisor responsiveness (The Bill and Melinda Gates Foundation's Integrated Planning and Advising for Student Success). Some initiatives focus on large-scale institutional practices like The Bill and Melinda Gates Foundation's Frontier Set, Excellence in Academic Advising from NACADA: The Global Community for Academic Advising, and the John N. Gardner Institute.

These initiatives and organizations share a focus on broad institutional measures to make the greatest impact on the greatest number of students. By design, the initiatives previously mentioned—and many institutional solutions that have resulted from these initiatives—frequently attempt to aid large numbers of students without attending to the unique circumstances of a particular student population or institution. Some of these initiatives analyze student information systems for efficiencies and data-driven conclusions that can positively impact student success. In some instances, simplifying university policies can increase efficiency, such as eliminating holds on student registration for all students. Some institutions implement policy changes that impact whether students apply for graduation or are automatically graduated when they meet their graduation requirements, thereby reducing the option for students to linger after they have earned their degree. These and similar policies impact academic advising in small and large ways, touching many aspects of the student experience by way of policy changes, technology improvements, or procedural corrections to accepted or historic practice.

Another example of a scalable intervention is the 15 to Finish component of the Complete College America Game Changer initiative. The 15 to Finish intervention requires institutions to encourage students to take at least 15 credit hours per semester. This approach helps students graduate in 4 years while keeping them busy and challenged throughout each semester. There are studies at some institutions—notably, the University of Hawai'i System—that show that students who register for at least 15 credit hours have higher completion rates compared to students taking between 12 to 14 credit hours (University of Hawai'i System, 2014, 2017). While there can be positive outcomes from implementing university or system-wide changes, interventions of this nature can prompt individual advisors and scholars to point out that widespread implementation is not in the best interest of students who may lack the financial or cultural capital needed to progress while taking 15 or more credit hours (Chan, 2020; Kemplin, 2014). Regardless of individual advising concerns, these changes exemplify university systems' willingness to make system-wide, state-wide, or institutional-type changes (e.g., suggestions for widespread policy changes across all Historically Black Colleges and Universities). Proponents of these massive sea changes can think of important and consequential changes on a large scale but may not consider that they are costly to the systems and institutions involved.

The Second Narrative: LGBTQA+ Student Completion and Retention

There are alternate narratives in higher education today that focus on improving access to graduation outcomes, not just enrollment. These narratives focus on inclusion and equity. The argument focuses on the importance of graduation of queer and trans students—among other special populations—as "the right thing to do." This perspective is rooted in years of effort to change campuses and improve graduation outcomes as a necessary improvement for traditionally disenfranchised students. In this alternate narrative, improved graduation rates are the result of increased sensitivity to queer and trans-inclusive policies (e.g., equity and inclusion statements, inclusive restrooms, and chosen name policies). These policies help queer and trans students gain a sense of belonging, which contributes to persistence and graduation. The researchers, educators, and advocates of and for LGBTQA+ students cited in the following paragraphs have written extensively on the conditions facing queer and trans students. These conditions relate to almost every aspect of the student experience, including, but not limited to, residence halls and housing, academic programs, restroom accommodations, queer and trans student organizations, the quantity and visibility of queer and trans staff and faculty members, participation in athletics, and organizations for students of color, among other focus areas.

The literature affirms the importance of LGBTQA+ student centers in providing safe spaces for queer and trans students to connect with one another, sharing on- and off-campus community resources, helping students feel welcome on campus, engaging in curricular discourse, positively influencing self-esteem, increasing sense of belonging on campus, and serving as examples of inclusion (Garvey et al., 2018; Nicolazzo, 2017; Pitcher et al., 2018; Rankin et al., 2019). The support offered by queer and trans student centers is especially important for students who have been cut off from their family as a result of their queer and trans identification (Garvey et al., 2018). Further, LGBTQA+ student centers positively impact persistence for trans students and queer and trans students of color when the center acts a safe space (Duran et al., 2019; Garvey, 2019; Goldberg, 2018). Additionally, queer and trans students of color that report lack of acceptance and negative experiences in college also report increased feelings of marginalization (Garvey, 2019).

In addition, faculty relationships are a critical component of queer and trans students feeling integrated into campus and academic life (BrckaLorenz et al., 2017; Wolf et al., 2017; Woodford et al., 2015). Faculty members are perceived as caring representatives of the institution when they provide curricular and career mentoring and support in the classroom (Garvey et al., 2018; Vaccaro, 2012; Woodford et al., 2015). Queer and trans students perceive faculty members positively when they try to learn about queer and trans student issues, use a student's chosen name, and hold themselves accountable when they misgender or misname students (Goldberg, 2018). Conversely, faculty members who repeatedly misgender and misname students are seen as marginalizing students, thus creating a stressful and anxiety-inducing classroom environment for queer and trans students (Goldberg, 2018; Nicolazzo, 2017).

Queer and trans students identify gender-blind housing and all-gender (or gender-neutral) restrooms as crucial parts of feeling safe and included on campus (Goldberg et al., 2018; Seelman, 2016). These structural accommodations and supports increase queer and trans students' sense of belonging and contribute to positive perceptions of a campus climate (Goldberg, 2018). The lack of such accommodations can be perceived by queer and trans students as microaggressions, which might be linked to poor academic outcomes (Woodford et al., 2017) and increased risk of suicidality (Goldberg, 2018).

Nondiscrimination campus policies, such as the inclusion of "gender identity" in the campus nondiscrimination statement, are important and are positively associated with persistence (Garvey, 2019; Goldberg, 2018). Another example of a positive policy change is the ability to change one's chosen name and gender marker to reflect one's identity. Queer and trans students at institutions with this capability report increased feelings of belonging and connection to the institution (Blumenfeld et al., 2016; Goldberg, 2018). Queer and trans students also identified access to health insurance that covers queer and trans students' health decisions along with access to counseling support services as important issues. Trans students are at higher risk of experiencing mental health issues, including depression, suicidal ideation, eating disorders, and other serious health issues, than their cisgender peers (Goldberg, 2018).

These examples of campus climate (i.e., the structures, policies, and environmental qualities that touch every aspect of a student's academic, cocurricular, and social life) are reflected in national studies that offer institutions a road map to improve queer and trans student persistence. The Campus Pride Index monitors several different areas that contribute to queer and trans student success, including policy inclusion, support and institutional commitment, academic life, student life, housing, recruitment and retention efforts, counseling and mental health support, and campus safety (Campus Pride Index, 2020). Goldberg (2018) identifies 10 focused recommendation areas: policies and protections for students; curriculum; trainings aimed at students; trainings aimed at faculty members and staff; inclusive name, gender, and pronoun policies; documents, forms, and records; restrooms; housing; queer- and trans-inclusive physical and mental health support; and specific focus on trans-inclusive spaces. The study on queer and trans student satisfaction conducted by Blumenfeld et al. (2016) shows that students assess campus climate within the context of their own individual context as well as comparatively to determine their overall satisfaction (e.g., the campus compared to the off-campus community or their satisfaction with their home department compared to the overall campus climate). In this study, students identified the following crucial issues: physical and emotional safety; faculty, staff, and peer support; institutional support such as registrar policies or health insurance benefits; the support available within or from their home department; institutional factors such as marginalization due to race, class, gender, and other intersecting identities; and the support or community offered by the city in which the institution is located (Blumenfeld et al., 2016).

A Complex Dialogue

Two separate conversations about student success exist, and each has serious ramifications for queer and trans students. One narrative focuses on large-scale change with minimal attention paid to specific issues facing marginalized LGBTQA+ students but has significant grant funding from national philanthropies as well as the support of state legislators; the other focuses intently on a myriad of intersectional issues impacting LGBTQA+ students but exists almost solely within queer and trans academic circles. Unless advisors and advising administrators are reading LGBTQA+ scholarship (including this text), they are likely to only encounter the national conversation on completion. Even if they are reading about LGBTQA+ student success, there is not a well-funded national conversation that coaches academic advisors and administrators on how to change institutional structures to serve LGBTQA+ students more effectively. How can advisors who are aware of these two narratives develop language that centers their individual and collective student experience in the dominant national discourse on progression and retention? The following vignette explores this very issue.

Vignette

While a state's board of regents is being scrutinized for declining graduation rates and increased costs, a well-known philanthropy has awarded a consulting contract to a national higher education nonprofit company that specializes in completion initiatives. As a result, the state has agreed to work with the nonprofit consultants to implement three new programs meant to improve graduation rates. A director of academic advising is representing her/his/their office—and the campus advising system—at a state meeting that will introduce the new initiatives. The director of advising is a former chair of the campus LGBTQA+ staff and faculty association, and in that role, he/she/they led an appointed task force to add the words "and expression" to the campus diversity statement, so that it now reads "gender identity and expression." It took 3 years to achieve this goal and was a difficult, wearying process. While listening to the lieutenant governor speak about the importance of student success, the director considers how these new initiatives and their corresponding resources can be used to further progress toward meeting the needs of LGBTQA+ students on their campus. The questions on the director's conference notepad include:

- What does the national or institutional data tell us about retention outcomes for first-generation queer and trans students?
- Why aren't our institutional surveys asking about gender identity and expression when we are collecting our own student data?
- Where are the trans student voices in our analysis of why students persist?
- How does our engagement with this national organization benefit individual students (namely, students who identify as queer or trans) if the focus, literature, and demographic data collection doesn't include them?
- While we are participating in this multicampus effort to retain students, how will the anticipated, scalable gains benefit all students including our most marginalized, least studied, and most vulnerable?

A Summation and Steps to Consider

It is unlikely that the college completion initiative will be the last nation-wide initiative higher education thought leaders will propose. In my 25 years working at U.S. higher education institutions, the completion and early-career education initiatives are merely the latest in a line of large-scale, research-backed, president-approved programs designed to address serious issues at colleges and universities. In the meantime, academic advisors and administrators, student affairs personnel, LGBTQA+ student services coordinators, and LGBTQA+ student leaders themselves continue the relentless advocacy work necessary for LGBTQA+ student success. As a marginalized voice at colleges and universities, it will be their/our role to "queer" the next national initiative designed to improve higher education for students so that it includes LGBTQA+ students.

The chapters in this book offer foundational knowledge and resources upon which to base future work. Caring and informed advisors, advising administrators, and central administrators can take the following steps and actions every day to transform our understanding and advocacy for LGBTQA+ students:

- Learn about your campus and where it stands on the Campus Pride Index, Goldberg's recommendations for structural and political change, or Blumenfeld's recommendations.

- Learn more about why your campus promotes "a completion agenda" and whether it can simultaneously make changes that increase the persistence of LGBTQA+ students on your campus.
- Ask how your campus makes a difference for queer and trans students—does it aid or hinder their completion, or both?
- If your campus participates in completion-focused conversations encouraged by your president, chancellor, or state legislature, what are ways you or your advising unit could impact the conversation about LGBTQA+ student success?
- Work with others to discern how you and your unit can talk about completion in a way that includes the persistence of all students at your institution.
- Ask what steps your campus can take that would promote persistence and reduce attrition for LGBTQA+ students as part of a completion focus.
- Take advantage of public forums, talks, "completion academies," webinars on completion, and other campus events to talk about barriers to persistence that impact a significant proportion of your student population.
- Read studies about LGBTQA+ student persistence. As part of your research, ask students on your campus about their experiences, challenges, and support structures.
- Explicitly tie LGBTQA+ student advocacy to promoting persistence— add persistence literature about queer and trans student populations to your campus' persistence library when your school creates a "completion-focused" online website or article repository.

References

Blumenfeld, W. J., Weber, G. N., & Rankin, S. (2016). In our own voice: Campus climate as a mediating factor in the persistence of LGBT students, faculty, and staff in higher education. In P. Chamness Miller & E. Mikulec (Eds.), *Queering classrooms: Personal narratives and educational practices to support LGBTQ youth in schools,* 208–229. Information Age.

BrckaLorenz, A., Garvey, J. C., Hurtado, S. S., and Latopolski, K. S. (2017). High-impact practices and student-faculty interactions for gender variant students. *Journal of Diversity in Higher Education, 10*(4), 350–365. https://www. academia.edu/33292706

Campus Pride Index. (2020). *Frequently asked questions.* http://www.campusprideindex. org/faqs/index

Chan, R. Y. (2020). *How does the 15 to finish initiative affect academic outcomes of low-income, first-generation students? Evidence from a college promise program in*

Indiana (Publication No. 27741431) [Doctoral dissertation, Indiana University]. ProQuest Dissertations & Theses Global. http://dx.doi.org/10.2139/ssrn.3319082

Duran, A., Pope, R. L., & Jones, S. R. (2019). The necessity of intersectionality as a framework to explore queer and trans student retention. *Journal of College Student Retention: Research, Theory, & Practice, 21*(4), 520–543. https://doi.org/10.1177/1521025119895510

Garvey, J. C. (2019). Critical imperatives for studying queer and trans undergraduate student retention. *Journal of College Student Retention: Research, Theory, & Practice, 21*(4), 431–454. https://doi.org/10.1177/1521025119895511

Garvey, J. C., BrckaLorenz, A., Latopolski, K. S., & Hurtado, S. S. (2018). High-impact practices and student-faculty interactions for students across sexual orientations. *Journal of College Student Development, 59*(2), 210–226. https://www.academia.edu/33838778/

Goldberg, A. E. (2018, August). *Transgender students in higher education.* The Williams Institute. https://williamsinstitute.law.ucla.edu/wp-content/uploads/1808-Trans-Higher-Ed.pdf

Goldberg, A. E., Kuvalanka, K. A., Budge, S., Benz, M. B., & Smith, J. Z. (2018). Mental health and health care experiences of trans students in higher educational settings: A mixed methods study. *The Counseling Psychologist 47*(1), 59–97. https://doi.org/10.1177/0011000019827568

Joslin, J. E. (2018, Winter). The case for strategic academic advising management. *Academic Advising Re-examined, 184,* 11–20. https://doi.org/10.1002/he.20299

Kemplin, S. (2014). *Redefining full-time in college: Evidence on 15-credit strategies.* Community College Research Center. https://ccrc.tc.columbia.edu/media/k2/attachments/redefining-full-time-in-college.pdf/

National Center for Education Statistics. (2017). *Digest of education statistics.* https://nces.ed.gov/programs/digest/d17/tables/dt17_326.10.ASP

Nicolazzo, Z. (2017). *Trans* in college: Transgender students' strategies for navigating campus life and the institutional politics of inclusion.* Stylus.

Pitcher, E. N., Camacho, T. P., Renn, K. A., & Woodford, M. R. (2018). Affirming policies, programs, and supportive services: Using an organizational perspective to understand college student success. *Journal of Diversity in Higher Education, 11,* 117–132. https://doi.org/10.1037/dhe0000048

Rankin, S., Garvey, J. C., & Duran, A. (2019). A retrospective of LGBT issues on US college campuses: 1990–2020. *International Sociology,* 1–20. https://doi.org/10.1177/0268580919851429

Seelman, K. L. (2016). Transgender adults' access to college bathrooms and housing and the relationship to suicidality. *Journal of Homosexuality, 63,* 1378–1399. https://doi.org/10.1080/00918369.2016.1157998

University of Hawai'i System. (2014). *Update on HGI and 15 to finish* [Presentation]. CCAO-CSSAO Joint Meeting. http://blog.hawaii.edu/hawaiigradinitiative/files/2014/05/ccao1405v2.pdf

University of Hawai'i System. (2017). *Hawai'i graduation initiative.* http://blog.hawaii.edu/hawaiigradinitiative/15-to-finish/

Vaccaro, A. (2012). Campus microclimates for LGBT faculty, staff, and students: An exploration of intersections of social identity and campus roles. *Journal of Student Affairs Research and Practice, 49*(4), 429–446. https://doi.org/10.1515/jsarp-2012-6473

White, E. R. (2015). Academic advising in higher education: A place at the core. *The Journal of General Education, 64*(4), 263–277. https://doi.org/10.5325/jgeneeduc.64.4.0263

Wolf, D. A. P. S., Perkins, J., Butler-Barnes, S. T., & Walker, T. A., Jr. (2017). Social belonging and college retention: Results from a quasi-experimental pilot study. *Journal of College Student Development, 58*(5), 777–782. https://doi.org/doi:10.1353/csd.2017.0060

Woodford, M. R., Joslin, J., Pitcher, E. N., & Renn, K. A. (2017). A mixed methods inquiry into trans* environmental microaggressions on college campuses: Experiences and outcomes. *Journal of Ethnic & Cultural Diversity in Social Work, 26,* 95–111. https://www.tandfonline.com/doi/full/10.1080/15313204.2016.1263817

Woodford, M. R., & Kulick, A. (2015). Academic and social integration on campus among sexual minority students: The impacts of psychological and experiential campus climate. *American Journal of Community Psychology, 555*(1–2), 13–24. https://doi.org/10.1007/s10464-014-9683-x

7

LGBTQA+ STUDENTS AND CAREER ADVISING

Carolyn Meeker, Richard A. Sprott, and Craig M. McGill

L esbian, gay, bisexual, transgender, queer, questioning, and asexual (LGBTQA+) students experience unique challenges related to their career development and preparation. For example, they might express heightened caution, concern, or apprehension when exploring and choosing a major, seeking a job or internship, constructing a résumé, and/or entering the job market (Greathouse, 2019). These concerns may be founded in anti-LGBTQA+ stigma related to specific professions (e.g., police bias against gay male law enforcement officers; Collins & Rocco, 2015; Greathouse et al., 2018), indecision about disclosing their sexual orientation or gender identity to a potential employer (Out & Equal Workplace Advocates, 2019), or fear of potential harassment or bias in the workplace (Human Rights Campaign [HRC], 2018). Employment discrimination at the local, state, and federal level has been a major concern for employees who identify as LGBTQA+ (Greathouse, 2019). Fortunately, strides are being made in the right direction as a ruling by the U.S. Supreme Court on June 15, 2020, extended the 1964 Civil Rights Act to protect LGBTQA+ employees.

With all the uncertainty for LGBTQA+ students in the job market, it is important, when discussing student career development, for advisors to understand three commonly used terms: *career advising, career counseling,* and *career coaching.*

- Career *advising*: A process "to help students make academic decisions that incorporate knowledge of academic/career relationships and possibilities" with a focus on integrating self, academic, and career information (Gordon, 2006, p. 13).

- Career *counseling*: A process "to assist students with career development problems," with the foremost goal being resolution (Gordon, 2006, p. 13). Although this process is not mental health counseling, it may be experienced as therapeutic.
- Career *coaching*: An active, focused, positive, and outcome-oriented approach that focuses on students' capabilities, helping them to practice and hone skills needed in the job search (National Association of Colleges and Employers [NACE], 2017).

In this chapter, we use advisor/advising to refer to any of these three activities. In so doing, we are writing to and for anyone who has an advising role in any capacity (e.g., faculty members, generalist primary-role, or a specialty role) that involves students' career development and decision-making. Queer (Q) and asexual (A) are included within the spectrum of marginalized LGBTQA+ identities, and we use LGBTQA+ within the chapter, unless the research focused on specific identities, such as lesbians (L) or gay males (G) only.

To help students navigate career decisions, advisors should be aware of how students' experiences inform their self-concepts and how their sexual orientation and gender identities can impact their perceptions of work and career options. Therefore, in this chapter, we provide an overview of the career advising needs of LGBTQA+ students, offering suggestions for how academic advisors can help students navigate these decisions. Additionally, we discuss concerns related to work environments and employment decisions, identity considerations, and implications for practice.

Work Environments and Employment Decisions

The atmosphere of a work environment greatly impacts one's career decisions. Unfortunately, people with marginalized sexual orientation and/or gender identities might experience harassment, discrimination, and prejudice in their educational and work environments (Fassinger, 2008). In fact, one study found that 31% of LGBTQ workers often felt unhappy or depressed at work and 20% searched for a different job because the workplace was not LGBTQ-inclusive (HRC, 2018). Additionally, people with multiple marginalized identities (e.g. sexually *and* racially marginalized people) must cope with additional social stressors within the workplace (Harris, 2014). An LGBTQA+ person may or may not "pass" as a heterosexual or cisgender person. Additionally, the degree of acceptance/tolerance an individual has for their own identities could affect their career decision and how they act within the workplace (Harris, 2014).

A critical factor for LGBTQA+ students to consider when pursuing careers and positions is whether or not to be "out" to (potential) employers and/or coworkers. In fact, the decision to be out has the potential for long-lasting consequences; even if one's current colleagues are accepting of LGBTQA+ identities, future coworkers may not be. Socialization is of critical importance in the workplace because it shapes personal relationships and establishes guidelines for everyday conduct (Van Maanen & Schein, 1979). Additionally, it provides a framework from which employees identify with their new organization (Van Maanen & Schein, 1979) and can make or break a career (Schein, 1988). Relationship-building can be the primary vehicle of the socialization process (Korte, 2009). Relationships develop through disclosing details about one's personal experiences, dispositions, past events, and future plans (Derlega & Grzelak, 1979). Therefore, if one's sexual orientation or gender identity could impact relationship-building, it is possible that an LGBTQA+ employee could experience not only dissatisfaction, but also discrimination in the workplace.

Another factor that can hamper socialization is the fear of negative coworker reactions. Anticipated stigma may restrict disclosure of personal information, disrupting the socialization process through the inability to build authentic relationships. In fact, 48% of LGBTQA+ workers are closeted (i.e., conceal their sexual orientation and/or gender identity) at work (HRC, 2018). Prominent reasons people might choose to conceal sexual orientation and/or gender identity include fear of being stereotyped, making others uncomfortable, and losing connections with coworkers. Additionally, there is a double standard regarding what is deemed appropriate to share in the workplace. Although 78% of non-LGBTQ workers report being comfortable talking to coworkers about their spouse, partner, or dating life, 59% of non-LGBTQ workers consider it unprofessional to talk about sexual orientation and gender identity in the workplace (HRC, 2018). These statistics indicate that even though non-LGBTQA+ workers are comfortable talking about non-LGBTQA+ relationships, they fail to recognize that everyone has a sexual orientation and gender identity that *impacts* discussions about spouses, partners, and dating. In effect, these statistics indicate that many non-LGBTQA+ workers inherently block the socialization of LGBTQA+ employees.

Not only could self-disclosure of sexual orientation and/or gender identity have a negative impact on workplace relationships, studies have shown that it also has a negative impact on securing employment. A study of discrimination against openly gay men in the United States found that résumés that listed experience in a gay campus organization had a 40% less chance of receiving a response from a potential employer (Tilcsik, 2011). This was particularly true in the southern region of the United States and with employers who emphasized the importance of stereotypically heterosexual male personality traits (e.g., decisiveness, assertiveness, aggressiveness, ambition).

In a historic decision on June 15, 2020, the U.S. Supreme Court ruled that the 1964 Civil Rights Act protects gay, lesbian, and transgender employees from discrimination based on sex; this extended protections that ban employment discrimination based on race, religion, national origin, or sex to LGBTQ populations. Prior to this, only 21 states and the District of Columbia prohibited employment discrimination based on sexual orientation or gender identity; several other states prohibited discrimination but only for public employees or for sexual orientation, not gender identity (HRC, 2020). Though strides have been made in the right direction, more work needs to be done to eliminate discrimination of LGBTQA+ persons.

Identity Considerations

To understand the critical importance of how identity impacts career decisions, it is first necessary to understand what identity is. In *Identity, Meaning, and Subjectivity in Career Development*, Gedro (2017) outlined five characteristics of identity:

- "Identity is *fluid*," rather than fixed and unitary.
- "Identity is *constructed*"; individuals assess how their sense of self was formed, where their perceptions came from, reinterpret prior experiences, and imagine their identities in new ways.
- "Identity is *multi-dimensional* and *matrixed*"; individuals' identities include demographic aspects, relationship and social roles, and organizational identities.
- "Identity is *recognizable* and *detectable* sometimes, but certainly not always."
- "Identities are *value-laden* and have capital or costs associated with them." (p. 132)

When an individual considers career options, they might consider how their personal sense of self—as a social being who has a variety of life roles (e.g., student, single mother) and identity characteristics (e.g., first-generation, lesbian)—impacts their decision-making. Identity characteristics such as race, ethnicity, gender, and sexual orientation impact one's sense of self, as do major life changes like marriage, divorce, or having children. Traditional career development models (e.g., Super's life-span model, 1990) do not take LGBTQA+ developmental factors into consideration, although LGBTQA+ career trajectories differ because of these factors (Gedro, 2009).

It is crucial for advisors to understand how these identities may affect LGBTQA+ persons. Identity characteristics intersect with work/career identity, and the resulting complexity means that there is not a standard formula for advising everyone. Each student will bring unique experiences and interests to advising sessions, and advisors can encourage students to share their stories about what led them to choosing their major, courses, and co-curricular activities, what interests and skills they are developing, and how they envision their future.

Multiple Interacting Identity Characteristics

Advisors should seek to understand how intersecting identities, particularly marginalized identities, affect their students' experiences and decisions. For example, a student's experience of being gay and coming from a recently immigrated family is different from a student's experience of being gay and whose family has been here for several generations. Similarly, a student's experience of being transgender and Black, Indigenous, or a Person of Color (BIPOC) is different from a student's experience of being transgender and White.

While there is no standard formula for advising, there are some structural identity factors that advisors can assess as a place to start. These structural factors include centrality, salience, and valence. *Centrality* focuses on how prominent the identity is to the person's sense of self (Dyar et al., 2015). For example, is the student's LGBTQA+ identity something they want to consider as a priority when making employment and career decisions, or is it less important to them when they think of their career options? The *salience* of the identity in the social environment also matters. How prevalent are issues of sexual orientation and/or gender identity in the work or school environment (Renn & Ozaki, 2010)? An advisor can collaborate with a student to assess how a particular work environment or field of work highlights or downplays sexual orientation or gender identity; the world of finance may downplay these characteristics, but the world of education may consider sexual orientation and gender identity to be relevant or salient. *Valence* of the identity asks whether the person has an internalized negative evaluation of being LGBTQA+, as in internalized homo/bi/trans/phobia (Frost & Meyer, 2009). An advisor will need to pay attention to the positive or negative attitudes the student holds about their own sexual orientation or gender identity.

Sexual/gender identities also intersect with racial/ethnic identities, and racial/ethnic identities intersect with work/career identities, leading to increased complexity with sometimes surprising outcomes. For example, the National Longitudinal Study of Adolescent to Adult Health (Harris &

Udry, 2018) reported racial/ethnic differences regarding positive attitudes towards school, with racial/ethnic marginalized students having lower positive attitudes than White students. However, race/ethnicity differences disappeared for students who were gay or lesbian (Battle & Linville, 2006). In other words, lesbian and gay students of color had significantly more positive attitudes toward school than their heterosexual counterparts. The ways in which two marginalized identity characteristics interact for an individual can have a surprising impact on their experiences at school, highlighting how important it is to take multiple identity characteristics into account when advising.

Socioeconomic status (SES) and social class also have the potential to predict career development variables, including students' educational and occupational aspirations (Eshelman & Rottinghaus, 2015). For example, a student with a lower SES is less likely to have high career aspirations. To focus on supporting students from all economic levels, colleges and advisors need to be aware of how students' social and cultural capital impact their awareness of and access to opportunities. Social capital refers to the investment in social relationships with expected returns in the marketplace (Holland, 2010). Cultural capital refers to a social relationship in a marketplace that involves cultural knowledge (i.e., education, how to navigate process of career development) that can increase status and power (Nora, 2004). Social and cultural capital will be different for an LGBTQA+ student from a family that has struggled with poverty than an LGBTQA+ student from a family that has always had resources, because of access, exposure, and family support around LGBTQA+ community resources and cultural events, for example.

To better understand potential forms of capital that can empower students, advisors can learn about Yosso's cultural wealth model. In the article "Whose Culture Has Capital? A Critical Race Theory Discussion of Community Cultural Wealth," Yosso (2005) explored communities of color as locations where members of socially marginalized groups have an array of cultural knowledge, skills, abilities, and contacts that often go unrecognized and unacknowledged. Yosso (2005) identified six forms of cultural capital that advisors can use to frame their interactions with students, particularly students of color:

- Aspirational capital: "the ability to maintain hopes and dreams for the future, even in the face of real and perceived barriers" (p. 79);
- Linguistic capital: "the intellectual and social skills attained through communication experiences in more than one language and/or style" (p. 79);

- Familial capital: cultural knowledge nurtured among family, sense of community history, memory, and cultural intuition;
- Social capital: students' networks of people and community resources;
- Navigational capital: students' skills in maneuvering through social institutions; and
- Resistance capital: "those knowledges and skills fostered through oppositional behavior that challenges inequality" (p. 80).

This framework of cultural wealth can be applied to all students, and particularly students who identify as LGBTQA+ and as low income and/or students of color.

Regarding the experiences of undocumented Latinx immigrant university students, Cervantes et al. (2015) shared students' recommendations for how colleges can improve support services. Colleges need to educate faculty members and staff about the barriers that undocumented students typically encounter, including experiences of nonvalidation, prejudicial attitudes, and equity in access to services. Two specific recommendations were for colleges to offer Undocumented Student Safe Zone workshops (similar to LGBTQA+ Safe Zone workshops) where information and education about undocumented students can be shared and for immigration-affirmative faculty members to add a "freedom to disclose" statement on their course syllabi. Other recommendations were for colleges to increase the availability of scholarships that do not require citizenship or residency status; create a list of faculty members, staff, and administrators who support undocumented students; and provide access to more jobs and postgraduation career opportunities. Along the same lines, Stebleton and Jehangir (2020) also demonstrated the need for additional institutional support for first-generation students' career and postgraduate development. This includes addressing a lack of cocurricular and leadership development (Rodriguez, 2018) and first-gen students being less likely to participate in internships, study abroad, or in campus leadership roles (Saenz et al., 2007). Colleges need to address how a lack of opportunities "are often tied to institutional barriers that have historically designed programs of this nature for the participation of White, middle-class students with limited attention to fiscal challenges, familial responsibilities, and collectivist identities that shape first-generation experiences" (Stebleton & Jehangir, 2020, p. 5).

Minority Stress

Minority stress is a type of social stress in which a person experiences a conflict between promoted values of a society and their lived experience

(Lazarus & Folkman, 1984). The concept "describes stress processes, including the experience of prejudice events, expectations of rejection, hiding and concealing, internalized homophobia, and ameliorative coping processes" (Meyer, 2003, p. 674). Minority stress is considered distinct (not the same general stressors experienced by most people in a society), chronic, and socially based. It should come as no surprise that minority stress can influence the career-lifespan trajectory for people with marginalized sexual orientation and gender identities. LGBTQA+ students in the early stages of exploring their sexual orientation and gender identity may put other areas of development (e.g., career decisions and exploration) on hold to cope with confusion and other stressors related to realizing one's sexual orientation and gender identity (Schmidt & Nilsson, 2006). Students experiencing sexual identity development may have difficulty with career development decisions amidst inner turmoil/distress and low levels of support (Lyons et al., 2010; Schmidt & Nilsson, 2006). Holding more than one marginalized identity characteristic (e.g., race, class, gender) may increase the impact of minority stress on career decision-making and development (see chapter 5). For instance, African Americans may receive support for their racial identity in their racial communities but may not receive support for their sexual orientation or gender identity from the same people (Harris, 2014). Different marginalized identity characteristics pose separate challenges that may influence an individual's career decisions (Harris, 2014). Perceived discrimination and social support can influence college adjustment and vocational indecisiveness for LGBTQA+ college students (Schmidt et al., 2011) and career development might be nourished with coping strategies, resilience, and career adaptability (Chung, 2011; Savickas, 2011).

Narrative Approach to Identity

Alongside a structural approach to identity that emphasizes the content of the identity, how it relates to other identities and roles, or the centrality of the identity to one's sense of self, there is a narrative approach to identity (Hammack & Cohler, 2009). The narrative approach examines how our stories about our past and possible future experiences help constitute or construct our sense of self. Some narrative approaches focus on how an individual's stories of past and future become resources to manage significant transitions in a person's career trajectory, such as the transition from school to work. Often, these stories make a point about the self, highlighting a person's values around work and career, to establish a sense of authenticity (Ibarra & Barbulescu, 2010). These stories also point to possible future selves, which can influence decisions about work and career (Ibarra, 1999). Self-narratives are tools for helping people cope and make sense of themselves as they move between old and new roles, explore new options, or establish themselves and find social acceptance in a new role.

LGBTQA+ students often have different narratives than their heterosexual peers. For some, a sense of self involves a master narrative of *struggle and success*, a story of self-discovery often involving overcoming the stigma attached to their LGBTQA+ identities. Other LGBTQA+ students might have a master narrative of *emancipation*, a story of challenging and confronting any label or categorization that society imposes on one's sexuality, thereby coming to self-actualization but challenging the larger society and even the LGBTQA+ community (Hammack & Cohler, 2009). These narratives can influence how an LGBTQA+ person conceals or discloses their sexual orientation and/or gender identity in the workplace; both concealment and disclosure have different costs, affecting one's career path (Read, 2009).

To be effective, advisors can listen to a student's story to better understand where they are coming from and where they want to go:

> Advisors listen with rapt attention as their students' stories unfold and in return tell stories of their own. This story telling is no idle chatter to pass the time pleasantly. Engaging in narratives may well be the most thorough and most efficient way that advisors have to come to understand the student before them and to be understood by that student. (Hagen, 2018, p. xvi)

By eliciting stories of early work or school success and listening for internalized negative voices about the self, advisors can co-create narratives with LGBTQA+ students that are more supportive of positive career development.

Career Values and Assessment Inventories

A person's values play a significant role in their career decision-making and development, so effective advising should help the student ascertain their values. For instance, it is important to know whether an individual aspires to extrinsic rewards (e.g., salary, designated parking, first-class travel) or intrinsic rewards (e.g., work/life balance, job-sharing). To help students understand their values, Brown (1995) proposed that career counselors use a values-based approach to assist their clients through occupational transitions. This approach helps clients identify, clarify, and prioritize their values using qualitative (client-counselor conversations) and quantitative (values inventories) approaches. Two assessments to consider utilizing are the life values inventory (Crace & Brown, 1996), which can be used to help students identify their values, and the Rokeach Value Survey (Rokeach, 1973) which can help to prioritize/rank these values.

Personality tests are also a helpful way to assess intrinsic student values. Two common assessments used to help students consider options and make decisions about their career development are the Strong Interest Inventory (Strong) and the Myers-Briggs Type Indicator (MBTI).

The Strong Interest Inventory, based on John Holland's (1959) theory of vocational personalities and work environments, helps individuals identify their interests by exploring six broad personality types: Realistic, Artistic, Investigative, Social, Enterprising, and Conventional. Each type is characterized by a collection of beliefs, values, interests, abilities, and preferred activities. The Strong also describes one's preferences for work style, learning environment, team orientation, leadership style, and risk-taking and ranks the top occupations (out of 260) most compatible with their interests (Hollatz-Wisely, 2016). Data suggest that the Strong is valid and reliable when used with members of the LGBT community and that there are gendered differences (men and women) in terms of occupational interests (Schaubhut & Thompson, 2016). Therefore, when completing the Strong, individuals are asked to indicate their gender (male/female). Not only does this reify a problematic binary system of gender, it might cause stress for gender nonconforming or nonbinary students. Advisors should be cognizant of this when describing the Strong and interpreting results and strive to use inclusive language. Advisors can also generate reports for either (or both) gender options, but this decision should be made by the student.

Another tool commonly used in career advising is the Myers-Briggs Type Indicator (MBTI) personality assessment. The MBTI provides a constructive framework to understand individual differences and strengths, allowing students to form a foundation for lifelong personal development. One's MBTI profile reveals how an individual perceives and interacts with the world, showing personality preferences in four dimensions: extroversion or introversion; sensing or intuition, thinking or feeling, and judging or perceiving. Each combination of four letters corresponds to one of 16 types with corresponding characteristics and vocational category. Alhough the MBTI illuminates helpful information about student personalities, it should also be used with caution. A 1993 study of the MBTI concluded that while it is a useful instrument, it must be applied carefully and should never be used to segregate people "in" or "out" of groups or teams—particularly in employment decisions (Wurster, 1993).

In general, when implementing any kind of assessment, it is important to understand the assessment's limits before implementing it into one's advising practice. Steps should be taken to understand the environment in which the assessments were founded; who the initial participants were, from which data was obtained; whether subsequent items were derived; and from what sociocultural lens the designers were working.

Implications for Practice

Many factors influence college students' choices about majors, coursework, and career planning. Some choices may make sense in the short term or in the context of other priorities, but these same choices may work against students' long-term career goals. Academic advisors are positioned to help students think through these issues, but they must be prepared to help students understand how their educational choices relate to career fields and refer students to resources for navigating employment options and opportunities (Gordon, 2006). Advisors are also faced with a wide range of individual differences among students that must be considered to provide effective advising.

Academic advisors can help LGBTQA+ students by understanding how multiple intersecting identities and self-perceptions might influence career development and decision-making processes. Advisors can address minority stress by encouraging/affirming students throughout their career exploration and decision-making (Dispenza et al., 2015). To better support students who are LGBTQA+, low income, and/or Black, Indigenous, or People of Color (BIPOC), advisors can learn about available resources and partner with offices and organization on campus (i.e., counseling center, career center) and off campus (i.e., professional associations, employment opportunities). For example, Federal TRIO Programs, which are designed to motivate and support students from disadvantaged backgrounds (i.e., low-income, first-generation, students with disabilities) to succeed in college, may provide workshops related to sexual orientation and gender diversity. In this case, the advisor can refer students to such workshops. If the TRIO program does not have such workshops, then perhaps advisors can request one or help create one. Advisors can also participate in workshops to learn about student populations, such as Deferred Action for Childhood Arrivals (DACA) and undocumented students. Additional resources are listed at the end of the chapter. Through all this, advisors need to assess the centrality, salience, and valence of the student's LGBTQA+ identity to offer effective advising and to be aware of how sexual/gender identities can be affected by students' racial/ethnic and class identities (Tillman-Kelly, 2015).

One way to acknowledge the complexity of identity in a student's life is to think about career advising through the lens of narrative theory and storytelling. A narrative approach calls for advisors to elicit a student's stories, identify current values and goals in those stories, and listen for possible selves that might be encouraged or challenged regarding decisions around coursework, majors, and career planning. Advisors can help students find their narrative and the way they wish to live their lives by assessing where each student is in their career development (e.g., having or lacking clear goals, ready to make decisions) and empowering students to plan accordingly and strategically (Gordon, 2006). Even students who have made realistic career decisions based on their academic abilities and talents might still need help researching career possibilities. All students need specific information related to career planning, such as how to search for internships and jobs, changes in the workplace, and what skills are marketable (Kummerow, 2000).

In addition to narrative approaches, values-based approaches and personality assessments may be useful. For example, LGBTQA+ students may pick a major and/or career based on their sexual orientation or gender identity, which may or may not be congruent with their strengths, talents, and aspirations (Gedro, 2009). For example, they may identify law enforcement as a field of interest, but not pursue it because they perceive it to be unwelcoming to LGBTQA+ employees. Students may "prematurely foreclose on career choices because of limited awareness or constriction of self-concept" (Prince, 1995, p. 169). The Strong and other assessments can be used to help LGBTQA+ students discover how their values and various other identity factors intersect (Prince & Potoczniak, 2015). For example, when helping students discover their academic and career identity and how to identify potential conflicts among values, roles, and workplace, advisors can use Brown's (1995) values-based approach or the results of personality assessments. Advisors should consider their student's identity characteristics and values while delivering the information, helping students feel empowered to seek resources and opportunities within their communities. Integrating narrative theory into advising sessions by allowing students to share their stories can foster a safe space where assessment results may be interpreted in ways that speak to the complexities of students' experiences, values, interests, aspirations, and skills.

Another factor advisors should consider when advising LGBTQA+ students is the workplace climate said students may soon enter. The workplace is unpredictable for LGBTQA+ people, so preparing students for this environment can require additional guidance and discussion. Advisors may not be prepared to answer such questions as "Should I be 'out' during an interview?" or "Where are the best places to work for gay accountants?" However, given the patchwork of state laws and the inconsistency of federal protection against discrimination, it is suggested that advisors understand and communicate information on the legal situation for LGBTQA+ students, to help students navigate their educational and career decisions. A helpful resource is the HRC's (2020) Corporate Equality Index. Advisors can use this tool to help LGBTQA+ students understand how workplace policies might affect them and how policies create a workplace culture that is welcoming or rejecting, which is an important consideration when addressing LGBTQA+ students' needs.

Another way that advisors can help prepare LGBTQA+ students is by developing Career Management. Career Management is one of eight broad competencies that employers expect college students to develop (NACE, 2017). Advisors can help LGBTQA+ students develop this competency by inviting them to reflect upon some considerations relating to their identities, values, and career goals. For example, in an article about LGBTQA+ students' readiness to reveal their identities, Anderson (2013) suggested self-assessment questions that advisors can share with students:

- If I choose to (withhold/disclose) this information, I might (feel/experience/be able to) _____.
- If I choose to (withhold/disclose) this information, my (employer/coworkers) might (feel/experience/be able to) _____.
- If I choose to (withhold/disclose) this information, my partner might (feel/experience/be able to) _____.
- It is (very/somewhat/not very/not at all) important for me to develop interpersonal relationships with my boss or coworkers.
- It is (very/somewhat/not very/not at all) important for my partner to attend company social events.
- Rate your perception of the overall climate/culture within this workplace (1 being "very hostile" and 5 being "very welcoming"). 1 2 3 4 5
- Rate your overall readiness to "come out" in the workplace (1 being "not at all ready" and 10 being "completely ready"). 1 2 3 4 5 6 7 8 9 10

These questions can be valuable to all students; they can also be adapted for individuals with various identity-based needs, (e.g., students who identify as polyamorous and/or gender nonconforming):

- If I choose to (withhold/disclose) that I have more than one partner, my coworkers might (feel/experience/be able to) _____.
- It is (very/somewhat/not very/not at all) important for me that my boss and coworkers use my pronouns, even though they don't match all my legal documentation.

Taking those responses into consideration, the advisor can help the student work through some potential dilemmas around their sexual orientation or gender identity and career considerations. For example:

1. **Using chosen or legal name:** Students must decide whether to use their chosen name instead of their given (legal) name in communications. Some documents (e.g., background checks, insurance paperwork) require the use of legal names. Other documents (e.g., résumés, cover letters) allow more flexibility. The students should ask themselves if the value of communicating their chosen name outweighs the potential risks. They may also need to consider whether they will use their given (legal) name in the application materials and then ask employers and coworkers to use their chosen name.

2. **Disclosing LGBTQA+ identity in application materials:** Students should consider whether to come out on a résumés, cover letter, and/or interview. In *Your Queer Career*, Folds (2013) discussed pros and cons. Some things that can be included (e.g., involvement in LGBTQA+ groups, awards) or asked about (e.g., employee affinity groups, inclusive practices) may imply a certain identity. In lieu of explicitly coming out, another tactic is to frame experiences with LGBTQA+ organizations and related skills and duties as commitment to diversity and/or service. The student should consider what value is added by explicitly linking activities to the LGBTQA+ context. They should assess whether intentionally outing themselves is beneficial to avoid working in a homo/bi/transphobic environment and how important it is that potential employers and coworkers know.

3. **Choosing professional attire**: A tip on a popular career advice website recommends to "Look at what your boss and other successful employees wear to work. Your observations will tell you about proper and expected business attire for your workplace" (Heathfield, 2019, para. 5). However, some people do not want to dress like everyone else. The student should consider how important it is for them to dress according to traditional/cisgender norms, particularly if another style makes them feel more comfortable or professional.

4. **Evaluating employer culture/fit:** Depending on the student's feelings regarding the previous considerations, they may wish to further explore if the employer is indeed a good fit. Students can use resources, such as the HRC (2020) Corporate Equality Index and the National Center for Transgender Equality (n.d.) research, and can scan company websites

to assess if the potential employer supports an inclusive environment, nondiscrimination policies and trainings, gender-neutral restrooms, participation in LGBTQA+ community events, recruitment of LGBTQA+ candidates, and so on. The student should consider how important is it to enjoy and feel safe and welcome in their work environment.

Students should work through these matters with assistance from an academic/career advisor. In some colleges, academic and career advisors may be the same role/person, while in other colleges, they may be completely separate.

Finally, as in all cases, the greatest work an advisor can do is to inform themselves first. To facilitate student growth and development, advisors can pursue professional development (Gedro, 2009; Pope et al., 2004). Specifically, advisors should receive training on how to integrate awareness of minority stress into their work with LGBTQA+ students to understand how students' experiences may influence their career decisions. Interventions could include self-examining biases, learning about LGBTQA+ development and culture, and intentionally becoming LGBTQA+ affirmative (Gedro, 2009).

In a time when "the world of work has grown increasingly complex and unpredictable, individuals have become increasingly responsible for their own career development" (Gedro, 2017, p. xiii). For many people, work is a core part of their identity and their living hours. By understanding the historical and current challenges this population faces, providing culturally responsive resources, and demonstrating LGBTQA+-affirming support and encouragement, advisors offer valuable guidance to students (Greathouse, 2019). Advisors can collaborate with students for success by helping them discover their values and passions and focusing attention on stories that enable positive career development.

Resources

The following resources are helpful tools for advisors working with LGBTQA+ students as they are considering their career decision-making and development. Please note that some of the information provided may change, as laws change.

- **Center for First-Generation Student Success** (https://firstgen.naspa.org/about-the-center). Mission: "The Center is the premier source of evidence-based practices, professional development, and knowledge creation for the higher education community to advance the success of first-generation students."

- **Human Rights Campaign (HRC) Corporate Equality Index**
  (https://www.hrc.org/campaigns/corporate-equality-index). Mission:

  By inspiring and engaging individuals and communities, the Human
  Rights Campaign strives to end discrimination against LGBTQ
  people and realize a world that achieves fundamental fairness and
  equality for all. HRC envisions a world where lesbian, gay, bisexual,
  transgender and queer people are ensured equality and embraced as
  full members of society at home, at work and in every community.
  (Human Rights Campaign, n.d.)

  While we recommend the Corporate Equality Index as a helpful
  resource, we also acknowledge the HRC's past harmful transphobic
  behaviors and do not endorse the organization specifically.

- **National Association of Colleges and Employers (NACE)** (https://
  www.naceweb.org/about-us). Mission:

  The National Association of Colleges and Employers empowers the
  community of talent acquisition and higher education professionals
  focused on the development and employment of college-educated
  talent by advancing equitable, evidence-based practices; creating
  leading content, research, and professional development opportunities; and enabling robust professional networks, while serving as the
  voice for the profession.

- **National Career Development Association (NCDA) Internet
  Sites for Career Planning** (https://www.ncda.org/aws/NCDA/pt/
  sp/resources). This is a list of free, current (updated regularly), and
  credible resources useful to career counselors, coaches, and specialists.
  It includes resources for self-assessments, general occupational
  information, industry and occupation-specific information, education
  topics, employment trends, job search, and special populations (e.g.,
  clients with disabilities, LGBTQA+, minorities).

- **National Center for Transgender Equality (NCTE)** (https://
  transequality.org/). Mission:

  The National Center for Transgender Equality advocates to change
  policies and society to increase understanding and acceptance of
  transgender people. In the nation's capital and throughout the country, NCTE works to replace disrespect, discrimination, and violence
  with empathy, opportunity, and justice. (NCTE, n.d.)

- **Out & Equal Workplace Advocates** (https://outandequal.org/) Mission: "Out & Equal is the global convener, thought leader and catalyst actively working to achieve workplaces of equality and belonging—supporting LGBTQ+ employees and leaders who thrive in their careers and lives and achieve greater impact on the world" (Out & Equal Workplace Advocates, n.d.).
- **The Global Community for Academic Advising, NACADA** (https://nacada.ksu.edu/). Mission: "NACADA promotes student success by advancing the field of academic advising globally. We provide opportunities for professional development, networking, and leadership for our diverse membership" (NACADA, 2019).
  a. NACADA Advising Community on Career Advising (https://nacada.ksu.edu/Community/Advising-Communities/Career-Advising.aspx)
  b. NACADA LGBTQA Advising and Advocacy Community (https://nacada.ksu.edu/Community/Advising-Communities/LGBTQA-Advising-and-Advocacy.aspx)
- For additional resources, see donahoe-rankin and Glenn vignette on page 110.

References

Anderson, R. A. (2013, November). Assessing the readiness to reveal: Resume writing strategies for LGBTQ students, *NACE Journal*. https://www.wcu.edu/WebFiles/Assessing_Readiness_Reveal.pdf

Battle, J. & Linville, D. (2006). Race, sexuality and schools: A quantitative assessment of intersectionality. *Race, Gender & Class, 13*(3/4), 180–199. https://www.jstor.org/stable/41675180

Brown, D. (1995). A values based approach to facilitating career transitions. *The Career Development Quarterly, 44*, 4–11. https://doi.org/10.1002/j.2161-0045.1995.tb00524.x

Cervantes, J. M., Minero, L. P., & Brito, E. (2015). Tales of survival 101 for undocumented Latina/o immigrant university students: Commentary and recommendations from qualitative interviews. *Journal of Latinx Psychology, 3*(4), 224–238. https://doi-org.ezproxy.fiu.edu/10.1037/lat0000032

Chung, Y. B. (2011). Work discrimination and coping strategies: Conceptual frameworks for counseling lesbian, gay, and bisexual clients. *The Career Development Quarterly, 50*(1), 33–44. https://doi.org/10.1002/j.2161-0045.2001.tb00887.x

Collins, J. C., & Rocco, T. S. (2015). Rules of engagement as survival consciousness: Gay male law enforcement officers' experiential learning in a masculinized industry. *Adult Education Quarterly, 65*(4), 295–312. https://doi.org/10.1177/0741713615585163

Crace, R. K., & Brown, D. (1996). Life values inventory. Life Values Resources.

Derlega, V. J., & Grzelak, J. (1979). Appropriateness of self-disclosure. In G. J. Chelune (Ed.), *Self-disclosure* (pp. 151–176). Jossey-Bass.

Dispenza, F., Brown, C., & Chastain, T. E. (2015). Minority stress across the career-lifespan trajectory. *Journal of Career Development, 43*(2), 103–115. https://doi.org/10.1177/0894845315580643

Dyar, C., Feinstein, B. A., & London, B. (2015). Mediators of differences between lesbians and bisexual women in sexual identity and minority stress. *Psychology of Sexual Orientation and Gender Diversity, 2*(1), 43–51. https://doi.org/10.1037/sgd0000063

Eshelman, A. & Rottinghaus, P. (2015). Viewing adolescents' career futures through the lens of socioeconomic status and social class. *The Career Development Quarterly, 63*, 320–332. https://doi.org/10.1002/cdq.12031

Fassinger, R. E. (2008). Workplace diversity and public policy. *American Psychologist, 63*, 252–268. https://doi.org/10.1037/0003-066X.63.4.252

Folds, R. B. (2013). *Your queer career: The ultimate career guide for lesbian, gay, bisexual, and transgender job seekers.* Riley B. Folds III.

Frost, D. M., & Meyer, I. H. (2009). Internalized homophobia and relationship quality among lesbians, gay men, and bisexuals. *Journal of Counseling Psychology, 56*(1), 97–109. https://doi.org/10.1037/a0012844

Gedro, J. (2009). LGBT career development. *Advances in Developing Human Resources, 11*(1), 54–66. https://doi.org/10.1177/1523422308328396

Gedro, J. (2017). *Identity, meaning, and subjectivity in career development: Evolving perspectives in human resources.* Palgrave Macmillan.

Gordon, V. N. (2006). *Career advising: An academic advisor's guide.* Jossey-Bass.

Greathouse, M. (2019, February 8). *Career considerations of LGBTQA students.* NACE Center for Career Development and Talent Acquisition.

Greathouse, M., BrckaLorenz, A., Hoban, M., Huesman Jr., R., Rankin, S., & Stolzenberg, E. (2018). *Queer-spectrum and trans-spectrum student experiences in American higher education.* https://doi.org/doi:10.7282/t3-44fh-3b16

Hagen, P. L. (2018). *The power of story: Narrative theory in academic advising.* NACADA.

Hammack, P. L., & Cohler, B. J. (2009). *The story of sexual identity: Narrative perspectives on the gay and lesbian life course.* Oxford University Press.

Harris, K. M., & Udry, J. R. (2018). *National longitudinal study of adolescent to adult health, 1994–2008.* DSDR. https://doi.org/10.3886/ICPSR21600.v21

Harris, L. N. (2014). Black, queer, and looking for a job: An exploratory study of career decision making among self-identified sexual minorities at an urban historically Black college/university. *Journal of Homosexuality, 61*(10), 1393–1419. https://doi.org/10.1080/00918369.2014.928170

Heathfield, S. M. (2019). *What is business attire? Definitions and examples of business attire.* The Balance Careers. https://www.thebalancecareers.com/what-is-business-attire-1918075

Holland, J. L. (1959). A theory of vocational choice. *Journal of Counseling Psychology*, 6(1), 35–45. https://doi.org/10.1037/h0040767

Holland, N. E. (2010). Postsecondary education preparation of traditionally underrepresented college students: A social capital perspective. *Journal of Diversity in Higher Education*, 3(2), 111–125. https://doi-org.ezproxy.fiu.edu/10.1037/a0019249

Hollatz-Wisely, C. (2016, January 19). *Gender and the Strong Interest Inventory: Two of the most common questions.* The Myers-Briggs Company. https://www.themyersbriggs.com/en-US/Connect-with-us/Blog/2016/January/Gender-and-the-Strong-Interest-Inventory-Two-of-the-Most-Common-Questions

Human Rights Campaign. (n.d.). *About: Our mission.* https://www.hrc.org/about

Human Rights Campaign. (2018). *A workplace divided: Understanding the climate for LGBTQA workers nationwide.* https://www.hrc.org/resources/a-workplace-divided-understanding-the-climate-for-lgbtq-workers-nationwide

Human Rights Campaign. (2020). *Corporate Equality Index 2020: Rating workplaces on lesbian, gay, bisexual, transgender and queer equality.* https://www.hrc.org/campaigns/corporate-equality-index

Ibarra, H. (1999). Provisional selves: Experimenting with image and identity in professional adaptation. *Administrative Science Quarterly*, 44, 764–791. https://doi.org/10.2307/2667055

Ibarra, H. & Barbulescu, R. (2010). Identity as narrative: prevalence, effectiveness, and consequences of narrative identity work in macro work role transitions. *Academy of Management Review*, 35(1), 135–154. https://doi.org/10.5465/AMR.2010.45577925

Korte, R. F. (2009). How newcomers learn the social norms of an organization. *Human Resource Development Quarterly*, 20(3), 285–306. https://doi.org/10.1002/hrdq.20016

Kummerow, J. M. (Ed.). (2000). *New directions in career planning and the workplace* (2nd ed.). Davies-Black.

Lazarus, R. S., & Folkman, S. (1984). *Stress, appraisal, and coping.* Springer.

Lyons, H. Z., Brenner, B. R., & Lipman, J. (2010). Patterns of career and identity interference for lesbian, gay, and bisexual young adults. *Journal of Homosexuality*, 57(4), 503–524. https://doi.org/10.1080/00918361003608699

Meyer, I. H. (2003). Prejudice, social stress, and mental health in lesbian, gay, and bisexual populations: Conceptual issues and research evidence. *Psychological Bulletin*, 129, 674–697. https://doi.org/10.1037/033-2909

NACADA. (2019). *Our vision and mission: NACADA mission.* https://nacada.ksu.edu/About-Us/Vision-and-Mission.aspx

National Association of Colleges and Employers. (2017, September 13). *Primary focus: Career coaching vs. career counseling.* https://www.naceweb.org/career-development/organizational-structure/primary-focus-career-coaching-vs-career-counseling/

National Center for Transgender Equality. (n.d.). *About: Mission.* https://transequality.org/about

Nora. A. (2004). The role of habitus and cultural capital in choosing a college, transitioning from high school to higher education, and persisting in college among minority and nonminority students. *Journal of Hispanic Higher Education, 3*(2), 180–208. https://doi.org/10.1177/1538192704263189

Out & Equal Workplace Advocates. (n.d.). *Archives: Mission.* https://outandequal. org/?s=in+the+global+covener&submit=

Out & Equal Workplace Advocates. (2019). *Workplace equality factsheet 2019.* https://outandequal.org/app/uploads/2019/03/2019-LGBTQ-Fact-Sheet.pdf

Pope, M., Barret, B., Szymanski, D. M., Chung, Y. B., Singaravelu, H., McLean, R., & Sanabria, S. (2004). Culturally appropriate career counseling with gay and lesbian clients. *The Career Development Quarterly, 53*(2), 158–177. https://doi.org/10.1002/j.2161-0045.2004.tb00987.x

Prince, J. (1995). Influences on the career development of gay men. *Career Development Quarterly, 44*(2), 168–178. https://doi.org/10.1002/j.2161-0045.1995.tb00683.x

Prince, J. P., & Potoczniak, M. J. (2015). Using psychological assessment tools with lesbian, gay, bisexual, and transgender clients. In S. H. Dworkin, & M. Pope (Eds.), *Casebook for counseling* (pp. 319–327). American Counseling Association. https://doi.org/10.1002/9781119221715.ch30

Read, M. M. (2009). Midlife lesbian lifeworlds: Narrative theory and sexual identity. In Hammack, P. L. & Cohler, B. J. (Eds.), *The story of sexual identity: Narrative perspectives on the gay and lesbian life course* (pp. 347–373). Oxford University Press.

Renn, K. A., & Ozaki, C. C. (2010). Psychosocial and leadership identities among leaders of identity-based campus organizations. *Journal of Diversity in Higher Education, 3*(1), 14–26. https://doi.org/10.1037/a0018564

Rodriguez, J. P. (2018). Building a first-generation community: First scholars at the University of Memphis. https://firstgen.naspa.org/blog/building-a-first-genera-tion-community-first-scholars-at-the-university-of-memphis

Rokeach, M. (1973). *The nature of human values.* Free Press.

Saenz, V. B., Hurtado, S., Barrera, D., Wolf, D., & Yeung, F. (2007). *First in my family: A profile of first-generation college students at four-year institutions since 1971.* Higher Education Research Institute and Cooperative Institutional Research Program, University of California, Los Angeles.

Savickas, M. L. (2011). Constructing careers: actor, agent, and author. *Journal of Employment Counseling, 48,* 179–181. https://doi.org/10.1002/j.2161-1920.2011.tb01109.x

Schaubhut, N. A., & Thompson, R. C. (2016). *Technical brief for the Strong Interest Inventory Assessment: Using the Strong with LGBT populations* (Updated version). CPP, Inc. https://ap.themyersbriggs.com/content/Research%20and%20White%20Papers/Strong/Tech_Brief_Strong_LGBT.pdf

Schein, E. H. (1988). Organizational socialization and the profession of management. *Sloan Management Review, 31,* 53–63. https://sloanreview.mit.edu/article/organizational-socialization-and-the-profession-of-management/

Schmidt, C. K., Miles, J. R., & Welsh, A. C. (2011). Perceived discrimination and social support: The influences on career development and college adjustment of LGBT college students. *Journal of Career Development, 38*(4), 293–309. https://doi.org/10.1177/0894845310372615

Schmidt, C. K., & Nilsson, J. E. (2006). The effects of simultaneous developmental processes: Factors relating to the career development of lesbian, gay, and bisexual youth. *Career Development Quarterly, 55*(1), 22–37. https://doi.org/10.1002/j.2161-0045.2006.tb00002.x

Stebleton, M. J., & Jehangir, R. R. (2020). A call for career educators to recommit to serving first-generation and immigrant college students: Introduction to special issue. *Journal of Career Development, 47*(1), 3–10. https://doi-org.ezproxy.fiu.edu/10.1177/0894845319884126

Tilcsik, A. (2011). Pride and prejudice: Employment discrimination against openly gay men in the United States. *American Journal of Sociology, 117*(2), 586–626. https://doi-org.ezproxy.fiu.edu/10.1086/661653

Tillman-Kelly, D. L. (2015). *Sexual identity label adoption and disclosure narratives of gay, lesbian, bisexual, and queer (GLBQ) college students of color: An intersectional grounded theory study* [Doctoral dissertation, Ohio State University]. file:///C:/Users/Marianna/Downloads/Tillman-Kelly_Dissertation_Final%20(1).pdf

Van Maanen, J., & Schein, E. H. (1979). Toward a theory of organizational socialization. In B. M. Staw (Ed.), *Research in organizational behavior* (pp. 209–264). JAI.

Wurster, C. D. (1993). *Myers-Briggs Type Indicator: A cultural and ethical evaluation.* The Industrial College of the Armed Forces, National Defense University. https://apps.dtic.mil/dtic/tr/fulltext/u2/a276674.pdf

Yosso, T. J. (2005). Whose culture has capital? *Race, Ethnicity and Education, 8*(1), 69–91. https://doi.org/10.1080/1361332052000341006

Conversations

Career Advising for LGBTQA+ Students in Nonlinear Career Paths

erin donahoe-rankin and Ashley Glenn

"Master advisors integrate academic advising and career advising" as Shaffer succinctly put it (Grites et al., 2016, p. 170).

To illustrate chapter 7, "LGBTQA+ Students and Career Advising," we offer an example of advising in practice. The following vignette illustrates the experiences of an LGBTQA+ student and academic advisor as they might engage in a career planning and decision-making conversation(s):

Eli is only 3 months away from college graduation, a feat that did not always feel within reach because of their journey as a queer, white, first-generation college student who grew up in a midsized city in the culturally conservative South. This region in the United States is often referred to as the "Bible Belt," known for its religiously conservative attitudes that dictate social norms—norms that are often reflected in political and legal terms, pervading individual interactions (Shelton, 2018). And although neither of Eli's parents attended college, they encouraged Eli's love of learning.

It was this support that gave Eli the confidence to seek out the high school's early college program, to speak with the high school guidance counselor regularly, and to pursue an associate's degree while in high school. Taking courses in history and government while volunteering with the county's peer court program gave Eli a glimpse into a career in law and advocacy. During Eli's senior year of high school, they came out to their family as a lesbian. Both parents shrugged off this news, saying that Eli was too young to know. After this talk, Eli's parents rarely asked about their personal life, only about school.

Eli still remembers how thrilled their parents were when they received the news: Eli had been accepted to the state's flagship university. With news of a full scholarship, Eli decided to stay in-state, not too far from home. As a freshman in college, Eli only visited home on the occasional weekend, becoming very involved in the LGBTQA+ community on campus and quickly making friends. Helping to plan Pride Week and spending time with other LGBTQA+ students felt like coming home, a home Eli hadn't known before.

As a first-year student, Eli decided to major in the liberal arts, focusing on prelaw and human rights. To complement their academic coursework, they carefully crafted professional experiences, including volunteering with a nonprofit focused on women's rights, obtaining a local internship with a law firm recognized in the state for their advocacy, and applying for a national internship with a state representative. Eventually, Eli accepted a position with a conservative congressman; although their political views differed, Eli knew they would learn much.

Through this professional experience, Eli discovered an interest in international law and national security, new strengths in strategy, and skills in data analysis they had not previously recognized. Living in Washington, DC, Eli witnessed a world very different from the town in which they grew up and from their college campus, which before had already felt like a more diverse and welcoming place. This experience not only altered Eli's professional interests but also gave a new perspective on gender identity. Now, having met folks with identities across a spectrum, Eli began to think deeply about their own gender—what it meant to them and whether the identity of female still truly fit.

Returning from their internship in their junior year, Eli changed coursework from social justice topics to seminars focused on international law and security. After a close friend suggested they speak with a counselor at the student health center, Eli began attending a gender identity support group at their university. Conversations there had Eli thinking more about how they expressed themselves and when they felt most comfortable. Having always dressed more according to societal norms associated with males, Eli recalled a grocery store clerk recently calling them "Mister." At the time, being mistaken as a man felt inaccurate, but something resonated in being identified as not female.

In their senior year, they began introducing themselves as "Eli" and using "they/them/theirs" as their chosen pronouns. They began taking steps to transition, changing their chosen name to Eli with university records. As they shared this news with friends, not everyone responded positively. However, one professor, Dr. Tamara Hogges, was especially supportive and openly encouraged Eli to use their experience to research the impact of nondiscrimination laws on transgender communities.

In Eli's final semester, their name had been changed within the university system and on their student card, but their official state ID still showed their dead name given and sex assigned at birth. Having researched how long it takes to officially change all legal documents, Eli is concerned that there will not be time enough for the name change to take effect before submitting job applications and is concerned about their next steps and what life after graduation will look like.

As they begin researching postgraduation opportunities, Eli is not sure which direction to go. Should they look for positions related to advocacy and human rights, a field where they have experience and feel most comfortable? Or should they pursue fellowships in the federal government so they can move closer toward a career within international law and security? Thinking about these white-collar work environments, Eli wonders if they will be accepted.

When Eli makes an appointment with their academic advisor, Kris, whom they have known since their first semester, the scheduling system asks: "reason for your appointment." Eli thinks it over and writes "graduation." In preparing for the appointment, Kris notes that Eli's graduation application is approved based on current enrollment, they are graduating *summa cum laude*, and should have already received their first email about commencement. Everything appears in order and ready to go, so Kris wonders what questions Eli might have.

Eli arrives for their appointment, and Kris goes over the basics of Eli's graduation status and next steps, adding they are excited for Eli and looking forward to sharing this occasion with them. Kris then asks, "So Eli, what questions do have for me?"

Eli's Questions

- Should I give my chosen name in my résumé, cover letter, and during the interview?
- With personal statements for applications, how personal should I get?
- When I talk about my past internship experiences, how should I talk about them? Can I share these experiences without the risk of outing myself?
- How will I talk with my past professors and supervisors about my transition and chosen name? What would be appropriate to share?
- Can I ask references to share only certain things or in a certain way? What if I haven't really kept in touch with them, how much do I need to share or clarify?
- How can I ask about the culture of a workplace or find out more about what it's really like to work there?
- Do I choose a career path where I have more experience and feels more familiar or choose the career that I want to move toward?

Academic Advising Considerations

While a referral to the campus career center or a similar resource should certainly be included, "assisting students with career concerns within an educational framework" is still part of academic advising; addressing Eli's questions, at least in part, can facilitate this "shared goal" and any subsequent referral (Grites et al., 2016; Ledwith, 2014). Advisors cannot anticipate and have a ready list of answers for every student situation, but an advisor should anticipate the need to be familiar with a variety of theories and approaches to inform the questions that may arise in the moment. While most advisors will have experience with student development theory, additional familiarity with topics such as queer theory, narrative theory, and planned happenstance theory could positively impact an advisor's response to Eli. Yes, Eli has very specific questions about their career and job search, but one might also look beyond these to the broader and, arguably, more difficult concerns these questions point to as a whole. In the rest of the vignette, we will provide examples for how the advisor might address Eli's questions using these theories.

We will begin by examining queer theory. Denton (2019) stated that queer theory, "challenges linear and stable notions of development," and its critiques help us, "consider how even well-intentioned knowledge production (e.g., scholarship, programs) exercises power in ways that may exclude students who do not fit current hetero- and homonormative binaries of sexual and gender identity" (p. 60). An advisor informed by queer theory is aware of the systemic, structural, and societal norms that impact Eli's questions. Subsequently, the questions an advisor might pose to Eli would reflect these contextual considerations. Additionally, advisors should recognize the relationship between the historical and ongoing social constructs queer theory critiques and their impact on those "climates less safe" or "unpredictable" for LGBTQA+ students entering the workplace as described in the previous chapter. As students consider viable career paths, it is understandable that they would also consider safety concerns, but often LGBTQA+ students will engage in what is called "occupational stereotyping," wherein the student's perception of careers as LGBTQA-friendly or not is determined before they ever speak to advisors or career professionals (Hughey et al., 2009). Understanding the role of sociohistorical and societal norms, and the critiques queer theory brings to them, provides Kris the opportunity to discuss with Eli a topic such as occupational stereotyping in a way that elucidates the phenomenon and positively reframes that conversation about careers in advocacy versus international law.

When a conversation is looked at from a third-person perspective, it tells a story, and stories are the purview of narrative theory. In *The Power of Story: Narrative Theory in Academic Advising,* Hagen (2018) calls attention to story as the way that both students and advisors convey meaning. Telling a story is not just about what happened when but creates a picture of the storyteller. Stories define and redefine the storyteller's relationship to themselves, to others, and the world around them. They take on sociohistorical context as the storyteller will interpret and reinterpret their own stories over time. In other words, people change and the stories they tell about themselves change, too. Framing Eli's circumstances through narrative theory allows a broader conversation about how graduation is instinctively and inherently a crossroads. The pursuit of a college degree always already includes the idea of an end, a completion, an exit. We should not be surprised that, upon achieving that end, students may yet feel some sense of loss or apprehension for what comes next. In Eli's case, the crossroads is not graduation alone. As Eli (re)defines or comes more fully into their identity, they also stand at a crossroads between past and future selves. Hagen (2018) called the crossroads a place of "discomfort and disequilibrium, where a new start can begin" (pp. 73–74). As the previous chapter highlights, the master narratives of "struggle and success" or "emancipation" may come into play. For Eli, their relationship to these narratives may be all the more complicated by their gender fluidity. To be present as and assumed to be white, straight, and male by others—even superficially—is a new and complex feeling. Eli may feel their gender presentation is more authentic, even freeing. Still, it also changes the way they are seen and, in a way, seen as part of the heteronormative patriarchy. Informed by narrative theory, an advisor can recognize and validate a student at the crossroads. Given the opportunity, Kris might also provide a positive space for Eli to talk through the narratives placed upon them by how others read their gender. Considering these narratives closely may help Eli better understand and imagine their everyday in the workplace.

An advisor, knowing that queer theory undermines the linear approach inherent to traditional student development and narrative theory demonstrates that "plot does not always unfold in a linear way" (Hagen, 2018), needs a career advising theory that doesn't contradict these ideas and can coexist with the ambiguities they embrace. Planned happenstance theory challenges "the notion that career planning is a logical and linear activity" (Hughey et al., 2009) and, as described by Mitchell et al. (1999), seeks to encourage curiosity, persistence, flexibility, and optimism in the uncertain world of career decision-making. To consider this theory in practice, remember Eli's interest in advocacy-related positions has not diminished—they have only added an interest in investigating options in government and international law. But with new ideas comes newfound ambivalence. Eli feels unsure about choosing a new path and worries whether it will be a welcoming atmosphere for them. As Eli's advisor, Kris would be served well to emphasize that unexpected opportunities may present themselves throughout one's life and career. Adjusting one's plans to account for these opportunities shouldn't be taken as straying from that path, rather it shows an "open-mindedness" and flexibility that Eli can employ now and in the future. Central to planned happenstance theory is reframing indecision in terms of curiosity and willingness to take risks in the face of unexpected chances (Mitchell et al., 1999). Ultimately, Eli can and should apply for a variety of positions. Applications only communicate one's interest in a particular job; they are not a commitment to the job itself. Encouraging Eli to consider what plans they might make in the event of different offers or opportunities might assist them in identifying what is most pressing or important for them at this time and offer a model for future career decisions.

Nonetheless, these are just possible interpretations of Eli's story and only one example of the convergence of theories an advisor might use. Advisors will recognize Eli as the author in this story and themselves, not as all-knowing experts or oracles, but sounding boards and interlocutors who can offer space for reflection and consideration. To do this well, advisors should cultivate an approach of epistemic humility as defined by Hagen (2018):

> Listening well involves questions, whether they are spoken or not. A skilled advisor listening to a student narrative unfold cultivates an attitude of questioning, rather than one of already knowing the answers. Champlin-Scharff & Hagen (2013) refer to this as "epistemic humility" (p. 235), a listening stance in which one does not already presume to know, a stance in which one rolls with uncertainty and ambiguity. (p. 39)

The advisor's role then is not to tell Eli or any (LGBTQA+) student what to do, but rather to offer insights, informed by these theories and approaches, as accessible connections between where the student is and where they may want to go. This may result in departing from the often-linear concept of students moving from first year through college to graduation and then career. "Listening well" will mean following the narrative bread crumbs students provide and being willing to deviate from well-worn advising paths, being prepared enough to know how to translate these abstract conversations into actionable next steps for students. In Eli's case, identifying actionable next steps means emphasizing the timeliness of connecting to university networks and resources prior to graduation. Therefore, Eli's advisor could propose the following "key questions," informed by chapter 7 and the theories reviewed previously.

Advisor Questions

- Talk me through why you feel you need to eliminate options now: What do you gain by doing so? What might you lose?
- College is all about discovering new things. How would you describe the relationship between the familiar/past passion and the discovery/new strengths? Are there connections you see?
- How do you feel about your professional life being an extension of your personal life? In an ideal world, what would you like this balance to look like?
- What career assessments have you already taken or would you like to take? What tools would assist you in reflecting about yourself, strengths, and skills?
- What is your ideal work environment? What are your work values?
- Resources exist to assist LGBTQA+ job seekers in finding out about workplace policies and culture. Are you familiar with the HRC Corporate Equality Index or Out & Equal Workplace Advocates?
- Have you contacted or met with a career coach or others at our career center? They can help you workshop résumés or cover letters, practice interviews, and find industry-specific insights. (Advisors should already be familiar with what their campus career center offers and any limitations that might impact graduating students.)
- What networks do you have right now? How can I help you navigate your networks, including identifying those who can help you prepare for talking to your references?
- Where can you begin to cultivate a network of professionals, alumni, and colleagues whom you will reach out to when similar questions arise?
- What are the narratives placed upon you by how others read your gender? How might this impact your everyday in the workplace?
- Which of your needs take precedence right now? What do you expect to take precedence as a recent graduate?

Reflecting on this student scenario, what additional questions might you ask Eli? What resources can you identify, on your campus or beyond, that might assist students with similar questions or concerns? What theories and approaches are you already familiar with that can inform your responses? What gaps might you identify in your own training or experience that you would like to address?

References

Champlin-Scharff, S., & Hagen, P. L. (2013). Understanding and interpretation: A hermeneutic approach to advising. In J. K. Drake, M. A. Miller, & P. Jordan (Eds.), *Academic advising approaches: Strategies that teach students to make the most of college* (pp. 223–239). John Wiley & Sons.

Denton, J. M. (2019). Queer theory: Deconstructing sexual and gender identity, norms, and developmental assumptions. In E. S. Abes, S. R. Jones, & D. L. Stewart (Eds.), *Rethinking college student development theory using critical frameworks* (pp. 55–63). Stylus.

Grites, T. J., Miller, M. A., & Voler, J. G. (2016). *Beyond foundations: Developing as a master academic advisor.* John Wiley & Sons.

Hagen, P. L. (2018). *The power of story: Narrative theory in academic advising.* NACADA: The Global Community for Academic Advising.

Hughey, K. F., Nelson, D., Damminger, J., & McCalla-Wriggins, B. (2009). *The handbook of career advising* (1st ed.). Jossey-Bass.

Ledwith, K. E. (2014). Academic advising and career services: A collaborative approach. *New Directions for Student Services, 2014*(148), 49–63. https://doi.org/10.1002/ss.20108

Mitchell, K. E., Levin, S., & Krumboltz, J. D. (1999). Planned happenstance: Constructing unexpected career opportunities. *Journal of Counseling & Development, 77*(2), 115–124. https://doi.org/10.1002/j.1556-6676.1999.tb02431.x

Shelton, S. A. (2018). "We're in the freaking Bible Belt": A narrative analysis of the complexities of addressing LGBTQ topics while teaching in the Deep South. In K. K. Strunk (Ed.), *Queering education in the Deep South* (pp. 3–14). Information Age.

8

LGBTQA+ STUDENTS AND MENTAL HEALTH

kristen a. langellier and Jennifer M. Gess

D
ue to the developmental nature of the traditional college age, most college students are experiencing myriad changes. These changes can include mental health issues, as many mental illnesses develop or become more prominent during young adulthood (Liu et al., 2019). College students also experience a higher risk of mental health difficulties due to the stresses and pressures of student life (Laidlaw et al., 2016). LGBTQA+ students face even further risk of mental health concerns, including higher rates of depression, anxiety, suicidality, and trauma- and stressor-related disorders. These mental health disparities may be related to the heightened discrimination and oppression experienced by LGBTQA+ persons (Grant et al., 2014). This chapter discusses common mental health concerns exhibited by LGBTQA+ college students and the ways these concerns manifest. Recommendations are provided for introducing counseling to students and helping them find LGBTQA+ affirmative, queer-competent counselors and resources in their community. Finally, a vignette is included to illustrate the information provided in the chapter.

The serious mental health challenges faced by LGBTQA+ students are best examined from an intersectional lens that recognizes minority stress using the socioecological perspective. The socioecological model is a contextual, multilevel model that provides a framework to consider various levels of systems and interactions between individuals and their environment. The socioecological model was developed from Bronfenbrenner's seminal work in 1979 on ecological systems, in which counseling psychologists explored relationships among individuals, communities, and society. The health-care field and school counseling community later expanded upon this approach to address social injustices (Furman & Gruenewald,

2004). The socioecological model helps delineate whether mental health difficulties are the result of challenges occurring in society or within the individual (Ratts et al., 2016). This distinction can be useful when working with LGBTQA+ students, as LGBTQA+ students experience greater discrimination and oppression than their cisgender and heterosexual peers.

The socioecological model also addresses intersecting identities, including race, ethnicity, gender, affectional orientation, economic status, religion, spirituality, and ability status, as well as the ways these aspects impact one's status in society (Harley et al., 2002). Intersectionality, first coined by legal scholar Kimberlé Crenshaw in 1989, was originally used to describe the multiple overlapping forms of discrimination African American women face (see chapter 5). Since Crenshaw's (1989) conception of intersectionality, many social justice movements have used the term to describe the overlapping oppressions experienced by marginalized populations. Intersectional identities are often impacted by multilevel systems and interactions, as outlined by the socioecological model. Specifically, the socioecological model focuses on five levels of influence: (a) intrapersonal, (b) interpersonal, (c) institutional, (d) community, and (e) public policy (Ratts et al., 2016). The intrapersonal level focuses on individual characteristics; the interpersonal level encompasses family, friends, peers, and colleagues; the institutional level considers schools, churches, work, businesses, and community organizations; the community level examines the norms and values of the community; and the public policy level addresses local, state, and federal policies and laws (Ratts et al., 2016). College students, including those who identify as LGBTQA+, have complex, multilayered identities, which academic advisors must take into account.

Finally, we believe academic advisors must incorporate an understanding of minority stress in their use of the socioecological model. Minority stress is the process by which LGBTQA+ people experience unique stressors which may lead to mental disorders (Meyer & Frost, 2013; see chapter 7, this volume). By using the socioecological model and incorporating intersectionality and the minority stress model in their approaches, academic advisors can work with students to best understand and support students' mental health concerns.

Common Mental Health Concerns of LGBTQA+ College Students

While mental health symptoms may manifest similarly across most people, there are also stark differences in the ways LGBTQA+ persons experience and express mental health concerns. LGBTQA+ people experience discrimination and oppression at rates higher than their cisgender, heterosexual peers, at the interpersonal, institutional, community, and public policy levels of influence (Asakura, 2018; Conron & Goldberg, 2020). LGBTQA+ people may internalize these negative experiences, leading to internalized homophobia or transphobia and heightened stress at the intrapersonal level. As a result, LGBTQA+ students experience greater risk of mental health concerns and may express more severe symptoms.

Depression

Depression is a common mental health concern on U.S. college campuses. Recent statistics regarding depression in the United States report an estimated 8% of adults over 20 years old struggle with depression for at least a 2-week duration (Brody et al., 2018). Although there is a dearth of literature and research regarding LGBTQA+ college students' mental health concerns, studies indicate those who experience prejudice and discrimination due to their sexual or gender identity often suffer from depression (Bissonette & Szymanski, 2019). Seventy-eight percent of college-aged individuals identifying as LGBTQA+ reported suffering from mental health challenges (Ketchen Lipson et al., 2019). This rate is considerably higher than that of their non-LGBTQA+ peers. Indeed, data from a meta-analysis of seven institutions suggest students who identify as LGBTQA+ experience depression at rates higher than their non-LGBTQA+ counterparts (Intrabartola, 2017). About 30% of students identifying as LGBTQA+ described experiencing a depressive episode severe enough to inhibit their normal day-to-day activities (Intrabartola, 2017). Signs of depression most often exhibited by young adults are both emotional and behavioral and may include:

- Feelings of sadness, evidenced by tearfulness or an expression of feeling empty or hopeless
- Anger or irritability, sometimes seemingly out of proportion with the event or situation
- Loss of interest in activities they previously enjoyed, such as hobbies, sports, or even day-to-day activities, such as cleaning, cooking, or going to a job, often evidenced by avoiding these activities
- Trouble sleeping, manifesting as either insomnia or sleeping too much
- Feelings of worthlessness, guilt, or shame, often exemplified by blaming self for things out of their control or outside of their responsibility
- Lack of energy such that they must exert significant effort for miniscule or mundane tasks (Mayo Clinic, n.d.-b)

In addition to recognizing the symptoms listed previously, awareness of the symptoms of depression in LGBTQA+ students as understood through the socioecological model will be beneficial for academic advisors. For example, a possible intrapersonal cause of depression is the student internalizing negative attitudes and beliefs related to their LGBTQA+ identity, which often leads to low self-worth and feelings of worthlessness and guilt (Grant et al., 2014). Examples of interpersonal situations that may lead to depression in LGBTQA+ students include increased loneliness and isolation, as well as students experiencing the need to conceal their true identities in order to feel safe (Bissonette & Syzmanski, 2019). Institutional concerns, such as campus climate issues, may also lead to increased symptoms of depression. Examples of institutional concerns include policies that impact LGBTQA+ students' sense of belonging on campus, including the absence of inclusive restrooms, gender-neutral forms, and LGBTQA+ inclusive faculty and staff professional development. Finally, possible community issues leading to depression in LGBTQA+ students include the extent to which the local environment provides opportunities for LGBTQA+ communities to be celebrated, such as annual pride festivals, affirming restaurants and bars, and supportive emblems and signs such as rainbows and "Safe Space" decals.

Anxiety

The American College Health Association (2018) found that 22.1% of college students reported being diagnosed with or treated for generalized anxiety disorder within the previous year. Similar to depression, the rates of anxiety diagnoses for LGBTQA+ college students are higher than those of their non-LGBTQA+ peers (Borgogna et al., 2019; Grant et al., 2014). Symptoms of generalized anxiety disorder can be emotional and/or physical (Mayo Clinic, n.d.-a). Emotional and behavioral symptoms of generalized anxiety disorder can change depending on the individual and may include:

- Continual worry or anxiety disproportionate to the situation; worry often consumes thoughts such that it borders on obsessive
- Planning for worst-case scenarios and persistent overthinking situations
- Heightened sense of threat in situations that are not threatening
- Poor reaction to ambiguous or uncertain circumstances
- Persistent worry and fear regarding decisions and choices

Possible physical signs can include:

- Persistent fatigue
- Irritability
- Sleep disturbances

- Tense or sore muscles
- Being easily startled
- Gastrointestinal symptoms such as nausea or diarrhea (Mayo Clinic, n.d.-a)

It is best to examine these mental health concerns through the socioecological framework. A possible intrapersonal cause of anxiety in LGBTQA+ people could be connected to the oppression and discrimination they face or have faced, leading them to expect oppression, discrimination, or even violence. Possible interpersonal causes are similar in that the expectation of oppression, discrimination, or violence causes hypervigilance and fear responses. In an interpersonal situation, anxiety could arise out of fear of interacting with certain individuals or groups on campus. An example of an institutional cause of anxiety could be the lack of safe spaces or gender-neutral bathrooms on campus. As with depression, a lack of polices that protect LGBTQA+ individuals on campus could also lead to anxiety. Similarly, community causes of anxiety may relate to the repeated exposure to oppression, discrimination, and potential violence LGBTQA+ students face, which leads to hypervigilance and fear.

Suicidality

In addition to heightened rates of depression and anxiety, LGBTQA+ college students are more likely to experience suicidal ideation than their non-LGBTQA+ peers (Lytle et al., 2014). Suicidal ideation, however, is difficult to assess due to the often unknown reasons for death. According to a study using data collected in 2013, 10% of transgender college students and 5% of cisgender LGBTQA+ students have attempted suicide (Woodford et al., 2018). Younger LGBTQA+ students face higher risks of suicide, with 47.7% of lesbian, gay, or bisexual (LGB) youth considering suicide in 2017 (Kann et al., 2018). In comparison, the rate of suicide attempts among the general college student population in 2015 was 9% (Liu et al., 2019). These high numbers reflect the challenges LGBTQA+ college students face and the lack of coping mechanisms provided in our pervasive hetero- and cis-normative culture.

Overall, LGBTQA+ college students experience statistically higher rates of discrimination and oppression at the interpersonal, institutional, community, and public policy levels, resulting in heightened minority stress and an increased risk of suicidal ideation. LGBTQA+ students also encounter both subtle discrimination and blatant violence at much higher rates than their cisgender, heterosexual peers (Edwards et al., 2015; Murchison et al., 2017). For example, at the interpersonal level, LGBTQA+ students may experience insensitive, demeaning insults from peers that dismiss the student's identity (e.g., "You're just saying you're genderqueer to get attention"), as well as physical violence and sexual assault (Edwards et al., 2015; Murchison et al., 2017). In fact, students who identify as LGBTQA+ experience higher rates of sexual assault (24.3%) compared to non-LGBTQA+ college students (11%; Edwards et al., 2015). Attempting to cope with discrimination and oppression may lead students to pursue risky behaviors like substance misuse and abuse, both of which are more prevalent among LGBTQA+ students than their peers (Kroshus & Davoren, 2016). Considering the impacts of the institutional and community levels of the socioecological model, there is a lack of experience and education among college campus administrators on the risk factors LGBTQA+ students experience and ways faculty and staff members can support LGBTQA+ students. Signs of suicidality in young people include:

- Frequently mentioning suicide, including mentioning wanting to be dead
- Having access or means to take one's life, such as access to guns or other weapons, pills, or sharp objects
- Isolating oneself and declining social opportunities more than usual
- Severe mood swings
- Saying goodbye to people as if they will not see them again
- Engaging in risky and self-destructive behavior (Mayo Clinic, n.d.-d)

Transgender students often experience more numerous and severe incidents of trauma related to prejudice and discrimination because of their gender identity (Burnes et al., 2016; Richmond et al., 2012). Transgender people have one of the highest rates of suicidality: according to the 2015 U.S. Transgender Survey, 82% of transgender people have had serious thoughts of killing themselves at some point in their life, and 40% of transgender people have attempted suicide in their lifetime, compared to 4.6% of the general population (James et al., 2016). Furthermore, transgender students face even higher risks of suicide attempt and completion than their cisgender LGBTQA+ peers (Effrig et al., 2011; Seelman, 2016). These numbers increase drastically when the transgender person has multiple marginalized identities (Grant et al., 2011). For example, 54% of transgender people with disabilities and 57% of American Indian transgender people have attempted suicide in their lifetime (James et al., 2016).

The socioecological lens helps us understand the reasoning behind these statistics. Transgender people experience pervasive violence and mistreatment, including high rates of verbal harassment (54%), physical attacks (24%), and sexual assaults (13%; James et al., 2016). Prior experiences of violence and discrimination, in turn, are associated with higher suicide rates (Clements-Nolle et al., 2006). Thirteen percent of transgender individuals who have sought professional guidance (e.g., psychologists, counselors, or religious advisors) were told to stop their gender transition, leading to higher rates of suicide attempts (James et al., 2016). Known as conversion therapy, this unethical, harmful practice of attempting to change an individual's internal gender identity is founded in fear and cisnormative expectations. It is important to recognize the harm of invalidating or otherwise not supporting transgender students' identities.

Lack of accessibility to safe restrooms is another stressor that leads to higher rates of suicidality among transgender individuals (Grant et al., 2011; Herman, 2013). Many transgender people experience harassment and violence in public restrooms, including being questioned about whether they belong in the men's/women's restroom and being told to leave (Seelman, 2016). Transgender people of color, transgender individuals with disabilities or who live in a rural area, and transgender people who were visibly perceived as transgender were found more likely to face harassment and violence in public restrooms, leading to higher rates of suicidality (Grant et al., 2011; Seelman, 2016). Academic advisors must recognize the importance of using a lens of intersectionality to understand the multiple layers of oppression faced by transgender students and their associated risks of suicidality.

Trauma and Stressor-Related Disorders

Trauma and stressor-related disorders are caused by exposure to traumatic or stressful events and subsequent psychological distress (American Psychiatric Association, 2013). After the traumatic or stressful event, the individual develops an associated stressor, trauma-related thoughts or feelings, and distress or functional impairment, among other criteria (American Psychiatric Association, 2013). The rates of trauma and stressor-related disorders, such as post-traumatic stress disorder (PTSD), among college students are higher than those of the general population due to students' heightened risk factors (Read et al., 2011). Risk factors for the general college population include higher rates of sexual assault (Rothman et al., 2019). LGBTQA+ students experience even higher rates of trauma and stressor-related disorders due to additional risk factors related to their sexual orientation and/or gender identity in college. Signs of trauma and stressor-related disorders in young people include:

- Unwanted, distressing memories of the traumatic event
- Nightmares about the traumatic event
- Avoiding anything that is a reminder of the traumatic event
- Feelings of hopelessness and emotional numbness
- Lack of interest in previously enjoyable activities
- Difficulties concentrating (Mayo Clinic, n.d.-c)

The effects of heteronormativity, cisnormativity, queerphobia, and transphobia are woven throughout schools and college campuses (Kosciw et al., 2013). Queerphobia and transphobia can include blatant threats and violence as well as subtle microaggressions. LGBTQA+ students may hear heterosexist language (e.g., "That's so gay!"), and transgender students may experience discrimination in the restrooms (e.g., being stared at, being asked if they're in the correct restroom, or being thrown out; Woodford et al., 2012). These experiences of minority stress lead to chronic psychosocial stress and could result in trauma and stress-related disorders. Transgender and asexual students experience an even higher risk of developing trauma and stress-related disorders.

Transgender college students. Transgender people often experience numerous and severe incidents of trauma related to prejudice and discrimination against their gender identity (Richmond et al., 2012). Transgender people of color experience even more violence and mistreatment than their white transgender counterparts. Furthermore, transgender people of color are three times more likely to live in poverty and four times more likely to be unemployed than the general population (James et al., 2016). They also experience heightened health disparities, such as greater risk of living with HIV, than the general population (James et al., 2016). It is clear transgender people experience greater challenges than cisgender individuals, and much of this is due to transphobia embedded within social systems, including barriers to quality health care; prejudicial policies at the local, state, and federal levels; and discrimination within schools (Beemyn, 2003; Seelman, 2014; Singh et al., 2013). As one transgender student explained:

> Every single day at college, I was harassed for being a visibly trans woman. People slowed their cars down to stare at me, they shouted slurs at me from their dorm windows, insulted me in class, and a lot more I'd rather not think about. It got so bad that I tried to kill myself twice over the course of three months. (James et al., 2016, p. 134)

Twenty-five percent of transgender college students who are out or perceived as transgender have experienced violence or harassment at school (James et al., 2016). This number increases when the student has additional marginalized identities: 37% of American Indian transgender students and 28% of Black transgender students have experienced verbal, physical, and/or sexual harassment at school. Exposure to stressful and traumatic events, such as verbal, physical, and sexual harassment leads to higher rates of psychological distress.

Sexual harassment is a traumatic experience over 11% of all college students and 23.1% of female-identified college undergraduate students experience (United States Bureau of Justice Statistics, 2015). Nearly half of transgender people have been sexually assaulted (James et al., 2016). According to one such student:

> I was sexually assaulted at my university . . . The university didn't do anything to help me . . . I lived in terror the entire time I was on campus. I was denied a rape kit because I was transgender and the police were completely uninterested. (James et al., 2016, p. 201)

The high prevalence of sexual violence on college and university campuses leads to increased rates of depression, anxiety, suicidality, and PTSD among students, particularly transgender students (Rothman et al., 2019).

Asexual college students. Asexuality is a natural variation in human sexuality which refers to individuals who do not experience the same level of sexual attraction as the general population (Parent & Ferriter, 2018). Asexual individuals are over four times more likely to report a diagnosis of PTSD than those who do not identify as asexual (Parent & Ferriter, 2018). Moreover, asexual people are more likely to experience sexual trauma than nonasexual people, which could be connected to their higher rates of PTSD (Parent & Ferriter, 2018). Understanding symptoms of trauma and stressor-related disorders, especially when working with asexual students, will allow advisors to support their students to the fullest capacity.

The Intersection of Academic Advising, Mental Health Concerns, and Professional Counseling

Academic advisors must be prepared to work with students exhibiting mental health issues, especially LGBTQA+ students (Larkin et al., 2015). Using the statistics presented and the socioecological model of conceptualizing the realities LGBTQA+ students face, it becomes clear there is a higher likelihood

LGBTQA+ students will exhibit mental health concerns. As such, advisors need to be prepared to understand these concerns through an intersectional approach. To assist advisors in working with LGBTQA+ students, a vignette focusing on a nonbinary student has been provided in the next section. LGBTQA+ communities encompass a broad spectrum of identities, and while it is impossible to address all these identities in one vignette, the hope is that this example will be translatable in working with students of various gender and sexual identities.

Vignette

Liu, a 19-year-old college freshman who identifies as nonbinary, is a first-generation student from a low-income background. Liu (they/them) is meeting with Kelani (she/her), their academic advisor. Kelani has become concerned about Liu's well-being, as she has noticed some changes in Liu's behavior over the course of the academic year. The university Liu attends is in a conservative region of the United States, and Liu's grades have slipped significantly in their second semester, resulting in academic probation. Additionally, Liu has a track scholarship and is on the university track team. The track coach has mentioned to Kelani that Liu has missed several practices and their performance has dropped.

Kelani has been wondering about Liu's experiences as a gender nonbinary person in this region of the country and whether their gender identity experiences are related to their current state of distress. Kelani has planned on bringing this up to Liu in their next meeting. Kelani is concerned about potential barriers to student support; the campus counseling center is overwhelmed and overloaded with student clients, as is the case in many campus counseling centers across the country. Additionally, Kelani wants to ensure she can find a long-term option for Liu, because her campus's counseling center is only able to provide short-term counseling across six sessions.

As she was planning her conversation with Liu, Kelani talked with the campus counselors to find out what she should say when recommending counseling services. Kelani is worried she will offend Liu or make them feel "crazy." The counselors reassured Kelani and provided some guidance for introducing Liu to counseling. These recommendations included continuing to use Liu's pronouns "they/them," working with Liu from a socioecological and intersectional lens, and providing information related to LGBTQA+ affirmative resources.

As the conversation began, Kelani focused on Liu's academic performance and the track coach's concerns. Kelani noticed that Liu seemed ashamed and spoke in a barely audible tone. They didn't make much eye contact with

Kelani, and their cheeks turned red when Kelani mentioned academic probation. Kelani asked how Liu's life was outside of school, which opened the door for a discussion of mental health concerns. Liu stated, "Actually, it sucks. The people in the town stare at me when I go to the grocery store. Some of my teachers use the wrong pronouns. I just feel really alone."

"It sounds like you are dealing with a lot—and anyone would struggle with this much on their mind," Kelani said, using a calm and compassionate tone.

Kelani remembered the counselors recommended she work with Liu from a socioecological, intersectional lens. Bearing this in mind, Kelani considered how Liu expressed challenges at the interpersonal level (e.g., teachers), institutional level (e.g., school, sports), and community level (e.g., grocery stores). Kelani also considered Liu's identity as gender nonbinary, as well as other aspects related to their intersecting identities, such as race, ethnicity, spirituality and religion, age, ability status, sexuality, and national origin background. She wondered how these multilevel, intersecting aspects of Liu's identity impact their mental health.

Liu continued, "It is a lot of stress. I moved here from a more progressive city, and even though my family isn't understanding of me, at least I had friends and community. Here, I'm completely alone. Since I moved here, all I want to do is sleep and stay in bed all day. It's so hard to get the energy to go to class."

"Liu, it sounds as though you are feeling pretty down and alone, especially since you're not experiencing acceptance at any level: from the community, the school, your family, and peers. That is all very heavy," Kelani responded. "I am wondering if you've ever seen a counselor before. A lot of the students I meet with see counselors, either here on campus or out in the community, as they want some extra support while going through so much at college."

"Yeah, I saw one when I was coming out a few years ago; my parents wanted me to go," Liu answered. "He wasn't very helpful. I felt misunderstood and like he didn't get my identity at all."

This admission was concerning to Kelani, as Liu's past experience with an unhelpful counselor could impact Liu's willingness to attend counseling. She remembered what the counselors at the college's counseling center told her—not everyone will be the right fit and sometimes people must meet several different counselors before they find the right one. Additionally, the campus counselors mentioned that counselors are increasingly doing extra work in order to become competent and affirming of LGBTQA+ individuals. Prior to Liu's arrival in her office, Kelani searched the websites the campus counselors mentioned in order to find a few off-campus counselors who were LGBTQA+ competent and affirming.

"That's terrible. I am sorry you had that experience," Kelani began. "My colleagues in the counseling office tell me that it's pretty common for people to take time finding the right fit. And they say counselors understand and expect that. I have researched a few people in the community, and I want to show you their websites. Would that be okay?"

Liu agreed, and Kelani opened the web page of a local counselor on her computer. "This counselor, Brady, has a pride flag and a trans flag on his web page. It says here that he specializes in working with LGBTQA+ people. I called him earlier and asked him a few questions to see if he truly is affirming, and he certainly seems to be. He said he's an active member of the state's Society for Sexual, Affectional, Intersex, and Gender Expansive Identities (SAIGE) division [and that he] regularly attends continuing education courses on working with queer and trans clients. Plus, he is willing to see a few clients from the college for free." Liu looked over his web page and read Brady's counseling philosophy statement. His counseling statement reflected the importance of honoring sexual diversity, celebrating the gender continuum, and being open and nonjudgmental. With Liu's agreement, Liu and Kelani called Brady to make an appointment using Kelani's office phone. Kelani was relieved Liu was going to get the help they deserve from a competent and affirming counselor.

Questions to Consider

- Consider your familiarity with using they/them as a gender-neutral singular pronoun. How might you increase your familiarity and comfort with this pronoun?
- As an advisor, do you maintain professional relationships with local LGBTQA+-affirming counselors? Consider to whom you might refer Liu for counseling if you were working with them at your institution.

Recommendations for Advising Practice

For many people, the presence of a social stigma against mental health issues can be a barrier to seeking counseling services. In fact, only one out of three college students attends counseling for help with mental health issues (Eisenberg et al., 2011). Academic advisors may be the first to learn about students' mental health issues, and it is therefore crucial that advisors possess the knowledge and frameworks necessary for addressing mental health. In particular, we recommend utilizing the socioecological model to support LGBTQA+ students with mental health issues.

At the intrapersonal level, academic advisors can provide a nonjudgmental space for students to express themselves openly. Paying attention to the language one uses can be beneficial in encouraging individuals to see a counselor; this could prove especially helpful for those who might self-stigmatize counseling or mental health issues (Jones, 2017). We suggest using people-first language such as "someone struggling with depression" rather than referring to people as their diagnosis or mental health concern. For example, saying "she's borderline" labels the individual by the diagnosis first, whereas "a woman with borderline personality disorder" positions personhood and individuality before diagnosis. In addition to using people-first language in a nonjudgmental space, academic advisors can normalize working with a counselor by employing simple shifts in language and moderating their tone of voice. Keeping a soft and empathic tone will help alleviate the student's feelings of judgment or shame (Jones, 2017). Academic advisors might begin the conversation with empathetic and innocuous phrases such as, "It seems like you are dealing with a lot" before moving into specific statements like, "A lot of students seek help at the counseling center or in the community. Have you ever gone to a counselor before?" These intrapersonal recommendations offer LGBTQA+ students the opportunity to be authentic in the academic advising setting.

The interpersonal level focuses on students' social networks and support systems, including college and university support systems. Academic advisors may benefit from maintaining awareness of on- and off-campus LGBTQA+ support groups. Many university campuses support a gay-straight alliance, sexuality and gender awareness student club, or campus pride group. However, some campuses do not permit such groups to exist due to religious or faith-based beliefs, and it is therefore imperative for academic advisors to be aware of off-campus, community-based LGBTQA+ support systems (see chapter 9). There may also be local LGBTQA+ support groups facilitated by licensed counselors.

The next level of the socioecological model is the institutional level, which includes schools, churches, businesses, and community organizations. Academic advisors are well-positioned on campus to help alleviate potential institutional concerns. For example, advisors can assist in the advocacy for gender-neutral restrooms on campuses or provide campus maps showing where the gender-neutral restrooms are located. Advisors can also recommend that college and university forms in or outside their department use gender-neutral language, such as "parent/partner/spouse" instead of "mother/father/husband/wife."

The community level of the socioecological model provides the opportunity to explore the norms and values of a college or university campus. One recommendation is to avoid language that labels an individual's emotions or reactions as "normal" or "abnormal." Avoiding judgment-based language can help lessen the student's feelings of shame and the stigmas associated with mental health issues. Research demonstrates that limiting usage of qualifying terms helps individuals accept mental health concerns (Jones, 2017). Specifically, for LGBTQA+ individuals, it should be noted that until 1973, the *Diagnostic and Statistical Manual of Mental Disorders (DSM)* included "homosexuality" as a mental disorder (Drescher, 2015). Consequently, we recommend avoiding the word *homosexuality* as a potentially triggering word. Avoiding language embedded in discrimination and oppression can help change the norms and values of the college or community campus to become more inclusive.

Finally, the public policy level of the socioecological model suggests academic advisors remain aware of the ways local, state, and federal policies and laws may be impacting LGBTQA+ students. For example, certain policies determine the criteria transgender student-athletes must meet in order to compete at the college or university level (Griffin & Carroll, 2011; see chapter 11). These criteria may be impossible for some transgender student athletes to meet, thus negatively impacting their mental health. Academic advisors can benefit from awareness of the impacts of such policies, especially because academic advisors are in the position to advocate for and support students.

Campus counseling centers tend to be overloaded with clients, and the wait to see a counselor may be longer than desired (Thielking, 2017). Therefore, it is good practice for academic advisors to be aware of queer-competent professional counselors in the community accepting student patients. Several resources exist that can be of use to academic advisors when recommending counselors to LGBTQA+ students, including information regarding counselors' professional development and competencies regarding queer issues. Those resources appear in the list that follows. In addition to knowing which counselors in their communities are queer-competent and LGBTQA+ affirming, we recommend academic advisors be mindful of potential barriers students from low socioeconomic statuses might experience in accessing mental health care. Many counselors will work within a sliding scale fee structure to accommodate low-income clients, and counselors typically make this information available on their website or will answer such questions over the phone.

Finally, it is important to remember the resiliency of LGBTQA+ students (Meyer, 2015). Considering the multiple layers of oppression and discrimination they have encountered from various sources across history, LGBTQA+ individuals continue to demonstrate remarkable strength. Academic advisors can focus on positive strengths among LGBTQA+ students while also acting as agents of change at multiple levels.

LGBTQA+ Affirmative Counselors

Locating LGBTQA+ affirmative counselors is imperative for academic advisors. There are many resources designed to help individuals find LGBTQA+ affirming counselors, including:

- American Association of Sexuality Educators, Counselors, and Therapists: www.aasect.org/referral-directory
- Gay and Lesbian Medical Association: www.glma.org
- Local LGBTQA+ community centers
- Planned Parenthood: www.plannedparenthood.org/get-care/our-services/lgbt-services
- Psychology Today: www.psychologytoday.com
- RAD Remedy: www.radremedy.org
- Society for Sexual, Affectional, Intersex, and Gender Expansive Identities (SAIGE): www.saigecounseling.org
- State division of the Association of LGBT Issues in Counseling: www.algbtic.org/our-branches/
- The Trevor Project: www.thetrevorproject.org
- Trans Lifeline: www.translifeline.org
- World Professional Association for Transgender Health: https://www.wpath.org

Some students may feel comfortable using the previously listed resources to find an LGBTQA+ affirming counselor independently. Doing so may empower the student to locate additional resources on their own. However, some students may be experiencing extra stressors and will benefit from having their academic advisor assist with finding an LGBTQA+ affirming counselor.

Academic advisors are advised to avoid assuming counselors on the previous lists are automatically LGBTQA+ affirming. We encourage more exploration and establishing relationships with LGBTQA+ affirmative counselors. The first step is to review the counselor's website. Are LGBTQA+ people represented? Does the website content celebrate LGBTQA+ people? Next, call the counselor and ask if they work with LGBTQA+ clients, how they approach working with LGBTQA+ clients, what their theoretical orientation is (which informs how they work with clients), and whether they are engaged in any LGBTQA+ counseling organizations or continuing education courses. Ask to see the counselor's forms and check to see whether the forms provide open spaces for gender and pronouns and if they use gender-neutral language when referring to individuals and relationships. Finally, look up reviews of the counselor and ask around. Consider asking other counselors you respect whether they know of and would recommend this particular counselor. This information will provide advisors and students with an understanding of the counselor's beliefs, practices, and level of knowledge regarding the unique struggles of LGBTQA+ individuals.

Conclusion

This chapter provided information as to the incidence and prevalence of common mental health concerns experienced by groups across the LGBTQA+ spectrum, demonstrating that LGBTQA+ individuals experience mental health-related concerns at rates significantly higher than their non-LGBTQA+ counterparts (Borgogna et al., 2019; Eisenberg et al., 2013; Grant et al., 2014). Conceptualizing these concerns from a socioecological framework can be useful to academic advisors, who will likely encounter mental health concerns in students with whom they work. Additionally, we posit that academic advisors can provide a valuable support system for students who are unsure or scared of seeing a counselor. Keeping in touch with any student for whom referrals have been made will also be of substantial help. The unique relationship between advisors and students presents an opportunity to explore the possibility of seeing a counselor in a safe and affirming environment. Regardless of a student's choice to see a counselor, the advisor can still provide the student with a potentially life-saving support system.

References

American College Health Association. (2018). *American College Health Association—National College Health Assessment II: Reference group executive summary spring 2018.* https://www.acha.org/documents/ncha/NCHA-II_Spring_2018_Reference _Group_Executive_Summary.pdf

American Psychiatric Association. (2013). *Diagnostic and statistical manual of mental disorders* (5th ed.). https://doi.org/10.1176/appi.books.9780890425596

Asakura, K. (2018). It takes a village: Applying a social ecological framework of resilience in working with LGBTQ youth. *Families in Society: The Journal of Contemporary Social Sciences, 97*(1), 15–22. https://doi.org/10.1606/1044-3894.2016.97.4

Beemyn, B. G. (2003). Serving the needs of transgender college students. *Journal of Gay & Lesbian Issues in Education, 1*(1), 33–50. https://doi.org/10.1300/J367v01n01_03

Bissonette, D., & Szymanski, D. M. (2019). Minority stress and LGBQ college students' depression: Roles of peer group and involvement. *Psychology of Sexual Orientation and Gender Diversity, 6*(3), 308–317. https://doi.org/10.1037/sgd0000332

Borgogna, N. C., McDermott, R. C., Aita, S. L., & Kridel, M. M. (2019). Anxiety and depression across gender and sexual minorities: Implications for transgender, gender nonconforming, pansexual, demisexual, asexual, queer, and questioning individuals. *Psychology of Sexual Orientation and Gender Diversity, 6*(1), 54–63. https://doi.org/10.1037/sgd0000306

Brody, D. J., Pratt, L. A., & Hughes, J. P. (2018). *Prevalence of depression among adults aged 20 and over: United States, 2013–2016* (NCHS Data Brief No. 303). [Data set]. National Center for Health Statistics. https://www.cdc.gov/nchs/data/databriefs/db303.pdf

Bronfenbrenner, U. (1979). *The ecology of human development: Experiments by nature and design.* Harvard University Press.

Burnes, T. R., Dexter, M. M., Richmond, K., Singh, A. A., & Cherrington, A. (2016). The experiences of transgender survivors of trauma who undergo social and medical transition. *Traumatology, 22*(1), 75–84. https://doi.org/10.1037/trm0000064

Clements-Nolle, K., Marx, R., & Katz, M. (2006). Attempted suicide among transgender persons: The influence of gender-based discrimination and victimization. *Journal of Homosexuality, 51*(3), 53–69. https://doi.org/10.1300/J082v51n03_04

Conron, K. J., & Goldberg, S. K. (2020, April). *LGBT people in the US not protected by state nondiscrimination statutes.* UCLA School of Law, Williams Institute. https://williamsinstitute.law.ucla.edu/wp-content/uploads/LGBT-ND-Protections-Update-Apr-2020.pdf

Crenshaw, K. (1989). Demarginalizing the intersection of race and sex: A Black feminist critique of antidiscrimination doctrine, feminist theory and antiracist politics. *University of Chicago Legal Forum, 1989*(1), 139–167.

Drescher, J. (2015). Out of DSM: Depathologizing homosexuality. *Behavioral Sciences, 5*(4), 565–575. https://doi.org/10.3390/bs5040565

Edwards, K. M., Sylaska, K. M., & Neal, A. M. (2015). Intimate partner violence among sexual minority populations: A critical review of the literature and agenda for future research. *Psychology of Violence, 5*(2), 112–121. https://doi.org/10.1037/a0038656

Effrig, J. C., Bieschke, K. J., & Locke, B. D. (2011). Examining victimization and psychological distress in transgender college students. *Journal of College Counseling, 14*(2), 143–157. https://doi.org/10.1002/j.2161-1882.2011.tb00269.x

Eisenberg, D., Hunt, J., & Speer, N. (2013). Mental health in American colleges and universities: Variations across student subgroups and across campuses.

The Journal of Nervous and Mental Disease, *201*(1), 60–67. https://doi. org/10.1097/nmd.0b013e31827ab077

Eisenberg, D., Hunt, J., Speer, N., & Zivin, K. (2011). Mental health service utilization among college students in the United States. *The Journal of Nervous and Mental Disease*, *199*(5), 301–308. https://doi.org/10.1097/nmd.0b013e3182175123

Furman, G. C., & Gruenewald, D. A. (2004). Expanding the landscape of social justice: A critical ecological analysis. *Educational Administration Quarterly*, *40*(1), 47–76. https://doi.org/10.1177/0013161X03259142

Grant, J. E., Odlaug, B. L., Derbyshire, K., Schreiber, L. R. N., Lust, K., & Christenson, G. (2014). Mental health and clinical correlates in lesbian, gay, bisexual, and queer young adults. *Journal of American College Health*, *62*(1), 75–78. https://doi.org/10.1080/07448481.2013.844697

Grant, J. M., Mottet, L. A., Tanis, J., Harrison, J., Herman, J. L., & Keisling, M. (2011). *Injustice at every turn: A report of the national transgender discrimination survey*. National Center for Transgender Equality and National Gay and Lesbian Task Force. https://www.thetaskforce.org/wp-content/uploads/2019/07/ntds_full.pdf

Griffin, P., & Carroll, H. (2011, August). *NCAA inclusion of transgender student-athletes*. NCAA Office of Inclusion. https://www.ncaa.org/sites/default/files/Transgender_Handbook_2011_Final.pdf

Harley, D. A., Jolivette, K., McCormick, K., & Tice, K. (2002). Race, class, and gender: A constellation of positionalities with implications for counseling. *Journal of Multicultural Counseling and Development*, *30*(4), 216–238. https://doi. org/10.1002/j.2161-1912.2002.tb00521.x

Herman, J. L. (2013). Gendered restrooms and minority stress: The public regulation of gender and its impact on transgender people's lives. *Journal of Public Management & Social Policy*, *19*(1), 65–80.

Intrabartola, L. (2017, October 25). *LGBTQ students think of suicide 4x as often*. Futurity. https://www.futurity.org/lgbtq-college-students-1584462/

James, S. E., Herman, J. L., Rankin, S., Keisling, M., Mottet, L., & Anafi, M. (2016). *The report of the 2015 U.S. transgender survey*. National Center for Transgender Equality. https://www.transequality.org/sites/default/files/docs/USTS-Full-Report-FINAL.PDF

Jones, M. (2017, November 20). *How to encourage someone to see a therapist*. National Alliance on Mental Illness. https://www.nami.org/Blogs/NAMI-Blog/November-2017/How-to-Encourage-Someone-to-See-a-Therapist

Kann, L., McManus, T., Harris, W. A., Shanklin, S. L., Flint, K. H., Queen, B., Lowry, R., Chyen, D., Whittle, L., Thornton, J., Lim, C., Bradford, D., Yamakawa, Y., Leon, M., Brener, N., & Ethier, K. A. (2018). Youth risk behavior surveillance: United States, 2017. *Morbidity and Mortality Weekly Report Surveillance Summaries*, *67*(8), 1–114. https://www.cdc.gov/mmwr/volumes/67/ss/ss6708a1.htm

Ketchen Lipson, S., Raifman, J., Abelson, S., & Reisner, S. L. (2019). Gender minority mental health in the U.S.: Results of a national survey on college campuses. *American Journal of Preventive Medicine, 57*(3), 293–301. https://doi. org/10.1016/j.amepre.2019.04.025

Kosciw, J. G., Palmer, N. A., Kull, R. M., & Greytak, E. A. (2013). The effect of negative school climate on academic outcomes for LGBT youth and the role of in-school supports. *Journal of School Violence, 12*(1), 45–63. https://doi.org/ 10.1080/15388220.2012.732546

Kroshus, E., & Davoren, A. K. (2016). Mental health and substance use of sexual minority college athletes. *Journal of American College Health, 64*(5), 371–379. https://doi.org/10.1080/07448481.2016.1158179

Laidlaw, A., McLellan, J., & Ozakinci, G. (2016). Understanding undergraduate student perceptions of mental health, mental well-being and help-seeking behaviour. *Studies in Higher Education, 41*(12), 2156–2168. https://doi.org/10.1080/ 03075079.2015.1026890

Larkin, R., Crumb, L., Fountain, Y., Glenn, C., & Smith, J. (2015). Managing mental health situations in the advising office. *Academic Advising Today, 38*(2). https://nacada.ksu.edu/Resources/Academic-Advising-Today/View-Articles/ Managing-Mental-Health-Situations-in-the-Advising-Office.aspx

Liu, C. H., Stevens, C., Wong, S. H. M., Yasui, M., & Chen, J. A. (2019). The prevalence and predictors of mental health diagnoses and suicide among U.S. college students: Implications for addressing disparities in service use. *Depression & Anxiety, 36*(1), 8–17. https://doi.org/10.1002/da.22830

Lytle, M. C., De Luca, S. M., & Blosnich, J. R. (2014). The influence of intersecting identities on self-harm, suicidal behaviors, and depression among lesbian, gay, and bisexual individuals. *Suicide and Life-Threatening Behavior, 44*, 384–391. https://doi.org/10.1111/sltb.12083

Mayo Clinic. (n.d.-a). *Anxiety disorders.* https://www.mayoclinic.org/diseases-conditions/anxiety/symptoms-causes/syc-20350961

Mayo Clinic. (n.d.-b). *Depression (major depressive disorder).* https://www. mayoclinic.org/diseases-conditions/depression/symptoms-causes/syc-20356007

Mayo Clinic. (n.d.-c). *Post-traumatic stress disorder (PTSD).* https://www. mayoclinic.org/diseases-conditions/post-traumatic-stress-disorder/symptoms-causes/syc-20355967

Mayo Clinic. (n.d.-d). *Suicide and suicidal thoughts.* https://www.mayoclinic.org/ diseases-conditions/suicide/symptoms-causes/syc-20378048

Meyer, I. H. (2015). Resilience in the study of minority stress and health of sexual and gender minorities. *Psychology of Sexual Orientation and Gender Diversity, 2*(3), 209–213. https://psycnet.apa.org/doi/10.1037/sgd0000132

Meyer, I. H., & Frost, D. M. (2013). Minority stress and the health of sexual minorities. In C. J. Patterson & A. R. D'Augelli (Eds.), *Handbook of psychology and sexual orientation* (pp. 252–266). Oxford University Press.

Murchison, G. R., Boyd, M. A., & Pachankis, J. (2017). Minority stress and the risk of unwanted sexual experiences in LGBQ undergraduates. *Sex Roles, 77*(3–4), 221–238. https://doi.org/10.1007/s11199-016-0710-2

Parent, M. C., & Ferriter, K. P. (2018). The co-occurrence of asexuality and self-reported post-traumatic stress disorder diagnosis and sexual trauma within the past 12 months among U.S. college students. *Archives of Sexual Behavior, 47*(4), 1277–1282. https://doi.org/10.1007/s10508-018-1171-1

Ratts, M. J., Singh, A. A., Nasar-McMillan, S., Butler, S. K., & McCullough, J. R. (2016). Multicultural and social justice counseling competencies: Guidelines for the counseling profession. *Journal of Multicultural Counseling and Development, 44*(1), 28–48. https://doi.org/10.1002/jmcd.12035

Read, J. P., Ouimette, P., White, J., Colder, C., & Farrow, S. (2011). Rates of DSM–IV–TR trauma exposure and posttraumatic stress disorder among newly matriculated college students. *Psychological Trauma: Theory, Research, Practice, and Policy, 3*(2), 148–156. https://doi.org/10.1037/a0021260

Richmond, K. A., Burnes, T., & Carroll, K. (2012). Lost in trans-lation: Interpreting systems of trauma for transgender clients. *Traumatology, 18*(1), 45–57. https://doi.org/10.1177/1534765610396726

Rothman, K., Georgia Salivar, E., Roddy, M. K., Hatch, S. G., & Doss, B. D. (2019, August 17). Sexual assault among women in college: Immediate and long-term associations with mental health, psychosocial functioning, and romantic relationships. *Journal of Interpersonal Violence,* 1–23. 886260519870158. https://doi.org/10.1177/0886260519870158

Seelman, K. L. (2014). Transgender individuals' access to college housing and bathrooms: Findings from the national transgender discrimination survey. *Journal of Gay & Lesbian Social Services, 26*(2), 186–206. https://doi.org/10.1080/10538720.2014.891091

Seelman, K. L. (2016). Transgender adults' access to college bathrooms and housing and the relationship to suicidality. *Journal of Homosexuality, 63*(10), 1378–1399. https://doi.org/10.1080/00918369.2016.1157998

Singh, A. A., Meng, S., & Hansen, A. (2013). "It's already hard enough being a student": Developing affirming college environments for trans youth. *Journal of LGBT Youth, 10*(3), 208–223. https://doi.org/10.1080/19361653.2013.800770

Thielking, M. (2017, February 8). Surging demand for mental health care jams college services. *Scientific American.* https://www.scientificamerican.com/article/surging-demand-for-mental-health-care-jams-college-services/

United States Bureau of Justice Statistics. (2015). *Campus law enforcement, 2011–2012.* https://www.bjs.gov/content/pub/pdf/cle1112.pdf

Woodford, M. R., Howell, M. L., Silverschanz, P., & Yu, L. (2012). "That's so gay!": Examining the covariates of hearing this expression among gay, lesbian, and bisexual college students. *Journal of American College Health, 60*(6), 429–434. https://doi.org/10.1080/07448481.2012.673519

Woodford, M. R., Weber, G., Nicolazzo, Z., Hunt, R., Kulick, A., Coleman, T., Coulombe, S., & Renn, K. A. (2018). Depression and attempted suicide among LGBTQ college students: Fostering resilience to the effects of heterosexism and cisgenderism on campus. *Journal of College Student Development, 59*(4), 421–438. https://doi.org/10.1353/csd.2018.0040

9

ADVISING LGBTQA+ STUDENTS AT CHRISTIAN-BASED INSTITUTIONS

Natalie S. Oliner

W ith the increase of LGBTQA+ representation in mainstream media, many Americans have witnessed a storyline that includes an LGBTQA+ individual navigating a conflict between their identity and another factor such as family approval, self-acceptance, or negative perceptions from their community or society. One such narrative media often portrays is an individual's personal conflict in reconciling their sexuality and/or gender identity with their religiosity. While these portrayals risk creating a stereotypical story, many LGBTQA+ individuals do struggle to accept their identity in light of their religious beliefs.

These struggles can occur during K–12 education and continue into a student's undergraduate career, where they will enter a formative environment in which they can explore and develop their identity. This exploration can be both taxing and rewarding for LGBTQA+ students at any college or institution, but LGBTQA+ students who attend religious-based institutions may encounter unique challenges in navigating and reconciling their sexual orientation, gender identity, and religiosity.

As of 2015, about 20% of higher education institutions in the United States were categorized as religiously affiliated. Various Christian denominations make up the majority of religious institutions (92%), while the remaining 8% are interdenominational (3.9%) and Jewish (4.1%; National Center for Education Statistics, 2016). Research on the perspectives of religious-based institutions toward LGBTQA+ students and their experiences at those institutions is scarce, and what exists tends to focus solely on Christian institutions. Given the minimal literature and dominant Christian representation among U.S. religious-based higher education institutions, this chapter focuses on advising LGBTQA+ students specifically at Christian-based institutions.

While I have never attended or been employed by a religious institution, I have always been intrigued by how religion influences social and individual perspectives and behaviors toward marginalized populations. Growing up as a White, pansexual, cisgender woman with agnostic beliefs and Jewish customs in the Southern United States, I witnessed prejudices toward Jews, Muslims, people of color, LGBTQA+ individuals, people with disabilities, and other marginalized communities. These experiences inspired me to pursue religious studies and sociology to examine cultural, social, and systemic oppression toward marginalized identities. Now, as an academic advisor and researcher, I work closely with LGBTQA+ students and have had extensive conversations with LGBTQA+ students at secular and religious institutions about their experiences and relationships with religion as well as the ways they navigate their identities on campus.

As I reflect on my own experiences, research, and work in academic advising, it is evident that academic advisors—especially those at Christian-based institutions where LGBTQA+ support may be minimal—are positioned to provide effective support systems for LGBTQA+ students. Advisors can impart support to LGBTQA+ students through intentional and meaningful reflection, compassionate interpersonal practice as students navigate their LGBTQA+ and religious identities, appropriate referrals and connections to LGBTQA+ and Christian resources, and deliberate campus-wide advocacy. After a brief overview of contexts for Christian higher education institutions in the United States and LGBTQA+ student experiences at those institutions, I provide a vignette of Sylvia, a bisexual student at a Christian-based university who is struggling to reconcile her sexual orientation and religious identity. Sylvia's story serves as a lens through which advisors can reflect, support, and advocate for LGBTQA+ students so they can thrive and be their authentic selves.

Contexts for Christian Higher Education Institutions in the United States

While LGBTQA+ students are at risk of experiencing discrimination or harassment at any college or university, Christian higher education institutions have characteristics that provide a unique context for LGBTQA+ students. Each college or university will vary in their levels of LGBTQA+ inclusivity, but some policies of religious institutions based on Christian values and scripture exist in tension with LGBTQA+ identities (Yarhouse et al., 2009).

Therefore, LGBTQA+ students at Christian institutions will likely have to navigate religious-based perceptions of the LGBTQA+ community, inclusive and discriminatory practices, and legal tensions.

Diverse Christian Perspectives of LGBTQA+ Students

Within the last decade, several researchers have measured perceptions toward the LGBTQA+ community by religiosity, yet this does not appear to be a topic that is consistently studied, updated, or revised (Chonody et al., 2013; Holland et al., 2013; Stratton et al., 2013). Several findings suggest pro-LGBTQA+ perceptions and attitudes are prevalent among liberal religious traditions and/or nonreligious individuals. Women also tend to hold more liberal perspectives toward the LGBTQA+ community compared to men (Holland et al., 2013). Additionally, junior- and senior-level students tend to adopt more liberal perspectives toward LGBTQA+ individuals compared to first-year and sophomore students, regardless of institutional size. This may be due to juniors and seniors having more exposure to diverse identities and experiences through coursework and socialization (Holland et al., 2013). However, while students' religiosity rates decrease with additional years of education, students' general levels of religiosity are likely higher at Christian institutions compared to non-Christian institutions (Astin et al., 2011).

Studies also show that strong evangelical beliefs and Christian religiosity often correlate with discriminatory views or behaviors toward LGBTQA+ individuals (Holland et al., 2013; Wilkinson & Roys, 2005). Similarly, personal and environmental factors, such as the ability to empathize with the LGBTQA+ community, identifying as an ally, and generally supporting social justice, can be predictors for pro-LGBTQA+ activism (Jones & Brewster, 2017). Therefore, if an institution operates according to anti-LGBTQA+ beliefs or creates barriers for faculty members, staff members, students, and administrators to identify and act as allies, the environment may be perceived as unwelcoming and unsupportive of LGBTQA+ students. While some Christian institutions include LGBTQA+ students in diversity and nondiscrimination policies, others exclude this population (Coley, 2017). LGBTQA+ students have a greater risk of encountering discriminatory messaging at a college or university that does not support LGBTQA+ identities (Barnes & Meyer, 2012). Specifically, an institution's adoption of a "communal orientation," which focuses on social justice through a theological lens, is a stronger predictor of institutions adopting inclusive policies and practices compared to institutions that integrate an "individualist orientation," which uses theology to focus on personal religiosity and devoutness

(Coley, 2017). Institutional perspectives and theological orientations set the tone for how students will experience the campus climate and will influence potential interpersonal and political barriers as LGBTQA+ students navigate their identities at Christian institutions.

While there is a history of tension between Christianity and LGBTQA+ individuals, Christians can adopt various stances on gender identity and sexual orientation that are not anti-LGBTQA+. Based on their interpretations of the Bible and other Christian teachings, some may view LGBTQA+ identities and behaviors as "sinful, unnatural, immoral, and perverse" (Vespone, 2016, p. 218), while others may choose to focus on the notion of God's unconditional love for all regardless of identity and behavior (Rodriguez, 2010). While Christianity is not inherently anti-LGBTQA+, many LGBTQA+ individuals have experienced rejection from Christian institutions or dissonance between their religious and LGBTQA+ identities, which can influence their experiences with their identities at Christian institutions (Love et al., 2005).

Inclusive and Discriminatory Practices

Campus Pride is a nonprofit organization of student leaders and organizations dedicated to improving the safety, inclusivity, support, and climate for LGBTQA+ college students. The organization achieves these goals by promoting institutions that are inclusive of LGBTQA+ identities. The organization's Campus Pride Index is an extensive database of institutions ranked on a five-star scale based on the institution's commitment to diversity and inclusion through its resources, policies, and practices (Campus Pride, 2020a). Examples of an institution's commitment include the presence of counseling groups and student organizations for LGBTQA+ students, LBGTQA+-inclusive professional development for faculty and staff members, gender-inclusive restrooms, the existence of an LGBTQA+ center, and nondiscrimination policies that explicitly include sexual orientation and gender identity. As of 2020, there are 25 religiously affiliated institutions listed in the Campus Pride Index out of more than 300 total colleges and universities (Campus Pride, 2020a).

In addition to praising institutions actively supporting and including LGBTQA+ students, Campus Pride also alerts students to institutions with problematic policies or a history of problematic actions that may not be as safe or inclusive of LGBTQA+ communities. This "worst list" allows individuals to search institutions by state, Title IX exemption status, religious/faith affiliation, and campus size (Campus Pride, 2020b). Each search result explains why an institution was placed on the list and details the institution's history with Title IX and other issues involving anti-LGBTQA+

policies and practices. Examples of "shameful" behaviors from institutions on this list include institutions actively working to dismantle state bills that protect LGBTQA+ students from discrimination at Christian institutions (e.g., SB 1146 in California), Title IX exemptions that allow institutions to discriminate on the basis of sexual orientation and gender identity, and messages from presidents or other campus leaders that actively support anti-LGBTQA+ policies (Campus Pride, 2020b). Of the 150 campuses listed on the worst list, almost all are Christian institutions.

Legal Tensions

There are many legal implications to consider when examining institutions that are exempt from protecting students (or staff members) based on sexual orientation or gender identity (e.g., Title IX exemptions) as well as institutions that require staff members and students to accept an institutional "faith statement" that may include anti-LGBTQA+ beliefs and values (Gjelten, 2018). Whether students or staff members personally identify as LGBTQA+ or are advocating on behalf of an LGBTQA+ individual, they need to balance the needs of LGBTQA+ and religious individuals as well as their institution's mission.

Several cases have begged serious questions, including: "What constitutes freedom of speech and religion when an individual holds religious views that do not support LGBTQA+ identities? Can LGBTQA+ staff members or students be fired or expelled due to their identity?" Cases like *Keeton v. Anderson-Wiley* (2011) ruled that the first amendment guarantees a person's freedom of speech and religion but not at the expense of another's rights. *Ward v. Polite* (2012) highlighted the distinction between holding beliefs and acting on them in a harmful way toward another, as well as the importance of educational programs that outline explicit policies for appropriate rules regarding practice and conduct.

Historically, LGBTQA+ individuals have had minimal protections in the workplace regarding nondiscrimination under federal law. Title VII and Title IX of the Civil Rights Act of 1964 provide protection against discrimination based on sex. However, it has been unclear whether sexual orientation and gender identity are included in these protections (Civil Rights Act, 1964). The June 15, 2020, Supreme Court ruling (*Altitude Express Inc. v. Zarda*, 2020; *Bostock v. Clayton County*, 2020; *R. G. & G. R. Harris Funeral Home Inc. v. Equal Employment Opportunity Commission*, 2020) clarified that sexual orientation and gender identity are covered under the category of sex, but it is uncertain whether this ruling will apply to Title IX protections. Additionally, some Christian schools have Title VII and IX exemptions due to claims the Civil Rights Act conflicts with religious beliefs (Gjelten, 2018). At the time of this writing, several cases are currently under review by the U.S. Supreme Court to address Christian institutions' ability to be exempt from antidiscriminatory policies so campus professionals can hire and terminate individuals based on their sexual orientation, gender identity, or other identities due to religious beliefs (*Our Lady of Guadalupe School v. Morrissey-Berru*, 2019; *St. James Catholic School v. Biel*, 2018). The results of these cases would have significant implications for Christian institutions and their ability to discriminate against LGBTQA+ staff members and students. As legislation evolves, it is important for advisors and students to have a thorough understanding of their legal rights as well as their institution's policies regarding protection against discrimination to avoid termination or expulsion.

LGBTQA+ Student Experiences at Christian Higher Education Institutions

LGBTQA+ students at any college or university can experience tension between their LGBTQA+ and religious identities; however, navigating religious beliefs and LGBTQA+ identity at a Christian institution can pose unique challenges (Craig et al., 2017; Love et al., 2005). These challenges can include the conflicts LGBTQA+ students experience between their LGBTQA+ and religious identities as they work to reconcile the two, navigating tensions related to the ways their LGBTQA+ identities are perceived on a Christian campus, and the implications these experiences can have on students' mental health.

LGBTQA+ and Religious Identity Conflict and Reconciliation

Certain anti-LGBTQA+ interpretations of religious teachings can lead an LGBTQA+ individual to experience an identity conflict while trying to reconcile LGBTQA+ and religious identities. Rodriguez (2010) suggested there are two types of conflicts that manifest: intrinsic and extrinsic. Intrinsic conflict refers to an individual's internal beliefs about themselves in relation to personal and religious values or ideas. Extrinsic conflict, in contrast, considers the external views and perspectives an individual witnesses in their community or society (Rodriguez, 2010). Both these types of conflicts can make it difficult for individuals to reconcile their LGBTQA+ identity with their religious identity.

A student who is experiencing intrinsic conflict might, for example, value their LGBTQA+ identity but struggle with their religious beliefs that seem to be in conflict with their sexual orientation or gender identity. Therefore, religiosity can influence tension with an individual's LGBTQA+ identity (Wolff et al., 2016). If an individual holds anti-LGBTQA+ religious beliefs and values, they may feel as though they are unable to reconcile their seemingly opposing identities and beliefs, and they may choose to ignore or repress one identity in favor of the other. Another individual, however, might adjust their understanding of religion and resituate their LGBTQA+ identity in a religious context, realizing their identities can overlap without having to hide their sexual orientation or gender identity (Love et al., 2005).

Each college student holds their own religious beliefs and perceptions. Regardless of sexual orientation or gender identity, college students are more likely to favor a more personal or individualized religion over a formal practice through religious institutions (Stoppa & Lefkowitz, 2010). Individuals separating institutional religion from spirituality is also increasingly common, with some individuals strongly identifying as spiritual rather than religious in the context of an organized, institutional religion (Rockenbach et al., 2012). This path of spirituality can provide a personal, less communal, and less formal practice for LGBTQA+ individuals. When considering LGBTQA+ students' possible extrinsic conflicts with their identities, this less institutionalized form of religion may be comforting, as there might be a lowered risk or threat of individuals rejecting them due to their sexual orientation or gender identity (Halkitis et al., 2009). With more varied and personalized forms of religious practice, non-LGBTQ+ college students might adopt accepting, less-biased views toward LGBTQA+ individuals. However, in a context with diverse perspectives, LGBTQA+ students must navigate their own religious identities (i.e., intrinsic conflicts) in addition to their non-LGBTQA+ peers' varying beliefs, which could lead to uncomfortable or discriminatory interactions or make evident potential non-LGBTQA+-inclusive mission statements and policies of their Christian institution (i.e., extrinsic conflicts).

Navigating LGBTQA+ Identity on a Christian Campus

The extent to which Christian institutions discuss LGBTQA+ identities can influence how LGBTQA+ students reconcile and navigate their identities on campus. For example, if administrators, faculty members, staff members, or students on campus discuss LGBTQA+ identities from a progressive, biological position (i.e., LGBTQA+ identity is inherent and natural), students and campus professionals are more likely to be accepting of LGBTQA+ identities. If, however, individuals view LGBTQA+ identity as a choice, they are less likely to be accepting or supportive of LGBTQA+ students (Haider-Markel & Joslyn, 2005; Wood & Bartkowski, 2004). Therefore, if a Christian campus maintains anti-LGBTQA+ policies and practices, LGBTQA+ students may experience more intrinsic and extrinsic identity conflicts than they would on a campus that upholds pro-LGBTQA+ policies and practices.

While certain discussions of LGBTQA+ identities—including perceptions of sexual orientation and gender identity being a choice—can be harmful, an absence of discussion can also pose challenges as LGBTQA+ students navigate their identities. If there is a lack of dialogue about LGBTQA+ identities on campus, LGBTQA+ students may feel like they are invisible, leading them to perceive living their authentic lives is unsafe (Craig et al., 2017; Wolff et al., 2017). Unwelcoming climates within a religious community can create an environment in which students are more likely to experience identity conflict and less likely to disclose their identity compared to other nonreligious groups such as family, peers, or colleagues (Legate et al., 2012).

When LGBTQA+ students do not have a comfortable or reaffirming space to disclose their identity, they may reject their identity by deciding not to "come out" or by trying to pass as non-LGBTQA+ individuals (Craig et al., 2017). In one study of 247 nonheterosexual students across 19 Christian colleges, almost 79% identified as heterosexual in public (Stratton et al., 2013). Because of this, LGBTQA+ students might actively avoid LGBTQA+ resources, and professionals may misgauge the numbers of LGBTQA+ and non-LGBTQA+ students on campus. However, if they are able to find a social network of LGBTQA+ peers, LGTBQA+ students can engage with a group that affirms their identity, provides support, and accepts them (Wolff et al., 2017). On the contrary, if LGBTQA+ individuals are part of a community that does not support their gender identity or sexual orientation, they may experience extreme self-hatred toward their LGBTQA+ identity (Harris et al., 2008).

Implications for Mental Health

Whether LGBTQA+ students are feeling isolated, unsafe, or struggling with their own religiosity and identity, all these stressors can affect students' mental health (Yarhouse et al., 2009). While LGBTQA+ students can encounter an uncomfortable environment at any institution, certain mandated involvement such as prayer or religious studies can be particularly stressful for students, as discussions therein may emphasize heteronormative gender identities in relation to religion (Craig et al., 2017). Leaders and other professionals on campus may support anti-LGBTQA+ policies, legislation, and practices such as conversion therapy or Title IX exemptions. If an LGBTQA+ student perceives these environments as unsafe or unwelcoming, they can experience increased levels of anxiety and stress (Iwasaki & Ristock, 2007) along with feelings of isolation or rejection (Vespone, 2016).

LGBTQA+ students at unsupportive Christian institutions may also experience severe identity conflicts as they navigate heightened levels of internalized homophobia (Barnes & Meyer, 2012), shame, self-hatred, and stigma related to their LGBTQA+ identities (Harris et al., 2008; Yarhouse et al., 2009). Students may also fully reject or compartmentalize their identities to avoid stigma and shame (Craig et al., 2017). Those who were instilled with more conservative religious values during their upbringing may experience increased levels of shame or self-hatred about their LGBTQA+ identities (Wilkerson et al., 2012). This can lead to anxiety, depression, feelings of inadequacy, guilt, or low self-esteem (Weber-Gilmore et al., 2011; see chapter 8, this volume). The barriers and stressors that arise while LGBTQA+ students work to resolve their LGBTQA+ and religious identities can have a significant impact on the students' mental health and, as a result, their ability to succeed and survive in college (Craig et al., 2017; Gold & Stewart, 2011). To better understand how various Christian perspectives and institutional climates can influence LGBTQA+ students' mental health, academics, personal relationships, and sense of belonging, the following vignette illustrates one student's journey in navigating her bisexual identity on a Christian campus.

A Vignette

Sylvia is a second-year student at Whittfield University, a religiously-affiliated institution in the Midwest. She was raised in a tight-knit family that attended church every Sunday. Sylvia's family celebrated her many academic and athletic accomplishments in high school—after all, she was an honors student who completed numerous advanced placement (AP) courses on top of being a star player on the varsity soccer and basketball teams.

In addition to her family, Sylvia also had a close group of friends in high school. She attended Bible studies and youth group social events with them. During her junior year, she dated a classmate, Dylan. As they neared senior year, they decided to break up since both knew they would likely attend different colleges and did not want to maintain a long-distance relationship.

Sylvia did not stress about her college search. She and her family always assumed she would attend Whittfield University like her brother and parents. She did not apply to other institutions for fear of upsetting her family, and she was comfortable continuing her family's legacy. As expected, she was admitted to the university and accepted into the honors program. While Sylvia was overjoyed when she received her letter, she felt uneasy about her future.

During her senior year of high school, Sylvia developed confusing feelings for one of the girls in her AP European History class. She recognized she was having feelings similar to when she first started dating Dylan. She did not know what to do. Growing up, she heard her family say that homosexuality was a sin, queer people needed to be cured, and a woman's role was to support her husband. Sylvia believed she could not share her newfound feelings with her parents. While her friends didn't make these comments as often, she knew their parents held similar views to her family, so she was scared her friends would share those views or, even worse, word of her feelings would get back to her parents. Sylvia decided to keep her feelings to herself but looked forward to exploring her identity in college.

Once at Whittfield, Sylvia sought opportunities to meet new people. She befriended two individuals from her first-year seminar class, Avi and Josh. After several weeks of hanging out, Avi came out to Sylvia as queer. Sylvia was taken aback by Avi casually mentioning her identity, but she also felt nervous because she had begun to develop feelings for Avi. Roughly a month later, they began dating. Sylvia made it clear she was not comfortable coming out to her family, friends, or anyone on campus—she had heard many anti-LGBTQA+ remarks from faculty members, staff members, administrators, and students. Avi, an out and proud LGBTQA+ student leader who tried to start an LGBTQA+ Christian student organization, understood and was supportive of Sylvia's process. However, Avi expressed frustration when she could not hold her girlfriend's hand around campus because Sylvia was uncomfortable at the idea of being outed. Sylvia did not want to receive harsh glares or hear discriminatory comments from students. During these disagreements, Sylvia would exclaim, "What if someone reports us? What if my parents find out? What if they start quoting Bible verses to us and everyone stares? What if being gay *is* a sin?" Sylvia had reason to be concerned—she had seen or heard of these things happening at school and around her hometown.

During the Fall semester of Sylvia's second year, she scheduled an advising appointment to discuss potential internship opportunities during the upcoming Summer semester. As she entered the office, her advisor noticed that Sylvia looked exhausted and fidgety. The advisor asked if she was okay. Sylvia stated that she was stressed about her upcoming test because she had not been sleeping well. After asking why she had not been sleeping well, her advisor observed her pausing and glancing at the rainbow ally sticker on the desk. She disclosed that her parents were visiting for homecoming and she was anxious because she had not told her parents that she was dating a girl. Additionally, she knew her girlfriend was frustrated about having to hide their relationship. The stresses from both situations caused her to lose sleep, which started to take a toll on her grades and could have potentially kept her from getting an internship or graduating on time. She began to cry as she expressed that she did not belong at Whittfield. She also explained that she was struggling with whether or not she should continue dating Avi because doing so went against her religious values and telling her parents could ruin their familial relationship.

Applications to Academic Advising

In addition to her concerns about repercussions with her family and academics, Sylvia is distressed by the intrinsic and extrinsic conflicts between her religious identity and sexual orientation. She feels isolated at Whittfield and torn about how to proceed with her academics, relationships, and overall path at the university.

In the following sections, I propose that advisors can be effective supports for LGBTQA+ students like Sylvia by reflecting on personal beliefs, taking appropriate steps to support students' religious and LGBTQA+ identities, sharing resources to help with identity conflict and connection, and advocating for LGBTQA+ student needs on campus.

Advisor Self-Reflection

Like students, advisors bring their religious beliefs, histories, and identities to interactions with others. An advisor "may struggle with sincerely held religious beliefs about LGBTQ [students], and may believe that changing or addressing sexual orientation or gender identity will relieve [students'] suffering" (Dessel et al., 2017, p. 17). However, this perspective is not affirming of students' identities. Therefore, it is critical that advisors reflect and become self-aware of their own perspectives, religiosity, and spirituality in order to consider how their personal experiences and beliefs influence their practice with LGBTQA+ students (see the Ally Narrative by Wendy K. Schindler in this volume).

Reflecting on one's own experience and perspective might include addressing some of the following questions:

- Do I identify as religious? Spiritual? How might that identity come across to a student who has encountered negative experiences with religion or religious communities?
- How do my religious or spiritual beliefs align or conflict with the institution's mission? How might an LGBTQA+ student with a different religious identity perceive the institution's mission?

- Whether my faith is accepting or disapproving of LGBTQA+ identities, how can I best support an LGBTQA+ student?
- How might I react if an LGBTQA+ student discloses a concern about interacting with someone who shares my religious beliefs?
- What factors in the advising and institutional environments—past or present—might be affecting an LGBTQA+ student's experiences?

Considering these questions can provide insight into an advisor's personal beliefs and perspectives as well as the ways they might respond to and support LGBTQA+ students. For example, if an advisor was raised under a similar religion or value system as Sylvia, they could provide less biased responses by reflecting on how their faith and beliefs might influence their reaction to Sylvia while striving to provide unconditional and holistic support. Advisors who identify as religious can also reflect on "common values of non-judgment, unconditional love, and social justice in order to work in an affirming manner with LGBTQ individuals" (Dessel et al., 2017, p. 22). This practice allows advisors to consider a common ground and focus on validating and supporting the student regardless of their religious beliefs related to LGBTQA+ identities.

Support Student Identities

Advisors can provide a supportive environment for LGBTQA+ students at Christian institutions in various ways. This can include affirming LGBTQA+ students' identities as they navigate conflict between their LGBTQA+ and religious identities, as well as creating safe spaces in one-on-one appointments. Additionally, advisors can become advocates by stressing the importance of visibility, engagement, and inclusivity of LGBTQA+ students on campus.

Affirm LGBTQA+ and Religious Identities

As students develop, they may experience intrinsic and extrinsic identity conflicts when attempting to reconcile their LGBTQA+ and religious identities. Since some Christian communities have shunned LGBTQA+ individuals (Yarhouse et al., 2009), it is critical advisors affirm LGBTQA+ students' identities and any dissonance they may be experiencing in their development. For example, Sylvia seems to be experiencing intrinsic identity conflict by wondering, "What if being gay is a sin?" She is also experiencing extrinsic conflict as a result of the comments she heard from her family and church community as well as her concern about others quoting Bible verses to her on campus. To help Sylvia address or navigate her conflict with her Christian upbringing and bisexual identity, an advisor might say, "It sounds like you are feeling distressed about being your authentic self and also holding true to your religious values. Tell me more about how you view your identities and perceive them as conflicting. In what ways do you think these identities may be able to overlap or complement one another?" Reflecting Sylvia's emotions and concerns and asking her to elaborate on her thoughts allows the advisor to remain neutral and guide her into unpacking her identities and the ways she views her two seemingly opposing identities as being able to relate to one another.

Emphasizing resilience is also helpful for students experiencing identity conflict, discrimination, or guilt (Zubernis et al., 2011). Highlighting the steps students have taken in understanding their identities, support systems they have developed, and barriers they may have overcome in experiencing discrimination are resilience-based approaches advisors can use when talking with LGBTQA+ students at Christian institutions (Zubernis et al., 2011). For example, Sylvia's advisor might applaud her forming a support group with Avi and Josh, her reflection on her identity, and instances where she demonstrated resilience when navigating her parents' or community's discriminatory remarks.

To have effective conversations about student identities and experiences, advisors should strive to create a safe and welcoming space for their advisees. Otherwise, students may feel uncomfortable, misunderstood, ashamed, or persecuted, creating mistrust of the advisor (or, more broadly, advising at the institution). Therefore, advisors should be cautious when broaching conversations around LGBTQA+ and religious identity so they do not create more stress or discomfort for students in addition to the tremendous adversity they may already be experiencing (Cornish et al., 2014).

Create Safe Spaces

To create a safe space, advisors must first acknowledge and validate a student's identity. This is critical at Christian institutions that do not directly acknowledge or discuss LGBTQA+ identities, experiences, and issues. Advisors can create safe spaces by normalizing conversations about LGBTQA+ matters and being supportive if the student discloses their identity. Having these supportive spaces within a religious community context can help students' psychological well-being (Lease et al., 2005).

In the vignette, Sylvia looked for an indicator that her advisor was an ally and a safe person with whom to disclose what she was going through. Perhaps Sylvia had not seen many ally stickers around campus due to a lack of allies, staff members' hesitation to display any open support for the LGBTQA+ community as a result of the institution's conflicting values, or a lack of awareness of LGBTQA+ allyship around the campus (McEntarfer, 2011). Seeing a sticker on her advisor's desk may have made Sylvia more comfortable with disclosing her identity and concerns (see chapter 10).

Advisors should also consider that individuals may feel more comfortable keeping to themselves despite perceiving their advisor or advising office to be safe. This may be because the student does not feel comfortable coming out in the broader, unwelcoming campus environment. However, closeted students might view their campus as less safe or welcoming than students who are publicly out (Gackowski, 2017). Since Sylvia is mostly closeted on campus, she may perceive the campus climate more negatively than an out LGBTQA+ student. Regardless, an advisor should validate her feelings by saying something like, "It sounds like you feel overwhelmed in your academic and personal life. That seems very stressful." The advisor could continue the conversation by adopting a strengths-based approach to highlight Sylvia's resilience and growth in navigating her identities or, perhaps, an appreciative advising approach by asking positive, open-ended questions to help guide Sylvia toward a desired personal or academic outcome.

Advocacy Within Advising
Christian institutions have historically omitted concrete policies and missions that include LGBTQA+ individuals (Paredes-Collins, 2014). Depending on a Christian institution's mission statement and perceptions toward LGBTQA+ individuals, advisors can advocate for the creation or improvement of inclusive language and policies regarding LGBTQA+ students. Whether working with administrators to change mission statements or simply by focusing on the advising unit's mission and goals, advisors can incrementally foster change (Bennett et al., 2019). Sylvia's advisor might ask her about particular experiences that make her feel like she does not belong. These might reflect her intrinsic identity conflict as she develops her own identity, or they may indicate a lack of campus acknowledgment or support of LGBTQA+ identities.

Advisors can also encourage students to be self-advocates—if they are comfortable doing so—by encouraging student involvement and activism on campus. Before encouraging self-advocacy, however, advisors and students should be mindful of campus policies and the potential ramifications of advocating for something that could result in termination or expulsion from the college. While it may be too risky for some students to participate, activism is a way LGBTQA+ students can find a purpose, community, and way to survive on campus (Gabriele-Black & Goldberg, 2019). Through this medium, students can advocate for LGBTQA+ organizations and support groups (Russell & Fish, 2016), inclusive policies, campus-wide professional development, events, and resources in the hopes of reducing discrimination and creating a more inclusive environment (Jones et al., 2016). Support groups can be a great resource for students to connect with one another, but advisors and students should be mindful of what an administration would allow based on the institution's mission and beliefs; advisors must also take into account the need to ensure the comfort, safety, and confidentiality of those who attend or join groups (Vespone, 2016). For example, directly calling for an LGBTQA+ meeting/group may be met with resistance, whereas using more general language, such as "Identity and Faith," may gain approval and help students feel more comfortable if they want to attend but are concerned about outing themselves (McEntarfer, 2011).

Regardless of the LGBTQA+ organization students advocate for, administration may outright resist attempts to create LGBTQ-inclusive resources (McEntarfer, 2011). Students and other activists would benefit from developing rapport with administrators and aligning the goals of the group with the institution's mission as much as possible. These activists may also gather allies and LGBTQA+-identifying individuals to advocate for the organization and inclusion of LGBTQA+ identities (Bennett et al., 2019; McEntarfer, 2011). Advisors can serve as allies and assist students by providing appropriate support and advocating alongside students.

Connect to Resources

If a college or university has existing LGBTQA+ and Christian resources on campus for LGBTQA+ students, it is beneficial to share them with students in case they are not aware of those opportunities (Wolff et al., 2017). The mere presence of these resources on campus can be a positive indicator that the institution recognizes and supports LGBTQA+ individuals, which may lead to more visible displays of support by campus professionals (McEntarfer, 2011). Additionally, LGBTQA+ student organizations on campus or in the community, especially those that combine LGBTQA+ and religious identities (Kocet et al., 2011), can be particularly useful in validating student identities and experiences while also serving as a support system that may help students work through their identity conflicts (Russell & Fish, 2016; Vespone, 2016).

LGBTQA+ students often highlight the absence of spaces to discuss their religion as an LGBTQA+ individual on Christian campuses (Gold & Stewart, 2011). Over the last decade, religious-based institutions have not commonly offered LGBTQA+ resources like LGBTQA+ centers (Fine, 2012). In the absence of campus resources, advisors can play a critical role by connecting students to community resources. Whittfield University, for instance, might not have a formal organization dedicated to LGBTQA+ students, but Sylvia's advisor could recommend she visit a multicultural center in the general community that holds social events for LGBTQA+ individuals.

However, advisors should also be aware that LGBTQA+ students might intentionally avoid joining groups or seeking resources for fear of being outed on campus (Yarhouse et al., 2009). Those who remain in the closet may struggle more to find community with like-minded or similarly identifying peers. Without a peer or student group outlet, students are left to find support on their own as they navigate any intrinsic and extrinsic conflicts that emerge from attempting to reconcile their LGBTQA+ and religious identities (Gold & Stewart, 2011). To further support students, advisors may mention the existence of queer theology, queer Christian autobiographies, queer history within Christianity, and other resources students can use anonymously or outside of the institution. Whether advisors take the time to research specific sources or encourage the student to do some researching of their own, this can serve as a low-stakes, anonymous way for LGBTQA+ students to explore the history, fields of study, and media that normalize the intersection of LGBTQA+ identity and faith (Vespone, 2016).

Churches that are openly accepting of LGBTQA+ identities may also have helpful resources. Whether students can find these resources online or in-person at local church communities, connecting students to others who share their identity and have experienced similar conflicts can help students find their fit and make meaning of their identity and Christian faith. Advisors can also consult with supportive faculty members, administrators, staff members, and religious authorities on campus who may be aware of specific LGBTQA+ and religious resources in the community (Kocet et al., 2011; Vespone, 2016). If applicable, a student's faith or spiritual practices may also provide comfort and strategies for coping with identity conflict or adversity (Yarhouse et al., 2009). However, students have different religious beliefs, so it is important that advisors understand an advisee's perspective on faith and religion before offering a faith-based recommendation or resource.

Campus Advocacy

Beyond unit-specific advocacy, advisors may be able to advocate for change at the campus level through their positions on campus-wide committees or through engagement with faculty members, staff members, and administrators (Rockenbach & Crandall, 2016). While this may be the ultimate responsibility of administration or other professionals on campus, advisors can provide helpful insight and support for LGBTQA+ causes. However, advisors and other college professionals may not receive support from administration when advocating for LGBTQA+ resources and policies, so advisors should be careful in how they advocate. There must be an appropriate balance between respecting the institution's mission and beliefs and striving to ensure the institution actively recognizes student identities and needs (Bennett et al., 2019; McEntarfer, 2011). When they are able to serve as advocates, having experiences with students like Sylvia equips advisors with concrete evidence that demonstrates why inclusive initiatives are necessary for students' sense of belonging and success. This advocacy emphasizes the importance of students' identities and faith in the community and advocates for including these overlapping identities instead of separating or silencing sexual orientation, gender identity, and religious or spiritual beliefs.

Developing LGBTQA+-inclusive programs and practices within advising can provide advisors with tangible suggestions for ways campus professionals can incorporate LGBTQA+ identities and perspectives into campus life. An advisor, for example, could advocate for an ongoing, campus-wide dialogue about LGBTQA+ identities and how they intersect with religion. This dialogue could include guest speakers or panelists who discuss their experiences as an LGBTQA+ individual of faith, campus administrators who highlight the college or university's dedication to creating a welcoming and inclusive environment, or students who are comfortable sharing their lived experiences on campus (Poynter & Washington, 2005).

Advisors might also recommend that faculty members across all disciplines become more intentional in incorporating LGBTQA+ experiences into their curriculum (Holland et al., 2013). Study groups (academic or religious) could dedicate time for peer discussions about diverse identities and experiences (Poynter & Washington, 2005). Faith leaders might conduct seminars that address LGBTQA+ topics. While this requires buy-in from various campus constituents, advisors can be leaders in stressing the importance and effectiveness of these practices, especially if they have evidence of their success within their advising practice.

Programming or resources through which various marginalized identities can congregate and engage with one another could be also beneficial for LGBTQA+ students at religiously based institutions, as students can participate without necessarily being singled out for their sexual orientation or gender identity (Rockenbach et al., 2016). By creating opportunities for LGBTQA+ and non-LGBTQA+ students to engage with one another, advisors, staff members, faculty members, and administrators can help create a more welcoming and inclusive environment for LGBTQA+ students and potentially improve the campus's perceptions of the LGBTQA+ community.

Conclusion

Colleges and universities provide important opportunities for students to explore and develop their identities, especially for LGBTQA+ students. However, this student population encounters distinctive challenges in their development and overall experience if they attend a Christian institution where they do not feel safe, acknowledged, included, and valued in the campus community. When attempting to support and advocate for LGBTQA+ students, academic advisors at Christian institutions should be mindful of their institution's potential legal right to discriminate against LGBTQA+ individuals based on the organization's religious beliefs. However, with appropriate approval from administrators and staff members, as well as adherence to institutional policies, advisors are uniquely situated to challenge and support LGBTQA+ students as they develop and navigate their undergraduate careers. By reflecting on one's personal religiosity, beliefs, and identities, making intentional efforts to recognize and support LGBTQA+ identities, connect students to LGBTQA+ and Christian resources, and advocating for inclusive policies and practices, academic advisors can positively influence LGBTQA+ student experiences at Christian-based institutions.

References

Altitude Express Inc., v. Zarda, No. 17-1623 (2nd Cir. Jun. 15, 2020).

Astin, A. W., Astin, H. S., & Lindholm, J. A. (2011). Assessing students' spiritual and religious qualities. *Journal of College Student Development, 52*(1), 39–61. https://doi.org/10.1353/csd.2011.0009

Barnes, D. M., & Meyer, I. H. (2012). Religious affiliation, internalized homophobia, and mental health in lesbians, gay men, and bisexuals. *The American Journal of Orthopsychiatry, 82*(4), 505–515. https://doi.org/10.1111/j.1939-0025.2012.01185.x

Bennett, L., Walton, M. K., & Boettcher, M. L. (2019). Social justice work at religiously affiliated and public institutions. *New Directions for Student Services, 2019*(168), 17–28. https://doi.org/10.1002/ss.20328

Bostock v. Clayton County, No. 17-1618 (11th Cir. June. 15, 2020).

Campus Pride. (2020a, April 25). *LGBTQ-friendly campus search.* Campus Pride Index. http://www.campusprideindex.org/searchresults/display/891467

Campus Pride. (2020b, April 25). *Worst list: The absolute worst campuses for LGBTQ youth.* Campus Pride Index. https://www.campuspride.org/worstlist/

Chonody, J., Woodford, M. R., Smith, S., & Silverschanz, P. (2013). Christian social work students' attitudes toward lesbians and gay men: Religious teachings, religiosity, and contact. *Journal of Religion & Spirituality in Social Work: Social Thought, 32*(3), 211–226. https://doi.org/10.1080/15426432.2013.801730

Civil Rights Act of 1964 § 7, 42 U.S.C. §2000e et seq (1964).

Coley, J. S. (2017). Reconciling religion and LGBT rights: Christian universities, theological orientations, and LGBT inclusion. *Social Currents, 4*(1), 87–106. https://doi.org/10.1177/2329496516651639

Cornish, M. A., Wade, N. G., Tucker, J. R., & Post, B. C. (2014). When religion enters the counseling group: Multiculturalism, group processes, and social justice. *The Counseling Psychologist, 42*(5), 578-600. https://doi.org/10.1177/0011000014527001

Craig, S. L., Austin, A., Rashidi, M., & Adams, M. (2017). Fighting for survival: The experiences of lesbian, gay, bisexual, transgender, and questioning students in religious colleges and universities. *Journal of Gay & Lesbian Social Services, 29*(1), 1–24. https://doi.org/10.1080/10538720.2016.1260512

Dessel, A. B., Jacobsen, J., Levy, D. L., McCarty-Caplan, D., Lewis, T. O., & Kaplan, L. E. (2017). LGBT topics and Christianity in social work: Tackling the tough questions. *Social Work & Christianity, 44*(1–2), 11–30. https://www.researchgate.net/publication/315706544_LGBTQ_Topics_and_Christianity_in_Social_Work_Tackling_the_Tough_Questions

Fine, L. E. (2012). The context of creating space: Assessing the likelihood of college LGBT center presence. *Journal of College Student Development, 53*(2), 285–299. https://doi.org/10.1353/csd.2012.0017

Gabriele-Black, K. A., & Goldberg, A. E. (2019). "I've heard there's some sort of underground group": LGBTQ activism on Evangelical Christian campuses. *Journal of Diversity in Higher Education.* Advance online publication. https://doi.org/10.1037/dhe0000163

Gackowski, I. (2017). *Perceptions of campus climate for lesbian, gay, and bisexual students at a religious college* (UMI No. 10616822) [Doctoral dissertation, Roosevelt University]. ProQuest Dissertations and Theses database.

Gjelten, T. (2018, March 27). *Christian colleges are tangled in their own LGBT policies* [Radio broadcast episode]. https://www.npr.org/2018/03/27/591140811/christian-colleges-are-tangled-in-their-own-lgbt-policies

Gold, S. P., & Stewart, D.-L. (2011). Lesbian, gay, and bisexual students coming out at the intersection of spirituality and sexual identity. *Journal of LGBT Issues in Counseling, 5*(3–4), 237–258. https://doi.org/10.1080/15538605.2011.633052

Haider-Markel, D. P., & Joslyn, M. R. (2005). Attributions and the regulation of marriage: Considering the parallels between race and homosexuality. *Political Science and Politics 38*(2), 233–240. https://doi.org/10.1017/S1049096505056362

Halkitis, P. N., Mattis, J. S., Sahadath, J. K., Massie, D., Ladyzhenskaya, L., Pitrelli, K., Bonacci, M., & Cowie, S.-A. E. (2009). The meanings and manifestations of religion and spirituality among lesbian, gay, bisexual, and transgender adults. *Journal of Adult Development, 16*(4), 250–262. https://doi.org/10.1007/s10804-009-9071-1

Harris, J. I., Cook, S. W., & Kashubeck-West, S. (2008). Religious attitudes, internalized homophobia and identity in gay and lesbian adults. *Journal of Gay & Lesbian Mental Health, 12*(3), 205–225. https://doi.org/10.1080/19359700802111452

Holland, L., Matthews, T. L., & Schott, M. R. (2013). "That's so gay!" Exploring college students' attitudes towards the LGBT population. *Journal of Homosexuality, 60*(4), 575–595. https://doi.org/10.1080/00918369.2013.760321

Iwasaki, Y., & Ristock, J. L. (2007). The nature of stress experienced by lesbians and gay men. *Anxiety, Stress and Coping: An International Journal, 20*(3), 299–319. https://doi.org/10.1080/10615800701303264

Jones, K. N., & Brewster, M. E. (2017). From awareness to action: Examining predictors of lesbian, gay, bisexual, and transgender (LGBT) activism for heterosexual people. *The American Journal of Orthopsychiatry, 87*(6), 680–689. https://doi.org/10.1037/ort0000219

Jones, T., Smith, E., Ward, R., Dixon, J., Hillier, L., & Mitchell, A. (2016). School experiences of transgender and gender diverse students in Australia. *Sex Education, 16*(2), 156–171. https://doi.org/10.1080/14681811.2015.1080678

Keeton v. Anderson-Wiley, 664 F. 3d 865 (11th Cir., 2011).

Kocet, M. M., Sanabria, S., & Smith, M. R. (2011). Finding the spirit within: Religion, spirituality, and faith development in lesbian, gay, and bisexual individuals. *Journal of LGBT Issues in Counseling, 5*(3–4), 163–179. https://doi.org/10.1080/15538605.2011.633060

Lease, S. H., Horne, S. G., & Noffsinger-Frazier, N. (2005). Affirming faith experiences and psychological health for Caucasian lesbian, gay, and bisexual individuals. *Journal of Counseling Psychology, 52*(3), 378–388. https://doi.org/10.1037/0022-0167.52.3.378

Legate, N., Ryan, R. M., & Weinstein, N. (2012). Is coming out always a "good thing"? Exploring the relations of autonomy support, outness, and wellness for lesbian, gay, and bisexual individuals. *Social Psychological and Personality Science, 3*(2), 145–152. https://doi.org/10.1177/1948550611411929

Love, P. G., Bock, M., Jannarone, A., & Richardson, P. (2005). Identity interaction: Exploring the spiritual experiences of lesbian and gay college students. *Journal of College Student Development, 46*(2), 193–209. https://doi.org/10.1353/csd.2005.0019

McEntarfer, H. K. (2011). "Not going away": Approaches used by students, faculty, and staff members to create gay-straight alliances at three religiously affiliated universities. *Journal of LGBT Youth, 8*(4), 309–331. https://doi.org/10.1080/19361653.2011.607623

National Center for Education Statistics. (2016). Table 303.90. *Digest of education statistics: 2016* (NCES 2017-094) [Data set]. https://nces.ed.gov/programs/digest/d16/tables/dt16_303.90.asp

Our Lady of Guadalupe School v. Morrissey-Berru, No. 19-267 (9th Cir, 2019).

Paredes-Collins, K. (2014). Campus climate for diversity as a predictor of spiritual development at Christian colleges. *Religion & Education, 41*(2), 171–193. https://doi.org/10.1080/15507394.2013.864206

Poynter, K. J., & Washington, J. (2005). Multiple identities: Creating community on campus for LGBT students. *New Directions for Student Services, 2005*(111), 41–47. https://doi.org/10.1002/ss.172

R. G. & G. R. Harris Funeral Homes Inc. v. Equal Employment Opportunity Commission, No. 18-107. (6th Cir. Jun. 15, 2020).

Rockenbach, A. N., & Crandall, R. E. (2016). Faith and LGBTQ inclusion: Navigating the complexities of the campus spiritual climate in Christian higher education. *Christian Higher Education, 15*(1–2), 62–71. https://doi.org/10.1080/15363759.2015.1106355

Rockenbach, A. N., Lo, M. A., & Mayhew, M. J. (2016). How LGBT college students perceive and engage the campus religious and spiritual climate. *Journal of Homosexuality, 64*(4), 488–508. https://doi.org/10.1080/00918369.2016.1191239

Rockenbach, A. B., Walker, C. R., & Luzader, J. (2012). A phenomenological analysis of college students' spiritual struggles. *Journal of College Student Development, 53*(1), 55–75. https://doi.org/10.1353/csd.2012.0000

Rodriguez, E. (2010). At the intersection of church and gay: A review of the psychological research on gay and lesbian Christians. *Journal of Homosexuality, 57*(1), 5-38. https://doi.org/10.1080/00918360903445806

Russell, S. T., & Fish, J. N. (2016). Mental health in lesbian, gay, bisexual, and transgender (LGBT) youth. *Annual Review of Clinical Psychology, 12*(1), 465–487. https://www.annualreviews.org/doi/10.1146/annurev-clinpsy-021815-093153

St. James Catholic School v. Biel, 911 F. 3d 603 (9th Cir., 2018).

Stoppa, T., & Lefkowitz, E. (2010). Longitudinal changes in religiosity among emerging adult college students. *Journal of Research on Adolescence, 20*(1), 23–38. https://doi.org/10.1111/j.1532-7795.2009.00630.x

Stratton, S. P., Dean, J. B., Yarhouse, M. A., & Lastoria, M. D. (2013). Sexual minorities in faith-based higher education: A national survey of attitudes, milestones, identity, and religiosity. *Journal of Psychology & Theology, 41*(1), 3–23. https://doi.org/10.1177/009164711304100101

Vespone, B. M. (2016). Integrating identities: Facilitating a support group for LGBTQ students on a Christian college campus. *Christian Higher Education, 15*(4), 215–229. https://doi.org/10.1080/15363759.2016.1186250

Ward v. Polite, 667 F. 3d 727 (6th Cir., 2012).

Weber-Gilmore, G., Rose, S., & Rubinstein, R. (2011). The impact of internalized homophobia on outness for lesbian, gay, and bisexual individuals. *The Professional Counselor: Research and Practice, 1*(3), 163–175. https://doi.org/10.15241/GWV.1.3.163

Wilkerson, J. M., Smolenski, D. J., Brady, S. S., & Rosser, B. R. (2012). Religiosity, internalized homonegativity and outness in Christian men who have sex with men. *Sexual and Relationship Therapy, 27*(2), 122–132. https://doi.org/10.1080/14681994.2012.698259

Wilkinson, W. W., & Roys, A. C. (2005). The components of sexual orientation, religiosity, and heterosexuals' impressions of gay men and lesbians. *Journal of Social Psychology, 145*(1), 65–83. https://doi.org/10.3200/SOCP.145.1.65-84

Wolff, J. R., Himes, H. L., Soares, S. D., & Miller Kwon, E. (2016). Sexual minority students in non-affirming religious higher education: Mental health, outness, and identity. *Psychology of Sexual Orientation and Gender Diversity, 3*(2), 201–212. https://doi.org/10.1037/sgd0000162

Wolff, J. R., Kay, T. S., Himes, H. L., & Alquijay, J. (2017). Transgender and gender-nonconforming student experiences in Christian higher education: A qualitative exploration. *Christian Higher Education, 16*(5), 319–338. https://doi.org/10.1080/15363759.2017.1310065

Wood, P. B., & Bartkowski, J. P. (2004). Attribution style and public policy attitudes toward gay rights. *Social Science Quarterly 85*(1), 58–74. https://doi.org/10.1111/j.0038-4941.2004.08501005.x

Yarhouse, M. A., Stratton, S. P., Dean, J. B., & Brooke, H. L. (2009). Listening to sexual minorities on Christian college campuses. *Journal of Psychology and Theology, 37*(2), 96–113. https://doi.org/10.1177/009164710903700202

Zubernis, L., Snyder, M., & McCoy, V. A. (2011). Counseling lesbian and gay college students through the lens of Cass's and Chickering's developmental models. *Journal of LGBT Issues in Counseling, 5*(2), 122–150. https://doi.org/10.1080/15538605.2011.578506

10

PROVIDING SUPPORT TO LGBTQA+ STUDENTS WHO HAVE EXPERIENCED SEXUAL VIOLENCE AND INTIMATE PARTNER VIOLENCE

Ryan Fette and Pat Tetreault

A dvisors work with a variety of students with diverse experiences and identities. One group of students in particular—sexual and gender minority (LGBTQA+) students—experience higher rates of harassment and discrimination, report more fear for their physical safety, and report experiencing higher rates of psychological stress after experiencing intimate partner violence than straight, cisgender students. In general, sexual violence and intimate partner violence also occur at higher rates for transgender and gender diverse individuals than for their LGB peers (Dank et al., 2014). Additionally, LGBTQA+ students are less likely to seek support or to report sexual violence and intimate partner violence due to minority stress (Calton et al., 2015). *Minority stress* is the stress members of marginalized groups experience from bias in addition to the stressors of everyday life (Meyer, 2003). Perceived or anticipated bias may impact victims' willingness to disclose their experiences to resource providers, law enforcement, and university officials.

Individuals who experience sexual violence or intimate partner violence may identify themselves as a victim or a survivor. The Rape, Abuse, & Incest National Network (RAINN) (2020) suggests using *victim* to describe someone "who has recently been affected by sexual violence," (para. 2) while *survivor* is used for someone "who has gone through the recovery process" (para. 3). RAINN encourages asking the person whether they identify as a victim or a survivor, but this may not be appropriate when responding to someone in crisis.

Working with sexual violence and intimate partner violence survivors requires knowledge of cultural and identity considerations as well as knowledge about their particular institution's policies responding to sexual misconduct laws, including Title IX of the Higher Education Reauthorization Act of 1972, Title VII of the Civil Rights Act of 1964, the Jeanne Clery Disclosure of Campus Security Policy and Campus Crime Statistics Act of 1990, and related regulations. The advisor's ability to apply this knowledge will improve support for survivors.

In addition to being well-informed about policies in place to help LGBTQA+ victims and survivors, advisors have the ability to foster relationships in which LGBTQA+ students feel comfortable disclosing sexual violence and intimate partner violence incidents in order to positively affect outcomes for survivors of all sexual orientations and gender identities. In this chapter, we will provide an overview of sexual violence and intimate partner violence for LGBTQA+ students as well as how sexual violence and intimate partner violence may be different for LGBTQA+ students than straight, cisgender students. A vignette and discussion will provide practical advice and consider nuances in students' situations based on their identities. We discuss how a more positive campus climate for LGBTQA+ individuals may mitigate sexual violence and intimate partner violence risk and better support LGBTQA+ survivors. A list of recommendations for responding to individual disclosures and improving campus climate and resources follows.

LGBTQA+ Students as Sexual Violence and Intimate Partner Violence Survivors

The 2015 National Intimate Partner and Sexual Violence Survey (NISVS) found that, in the United States at the time of survey, almost half of women and a quarter of men had experienced sexual violence in their lifetimes (Smith et al., 2018). Additionally, in 2015, about one third of the population in the United States had experienced intimate partner violence (Smith et al., 2018). Unfortunately, as gender identities were not reported, it is difficult to determine how transgender and gender diverse individuals responded to the survey. The categories of men and women may have only included cisgender men and women, or the categories may have included both cisgender and transgender individuals. Similarly, the experiences of individuals who identified outside of the cisgender binary were not apparent from this information.

Noting this limitation, the NISVS still contains useful information. Individuals who had experienced sexual violence or intimate partner violence were asked their age at the time of the first incident. The majority of individuals had been victimized either before they were 18 years old or between the ages of 18 and 24. This demonstrates that many students come to college after having already experienced victimization, and many students will also experience victimization during their college careers. Understanding the impact of these experiences will facilitate our ability to advise students in ways that support their academic success. The need to understand the impact of identities on survivors of sexual violence and intimate partner violence is particularly important in serving LGBTQA+ students, who face higher rates of sexual violence and intimate partner violence.

While understanding that prevalence rates for sexual violence and intimate partner violence may vary among groups of individuals based on identity can be helpful, it is important to remember that individuals of all sexual orientations and gender identities are at risk. However, lower rates of sexual violence are reported by straight, cisgender students than by LGBTQA+ students (Coulter & Rankin, 2017; Ford & Soto-Marques, 2016; Johnson et al., 2016). Additionally, it is important to note that there are a variety of identities within the LGBTQA+ community that will cause researchers' findings to vary depending on which identities have been grouped for analysis. For example, comparing "bisexuals" to "gays and lesbians," comparing "gay and bisexual men" to "lesbian and bisexual women," or comparing "bisexual women," "bisexual men," "lesbians," and "gay men" as separate categories would all produce different results.

Individuals who identify as bisexual, queer, pansexual, or questioning have been found to be at higher risk for sexual violence than straight, gay, and lesbian individuals (Eisenberg et al., 2017; Johnson et al., 2016) In fact, one in four bisexual students have experienced sexual violence (Cantor et al., 2019). Lesbians are at lower risk for sexual violence than straight women (Ford & Soto-Marquez, 2016), while bisexual, queer, and pansexual women are at higher risk than straight women (Eisenberg et al., 2017). Conversely, gay and bisexual men are at higher risk for sexual violence than straight men (Ford & Soto-Marquez, 2016). Similarly, transgender students are more likely to experience sexual violence than cisgender students (Cantor et al., 2019; Coulter & Rankin, 2017; Johnson et al., 2016). While sexual violence is not generally thought of as an LGBTQA+ concern, the reality is that many members of the community are at higher risk than their straight, cisgender peers, which means that having LGBTQA+-affirming resources for sexual violence and intimate partner violence survivors is needed to support their academic and personal success.

In addition to a higher sexual violence risk, LGBTQA+ individuals are also at higher risk for intimate partner violence victimization. Lesbian, gay and bisexual individuals reported significantly higher rates of intimate partner violence victimization than heterosexual individuals, and transgender individuals reported significantly higher rates than cisgender individuals (Dank et al., 2014). Approximately one third of LGBTQA+ individuals had experienced intimate partner violence in the past 2 years (Edwards et al., 2015) and more lesbian, gay, and bisexual students had experienced intimate partner violence than heterosexual students (Edwards & Sylaska, 2013). These facts illustrate that LGBTQA+ individuals are at a higher risk of intimate partner violence than straight, cisgender individuals.

In addition to the tactics used against straight, cisgender individuals, abusers may use additional tactics against LGBTQA+ individuals. An abusive partner might threaten to disclose a victim's sexual orientation or gender identity (Calton et al., 2015). Abusive partners might also leverage vulnerabilities created by heterosexism, cisgenderism, and transmisogyny against victims, using bias from individuals, groups, and social institutions for the abuser's purposes of maintaining control and encouraging self-blame (National Coalition Against Domestic Violence, 2018).

Race, disability, and other personal characteristics also interact with sexual orientation and gender identity to impact victimization. Gender identity compounds the effects of race/ethnicity and sexual orientation on victimization (Coulter et al., 2017), which is demonstrated by higher rates of sexual assault reported by transgender individuals than by cisgender people. Black transgender people also report higher levels of sexual assault than White transgender people, suggesting that the combination of cissexism and racism leads to greater violence against individuals who have multiple marginalized identities. These differences underscore the need to ensure that programs and services designed to address sexual violence and intimate partner violence prevention and victim services take into account inclusion of all identities.

Having explored how sexual orientation and gender identities impact victims' experiences with sexual violence and intimate partner violence, we can discuss how resulting outcomes for LGBTQA+ survivors differ from those of their straight, cisgender peers. In addition to the stress caused by experiencing violence, LGBTQA+ individuals also experience minority stress. Minority stress occurs in response to: (a) external events and conditions, (b) expectations that stressful external events will happen, and (c) internalization of the negative attitudes of the dominant culture about LGBTQA+ people (Meyer, 2003; see also Meyer, 1995, and Meyer & Dean, 1998).

In addition to minority stress, *internalized heterosexism* (Balsam, 2001) also impacts LGBTQA+ survivors. Internalized heterosexism manifests as "negative attitudes about homosexuality directed toward the self or the relationship" (Rostosky et al., 2007, p. 396). Internalized heterosexism impacts sexual violence and intimate partner violence victims by contributing to self-blame for the violence they have experienced. As an illustration, negative stereotypes about gay and bisexual men's sexuality may create barriers for gay and bisexual men as they process sexual violence experiences for themselves and consider telling others. Gay and bisexual men may have difficulty labeling unwanted sexual experiences due to stereotypes that men—and particularly men who have sex with other men—should "want" all sexual experiences and may feel guilt or shame because they were unable to prevent the assault (Donne et al., 2018). Gay and bisexual men may fear that others believe negative stereotypes and will not be supportive, which illustrates how expectations of heterosexism can contribute to minority stress (Donne et al., 2018).

Another consideration in addressing sexual violence and intimate partner violence for LGBTQA+ students is Title IX of the Higher Education Reauthorization Act of 1972. Title IX prohibits sex discrimination, including sexual violence and intimate partner violence in federally funded education programs in the United States, and gives the Department of Education authority to ensure colleges and universities are addressing sexual violence and intimate partner violence. New Title IX regulations took effect August 14, 2020 (United States Department of Education, 2020). Unfortunately, at the time of publication, there was not sufficient time to give the new regulations the careful consideration needed for meaningful discussion. However, pending litigation and the fall 2020 election had the possibility of modifying the regulations and how the Department of Education interpreted them. The authors believe that any information provided is accurate. However, advisors should check with their campus experts to confirm the institution's requirements and best practices for responding to survivors of sexual violence and intimate partner violence.

Most relevant to advisors in the new regulations is the potential for change in which college and university officials are required to report sexual misconduct to an institution's Title IX coordinator. Prior to the release of new Title IX regulations, most institutions designated almost all employees as Title IX responsible employees, who were required to report sexual misconduct to the institution's Title IX coordinator. The new regulations appear to have a narrower expectation of which university officials are required to report sexual misconduct. An institution must identify officials with authority to address sexual misconduct, and those officials are required to report incidents to the Title IX coordinator (Nondiscrimination on the Basis of Sex in Education Programs or Activities Receiving Federal Financial Assistance,

2020). Institutions may or may not identify advisors as officials with authority; however, having additional responsibilities related to supervising staff or working with a campus activity may create such authority. Advisors should pay close attention to their institution's policies and procedures.

Vignette and Discussion

Building on the literature about the impact of sexual orientation and gender identity and other identities on students' experiences with and the outcomes of sexual violence and intimate partner violence, we present a vignette to illustrate how these concepts can be used in practice. In the vignette and discussion, the gender identities of Skyler and Payton are not known. We will use they/them/their when referring to these individuals. For reference, Skyler is the survivor and Payton is the alleged perpetrator.

Skyler makes an appointment to speak with you, an advisor. During their meeting, Skyler mentions a drop in academic performance during the current semester. You ask Skyler what was challenging about the semester. Skyler discloses their significant other, Payton, insisted on having sex even after Skyler said "no." This occurred earlier in the semester, and Skyler has been struggling since the incident. The advisor did not expect Skyler to disclose this information and needs to quickly determine how to respond.

There are many ways an advisor can respond in this or a similar situation. Guidelines and resources will often vary depending on the college or university's policies related to sexual violence and intimate partner violence and the resources available both on and off campus. What should be consistent is that an advisor responds in supportive and affirming ways to students of all sexual orientations and gender identities. Use of inclusive language with all students, not only those you know or believe are LGBTQA+, is an important step in building credibility with survivors. Realizing that you may not be aware of the sexual orientations and gender identities of survivors or perpetrators may prevent you from making assumptions that can negatively impact your relationship with the survivor or inhibit the survivor from getting appropriate help.

To follow, we pose some questions about responding to Skyler to help you prepare for assisting LGBTQA+ students experiencing sexual violence and intimate partner violence:

- What should your initial response to Skyler be?
- What are the immediate concerns and needs that Skyler has?
- What sort of support should you offer?

- When do you share that you are a mandatory reporter with students (if you are)?
- How much information should you ask for?
- What information should remain confidential?
- Should you do a preliminary investigation on your own when you are required to report incidents to law enforcement or your Title IX coordinator, or when you are assisting a student to make a report?
- What follow-up is appropriate after addressing the initial situation?
- How might a student's sexual orientation or gender identity impact their choice of person to ask for help, or whether to ask for help at all?
- How could assumptions about the student's sexual orientation or gender identity be damaging?
- What other considerations might the student's sexual orientation, gender identity, and additional identities suggest?

In thinking through your response to Skyler, consider that initial responses to a student disclosing sexual violence or intimate partner violence will impact the student's willingness and ability to access resources. Students who have had negative reactions when "coming out" about their sexual orientations or gender identities may be more reluctant to disclose incidents of sexual violence and intimate partner violence. Nonjudgmental and affirming responses to disclosures are helpful. Some phrases you could say are "I'm sorry that happened to you" or "I appreciate your courage in sharing with me." Maintain a calm demeanor. Make it clear that sexual violence or intimate partner violence are not the survivor's fault.

An advisor's first instinct may be to gather as much information about the situation as possible. However, soliciting information may trigger mandatory reporting requirements and take choices away from the student. Advisors may or may not be required to report sexual misconduct. Helping students understand what an advisor must report allows students to make informed decisions about disclosing incidents. Additionally, reporting requirements should be shared as quickly as possible.

Another reason not to encourage the student to share more information than is necessary is because reducing the number of times the student is asked to describe the details of the incident will generally lower the likelihood or severity of revictimization, or causing additional trauma by having the individual relive their experience of violence. The student may have to recount the details of their experience several times if they decide to pursue the matter through criminal prosecution, civil litigation, or the institution's sexual misconduct process.

An advisor may also feel like they should gather additional information by talking to other parties before making a report to police or a Title IX coordinator. However, this may lead to the perpetrator learning about the investigation. Law enforcement may use the element of surprise to prevent a perpetrator from destroying evidence or telling witnesses what to say when interviewed. Improperly collecting or damaging electronic evidence, such as text messages, may lead to problems for an investigation as well. A best practice would be to report the incident and only collect additional information when requested to do so. This also helps ensure confidentiality. An advisor should only reveal a student's sexual orientation or gender identity if the student asks them to share that information or with the student's permission. Even when reporting same-gender sexual violence or intimate partner violence, information identifying the perpetrator can be shared without providing information about the victim's sexual orientation and gender identity.

As you consider how to initially respond to Skyler's disclosure, there are two primary concerns: assessing safety and connecting Skyler with advocacy services.

First, we will discuss what advocacy services are—as an advocate can assist you and the student in determining safety needs. Victim advocates are confidential resources, trained to help victims manage trauma responses, navigate medical, legal, and institutional processes, and provide referrals to other resources. Survivors who have the support of an advocate are more likely to file a report with law enforcement, receive more helpful information and services, and experience less secondary trauma when interacting with medical and legal systems (Campbell, 2006). For advisors, involving an advocate ensures that the student's needs are being met by a colleague who is specifically trained in responding to sexual violence and intimate partner violence. Explain to Skyler who advocates are and how they can help. Ask Skyler if they would like to contact an advocate and offer to help make the phone call. Where walk-in services for victims are nearby, consider walking with Skyler to the location. If an advocate will come to Skyler, offer to stay with Skyler while they wait. If Skyler does not wish to speak with an advocate, honor Skyler's wishes. See the next section about how to follow up with students who decline services.

In addition to connecting Skyler with an advocate, it is important to ascertain whether Skyler is safe. Determining a student's physical safety is a vital part of responding to the disclosure. Directly ask Skyler if they currently feel safe or have reason to believe they are in danger. If there is any doubt about the student's safety, contact campus security or local law enforcement. Always call 911 or campus police when physical danger is imminent. If you are not sure about your institution's protocol, you should consult with your campus experts *before* a situation arises. If you are working with students outside of the United States, consult with your campus experts to determine appropriate safety planning and resources. If Skyler is reluctant to contact law enforcement, explain that you are acting to ensure their safety and that you have a duty to report imminent risk of harm to authorities. Be aware that many students may have negative perceptions of, or have had negative experiences with, police and may find interacting with law enforcement to be frightening. If Skyler is uncomfortable with police, offer to stay with Skyler when the police respond. When victim advocates are available, they can also assist students in interacting with law enforcement. If you are not sure what your institution's protocol is for a situation where a student may be at risk of harm, you should consult with your campus experts *before* a situation arises.

Additional considerations to reduce risk for further victimization may involve shelter options, protection orders, and safety planning. Generally, assistance from local experts will be necessary to engage these services. Victim advocates, student legal services, shelter staff, and community advocacy organizations may be able to help. If Skyler has concerns about negative treatment by the legal system, being outed, or not having LGBTQA+ inclusive services available, these barriers need to be addressed. Skyler's concerns are valid and should not be minimized. One of the best ways to help Skyler is to know about LGBTQA+ affirming service providers. Again, you may not know Skyler's sexual orientation and gender identity. Referring all students to inclusive resources, when available, is the best course of action.

In situations in which a victim advocate is not available or a student declines advocacy services, encourage the student to seek medical and mental health services related to the sexual violence or intimate partner violence. Physical and psychological health-care needs may be immediate or longer-term. Some medical concerns include physical harm, sexually transmitted infections (STIs), pregnancy, and psychological care for trauma. More information about mental health resources for LGBTQA+ students can be found in chapter 8 of this book. Assisting victims is a sensitive task, and advisors can seek out informed resources on the internet, at victim advocacy centers, and through LGBTQA+ organizations. Advisors can use their expertise to refer students to campus and community medical and mental health-care providers, especially those which are LGBTQA+ inclusive.

While referring Skyler to health resources is important, asking questions related to specific health topics may be intrusive. Acknowledge to Skyler that physical and mental health care is often necessary and you can help connect them to resources. However, let Skyler guide the conversation from there. You can offer to help Skyler access services by making phone calls and helping to make appointments. Creating a plan with Skyler to access resources can be helpful, but individuals experiencing trauma may have difficulty engaging in planning. However, advisors should not insist on providing unwanted assistance and should be very clear that they are not serving as a victim advocate, legal representative, or in any other role for which they have not been trained.

Victims may have questions about who will learn about their experience of sexual violence or intimate partner violence if they access services. Skyler may be concerned about their parents or friends learning about the incident. Another concern may be that Payton will find out that Skyler told someone. Victims may be hesitant to take measures that will impact the perpetrator for a variety of reasons, including: feeling responsible for the violence, not wanting the perpetrator to be punished, or fearing retaliation from the perpetrator or others. Confidentiality is a complex topic with many nuances, so it is wise to err on the side of caution. Encourage Skyler to ask service providers about confidentiality when they access services. You can also call service providers and ask about confidentiality while Skyler listens, without divulging Skyler's identity. Consider calling your local victim advocacy agency or a national victim assistance hotline for guidance, such as the Rape, Abuse & Incest National Network (RAINN) National Sexual Assault Hotline, which can be reached at 1-800-656-HOPE.

In addition to hotline information, it is helpful to provide print resources to all students willing to accept them. Print resources provide a physical reminder of information shared about support services. Students who are in a trauma-response mode and some students with disabilities may benefit from having the information available in writing. For students who decline services, a printed resource can be a way to mention it is okay for the student to change their mind later. Let Skyler know that they have time to think about their options and that they can make and reevaluate their decisions as circumstances change.

Follow up with the student to make sure that they have received the information they need. Victims may not be responsive to follow up, and respecting their wishes is important. When interacting with the student, you can continue to show care by asking how the student is without mentioning the situation or asking any follow-up questions about it. If the survivor continues engaging, find out if the survivor has unmet needs. Balancing boundaries with providing caring support may be a challenge. Despite attempts to tell a student you are not a counselor or victim advocate, you may need to remind them of the limits of your scope of practice and redirect them to appropriate resources. When you have concerns about establishing boundaries with students, consult with your colleagues or supervisor for assistance.

When a student reveals they have experienced sexual violence or intimate partner violence, the student's sexual orientation and gender identity are factors in how they are impacted by the experience. While we cannot discuss every possible impact on every identity, we would like to look at how sexual orientation and gender identity might shape Skyler's situation. Due to heterosexism and cissexism in society, Skyler may choose not to disclose their sexual orientation or gender identity, even to an advisor they trust. Being outed could disrupt personal relationships, lead to workplace discrimination, housing discrimination, and additional abuse from the perpetrator or others. Skyler may be afraid that their parents will find out.

However, research shows that students who conceal their identities are more anxious, more depressed, and report higher levels of hopelessness (Tetreault et al., 2019). Skyler's prior experiences with bias or discrimination related to sexual orientation and gender identity will influence their decision to seek help (Donne et al., 2018; Tetreault et al., 2013). Fortunately, advisors who make students feel at ease related to sexual orientation and gender identity may be more likely to be seen as sources of support for LGBTQA+ students who experience sexual violence and intimate partner violence. Perceived similarity in identities, coupled with a specific skill set, may increase comfort or perceptions of trustworthiness, which may in turn facilitate disclosure (Donne et al., 2018). An LGBTQA+ survivor may make decisions about disclosing to a professional based on their relationship with that professional and their belief in the professional's acceptance of their identities. The student's perception of the professional's understanding of victim advocacy or related services may be a lesser concern. The authors' experience indicates that LGBTQA+ students will turn to a variety of people on campus for support, and, in the best-case scenarios, those individuals will be prepared to respond with understanding and the ability to refer to appropriate resources.

In addition to social support, intersections of identity can pose challenges for students because most services have been developed to address a single component of a student's identity rather than addressing all components simultaneously. While awareness of intersectionality is improving, we all need to be conscious of how we provide services so that all individuals feel comfortable seeking services and support.

When considering seeking help, an additional challenge LGBTQA+ survivors of sexual violence and intimate partner violence may face is not knowing whether a victim advocacy organization is supportive of LGBTQA+ individuals (Calton et al., 2015). For example, a community may have limited shelter options for intimate partner violence victims with the local shelter serving cisgender women. Transgender and nonbinary individuals may have difficulty accessing single-gender shelters, and there may not be shelter options for men. Although short-term shelter (3-day stay in a hotel) may be available in certain circumstances for anyone experiencing intimate partner violence, individuals may not know about these resources or trust that the organizations providing them are LGBTQA+ affirming. As many students are not aware of the available resources, advisors can put students in touch with Title IX coordinators and victim advocates who can work with campus housing to arrange emergency shelter. When affirming and knowledgeable services for LGBTQA+ students are not available through campus or community sexual violence and intimate partner violence resources, referral to community LGBTQA+ organizations may be appropriate. However, in many communities, LGBTQA+ organizations are volunteer- and peer-led and may not have the expertise or ability to provide services to sexual violence and intimate partner violence survivors.

To address these concerns, there are national organizations that can provide helpful information. In addition to the Rape, Abuse & Incest National Network's National Sexual Assault Hotline, the National Coalition Against Domestic Violence (NCADV) website contains information about intimate partner violence impacting the LGBTQA+ community, including the use of internalized bias against victims and how prior traumatization from bullying or hate crimes impacts help-seeking behavior. While the NCADV acknowledges that the intimate partner violence awareness movement has focused primarily on heterosexual relationships, the coalition does highlight barriers to LGBTQA+ persons getting help: myths that same-sex intimate partner violence is mutual, lack of appropriate training and knowledge on the part of service providers, anti-LGBTQA+ bias on the part of those providing services, the negative consequences for being outed, and the lack of LGBTQA+ inclusive resources. The Human Rights Campaign (HRC) also has a list of national resources for survivors and professionals working with LGBTQA+ people on their website.

Campus Climate, Sexual Violence, and Intimate Partner Violence

More inclusive environments may protect LGBTQA+ and other minority students in specific ways (chapter 17 provides more information about campus climate for LGBTQA+ individuals). For example, perpetrators may be less likely to victimize LGBTQA+ individuals, bystanders may be more likely to intervene against violence directed toward LGBTQA+ individuals, and LGBTQA+ people may feel more empowered to engage in self-protective behaviors (Longobardi & Badenes-Ribera, 2017). Advisors can influence campus climate and indirectly reduce harm to LGBTQA+ students by influencing campus policies and practices. Some examples would be: ensuring optional questions on forms for name in use, pronouns, and nonbinary gender markers, ensuring LGBTQA+ information exists in relevant curricula and campus programs, and conducting routine campus climate surveys about sexual violence and intimate partner violence, which include optional identity questions about sexual orientation and gender identities, so that the experiences of LGBTQA+ students are captured. When data are collected about LGBTQA+ student experiences, ensure the data are shared in presentations and reports.

Recommendations and Reminders

- Know your institution's protocol for situations where students are at risk of imminent harm from sexual violence and intimate partner violence.
- If you are required to report sexual misconduct, make sure you let students know that you are a mandated reporter and let them know what that means.
- Recognize the importance of confidentiality and privacy.
- Be familiar with resources for survivors.
- Understand how identities impact students' experiences and perceptions.
- Have visible signs of inclusion in your workspace and electronic communications.
- Seek out educational opportunities related to preventing sexual violence and intimate partner violence directed toward LGBTQA+ students and responding competently when disclosures are made.
- Understand distinctions between sexual orientation, gender identity, and gender expression.
- Understand current terminology and concepts and continue learning as information changes over time.
- Attend a workshop on creating inclusive spaces, brave space, or ally development.
- Use the name and pronouns that an individual wants you to use for them.
- Do not ask survivors to relive their trauma by explaining it to you.
- Acknowledge and continue reflecting on how your dominant identities influence your interactions with students and how you can use your power and positionality to advocate.

- Amplify the voices of survivors; do not speak for them.
- Engage in prosocial bystander behaviors, specifically intervening to prevent sexual violence and intimate partner violence.
- Remember that self-care is important and to seek out support for yourself.

Conclusion

When considering the impact of sexual violence and intimate partner violence on individuals, it is important to accept that every person deserves to live a life free from violence. The prevalence of sexual violence and intimate partner violence among college students and its disproportionate, negative impact on LGBTQA+ students are ongoing and underrecognized issues. Sexual orientation and gender identity are not the only identities that shape an individual's experience of victimization or influence the likelihood that an individual may be victimized. An individual's personal characteristics—such as race, having a disability, experiencing homelessness, prior experiences with violence, and so on—will also inform decisions to disclose, access formal support services, or report the incident(s) to authorities. Unfortunately, bias or lack of knowledge about LGBTQA+ identities can influence the reactions of formal support services, authorities, and those to whom the person discloses the incident.

Advisors can play a powerful role by providing competent assistance to students of all sexual orientations and gender identities. For advisors on campuses or in areas with well-developed resources for LGBTQA+ survivors, this will mean familiarizing oneself with what is currently available. For advisors in areas where LGBTQA+ resources are not as prevalent, it is important for advisors to work with campus and local leaders to ensure such resources become available. Advisors can change campus cultures by caring enough to become well-informed on relevant topics, advocating for sexual violence and intimate partner violence prevention efforts, supporting survivors, and doing their part to create a more inclusive campus climate for LGBTQA+ students. We all can make a difference.

References

Balsam, K. F. (2001). Nowhere to hide: Lesbian battering, homophobia, and minority stress. *Women and Therapy, 23,* 25–38. https://doi.org/10.1300/J015v23n03_03
Calton, J. M., Bennett Cattaneo, L., & Gebhard, K. T. (2015). Barriers to help seeking for lesbian, gay, bisexual, transgender, and queer survivors of intimate

partner violence. *Trauma, Violence, & Abuse, 17*(5), 585–600. https://doi.org/10.1177/1524838015585318

Campbell, R. (2006). Rape survivors' experiences with the legal and medical systems: Do rape victim advocates make a difference? *Violence Against Women, 12*(1), 30–45. https://doi.org/10.1177/1077801205277539

Cantor, D., Fisher, B., Chibnall, S., Harps, S., Townsend, R., Thomas, G., Lee, H., Kranz, V., Herbison, R., & Madden, K. (2019). *Report on the AAU campus climate survey on sexual assault and misconduct.* American Association of Universities. https://www.aau.edu/sites/default/files/AAU-Files/Key-Issues/Campus-Safety/Revised%20Aggregate%20report%20%20and%20appendices%201-7_(01-16-2020_FINAL).pdf

Coulter, R. W. S., Mair, C., Miller, E., Blosnich, J. R., Matthews, D. D., & McCauley, H. L. (2017). Prevalence of past-year sexual assault victimization among undergraduate students: Exploring differences by and intersections of gender identity, sexual identity, and race/ethnicity. *Prevention Science, 2017*(18), 726–736. https://doi.org/10.1007/s11121-017-0762-8

Coulter, R. W. S., & Rankin, S. R. (2017). College sexual assault and campus climate for sexual- and gender-minority undergraduate students. *Journal of Interpersonal Violence, 35*(5–6), 1351–1366. https://doi.org/10.1177/0886260517696870

Dank, M., Lachman, P., Zweig, J. M., & Yahner, J. (2014). Dating violence experiences of lesbian, gay, bisexual, and transgender youth. *Journal of Youth and Adolescence, 43*(5), 846–857. https://doi.org/10.1007/s10964-013-9975-8

Donne, M. D., DeLuca, J., Pleskach, P., Bromson, C., Mosley, M. P., Perez, E. T., Mathews, S. G., Stephenson, R., & Frye, V. (2018). Barriers to and facilitators of help-seeking behavior among men who experience sexual violence. *American Journal of Men's Health, 12*(2), 189–201. https://doi.org/10.1177/1557988317740665

Edwards, K. M., & Sylaska, K. M. (2013). The perpetration of intimate partner violence among LGBTQ college youth: The role of minority stress. *Journal of Youth and Adolescence, 42*(11), 1721–1731. https://doi.org/10.1007/s10964-012-9880-6

Edwards, K. M., Sylaska, K. M., Barry, J. E., Moynihan, M. M., Banyard, V. L., Cohn, E. S., Walsh, W. A., & Ward, S. K. (2015). Physical dating violence, sexual violence, and unwanted pursuit victimization: A comparison of incidence rates among sexual-minority and heterosexual college students. *Journal of Interpersonal Violence, 30*(4), 580–600. https://doi.org/10.1177/0886260514535260

Eisenberg, M. E., Lust, K., Mathiason, M. A., & Porta, C. M. (2017, August 21). Sexual assault, sexual orientation, and reporting among college students. *Journal of Interpersonal Violence.* 36 (1–2), 62–82. https://doi.org/10.1177/0886260517726414

Ford, J., & Soto-Marquez, J. G. (2016). Sexual assault victimization among straight, gay/lesbian and bisexual college students. *Violence and Gender, 3*(2), 107–115. https://doi.org/10.1089/vio.2015.0030

Human Rights Campaign (2020). *Sexual assault and the LGBTQ community.* https://www.hrc.org/resources/sexual-assault-and-the-lgbt-community

Johnson, L. M., Matthews, T. L., & Napper, S. L. (2016). Sexual orientation and sexual assault victimization among US college students. *The Social Science Journal, 53*(2), 174–183. https://doi.org/10.1016/j.soscij.2016.02.007

Longobardi, C., & Badenes-Ribera, L. (2017). Intimate partner violence in same sex relationships and the role of sexual minority stressors: A systematic review of the past 10 years. *Journal of Child and Family Studies, 26,* 2039–2049. https://doi.org/10.1007/s10826-017-0734-4

Meyer, I. (1995). Minority stress and mental health in gay men. *Journal of Health and Social Behavior, 36*(1), 38–56. www.jstor.org/stable/2137286

Meyer, I. H. (2003). Prejudice, social stress, and mental health in lesbian, gay, and bisexual populations: Conceptual issues and research evidence. *Psychological Bulletin, 129*(5), 674–697. https://doi.org/10.1037/0033-2909.129.5.674

Meyer, I. H., & Dean, L. (1998). Internalized homophobia, intimacy, and sexual behavior among gay and bisexual men. In G. M. Herek (Ed.), *Stigma and sexual orientation: Understanding prejudice against lesbians, gay men, and bisexuals* (pp. 160–186). SAGE.

National Coalition Against Domestic Violence. (2018, June 6). *Domestic violence and the LGBTQ community.* https://ncadv.org/blog/posts/domestic-violence-and-the-lgbtq-community

Nondiscrimination on the Basis of Sex in Education Programs or Activities Receiving Federal Financial Assistance, 85 Fed. Reg. 30026 (2020) (to be codified at 34 C.F.R. pt. 106.30).

Rape, Abuse & Incest National Network. (2020). *Key terms and phrases.* https://www.rainn.org/articles/key-terms-and-phrases

Rostosky, S. S., Riggle, E. D. B., Gray, B. E., & Hatton, R. L. (2007). Minority stress experiences in committed same-sex relationships. *Professional Psychology: Research and Practice, 38*(4), 392–400. https://psycnet.apa.org/doi/10.1037/0735-7028.38.4.392

Smith, S. G., Zhang, X., Basile, K. C., Merrick, M. T., Wang, J., Kresnow, M., & Chen, J. (2018). *The national intimate partner and sexual violence survey (NISVS): 2015 data brief—updated release.* National Center for Injury Prevention and Control, Centers for Disease Control and Prevention. https://www.cdc.gov/violenceprevention/datasources/nisvs/2015NISVSdatabrief.html

Tetreault, P., Fette, R., & Holt, N. (2019). *LGBTQA+ student assessment 2017.* Data presented to the Chancellor, University of Nebraska-Lincoln. https://health.unl.edu/lgbt

Tetreault, P., Fette, R., Meidlinger, P., & Hope, D. (2013). Perceptions of campus climate by sexual minorities. *Journal of Homosexuality, 60*(7). 947–964. https://doi.org/10.1080/00918369.2013.774874

United States Department of Education. (2020, May 6). *Secretary DeVos takes historic action to strengthen Title IX protections for all students.* https://www.ed.gov/news/press-releases/secretary-devos-takes-historic-action-strengthen-title-ix-protections-all-students

Ally Narrative

Janie Valdés

Growing up in a big city exposed me to a lot of different types of people at a very young age. I remember going to my local Dairy Queen and seeing two men showing a level of intimacy that I had not seen before. Similar to my parents' intimate interactions, the men were humorous, lighthearted, and caring toward one another. They displayed physical intimacy. I could not stop staring at them. In a Hispanic neighborhood in the 1970s, where most men were expected to be "macho," this was clearly not the norm as seen in the responses of patrons who were visibly uncomfortable, some physically moving away from the men. What stayed with me from this experience was my father's reaction. He never spoke derogatorily about the men. Instead, he reminded me that staring at others was not polite. Throughout my childhood and teenage years, he and my mother often reminded me that people were simply different from one another (whether that pertained to sexual orientation, race, or ethnicity) and life was to be lived freely. For two people who had been exiled from their country, losing family, friends, and livelihood, there was little left to judge—and I was the ultimate beneficiary of their openness and empathy.

My defining moment in *allyhood* came years later when a girlfriend in high school made advances toward me. I shared with her that, although "I was not like that," I was also not offended by the advance, nor did I think it should change our friendship. What the advance did was open my eyes to the negative stereotyping that some of our peers had about her and about me by mere association. I was okay saying that I was not a lesbian, but I learned to say—with greater conviction—that there was nothing wrong with being lesbian or gay, bisexual, transgender, or questioning.

I have called out the inappropriateness of a homophobic joke where the response is usually, "Oh, you can't take a joke" or "I did not mean anything bad by it; do not take things so seriously." Although I am still unable to remain quiet if I see outright injustice or insult, as I got older, I found more productive ways to spend energy and time supporting the LGBTQA+ community—patronizing our local gay men's chorus, cosponsoring an

LGBTQA+ student conference at my university, and serving on equity and inclusivity committees, to name a few examples.

However, I continue to learn the most from our students; they are in the best position to teach me about their experiences in the modern world and how I might be of support from my own place of privilege. In fact, when I worked on a grant project for students who age out of the foster care system or experience homelessness, it was the students themselves who enlightened me about the prevalence of LGBTQA+ youth who are kicked out of their homes due to their family's rejection.

From my experience as an ally, I have three pieces of advice for others seeking to be more supportive:

1. *Be self-aware.* What are your beliefs, perceptions, stereotypes, and understandings, and are you willing to question and adjust those? Do you understand, embrace, or reject your privilege or the places of privilege for others? At minimum, do you know to whom you should refer students should they share with you any struggles about their sexuality?

2. *Never stop learning.* Take advantage of opportunities to attend trainings and workshops that can inform, challenge, and enlighten you. Listen to and learn from your colleagues and your students, and do not be afraid to ask questions. In the late 1990s, as part of a university-wide diversity training, one of our senior leaders shared his coming out story. He said, "As a young man, if I could come out to the entire world at once, I would have because what is exhausting is having to constantly question and decide [when and who] to come out to and whether it is safe to do so." I never forgot his bravery or his story. Over the many years that have passed since, I have listened to similar stories from students who have been brave enough to come out to me in the confines and comfort of our advising session.

3. *Get involved.* Join campus groups and organizations where you can meet with diverse members of the LGBTQA+ community and allies. These can go a long way to raise your awareness of the many ways to support initiatives and programs. There is strength in numbers and strength in *you* to proudly demonstrate your allyhood!

Ally Narrative

Cody Harrison

My ally journey began like many other LGBTQA+ people growing up in the South: in a conservative, Christian household. Queerness, in any form, was not an option and was never even an idea I entertained. I knew gay people existed—I even had a lesbian cousin—but all information surrounding the LGBTQA+ community came in the form of jokes, the messages of sinfulness, or the ending of the weekly viewings of *Glee* with the family after "that gay episode." Attending a public liberal arts institution exposed me to more freedom of thought and expression than I could have ever fathomed. This exposure allowed me to begin a deep dive into my thoughts and feelings about religion (one of my majors, it would turn out), sexuality, gender, sex (both the noun and the verb), and learning to make my own choices instead of the choices I thought my parents would want me to make. The journey was not comfortable, and I'm glad that it wasn't; I learned more from the bumpy road than I would have from a less challenging path. By my senior year of undergrad, I came out to myself and to some of my closest friends, and I redefined the role religion played in my life. Graduation led me to live with my parents again for a year while I decided on a graduate program. Transitioning back to a conservative area with family led me to maintain a more secretive gay life. After the year ended, I returned to my undergraduate institution for a graduate program. By the end of grad school, I was able to come out to most of my immediate family and most of my friends. In the professional world, I have been able to come out and present myself as a gay man to my colleagues, my students, and my new friends and acquaintances. None of this would have been possible without allies and other LGBTQA+ identifying people and resources.

As I was growing in my identity as a gay man, I was taught the "A" in LGBTQA+ did not stand for ally because an ally is not someone who is part of the queer community. Instead, an ally should be working outside of the community to aid those within it. At its most basic definition, an *ally* is someone with power and privilege who stands up for/supports those without that power and privilege. With further education and self-reflection,

I realized that even members within the community (including myself) *could* be an ally for other community members (i.e., gay, lesbian, bisexual, etc.) because power dynamics still exist even within marginalized groups. For example, when thinking about intersecting identities, my whiteness and (cis)maleness gives me more opportunity to stand for, support, and defend my non-white, female, and trans/nonbinary/nonconforming community members. This realization helped me realize just how uneducated I really was about the rest of my community. My ignorance drove me to learn more through articles, trainings, and conversations about the group of people I consider to be family since my biological family isn't always the most supportive. Just like other allies and ally work, I needed to do this research on my own. I knew I couldn't just find a queer person of color and expect them tell me all the things I needed to know. Allies do their own learning rather than leaning on those who are already overburdened. This research, along with my continued education on the topic, has enabled me to become a better ally within the community. I know more than I did when I was just coming out, but there is still a lot for me to learn and incorporate into my everyday life. I call myself an ally for some members of our community. However, there are other members to whom I know I can only call myself a friend, someone with good intentions and love, but not enough education to truly offer what an ally should offer. I will continue to learn and grow in order to change that.

My advice for other allies? Recognize where you are an ally and where you are a friend, and work to turn that friendship into allyship. Find articles, training, presentations, podcasts, books by queer authors (nonfiction and fiction alike), and so on to educate yourself about the rest of your community. Help educate others as they journey to become an ally. Be ready and willing to make mistakes, learn from them, and work hard not to make them in the future. It's not an easy journey but definitely a rewarding one.

PART THREE

ADVISING LGBTQA+ STUDENT POPULATIONS

II

ADVISING LGBTQA+ STUDENT-ATHLETES

Donna J. Menke, Craig M. McGill, Josh Fletcher, and Meghan Pfeiffer

Growing awareness of LGBTQA+ issues and rights have helped garner acceptance of marginalized sexual orientations and gender identities in sport in the 21st century. Some examples of strides forward include: advocacy efforts to support the LGBTQA+ community by increasing visibility of LGBTQA+ athletes, the National Collegiate Athletic Association's (NCAA) adopting inclusion as a core value and releasing policy and best practice recommendations for LGBTQA+ student-athletes, and increasing nonprofit organizations (e.g., Athlete Ally, Campus Pride, LGBT SportSafe) that encourage heterosexuals to become allies in support of LGBTQA+ athletes and stop anti-LGBTQA+ discrimination in sport (Griffin, 2014). Despite these advances, homophobia is still very prevalent in sport, so additional work is needed for full inclusion to become the new norm. In fact, intercollegiate athletics is "one of the last bastions of cultural and institutional homophobia in North America" (Anderson, 2005, p. 13). Consequently, student-athletes who identify as LGBTQA+ face discrimination, isolation, and emotional turmoil (Griffin, 2012).

In many cases, the strife LGBTQA+ students face is due to lack of support at the institutional level. Over the last few years, postsecondary institutions have made diversity and inclusion a fundamental part of their mission with the goal of creating an environment that aims to be inclusive of all students (Griffin & Taylor, 2013). However, despite increased efforts to ensure that all students have equal opportunities to achieve their academic goals, institutions are not always prepared to adequately support diverse students. Institutions are often unprepared to provide proper support in response to homo/bi/trans/phobia, which impacts the psychological, academic, and athletic development of student-athletes. Although some might dismiss sexual orientation and gender identity as a private matter, a student-athlete's inability to be open about who they are and to develop their identity in a healthy, normal way poses serious harm to their emotional and psychological well-being, not to mention the toll it takes on their athletic and academic performance (Wolf-Wendel et al., 2008).

In addition to lack of institutional support, student-athletes' perceptions of academic and sport environments play a major role in their success (Rankin et al., 2016). Unfortunately, much remains to be explored regarding the experiences of LGBTQA+ student-athletes and the practices and conditions that promote student development, sense of belonging, comfortability, and inclusivity on college campuses (Stewart & Howard-Hamilton, 2015). Although the field of academic advising has addressed considerations for advising student-athletes (e.g., Leslie-Toogood & Gill, 2008; Menke, 2013) and LGBTQA+ students (e.g., Forest, 2006; Joslin, 2007; Self, 2007), only two publications address the intersection of these populations (Menke et al., 2015; Wolf-Wendel et al., 2008). Now more than ever, student-athletes are coming out during college, and academic advisors need to be knowledgeable and equipped to help them deal with the challenges they face. In this chapter, we will discuss higher education environments and LGBTQA+ student-athletes, intersectional considerations of athletic identity, implications for higher education policy and academic advising practice, and recommendations for future research.

Higher Education Environments and LGBTQA+ Student-Athletes

Campus environments shape the campus climate and impact the experiences of those who exist in those environments (Renn & Patton, 2010). Research on campus climate exclusively focuses on "the overall ethos or atmosphere of a college campus, mediated by the extent to which individuals feel a sense of safety, belonging, engagement within the environment, and valued as members of a community" (Renn & Patton, 2010, p. 248). Campus climate studies provide baseline data to gauge LGBTQA+ students' insights, attitudes, perceptions, and experiences in higher education. In fact, Rankin et al. (2016) examined the quality of the relationships with athletic administrators, athletic academic advisors, coaches, and athletic trainers and found that positive interactions with those individuals contributed to student-athletes' academic and athletic success. Other research suggests that if a campus was perceived to be inclusive for LGBTQA+ individuals, then the athletic department was also perceived that way (Greim, 2016). Unfortunately, one study revealed that, compared to heterosexual counterparts, LGBTQA+ students experienced greater harassment and discrimination based on sexual identity (Rankin et al., 2010). In another study, Rankin and Merson (2012) found that LGBTQA+ student-athletes have worse perceptions of campus climate than their heterosexual/cisgender counterparts and believe athletic departments do not always address discrimination or have enough diversity in athletic leadership.

LGBTQA+ student-athletes have many environments in which they form their perceptions of campus climate, including within the team, athletic department, and campus (i.e., classrooms, student union, and on ground), and those environments can be accepting, neutral, or hostile. If a campus is committed to an intercollegiate athletics experience in which "student-athlete health and well-being are the highest priority," there must be a commitment to the "physical, social, and psychological health and well-being of students of all sexual orientations and gender identities/expressions" (Griffin & Taylor, 2013, p. 3).

The following are two examples where the campus climate had a positive effect on student-athlete experience. One of us (Josh) was a former Division I collegiate springboard diver. The support of his coaches and teammates made a tremendous difference in his positive experience. Being able to speak openly about his experiences as a gay man changed the culture of the team, the language used formally and informally inside and outside of practice, and opened the door for other LGBTQA+ student-athletes to share their authentic selves. The same was true for Meghan, a former Division I women's soccer player; the support of her coaches and teammates played the largest role in her positive experience. Her coaches created a team culture where all individuals were valued and celebrated on and off of the field, which in turn increased the level of comfort and inclusivity she felt. In addition, she had openly lesbian teammates and an assistant coach, so, rather than feeling ostracized for being part of the LGBTQA+ community, she had other people in her immediate environment who provided a level of relatability that was invaluable during her tenure as a student-athlete. Additionally, the athletic department at her former institution hosted pride nights and made a "You Can Play" video in support of LGBTQA+ student-athletes. As a result of these ongoing initiatives in support of her community, she felt a heightened sense of belonging because she knew that the athletic department valued the inclusion of all and exclusion of no one. These are just two examples of how the athletic department can create a positive student-athlete experience.

Unfortunately, not all institutions have addressed LGBTQA+ student-athlete inclusion, which can negatively affect athletic and academic performance. As intercollegiate athletics is an integral part of higher education, its administrators, coaches, and staff have an ethical obligation to create inclusive, supportive environments where all student-athletes can thrive athletically and academically. At present, athletic departments tend to be characterized as cultures of heteronormativity and heterosexism, which can lead to "individual expressions of sexual prejudice" (Cunningham, 2015, p. 44). Factors contributing to homonegativity in college sports include athletes, coaches, and others involved not having had the necessary exposure to different sexualities and gender expressions; the strict (traditional) definition of masculinity; and the focus on "team" and "community" causing individual development to be neglected and ignored (Wolf-Wendel et al., 2008). Development is especially overlooked in team-oriented sports because they operate under an umbrella of team loyalty to the organization or athletic department. Lack of institutional support of LGBTQA+ student-athletes often results in an "athletics climate where LGBTQA+ administrators, student-athletes, and coaches hide their identities to avoid discrimination or harassment, [which] can negatively affect athletic and academic achievement" (Griffin & Taylor, 2013, p. 2). When LGBTQA+ student-athletes feel the need to hide their sexual orientation or gender identity out of fear of rejection, the climate is unhealthy and does not promote well-being. In fact, environments where LGBTQA+ student-athletes cannot openly speak about their orientation is a form of covert discrimination (Pfeiffer, 2018). In contrast, inclusive environments not only put down such discriminatory actions, they also promote overall student-athlete well-being.

Just as campus climate impacts athletic departments, the climate within the athletic department impacts teams. The relationships college athletes have with their coaches and athletic trainers establish whether the climate is healthy or unhealthy. A climate that forces LGBTQA+ athletes to remain closeted has a negative impact on the individual student-athlete. For example, male sports such as football and basketball have often held strong beliefs about masculinity (Stack & Staurowsky, 1998). This is problematic for gay men who are often stereotyped as effeminate and then ostracized for not meeting the masculine heterosexual expectation. Moreover, although there has been a larger acceptance of gay men on athletic teams in recent years (Fenwick & Simpson, 2017), "collegiate athletics has historically been considered an area of extreme prejudice and discrimination related to sexual orientation" (Oswalt, 2016, p. 237). As a result, male athletes may be hindered in exploring and developing their sexuality as a result of negative attitudes persisting in their athletic environment.

Female athletes face the stereotype that they are all lesbians and are viewed as unfeminine due to their athletic skill (Waldron, 2016). Women in sport have been held to hegemonic femininity, that is to say, stereotypical feminine characteristics: "emotional, passive, dependent, maternal, compassionate, and gentle" (Krane, 2001, p. 117). When women do not perform the heteronormative female role, they experience prejudice and discrimination. When female athletes do come out, the public response is typically indifference, which reflects the assumption that being a lesbian in sport is a common stereotype (Griffin, 2014). Left unchallenged, these assumptions are used to "validate practices of social inequality within sport environment" that keep student-athletes closeted (Waldron, 2016, p. 338). The pressure to perform in a world that values masculinity in men while devaluing masculinity in women can create internal conflict for athletes.

Another subpopulation that often faces stereotypes and discrimination with a lack of support resulting in social isolation are Black athletes on college campuses (Baker & Hawkins, 2016). Black athletes (particularly male athletes in the revenue-producing sports of football and basketball) are believed to be interested solely in sport with no interest or ability in academics. Black families and communities often emphasize athletics over academics and encourage athletic participation for entry into lucrative professional sports (Baker & Hawkins, 2016). These challenges are exacerbated for student-athletes with double minority statuses. Gay and lesbian athletes of color must also cope with cultural views that devalue LGBTQA+ statuses. This can further add to the isolation felt by student-athletes of color.

A subpopulation that is surrounded with controversy is the transgender student-athlete. Specifically, transgender controversy issues in sport frequently center on issues of competitive fairness. Because sports are often designated as either "male" or "female," concerns about transgender athletes arise based on erroneous assumptions. Societal beliefs of dichotomous sexual and gender identities influence concerns that allowing athletes to participate in sport based on their gender identity, and not assigned biological sex, threatens fair play in college athletics. However, medical evidence challenges this stereotype "pointing to physical variation that appears across athletes" (Gray et al., 2018, p. 46). In other words, skill level varies by individual athlete, not biology. Some believe that a male-to-female transgender athlete competing in a women's sport will take opportunities away from women and will have an unfair competitive advantage.

In response to these concerns, the NCAA (2011) has established guidelines by which transgender athletes may compete with teams based on their gender identity and has established guidelines for mixed sex teams. Women's sports teams with one or more male members or men's sports teams with one or more female members are defined in the guidelines as mixed teams. In addition, these guidelines take into account the hormone therapies used in gender transitions. For example, testosterone is a banned substance in NCAA sports competition but is a common part of the medical procedure for transitioning transgender athletes. For trans male athletes, once testosterone therapy has begun, the athlete can no longer compete on women's teams, but can compete on men's teams (NCAA, 2011). Transwomen athletes have more stringent guidelines: They are permitted to participate on men's teams unless they are using testosterone suppression medication. Once they begin this therapy, they must wait 1 year before being allowed to participate on a women's team. However, transgender athletes can receive a medical exemption to the rules regarding this banned substance, allowing them to compete in their sport in their respective gender division.

Although these guidelines address the concerns of the general public, they provide a unique form of alienation for trans students because they force LGBTQA+ people to identify themselves as such. As "silent sufferers," it is impossible to say how many athletes are forced to mask their true identity in hopes of passing as heterosexual and/or cisgender. Due to physical characteristics, transgender athletes may have more physical markers of their identities than sexual minorities. This might create challenges for transgender athletes and for the coaches, teammates, advisors, faculty, and others who support them. Transgender individuals are frequent targets for harassment, and they are often victims of violence. Athletic departments can create a welcoming climate for transgender athletes by establishing clear guidelines, educating staff on issues facing transgender athletes, and using and encouraging the use of proper pronouns for transgender athletes (Gray et al., 2018).

Intersectional Considerations of Athletic Identity

Intercollegiate athletics has propagated a subculture that emphasizes athletics over academics. Although student-athletes often begin their college experience idealistic about their academic future, they are often met with pressure from teammates to conform to a more prominent athletic identity (Rubin & Moses, 2017). Achieving high levels of athletic and scholastic performance is expected by college administrators, coaches, and fans, but the environments are not always conducive to an LGBTQA+ student and their academic and athletic development. LGBTQA+ student-athletes are twice as likely as their peers to experience harassment, and that harassment frequently comes from coaches and teammates during practice sessions (Rankin & Merson, 2012). This harassment has implications for the presence of homo/bi/trans/phobia in intercollegiate athletics, particularly within team sports (Griffin, 2012). The pressure of performing at a high level coupled with the visibility of being an athlete on campus and in the community—particularly at the NCAA Division I level—creates an environment where college athletes feel as if they are "living in a little bubble" (Menke, 2016, p. 16). Consequently, athletes may disengage with other aspects of their academic careers (Benson, 2000).

In addition to athletic and academic pressure, many students are trying to understand the way their identities intersect. A student's athletic identity intersects with other identity characteristics in complicated ways. Individuals are not one-dimensional, and as such, identity is constructed from a multitude of identity characteristics. Sexual orientation and gender are identity characteristics, but not everyone who identifies as LGBTQA+ experiences gender or sexual identity in the same way. Identity is how one views oneself (Beron & Piquero, 2016). *Athletic identity* is the extent to which a person identifies as an athlete (Brewer et al., 1993). The strength of the identity characteristic (e.g., gay, female) speaks to the salience for the person's overall identity. An athlete may identify as male or female, gay or straight, and they may have a strong or weak athletic identity. There are many factors that influence the salience of a student's athletic identity, including campus interactions (with faculty members, campus and athletic academic advisors, coaches, teammates, trainers, students, and academic and athletic administrators), comfort level with teammate diversity, and experiences within the physical campus environment. Some research suggests Division I student-athletes have more salient athletic identities than their Division II peers (Rankin et al., 2016). However, athletic identity tended to be less salient for LGBTQA+ student-athletes (Rankin et al., 2011). The various identity characteristics each student possesses influences their lived-experience and development as a student and as an athlete.

The experiences of transgender student-athletes are especially complex, with no single trans experience (Semerjian & Cohen, 2006). Because sports are often segregated by binary sex categories (i.e., male or female), transgender athletes are forced to identify by sex and not gender identity to participate. This can cause dissonance, as transgender individuals sometimes see their gender identity as either changing, fluid, or nonbinary. Few policies are in place to allow transgender athletes to compete in the most appropriate arena. This forces most athletes to choose a sport based on their sex assigned at birth and then to adapt appropriate "norms," because in American society, "variant sexual identity can be accepted as long as gender conventions are not crossed" (Lucas-Carr & Krane, 2012, p. 30).

Vignette

The following vignette is designed to introduce some of the obstacles and challenges transgender student-athletes may face when making the decision to disclose their identity. We have provided some questions to consider when working with transgender athletes. However, it is important to note that there is not a one-size-fits-all response to the vignette. Each student-athlete must be responded to in a way that best fits their unique situation.

Sara is a 20-year-old Latina athlete from a large Southern city, competing on a full scholarship on the men's track team. Sara has been seeing a therapist for several years and is starting to feel more comfortable sharing her identity and chosen pronouns as a transwoman in select social settings. Despite significant fear of rejection, Sara has recently shared with her close friends and immediate family that she is transgender and uses feminine pronouns. Her family has conflicting feelings trying to understand and accept her identity, while cherishing the memories and future plans they had for her. Ultimately, her family is making the effort to educate themselves to better support Sara, but recommend she not share her identity with extended family who are very conservative, both religiously and politically, and also vocally unaccepting of LGBTQA+ people. They also fear she will meet significant discrimination on the track team if she chooses to pursue any type of social or medical transition while in college.

During off season, Sara schedules a meeting with an assistant coach to share that she is transgender and considering a social and medical transition. To her surprise, her assistant coach is very supportive. During their conversation, however, Sara learns that she cannot compete on the men's track team if she begins testosterone suppression medication as she had planned to do with guidance from her therapist. To her additional surprise, she would not be eligible to compete on the women's track team for at least 1 year after starting medication. She leaves the meeting considering what she believes to be her two options: put a hold on any type of medical transition until after she's done competing on the men's team or wait 1 year without her scholarship and then hopefully compete on the women's team.

Sara's therapist recommended finding other transwomen who might be able to share their experiences in order to build community. Sara reaches out to her institution's LGBTQA+ resource center in hopes of connecting to others in a more private capacity than a large student organization meeting. The LGBTQA+ resource center staff connects her with a student leader, Monica, who is willing to meet one-on-one to share her experience as a transwoman of color on campus. During the meeting, Sara is relieved to hear Monica share her own journey of coming to terms with her gender identity and navigating difficult conversations with family and friends. Although Sara attempts to explain the various policies she had learned from the meeting with her assistant coach, as well as her love of competition and representing the university at the highest level of competition for college athletes, Monica cannot comprehend the consequences or pressures Sara experiences when competing as a student-athlete. Sara leaves their meeting with feelings of hope after meeting a fellow trans student living her truth in a genuine and authentic way, but she is also discouraged about not feeling she had connected to anyone who related to her experience as a transgender student-athlete of color.

Sara is faced with numerous pressures as the track season is about to begin. She is neither able to find support that understands her athletic identity and goals within the LGBTQA+ community nor in the athletic community for fear of outing herself or risking her chances of competing. She wants to be her most authentic self and share her identities with her coaches and teammates but knows transwoman athletes face significant eligibility barriers when competing in binary-based sports (i.e., men's or women's track). Sara has explained all of this to her advisor and is looking for additional guidance.

Elements for Advisor Consideration:

- Knowing that a student-athlete's inability to be open about who they are poses serious harm to their emotional and psychological well-being, as well as their athletic and academic performance, what approach would you take when suggesting Sara speak with her coach and teammates?
- What additional support offices, policies, or services might your campus offer that would be helpful in directing Sara?
- Consider your institution's various student affairs offices, nondiscrimination policies, counseling services, intergroup dialogue contacts, and equity and inclusion offices who might be able to provide additional information.

In the next section, we offer additional information that we hope will help advisors navigate the nuances of Sara's unique story.

Implications for Campus Policy and Advising Practice

Although this chapter is geared toward academic advisors, we must also discuss the larger landscape of campus climate. This is especially true since athletics transcend the academic spaces of campuses. Thus, we offer implications for higher education campus policy and then for academic advising practice.

At a broad level, institutions of higher education must work to make campus environments safer and more inclusive for students. Examples of widespread support for the LGBTQA+ community on college campuses include pro-LGBTQA+ resource centers, clubs, safe spaces, events, nondiscrimination policies for sexual orientation and identity, LGBTQA+-focused curriculum, and ally training programs. Although campus climates shift as societal perceptions of LGBTQA+ issues evolve, subtle forms of LGBTQA+ bias permeate college campuses in the form of microaggressions, "everyday, sometimes unintentional, words and actions that invade, silence, and make invisible LGBTQA+ identities and experiences" (Renn & Pitcher, 2016, p. 241). Therefore, advocating for LGBTQA+ students within athletic departments can be accomplished by hosting awareness and training sessions specifically for athletic departments, collaborating with athletic academic advisors, and providing resources to coaches and administration. These resources can be sourced from organizations such as Athlete Ally, LGBT SportSafe, You Can Play Project, TransAthlete, Women's Sports Foundation, and Campus Pride. Advisors, coaches, and administrators play an integral role in creating a climate of respect for LGBTQA+ student-athletes; thus, one can call upon these organizations to obtain information on how to understand and address obstacles to inclusion for LGBTQA+ student-athletes and how to build environments of inclusion. As in Sara's case, an assistant coach played a pivotal role in helping her understand policy and procedures for transgender athletes.

LGBTQA+ student-athletes' experiences are dynamic and varied, and their perceptions are shaped by a web of relationships with various campus stakeholders, including faculty, staff, administrators, coaches, and peers (Rankin et al., 2011). In striving to create effective strategies for combating homo/bi/trans/phobia, campus stakeholders must consider the unique circumstances of each individual group, the intersection of other identities (e.g., race, ethnicity), and their impact on one's gender and/or sexuality. For instance, the issues that transgender athletes like Sara face might be new to some higher education scholars, teachers, and practitioners. Campuses must assess the impacts of various campus entities—including athletics—to see if they provide safe and welcoming environments for transgender athletes. Because educators value diversity and inclusion, denying transgender athletes the same opportunities would go against the mission of most educational institutions and the NCAA's core values. The NCAA calls for institutions to provide equal opportunities to transgender athletes, to demonstrate that they value diversity by including and respecting transgender athletes, and to work collaboratively between the athletic department and families of the transgender athletes to provide safer environments for them to study and compete (NCAA, 2011). To support this goal, advisors should work collaboratively with trans student-athletes to understand what they need to feel supported.

As more institutions make strides to create a safe environment for LGBTQA+ students on a broader institutional level (e.g., revising institutional nondiscrimination policies, developing living communities for nonhetero-sexual students and allies), it is the micro cultures (e.g., classrooms, student organizations, athletic environments) where climate is experienced "most tangibly" (Stewart & Howard-Hamilton, 2015, p. 124). Since there is no monolithic academic and athletic culture (Anderson & Bullingham, 2015, p. 650), campus climate studies should be conducted annually to gauge how LGBTQA+ student-athletes are experiencing campus environments and whether these experiences impede their success. For instance, institutions could bring professional consultants to campus every 3 years (or so) to assess and recommend how athletic departments could survey their students about their experiences. Time could be given during team meetings, compliance meetings, and so on to assess the perceptions of LGBTQA+ and heterosexual student-athletes' experiences and perceptions of inclusivity.

Academic advisors are in a position to be strong catalysts for creating a safe and welcoming environment. Pfeiffer (2018) found that lesbian Division I student-athletes who had positive relationships with athletic academic advisors maintained high academic achievement (e.g., dean's list, conference honor roll) while meeting the demands of being a Division I student-athlete. For these participants, athletic advisors served as one of the main sources of personal and academic support. Advisors helped these student-athletes balance their academic demands by providing them with ongoing support such as monitored study hall, tutoring, academic mentoring, and sessions with the institution's sports psychologist and/or a counseling center staff psychologist. Because student-athletes may stay closeted to coaches and team-mates, academic advisors can play a crucial supportive role in the success of LGBTQA+ student-athletes.

When working with LGBTQA+ student-athletes like Sara, advisors may consider taking a holistic approach to understanding how the intersection of sexual, gender, race/ethnicity, and athletic identity characteristics shape the student's overall experience. An intersectional approach involves being culturally conscious, taking into consideration the complexities of various communities, and using social justice as a framework for social change: "Because intersectional work validates the lives and stories of previously ignored groups of people, it is seen as a tool that can be used to help empower communities and the people in them" (Dill & Zambrana, 2009, p. 12). We believe this approach will encourage students to show up in advising offices more frequently without the fear of having to silence parts of who they are. Advisors can do this by validating the feelings she is experiencing, while asking follow-up questions about what she needs at this time. It is important for academic advisors to allow Sara to lead the conversation and tell her own story. At times, academic advisors are looking to provide answers to complex problems, but, for many students, having a dedicated space to openly tell their story can be just as helpful. In considering appropriate referrals for Sara, academic advisors should consider what their institutions already offer. While offices of equity and inclusion vary, looking into nondiscrimination policies can be a good start in determining the level of legal support for sexual orientation, gender identity, and gender expression. Some institutions will have a dedicated LGBTQA+ resource center, while others will provide social services through an office of diversity. Academic advisors should consider their institution's student affairs offices, counseling services, intergroup dialogue contacts, and student-led organizations with specific focus on gender and sexuality. Connecting with other staff in these areas can be a great resource for academic advisors to continue their own education, while also gathering information for Sara or future students.

In addition, advisors can create safe spaces by disclosing their own sexual orientation (whether queer-identified or not), making themselves relatable, offering gestures of support and advocacy, placing pro-LGBTQA+ artifacts in their offices, and using inclusive language (Pfeiffer, 2018). For students like Sara, academic advisors can also simply listen and provide a space for students to validate their feelings without necessarily providing solutions. Advisors can also show their commitment outside of advising sessions by displaying LGBTQA+ signs, stickers, and resources (e.g., LGBTQA+-friendly magazines) in the waiting room, using bystander intervention skills (e.g., communicating concern when harmful language is used), and fostering an inclusive advising office free of homo/bi/trans/phobia. Through professional development opportunities, advisors can learn appropriate and inclusive language, become familiar with specific challenges faced by different groups of LGBTQA+ students, and engage in dialogue with other trainees who are experiencing the same difficulties and triumphs. This might include formalized trainings (e.g., ally training programs), webinars, and conference sessions. Through continued professional education, advisors will be more prepared to address LGBTQA+ issues in advising sessions and throughout campus.

Future Research

The gulf between LGBTQA+ empirical and theoretical scholarship and the work of athletic department administrators, coaches, and activists impedes progress toward inclusion in intercollegiate athletics (Cunningham, 2012). For instance, the "limited research on sexual identity in intercollegiate athletics suggests that the sport environment does little to encourage and support nonheterosexual identities" (Rankin et al., 2016, p. 704). The lack of scholarship in the advising literature regarding the intersections of LGBTQA+ student-athletes is a testament to this need. More research should investigate the intersection of gender and sexual identity with race and ethnic identity (Griffin, 2012). For example, the few studies that do exist focus on Black men who are socialized to behave in ways that are not only hyper-masculine, but also hyper-heterosexual (Harris et al., 2011; Southall et al., 2010). The literature says little about the experiences of lesbian, bisexual, and transgender individuals of color. Despite the demonstrated issues with homo/bi/trans/phobia in college athletics, little research investigating how these phobias affect college students is available. More studies on homo/bi/trans/phobia will enhance our understanding of the struggles of LGBTQA+ student-athletes. Knowledge of how these identities interact can help athletic administrators and academic advisors create safe and welcoming environments for LGBTQA+ student-athletes.

Conclusion

Despite sincere efforts to provide welcoming environments, some institutions are not immune to negative societal attitudes about LGBTQA+ issues, and discriminatory behaviors lead to hostile environments (Williams, 2013). Change among sport organizations and institutions is slow, and until policies have consequences for noncompliance, the sport climate for LGBTQA+ students will not improve (Griffin, 2014). Denial of the prevalence of homo/bi/trans/phobia has plagued collegiate athletics for years; silencing and closeting members of the LGBTQA+ community stunts their development and impacts team performance (Wolf-Wendel et al., 2008). The support of athletic academic advisors is integral to how comfortable and included LGBTQA+ student-athletes feel in athletic and academic environments. Thus, it is critical that athletic academic advisors who work with LGBTQA+ student-athletes have access to resources that will help them better engage with and support these students who may face obstacles that can impede their athletic and academic success.

References

Anderson, E. (2005). *In the game: Gay athletes and the cult of masculinity.* State University of New York Press.

Anderson, E., & Bullingham, R. (2015). Openly lesbian team sport athletes in an area of decreasing homohysteria. *International Review for the Sociology of Sport, 50*(6), 647–660. https://doi.org/10.1177%2F1012690213490520

Athlete Ally. (2017, January 5). *Athlete Ally lauds NCAA's decision to move championships from North Carolina.* https://www.athleteally.org/athlete-ally-lauds-ncaas-decision-move-championships-north-carolinaNC

Baker, A. R., & Hawkins, B. J. (2016). Academic and career advancement for Black male athletes at NCAA division I institutions. *New Directions for Adult and Continuing Education, 2016*(150), 71–82. https://doi.org/10.1002/ace.20187

Benson, K. F. (2000). Constructing academic inadequacy: African American athletes' stories of schooling. *Journal of Higher Education, 71*(2), 223–246. https://doi.org/10.2307/2649249

Beron, K. J., & Piquero, A. R. (2016). Studying the determinants of student-athlete grade point average: The roles of identity, context, and academic interests. *Social Science Quarterly, 97*(2), 142–160. https://doi.org/10.1111/ssqu.12235

Brewer, B. W., van Raalte, J. L., & Linder, D. E. (1993). Athletic identity: Hercules' muscle or Achilles heel? *International Journal of Sport Psychology, 24*, 237–254.

Cunningham, G. B. (2012). Bridging the gap: Researchers and activists pursuing LGBT equality in sport. In G. B. Cunningham (Ed.), *Sexual orientation and gender identity in sport: Essays from activists, coaches, and scholars* (pp. 69–77). Center for Sport Management Research and Education.

Cunningham, G. B. (2015). LGBT inclusive athletic departments as agents of social change. *Journal of Intercollegiate Sport, 8*, 43–56. https://doi.org/10.1123/jis.2014-0131

Dill, B. T., & Zambrana, R. E. (2009). Critical thinking about inequality: An emerging lens. In B. T. Dill and R. E. Zambrana (Eds.), *Emerging intersections: Race, class, and gender in theory, policy, and practice* (pp. 1–21). Rutgers University Press.

Fenwick, D., & Simpson, D. (2017). The experience of coming out as a gay male athlete. *Journal of Sport Behavior, 40*(2), 131–155.

Forest, L. (2006, December 1). Advising gay, lesbian, bisexual, and transgender students. *Academic Advising Today, 29*(4). https://nacada.ksu.edu/Resources/Academic-Advising-Today/View-Articles/Advising-Gay-Lesbian-Bisexual-and-Transgender-Students.aspx

Gray, A., Crandall, R. E., & Tongsri, J. (2018). Transgender student-athletes and their inclusion in intercollegiate athletics. *New Directions for Student Services, 2018*(163), 43–53. https://doi.org/10.1002/ss.20269

Greim, R. D. (2016). *You can play, but can you be yourself? How LGBT and non-LGBT student-athletes perceive the climate of NCAA Division I athletic departments* (Publication No. 10127826) [Doctoral dissertation, University of Missouri–Kansas City]. ProQuest Dissertations and Theses Global.

Griffin, P. (2012). LGBT equity in sports: Celebrating our successes and facing our challenges. In G. B. Cunningham (Ed.), *Sexual orientation and gender identity in sport: Essays from activists, coaches and scholars* (pp. 1–12). Center for Sport Management Research and Education.

Griffin, P. (2014). Overcoming sexism and homophobia in women's sports: Two steps forward and one step back. In J. Hargreaves & E. Anderson (Eds.), *Routledge handbook of sport, gender, and sexuality* (pp. 265–274). Routledge.

Griffin, P., & Taylor, H. (2013). *Champions of respect: Inclusion of LGBTQA+ student-athletes and staff in NCAA programs.* National Collegiate Athletic Association.

Harris, F., III., Palmer, R. T., & Struve, L. E. (2011). "Cool Posing" on campus: A qualitative study of masculinities and gender expression among Black men at a private research institution. *The Journal of Negro Education, 80*(1), 47–62. http://www.jstor.org/stable/41341105

Joslin, J. (2007). Lesbian, gay, bisexual, transgender, and queer students. In L. Huff & P. Jordan (Eds.), *Advising special student populations: Adult learners, community college students, LGBTQA+ students, multicultural students, students on probation, undecided students* (pp. 87–99). NACADA.

Krane, V. (2001). We can be athletic and feminine, but do we want to? Challenging hegemonic femininity in women's sport. *Quest, 53*, 115–133. https://doi.org/10.1080/00336297.2001.10491733

Leslie-Toogood, A. L., & Gill, E. (Eds.). (2008). *Advising student-athletes: A collaborative approach to success.* NACADA. https://nacada.ksu.edu/Resources/Clearinghouse/View-Articles/Advising-Student-Athletes.aspx

Lucas-Carr, C., & Krane, V. (2012). Troubling sport or troubled by sport. *Journal for the Study of Sports and Athletes in Education, 6*(1), 21–44. https://doi.org/10.1179/ssa.2012.6.1.21

Marine, S. B. (2011). *Stonewall's legacy: Bisexual, gay, lesbian, and transgender students in higher education.* Wiley.

Menke, D. J. (2013). Student-athletes in transition: Applying the Schlossberg model. *Academic Advising Today, 36*(3). http://www.nacada.ksu.edu/Resources/Academic-Advising-Today/View-Articles/Student-Athletes-in-Transition-Applying-the-Schlossberg-Model.aspx

Menke, D. J. (2016). Inside the bubble: A look at the experiences of student-athletes in revenue-producing sports during college and beyond. *Journal for the Study of Sports and Athletes in Education, 10*(1), 16–32. https://doi.org/10.1080/19357397.2016.1160695

Menke, D., McGill, C. M., & Fletcher, J. (2015). *Advising lesbian, gay, bisexual, transgender, and queer student athletes.* NACADA Clearinghouse. http://www.nacada.ksu.edu/Resources/Clearinghouse/View-Articles/Advising-LGBTQA-Athletes.aspx

National Collegiate Athletic Association. (2011). *NCAA inclusion of transgender athletes.* http://www.ncaa.org/sites/default/files/Transgender_Handbook_2011_Final.pdf

Oswalt, S. B. (2016). College athletes. In A. E. Goldberg (Ed.), *The SAGE encyclopedia of LGBTQA studies* (pp. 237–239). SAGE.

Pfeiffer, M. E. (2018). *Exploration of the experiences of self-identified lesbian division I student-athletes in the United States* (Publication No. 2049711866) [Doctoral dissertation, University of Memphis]. ProQuest Dissertations and Theses Global.

Rankin, S. R., & Merson, D. (2012). *Campus pride 2012 LGBTQA national college athlete report.* Campus Pride. https://www.campuspride.org/wp-content/uploads/CampusPride-Athlete-Report-Exec-Summary.pdf

Rankin, S. R., Merson, D., Garvey, J. C., Sorgen, C. H., Menon, I., Loya, K., & Oseguera, L. (2016). The influence of climate on the academic and athletic success of student-athletes: Results from a multi-institutional national study. *The Journal of Higher Education, 87*(5), 701–730. https://doi.org/10.1353/jhe.2016.0027

Rankin, S. R., Merson, D., Sorgen, C. H., McHale, I., Loya, K., & Oseguera, L. (2011). *Student-athlete climate study (SACS) final report.* Center for the Study of Higher Education, The Pennsylvania State University. https://www.ncaa.org/sites/default/files/SACs%2BReport%2BFinal%2B11-6-2012.pdf

Rankin, S. R., Weber, G., Blumenfeld, W., & Frazer, S. (2010). *2010 state of higher education for lesbian, gay, bisexual & transgender people.* Campus Pride. https://www.campuspride.org/wp-content/uploads/campuspride2010lgbtreportssummary.pdf

Renn, K. A., & Patton, L. (2010). Campus ecology and environments. In J. D. Schuh, S. R. Jones, & S. L. Harper (Eds.), *Student services: A handbook for the profession* (pp. 242–256). Jossey-Bass.

Renn, K. A., & Pitcher, E. N. (2016). College students. In A. E. Goldberg (Ed.), *The SAGE encyclopedia of LGBTQA studies* (pp. 239–244). SAGE.

Rubin, L. M., & Moses, R. A. (2017). Athletic subculture within student-athlete academic centers. *Sociology of Sport Journal, 34*(4), 317–328. https://doi.org/10.1123/ssj.2016-0138

Self, C. (2007). Advising lesbian, gay, bisexual, and transgender first-year students. In M. S. Hunter, B. McCalla-Wriggins, & E. R. White (Eds.), *Academic advising: New insights for teaching and learning in the first year* (pp. 213–221). National Resource Center for the First-Year Experience and Students in Transition.

Semerjian, T. Z., & Cohen, J. H. (2006). "FTM means female to me:" Transgender athletes performing gender. *Women in Sport and Activity Journal, 15*(2), 28–43. https://doi.org/10.1123/wspaj.15.2.28

Southall, R. M., Anderson, E. D., Nagel, M. S., Polite, F. G., & Southall, C. (2010). An investigation of ethnicity as a variable related to US male college athletes' sexual orientation behaviours and attitudes. *Ethnic and Racial Studies, 34*(2), 293–313. https://doi.org/10.1080/01419870.2010.4954090

Stack, A. L., & Staurowsky, E. J. (1998). *College athletes for hire: The evolution and legacy of the NCAA's amateur myth.* Praeger.

Stewart, D. L., & Howard-Hamilton, M. F. (2015). Engaging lesbian, gay, and bisexual students on college campuses. In S. J. Quaye & S. R. Harper (Eds.), *Student engagement in higher education: Theoretical perspectives and practical approaches for diverse populations* (2nd ed., pp. 121–134). Routledge.

Waldron, J. J. (2016). It's complicated: Negotiations and complexities of being a lesbian in sport. *Sex Roles, 74,* 335–346. https://doi.org/10.1007/s11199-015-0521-x

Williams, D. (2013). *Strategic diversity leadership: Activating change and transformation in higher education.* Stylus.

Wolf-Wendel, L., Bajaj, A., & Spriggs, T. (2008). Responding to the needs of lesbian, gay and bisexual student-athletes and their team members. In A. Leslie-Toogood & E. Gill (Eds.), *Advising student-athletes: A collaborative approach to success* (pp. 31–36). NACADA.

12

ADVISING LGBTQA+ STUDENTS IN STEM MAJORS

Natalie S. Oliner and Craig M. McGill

Academic advisors and college student personnel are often trained using research on supporting underrepresented student populations, like women in science, technology, engineering, and mathematics (STEM) majors and lesbian, gay, bisexual, transgender, queer/questioning, and asexual (LGBTQA+) students in postsecondary education. However, there is little discussion about the intersection of advising LGBTQA+ students in STEM fields. What happens when gender identity, gender expression, and sexual orientation are considered when examining student experiences? How do the experiences of masculine cisgender gay men, for example, differ from those of feminine cisgender heterosexual women in STEM fields? Or, how do the experiences of transgender women in STEM differ from those of transgender men? How do these collective experiences differ from heterosexual cisgender men or women?

STEM disciplines are often characterized as objective and neutral. This characterization, as well as historical career trajectories in which men entered the workforce and women adopted domestic lifestyles, assisted in creating a STEM gender gap. Once women began to pursue nondomestic occupations, they often studied caretaking or supportive/clerical disciplines while men continued to dominate STEM and other fields. Despite a presence of all genders in the workforce, STEM fields still tend to be composed of men, although gender ratios vary according to each STEM subfield (e.g., women tend to be more represented in biological sciences, which aligns with social stereotypes of women pursuing nurturing, human-centric careers; Hill et al., 2010; Sax et al., 2016; Stout et al., 2016). This male domination establishes a more conservative, heteronormative environment in STEM that creates

199

barriers for underrepresented identities in relation to race, gender (identity and expression), and sexual orientation (Cech & Waidzunas, 2011).

An ample amount of literature outlines the barriers women and underrepresented racial identities experience in STEM, but there is limited empirical research that focuses on LGBTQA+ students and individuals that identify along the vast gender spectrum. This includes transgender, genderqueer, and other gender nonconforming (GNC) individuals who do not adhere to the gender binary of man/masculine or woman/feminine. With minimal literature on LGBTQA+ students in STEM, and even less on how to advise these students, we aim to illuminate issues LGBTQA+ students encounter within STEM learning environments. After reviewing the STEM climate, and challenges LGTBQA+ students face within it, we situate our analysis of the issues around a vignette. Throughout the analysis, we suggest that the approaches for working with women in STEM provide efficient strategies for advising LGBTQA+ students in STEM.

As a way of positioning ourselves, we have been working as academic advisors for several years. Natalie identifies as a cisgender pansexual White woman who is culturally Jewish, a third-generation college student, and from the American South. Craig is a cisgender gay White man, and a fourth-generation college student from a middle-class family in the American Midwest. We acknowledge numerous layers of privilege in our identities.

Challenges of LGTBQA+ Students in STEM

Despite changing times, LGBTQA+ people still face many obstacles on college campuses. However, LGBTQA+ STEM students may experience especially unique challenges. For instance, in one study, LGB engineering students spent a significant amount of energy constructing a self that was acceptable in their environment (Cech & Waidzunas, 2011). The technical/social dualism plays an important role in students' lives as they may believe that the feelings they are grappling with are irrelevant to anything they experience in school (Cech, 2013). One aspect of this dualism is the mapping of gendered stereotypes that portray gay men as feminine and lesbian women as masculine. To deal with the complexities of their identities, the participants resorted to various coping methods to navigate their heteronormative environments. As a result, two ideologies prevailed. The first was "depoliticization," an ideology that views social or political issues as irrelevant or antithetical to engineering work while technical competencies are championed (Cech, 2013). The second is a belief in the meritocratic ideology, which posits that one achieves success through talent and hard work. It also legitimizes social inequality and relieves engineers of social responsibility. The profession, thus, shapes individuals from varied backgrounds into a mainstream ideology of thinking, and in the process, alienates many who do not fit into the dominant paradigm.

Additionally, opportunities to be more inclusive of all people in STEM course content is often prevented by a traditionalist view of the world. Lessons are often taught in absolutes. For instance, animal behavior is presented in a dichotomous framework wherein males act in one way and females act in another. Other examples include the interchangeability of the terms *gender* and *sex* the focus on evolution and reproduction in biology courses, and the disease model that explains any variance as an abnormality. Discussions about sexually transmitted infections focus on heterosexual transmission with little acknowledgment of why homosexual men are at higher risk of infection. These discussions establish a social stigma against anyone who may not fit into the heteronormative box (Dermer et al., 2010; Linley et al., 2018).

STEM students are typically concerned with at least two relational domains: professors and peers. Advisors need to understand the significance of each so they can better support students and help them navigate these domains.

Regardless of what a student plans to do postgraduation, a well-developed relationship with a faculty member is critical in the STEM fields. Students require an excellent letter of recommendation to enter competitive graduate or professional programs. In an ideal world, students could feel free to open up to their advisors and faculty members, but LGBTQA+ students may not be willing to take a chance in heteronormative environments. Additionally, students may fear that faculty members will view their sexuality as irrelevant to their work (Cech & Waidzunas, 2011). Thus, LGBTQA+ students are often left to make assumptions as to why a professor left potentially relevant material out of the course content: Was it the professor's discomfort or perception of irrelevancy? Were they simply trying to avoid controversy?

The second relational domain is other students. Because STEM courses generally lack a focus on social issues (Cech, 2013), LGBTQA+ STEM students may find it difficult to relate to other LGBTQA+ students because those peers may not be "out" or because they are simply unaware of potential LGBTQA+ content missing from classes. Additionally, extensive time requirements for labs and studying may leave students with less time to find safe spaces to connect with LGBTQA+ students, form relationships, and be included in social circles:

> There are things that people don't talk about in engineering, like being strong, or being open . . . Anything out of the ordinary, people just don't talk about. It's like this cloud . . . if it's not engineering-related, it's pushed to the side and not talked about. (Cech & Waidzunas, 2011, p. 11)

This "cloud" illustrates what LGBTQA+ STEM students may experience when trying to bond and make connections with other students. They feel the need to compartmentalize their LGBTQA+ and STEM identities because peers (and professors) might deem their identity as irrelevant, causing students to feel unsafe or uncomfortable.

Even in common meeting spots (e.g., resource centers on campus), students may have trouble identifying and connecting with LGBTQA+ students in the arts, humanities, education, and social sciences where sexuality and identity discussions are more common and accepted. Heteronormative environments give permission to those belonging to the dominant culture to isolate marginalized individuals. Heteronormality is even encountered in applying technical concepts:

> One of my friends who is a mechanical engineer was describing the body as a mechanical engine that only functions under various strains and stresses and relationships. And he didn't think that gayness was one of those relationships . . . basically, "the man is the plug and the woman is the outlet and if there are two plugs, how is [anything] going to charge?" (Cech & Waidzunas, 2011, p. 10)

Unwittingly, this person used engineering concepts to champion heterosexuality and de-legitimize homosexuality. Comments such as these can also make LGBTQA+ students feel unsafe and devalued, leading them to further compartmentalize their identities.

Ultimately, these negative environments may impact retention within STEM majors and the university. For instance, many gay men "prematurely foreclose on career choices because of limited awareness or constriction of self-concept" (Prince, 1995, p. 169). Understanding societal contexts and their ramifications for identity factors will help advisors better serve their students (Gedro, 2009).

The following vignette illustrates a possible example of what an LGBTQA+ student might experience when navigating STEM fields, in and outside of the classroom. Both queer theory (see chapter 4) and intersectionality (chapter 5) provide insight into this scenario. Each framework highlights the intersecting identities of students (intersectionality), especially of those students who identify as queer, and how they navigate oppressive systems.

Vignette

Johnny is a cisgender Latino male who was adopted at birth by a White family from a small rural community in the Midwest. In high school,

Johnny was a high-achieving student as well as a talented football and basketball player. He was involved in several clubs, volunteered regularly with his church youth group, and tutored middle-school students in math and science. Despite his popularity and athleticism, Johnny never had a serious girlfriend in high school and showed little interest in dating. Upon graduation, Johnny decided to attend a large, public research institution on the other side of the country. He had not yet come out to anyone as gay, but he knew it was only a matter of time once he went away to college.

During his first year of college, Johnny enjoyed his premed courses, and also appreciated learning about diverse identities and cultures through his general education courses. However, he became curious in his gender studies course when the topic turned to intersectionality in relation to gender identities, gender expressions, and sexual orientations. Specifically, he was concerned about how his own sexual orientation intersected with his race and religion. Despite the love he received from his politically conservative family, Johnny never felt *whole*. The content he learned produced dissonance relating to what he was taught about sex, sexual orientation, gender, and religion. Having no Latino racial or cultural influences from his family or peers, he never thought about what it meant to be Latino, Catholic, *and* gay. As a result, Johnny joined clubs on campus (one LGBTQA+-specific organization, the other for men of color), began dating men, and became a fierce advocate for trans rights. In addition to exploring his sexuality for the first time, Johnny also considered how he might merge his interests in LGBTQA+ issues with his premed biology major. After attending an LGBTQA+ healthcare seminar that his physiology instructor advertised, he became passionate about working with people seeking gender-affirming surgery.

At the beginning of Johnny's junior year, Johnny scheduled a meeting with his faculty advisor, Dr. Ashley Michaels, to discuss preparing for the Medical College Admission Test (MCAT), internship opportunities, and applying to medical school. Johnny developed a rapport with Dr. Michaels during his first 2 years at college and knew she was aware of his dedication to his academics as evidenced by his impressive 3.75 GPA, so he hoped she would agree to write him a letter of recommendation. During their conversation, Johnny wanted to mention his interest in working with trans individuals and disclose his sexual orientation, but he was not sure how she would react. Dr. Michaels' letter of recommendation would be paramount to his medical school application, so he did not want to share any information that might hinder her willingness to write a letter. About halfway through the meeting, Johnny mustered the courage to tell Dr. Michaels about his sexual orientation and his interests in trans work. Although she was courteous, Dr. Michaels implied that his identity and interests were separate issues from Johnny's science coursework and if he really wanted to go to medical school, he should focus on his studies. While relieved Dr. Michaels agreed to write his letter of recommendation, Johnny left disappointed, wondering if Dr. Michaels actually supported him and whether he would be able to pursue his passion in working with trans individuals. Dr. Michaels simply didn't "get it."

At the end of his junior year, Johnny decided to return home for the summer to shadow the family physician, Dr. Smith. Although Johnny realized this was an opportunity for him to gain valuable shadowing experience, he felt uneasy because he witnessed Dr. Smith express subtly racist remarks in the past. In addition, Johnny was anxious about being away from the queer and Latinx communities that became integral support systems for him while at college.

As he prepared for his summer internship, Johnny became more shaken—if a generally warm faculty advisor reacted negatively toward his identity and areas of interest, how would the older men in the department, the family doctor, or medical school professionals respond? He felt disheartened that an issue so essential to him was considered cursory, at best, and career-ruining, at worst. Nonetheless, Johnny began researching gender confirmation surgery and the potential needs of patients. He became fascinated by the process and stunned by how much his anatomy course raised his thinking about this social issue. Additionally, as Johnny considered his own identities and possible contribution to the field, he became acutely aware of the low representation of gay Latino physicians. His lab experiences and independent search about the profession caused Johnny anxiety and made him feel like an imposter. However, he also felt energized about his future. Johnny had so many questions and wanted to discuss them with another faculty member, but fearing their response, Johnny decided to focus on his homework, where he could temporarily retreat from the pressures of his future.

Analysis of Issues

What might an academic advisor do to help Johnny sort through these issues? Johnny's experience highlights important academic, personal, and professional issues LGBTQA+ STEM students often navigate.

Before reading this section, we encourage a review of the Appendix. Consider the questions there and then consider what you would do when working with Johnny and other LGBTQA+ students in STEM. Using Johnny's experiences and the existing literature on LGBTQA+ and STEM students, we discuss issues related to academic guidance, identity navigation, stereotype threat and representation, organizations and mentorship, and professional development.

Academic Guidance

Johnny is enduring significant stress as he struggles with his racial and queer identity in his personal, academic, and professional life, especially regarding his interest in attending medical school to be able to work with trans people. When advising a student like Johnny, it is important to openly acknowledge his various identities and his multiple stressors as well as to inquire about his support systems and well-being. Johnny's identity as a gay Latino man is prominent throughout his personal, academic, and professional paths. Therefore, it is important to affirm his sexual orientation, race, and other identities. An advisor could help Johnny search for academic and professional opportunities to work with LGBTQA+ patients while also connecting him with medical mentor programs for LGBTQA+ and/or Latinx students. By discussing various pathways to pursue his passions and connect with professionals who share his identity, Johnny's advisor would provide him support to pursue work that does not require him to compartmentalize his identity.

Identity Navigation

Intersectionality highlights the different ways our multiple identities and the social systems we live in affect our lived experiences. These experiences can be particularly strenuous when an individual has a marginalized identity (or identities) and must navigate an oppressive system or institution (Jones, 2015). Johnny struggles to navigate the constructed norms within his STEM environment as a gay Latino man, feeling he needs to keep his personal identity separate from his work. Unfortunately, when talking to his faculty advisor, Johnny attempted to integrate his identities with his coursework and career goals, but Dr. Michaels told him to compartmentalize his identities. She even suggested his nonscience coursework and commitment to social justice issues were irrelevant to the work that really mattered for his career. Interactions like these make students feel they must hide their identities and separate their personal identities from their work. However, managing one's identity ("passing" and "covering") by trying to keep one's life "compartmentalized" can have an emotional and educational toll on LGBTQA+ students (Cech & Waidzunas, 2011). This is especially true in heteronormative and unwelcoming environments like engineering, which can lead LGBTQA+ students to feel isolated, anxious, and unable to succeed in their chosen academic and career path (Cech & Waidzunas, 2011).

While considering his gay identity and queer medical research topic, Johnny is also concerned about returning to his predominantly White hometown after an academic year where he connected with other students of color. With low representation of Latinx medical professionals in his rural community, Johnny realizes he will continue to enter predominantly White spaces. After struggling with his identity in terms of his family and home community, learning STEM course content that ignores or conflicts with his identity, and having his identity dismissed by a faculty advisor, Johnny is hesitant to be open (or "out") at school and in the medical field, especially as a gay Latino man. Therefore, Johnny must manage different identities simultaneously (bifurcation), which can lead to burnout (Smith, 1987).

GNC students can also experience similar but unique barriers regarding identity management and anxiety. Even if a student is confident in their ability to pass as a cisgender individual, they are still potentially hiding a part of themselves. Like LGB students, GNC students may also feel the need to keep their identities hidden, particularly in majors and fields that have conventional and conservative gender norms (Cech & Waidzunas, 2011; Chung, 2001; Forest, 2006). For example, business schools often require men to wear suits and women to wear dresses or skirts for class presentations without considering those who do not fit into our society's dichotomous gender categories (Nicolazzo, 2016). This requirement can encourage students to adopt a mindset that their identity must be kept completely separate from their academic and professional life (Cech & Waidzunas, 2011; Chung, 2001; Forest, 2006; Moorhead, 2005). In fact, one student remarked, "In the business world, you're supposed to suppress your personal life anyways—it's like it's not part of your job" (Moorhead, 2005, para. 14). This bifurcation can be anxiety-inducing for students as they have to constantly manage what they say and how they act, while hiding their authentic selves when at school or work (Cech & Waidzunas, 2011; Chung, 2001). After having connected with other queer students of color, Johnny might have learned to become more comfortable with his university surroundings. Therefore, returning home may disrupt his newfound confidence and connection with other people of color.

Stereotype Threat and Representation

Another factor to consider is that LGBTQA+ STEM students may suppress certain identity characteristics to avoid stereotype threat (Pronin et al., 2004). STEM environments are frequently composed of White heterosexual cisgender males. While Johnny's academic field—biology—is sometimes an exception to this norm, the STEM environment can still be unwelcoming to non-White, nonheterosexual, and noncisgender individuals. When examining enrollment, retention, and graduation rates of women and underrepresented racial identities in STEM majors, researchers highlight stereotype threat as one explanation for the continuing trend of White men making up most of the STEM workforce (Shapiro & Williams, 2011; Steele et al., 2002; Stout et al., 2016). Stereotype threat (i.e., the apprehension that one's performance will align with a common (mis)conception or stereotype about their gender or race) can emerge in various ways (Shapiro & Williams, 2011; Steele et al., 2002). For example, a woman might perform poorly on a mathematics exam if prompted to disclose her gender at the beginning of the exam because she internalized the idea that women are not successful in math (Grossman & Porche, 2014; LaCosse et al., 2016; Robnett, 2016; Spencer et al., 1999). Should the theory of stereotype threat hold true for women and other minorities in STEM, LGBTQA+ students likely also experience difficulty finding their place in and navigating through historically conservative STEM fields (Cech & Waidzunas, 2011).

Johnny identifies as a man, which puts him in the gender majority within STEM majors, but his identity as a gay Latino man may cause him to question his ability to succeed in the predominantly White heterosexual medical field. He may also struggle to be his authentic self while pursuing his interest in working with trans people. In particular, he has learned about the machismo stereotype and, at times, feels pressure to perform hypermasculinity. Expectations of gender appearances and performance may also affect trans students who can feel like outsiders at risk of being targeted if their coworkers discover their gender identity. This constant attention to passing and fear of being "found out" can create an extreme psychological strain and cause students to experience poor well-being from a sense that they do not belong, especially when they do not know others who share their identity in the field.

Organizations and Mentorship

LGBTQA+ STEM students likely do not have LGBTQA+ role models in the STEM disciplines due to the invisibility of LGBTQA+ members and the field's systemic marginalization of LGBTQA+ persons. Additionally, faculty members, classmates, and coworkers might view being "out" in the classroom or at work as inappropriate, unprofessional, irrelevant, "private business," or as an attempt to push a political agenda. Thus, LGBTQA+ students assume the professional code is to stay silent, leaving them to navigate the heteronormative environments on their own.

Fortunately, organizations have developed initiatives to support underrepresented students in STEM due to the lack of gender, racial, and sexual orientation diversity in the field. For example, organizations such as the Society of Women Engineers (SWE), the National Society of Black Engineers (NSBE), the Society of Hispanic Professional Engineers (SHPE), and oSTEM: Out in Science, Technology, Engineering, and Mathematics, Inc. provide opportunities for underrepresented individuals to gather in a safe, supportive space where they can discuss academic and professional issues that are related to navigating their identity in STEM.

Although these organizations continue to make a significant impact in STEM fields, these populations are still underrepresented. Therefore, representation and mentorship are crucial in continuing to increase STEM pursuit, retention, and success. McGill and Woudenberg (2012) tailored Hill et al.'s (2010) recommendations for increasing women in STEM fields. We are adapting them to be inclusive of all racial, sexual, and gender marginalized students:

- Encourage students with racial, sexual, or gender marginalized identities to consider a STEM major when participating in high school college fairs or conducting campus visits.
- Send inclusive messages in marketing materials, curriculum, and mission/vision statements.
- Speak with faculty members about stereotype threat and benefits of growth mindset.
- Advocate for diverse representation of faculty and staff mentors.
- Find ways to proactively support marginalized students in STEM majors.
- Counter bias and raise awareness about systemic inequality and oppression.
- Learn about your own implicit biases.

With these strategies, advisors can help increase the support and visibility of racial, sexual, and gender marginalized students in STEM fields. For example, STEM professionals can meet with LGBTQA+ student groups in the K–12 system and encourage them to consider pursuing STEM. STEM personnel can also provide professional development opportunities for higher education staff and faculty to be inclusive and supportive and to discuss topics like stereotype threat. When STEM professionals and advisors are educated about the unique barriers of different types of identities, it is more likely that a school will be more welcoming and supportive for LGBTQA+ students like Johnny.

One such way to support LGBTQA+ STEM students is to promote involvement in student organizations and connection to mentors. Although all underrepresented students can benefit from mentors, LGBTQA+ STEM students can experience unique barriers based on their identity. For example, one study found that male-to-female (MtF) trans students had fewer mentors and leadership roles on campus, suggesting these students lost their male privilege and were forced to navigate social norms where women experience more difficulty entering leadership roles, especially in male-dominated fields (Dugan et al., 2012). Therefore, it is crucial that advisors encourage LGBTQA+ and other marginalized STEM students to get involved in organizations like oSTEM, SWE, NSBE, and SHPE. It is also important for advisors to recommend resources for connecting these students to mentors, especially those who are out as LGBTQA+. Advisors, faculty members, and organizations should also encourage dialogue about heteronormativity in the same way they are beginning to encourage discussions about gender and race/ethnicity (Joslin, 2007).

Professional Development

The recommendations and strategies for working with LGBTQA+ STEM students often mirror other marginalized groups (McGill & Woudenberg, 2012), but these strategies can carry different weight and meaning based on the particular population. For example, many professionals have a working knowledge of gender typically referring to men and women and sex referring to male and female, but professionals often need further education about individuals who do not identify within those binaries. Advisors and other higher education professionals might have to advocate for LGBTQA+ and racially marginalized students like Johnny because STEM faculty members, staff, and professionals may not be as familiar with these students' identities, experiences, and needs as they might be with White, cisgender, and/or heterosexual student experiences. One way to advocate would be to correct a faculty member who does not use a student's personal pronouns. Increasing higher education professionals' awareness of the needs of LGBTQA+ STEM students can lead to improved campus policy, campus organizations, and campus culture.

Additionally, advisors need to be cognizant of the ways marginalized identities are discussed or depicted within STEM fields—e.g., women being included in marketing materials (positive) or people of color being tokenized (negative). Similarly, when working with LGBTQA+ STEM students, advisors should "increase visibility," "promote understanding," "facilitate and support" students and LGBTQA+ initiatives, and "speak up" (Moorhead, 2005, para. 20). In addition to referring students to specific resources and advocating for LGBTQA+ students within the department, institution, or field more broadly, advisors must also be reflective and continue their professional development to best support students on an interpersonal level (McGill, 2013).

When working with students like Johnny, it is important to be educated about the multiple dimensions of a student's identity and what those identities mean to them. In addition, advisors should be aware of their support system and well-being. For example, Johnny may only disclose that his faculty advisor is not supportive of his identity during a discussion related to needing a letter of recommendation. While discussing how to request a recommendation letter, advisors should check in with students about how they feel regarding their experience with a professor and ask if they are experiencing any additional stressors.

Through ongoing personal and professional development, advisors can develop the knowledge and skills needed to support LGBTQA+ students as they navigate the historically conservative norms of STEM fields. Connecting LGBTQA+ STEM students to resources also helps create a supportive environment. This can include creating and promoting a space where LGBTQA+ STEM students feel comfortable expressing their identity, like the University of Louisville's J. B. Speed School of Engineering "Speed Spectrum" organization for LGBTQ and ally engineering students (Oliner, 2016). To help create an inclusive environment for LGBTQA+ STEM students and support their holistic success, advisors can celebrate LGBTQA+-identifying STEM professionals and their contributions to their fields (the National Organization of Gay and Lesbian Scientists and Technical Professionals [NOGLSTP] has compiled a list), partner with multicultural program offices to increase awareness through LGBTQA+ education and professional development for faculty members and staff, and connect students to professional organizations (oSTEM for fellow student support) and "out" faculty members (MentorNET for mentorship from professionals and faculty members). These practices reflect advisors' concern for the whole student—beyond academics—which is central to NACADA's core values of caring and inclusivity (NACADA, 2017). Advisors should continually hold themselves accountable by being educated about and trained on the latest trends and experiences of LGBTQA+ STEM students.

References

Cech, E. A. (2013). The (mis)framing of social justice: Why ideologies of depoliticization and meritocracy hinder engineers' ability to think about social injustices. In J. Lucena (Ed.), *Engineering Education for Social Justice* (pp. 67–84). Springer.

Cech, E. A. & Waidzunas, T. J. (2011). Navigating the heteronormativity of engineering: The experiences of lesbian, gay, and bisexual students. *Engineering Studies, 3*(1), 1–24. https://doi.org/10.1080/19378629.2010.545065

Chung, Y. B. (2001). Work discrimination and coping strategies: Conceptual frameworks for counseling lesbian, gay, and bisexual clients. *The Career Development Quarterly, 50*(1), 33–44. https://doi.org/10.1002/j.2161-0045.2001.tb00887.x

Dermer, S. B., Smith, S. D., & Barto, K. K. (2010). Identifying and correctly labeling sexual prejudice, discrimination, and oppression. *Journal of Counseling & Development, 88*(3), 325–331. https://doi.org/10.1002/j.1556-6678.2010.tb00029.x

Dugan, J. P, Kusel, M. L, & Simounet, D. M. (2012). Transgender college students: An exploratory study of perceptions, engagement, and educational outcomes. *Journal of College Student Development, 53*(5), 719–736. https://doi.org/10.1353/csd.2012.0067

Forest, L. (2006, December). Advising gay, lesbian, bisexual, and transgender students. *Academic Advising Today. 29*(4), 7–17. https://nacada.ksu.edu/Resources/Academic-Advising-Today/View-Articles/Advising-Gay-Lesbian-Bisexual-and-Transgender-Students.aspx

Gedro, J. (2009). LGBT career development. *Advances in Developing Human Resources, 11*(1), 54–66. https://doi.org/10.1177%2F1523422308328396

Grossman, J. M. & Porche, M. V. (2014). Perceived gender and racial/ethnic barriers to STEM success. *Urban Education, 49*(6), 698–727. https://doi.org/10.1177/0042085913481364

Hill, C., Corbett, C., & St. Rose, A. (2010). *Why so few? Women in science, technology, engineering, and mathematics.* American Association of University Women.

Jones, S. R. (2015). *Intersectionality in educational research.* Stylus.

Joslin, J. (2007). Working with lesbian, gay, bisexual, transgender, and queer students. In P. Jordan & L. Huff (Eds.), *Advising special populations*, Monograph #17 (pp. 87–95). NACADA.

LaCosse, J., Sekaquaptewa, D., & Bennett, J. (2016). STEM stereotypic attribution bias among women in an unwelcoming science setting. *Psychology of Women Quarterly, 40*(3), 378–397. https://doi.org/10.1177/0361684316630965

Linley, J. L., Renn, K. A., & Woodford, M. R. (2018). Examining the ecological systems of LGBTQ STEM majors. *Journal of Women and Minorities in Science and Engineering, 24*(1), 1–16. https://doi.org/10.1615/JWomenMinorScienEng.2017018836

McGill, C. M. (2013, December). LGBTQA allyhood: Academic advisors reflect. *Academic Advising Today, 36*(4). https://nacada.ksu.edu/Resources/Academic-Advising-Today/View-Articles/LGBTQA-Allyhood-Academic-Advisors-Reflect.aspx

McGill, C. M., & Woudenberg, D. L., (2012, June). *Gender matters in STEM majors!* NACADA Clearinghouse of Academic Advising Resources. http://www.nacada.ksu.edu/Resources/Clearninghouse/View-Articles/Gender-issues-in-STEM-majors.aspx

Moorhead, C. (2005). *Advising lesbian, gay, bisexual, and transgender students in higher education.* NACADA Clearinghouse of Academic Advising Resources. http://nacada.ksu.edu/tabid/3318/articleType/ArticleView/articleId/1156/article.aspx

NACADA: The Global Community for Academic Advising. (2017). *NACADA core values of academic advising*. https://www.nacada.ksu.edu/Resources/Pillars/CoreValues.aspx

Nicolazzo, Z. (2016). *Trans* in college: Transgender students' strategies for navigating campus life and the institutional politics of inclusion*. Stylus.

Oliner, N. (2016, Winter). Speed spectrum: A LGBTQ and ally engineering student organization. *Intersections, 1*(1), 7. https://en.calameo.com/books/00467790863e168b836cc

Prince, J. (1995). Influences on the career development of gay men. *Career Development Quarterly, 44*(2), 168–178. https://doi.org/10.1002/j.2161-0045.1995.tb00683.x

Pronin, E., Steele, C. M., & Ross, L. (2004). Identity bifurcation in response to stereotype threat: Women and mathematics. *Journal of Experimental Social Psychology, 40*(2), 152–168. https://doi.org/10.1016/S0022-1031(03)00088-X

Robnett, R. D. (2016). Gender bias in STEM fields. *Psychology of Women Quarterly, 40*(1), 65–79. https://doi.org/10.1177/0361684315596162

Sax, L. J., Kanny, M. A., Jacobs, J. A., Whang, H., Weintraub, D. S., & Hroch, A. (2016). Understanding the changing dynamics of the gender gap in undergraduate engineering majors: 1971–2011. *Research in Higher Education, 57*, 570–600. https://doi.org/10.1007/s11162-015-9396-5

Shapiro, J. R., & Williams, A. M. (2011). The role of stereotype threats in undermining girls' and women's performance and interest in STEM fields. *Sex Roles, 66*(3–4), 175–183. https://doi.org/10.1007/s11199-011-0051-0

Smith, D. E. (1987). *The everyday world as problematic*. Northeastern University Press.

Spencer, S. J., Steele, C. M., & Quinn, D. M. (1999). Stereotype threat and women's math performance. *Journal of Experimental Social Psychology, 35*(1), 4–28. https://doi.org/10.1006/jesp.1998.1373

Steele, C. M., Spencer, S. J., & Aronson, J. (2002). Contending with group image: The psychology of stereotype and social identity threat. *Advances in Experimental Social Psychology, 34*, 379–440. https://doi.org/10.1016/S0065-2601(02)80009-0

Stout, J. G., Grunberg, V. A., & Ito, T. A. (2016). Gender roles and stereotypes about science careers help explain women and men's science pursuits. *Sex Roles, 75*, 490–499. https://doi.org/10.1007/s11199-016-0647-5

APPENDIX 12.A QUESTIONS FOR VIGNETTE

Environmental Considerations

- What are some significant stressors in Johnny's environment? How might these stressors complicate his academic experience?
- What might an advisor do to help Johnny when he is seeking a letter of recommendation from a faculty member who does not support his gay identity or work interest?

Identity Navigation

- How does intersectionality help to explain Johnny's navigation of his identity?
- Which identities seem to be accepted by STEM professionals? Which identities have been relegated to be of less importance?
- How might compartmentalizing various aspects of his identity impact Johnny?
- If an advisor recognizes Johnny is having difficulty compartmentalizing and managing different identity factors, what might they recommend?

Stereotype Threat and Representation

- How can advisors work with students who have internalized misconceptions based on their identity factors (e.g., women not being good enough in math to succeed in STEM disciplines)?
- How else might stereotype threat be a concern to the wellbeing of LGBTQA+ STEM students?

Organizations and Mentorship

- How might LGBTQA+ STEM students be impacted without LGBTQA+ role models within their disciplines?
- What are some tools LGBTQA+ STEM students might use when working with people who think their identities are irrelevant to the job?
- What are some resources or organizations advisors could share with LGBTQA+ STEM students?
- How might advisors work with LGBTQA+ students to make them feel comfortable enough to remain in STEM majors?
- How might getting involved with STEM organizations improve LGBTQA+ student experiences?

Intrapersonal/Reflective Practice*

- How does an LGBTQA+ STEM student's experience differ from my own?
- Am I making assumptions about a student based on visible and invisible areas of diversity?
- How do my assumptions about all students on this campus seem to fit or not fit this student?
- What student characteristics contribute to academic successes or challenges?
- What types of support does this student (and this campus) possess to address specific areas of diversity?

*These questions are adapted and/or directly quoted from Archambault, 2015, pp. 189–191.

Departmental Culture

- How might have Dr. Michael's approach with Johnny been different? What could she have done to better support Johnny?
- If an advisor overhears a faculty member use an incorrect pronoun for one of their students, what might they do?
- If an advisor hears that one of the departmental faculty members refuses to accept a student's chosen pronoun, what might they do?

Reference

Archambault, K. L. (2015). Developing self-knowledge as a first step toward cultural competence. In P. Folsom, F. Yoder, & J. E. Joslin (Eds.), *The new advisor guidebook: Mastering the art of academic advising* (2nd ed.; pp. 185–201). Jossey-Bass.

13

ADVISING TRANS STUDENTS

Resisting Tropes and Supporting Resilience

C. J. Venable and Kyle Inselman

Trans students have become the subject of increasing interest in higher education scholarship, although higher education research on trans people is not new. In the past, resources for academic advising addressed a monolithic "LGBTQA+ student," focusing primarily on the concerns of students who are not straight (e.g., Harding, 2008) or relying on theoretical frameworks for understanding sexual orientation (e.g., Joslin, 2007) but not gender identity. Because both cis and trans people can identify as lesbian, gay, bisexual, queer, and other marginalized sexual orientations, much of the work centered on the LGBTQA+ community speaks only to the LGB or Q identities held by some trans people. In this chapter, we highlight the need to consider trans students as both unique from others in the LGBTQA+ community and as holding multiple identities and interlocking oppressions, such as LGBQ or heterosexual identity. While trans people have always been part of the LGBTQA+ community, there are numerous experiences exclusive to trans people that cis (nontrans) people do not encounter.

Gender identity is separate from sexual orientation; for example, a trans lesbian woman and a cis lesbian woman share both gender identity and sexual orientation but differ in trans or cis status. This distinction requires specific attention to how the experiences of trans people differ from those of cis people. At the same time, it is also important to recognize the different experiences among, for example, white, Black, and Latinx trans gay men, or between Deaf and hearing cis bisexual women. Differences in trans or cis status, gender identity, sexual orientation, race, and ability affect individuals' experiences and the ways they are impacted by multiple interlocking systemic oppressions and barriers, a phenomenon Kimberlé Crenshaw (1989) referred to as intersectionality (see chapter 5). Therefore, while this chapter focuses on the specific impacts being trans can have on a student's life, we must recognize that trans or cis status is only one part of an individual's positionality. While it is important that we discuss the needs of trans students *as trans students*, we know students do not live their lives as a collection of siloed identities. Advisors should treat students as individuals while remaining aware of the compounding factors that multiple marginalization may have on any student's experience.

In this chapter, we use *trans* to encompass a broad set of people under what is commonly called the *trans umbrella*, which includes people of many identities whose gender identity differs from that typically associated with their sex assigned at birth. Some use an asterisk after the word *trans* to act as a visual signifier of inclusion of a wide variety of identities under the trans umbrella. However, the asterisk is "a contested term with an ambiguous history" (Inselman, 2017, p. 3), and its use has fluctuated in recent years (Steinmetz, 2018). While we do not use the asterisk, we retain its usage in direct quotes from authors who do. Some terms advisors may hear trans students use to describe themselves include *trans woman, trans man, genderqueer, nonbinary, agender*, and *Two Spirit*, among many more.

With this vast diversity of individuals under the trans umbrella, we propose that the ideal approach for advising trans students is not simply following a list of best practices but rather shifting one's thinking about trans students. Best practices are temptingly easy to consider as a simple checklist and may therefore be applied without consideration of the specific context. Consider the best practice of asking students in a class to introduce themselves with their pronouns. This practice serves to normalize the notion that one's gender identity cannot be assumed based on one's appearance, theoretically creating a space where trans people's pronouns and identities can be respected in the same manner as cis people's. However, as Jaekel and Catalano (2019) noted, pronouns might be ignored or instead become an endpoint for ally work when "the bar of inclusion was set so low that liberation seemed to end at pronouns" (p. 151). Uncritically introducing a practice such as the "pronoun go-around" without focusing on why and what else must be done to fully include trans people turns the best practice into a minimal practice. In this chapter, we encourage an approach that reduces the chance of advisors settling for minimal practices in advising trans students.

We also write from the understanding that academic advising is about relationships and relationships take many forms. When working with trans students in particular, we advocate for advisor-student relationships based in agency and empowerment rather than the positional power of advisors over students. Approaches to advising that center student agency, such as those using self-authorship (Schulenberg, 2013) or appreciative inquiry (Bloom et al., 2013), may offer more potential for socially just relationships with trans students than those that assume advisors should make decisions about what students need based only on analytics or intuition.

Tropes and Structural Barriers

Advisors' understandings of trans students and their lives are culturally shaped. One important and damaging trope is the "caricature of the tragic/pathetic trans* individual" (Nicolazzo, 2014, p. 25; see also Serano, 2007). This portrayal of trans experience highlights the struggles trans people may face in a society that values cisgender identity and systematically subjects trans people to scorn, harassment, and violence; trans identity thus becomes synonymous with a tragic inability to survive, let alone thrive. In an example of the deficit-minded approach, advisors and advising administrators falling into this trans-as-tragic trope understand trans students only through the challenges they face or the ways trans students experience inequitable outcomes, without intentional consideration of the structural barriers that create such outcomes. For these professionals, the sum total of their knowledge about trans people is that they live miserable lives full of harsh discrimination caused by their trans identity.

We reject this deficit-focused portrayal of trans college students and encourage advisors to do the same. Although we do wish to make advisors aware of some of the key barriers trans students face, we want to emphasize that these barriers are *structural*. This means that while trans students (like all students) will face challenges, make mistakes, and enjoy successes, these experiences are shaped by larger forces that specifically affect trans students in different ways than cis students. The structural barriers trans students face are the result of institutional cisgenderism (Seelman, 2014), a system of oppression within higher education institutions that makes cisgender identity the default and marks transgender identity as an unacceptable deviation from the norm. Institutional cisgenderism permeates higher education through cultural norms and administrative systems that were built with the assumption only cisgender people exist.

Institutional cisgenderism causes marginalization of trans students, staff members, and faculty members that permeates the collegiate environment; such marginalization is more pronounced for trans students than for their cis LGBQ counterparts (Dugan et al., 2012; Seelman et al., 2012). Trans students may experience discrimination, harassment, and a low sense of belonging in the classroom (Pryor, 2015), housing (Chang &

Leets, 2018; Pryor et al., 2016), health and counseling centers (Goldberg et al., 2019), athletics (Gray et al., 2018), and other areas of campus. The institution as a whole may perpetuate trans students' marginalization by maintaining student records and nondiscrimination policies that are not trans-inclusive (Goldberg et al., 2018; Inselman, 2017). After graduation, this marginalization can persist in the job search and workplace (McFadden & Crowley-Henry, 2016), as evidenced by the disproportionately high rates of unemployment faced by the trans community (James et al., 2016). The effects of these experiences compound for trans students with multiple marginalized identities, especially for trans students of color, who may also experience marginalization *within* LGBTQA+ spaces (Inselman, 2017; Nicolazzo, 2016). Students' experiences of marginalization may lead to lower persistence toward degree completion, particularly for trans women and AMAB (assigned male at birth) nonbinary students (Inselman, 2017), who are already likely underrepresented in higher education (Goldberg et al., 2018; Inselman, 2017). However, despite these barriers, some studies have found that trans people overall have achieved higher levels of education than cis people (Grant et al., 2011; James et al., 2016).

While the widespread marginalization of trans people is clearly unacceptable, these challenges are often all advisors know about trans students. Trans students become understood as tragic figures, all of whom must be facing any challenge a student could face. They may even be perceived as the source of their own problems; trans people have been castigated as unproductive and overly concerned with personal issues, like gender transition, over other responsibilities (Irving, 2008). Instead, trans students' challenges should be understood in the context of institutional cisgenderism alongside other structural oppressions like white supremacy. These systems operate beyond any individual person and demand larger social and organizational change to address (Pope et al., 2014).

Rather than relying on the assumptions embedded in the trans-as-tragic trope, we offer another way for advisors to think about trans students and how they can work alongside trans students in ways that subvert these oppressive systems. We turn to resilience as an approach to consider the agency of trans students and then offer suggestions for ways advisors can facilitate resilience through their work.

Supporting Resilience in Advising

Given the vast diversity of identities held by trans students, including gender identities and intersecting positionalities, there is no "one size fits all" best practice for advising trans students. Instead, a resilience-enhancing approach allows advisors to support trans students of all backgrounds. In this section, we define *resilience*, review the current literature on resilience in trans youth and students, and illustrate how advisors can support trans students in the practice of resilience.

Resilience is understood as a trait or skill that allows individuals "to bend but not break, bounce back, and perhaps even grow in the face of adverse life experiences" such as stress, trauma, or tragedy (Southwick et al., 2014, p. 2). Resilience can take many forms, including broad types of resilience as well as individual resilience practices. Singh (2018) described resilience for trans and queer people as being composed of three types: intrapersonal resilience, interpersonal resilience, and community resilience. She described these types of resilience as practices to take care of oneself (intrapersonal resilience), practices that involve the support of other people in one's life (interpersonal resilience), and practices one "can develop from being part of a collective group who share identities, values, or some other commonality" (p. 3), such as being trans or queer (community resilience). In defining resilience, Southwick et al. (2014) noted "it is important to specify whether resilience is being viewed as a trait, a process, or an outcome, and it is often tempting to take a binary approach in considering whether resilience is present or absent" (p. 2). However, this binary approach is severely limiting, as individuals could demonstrate resilience in some aspects of their lives but not in others (e.g., at school or home), or may find some actions resilience-enhancing during some times of their lives but not others (e.g., in childhood or adulthood).

In researching trans students, Nicolazzo (2017) described resilience "as a verb" (p. 88), which is a way to recognize the limits of the binary approach and position resilience as an active practice rather than an attribute one either possesses or lacks. An important aspect of this positioning is the recognition that "one may be able to practice resilience with varying degrees of success" (p. 88), which emphasizes the iterative process of exercising resilience and evaluating the effectiveness of one practice over another. The goal of this process, according to Nicolazzo, is "not about getting better at the practice, but figuring out where and with whom one can best be successful and, thus, best navigate the collegiate environment" (p. 89). Describing resilience as a verb reframes resilience away from a practice of putting up with discrimination or hostile environments and toward a practice of recognizing and utilizing one's own agency to define and pursue success in the way best fit for the individual.

The use of agency is critical for trans resilience. A practice that enhances resilience for trans people in particular includes the ability to define and label one's own gender identity (Singh et al., 2011; Singh et al., 2014). Crucial to this practice is the support of others; Singh et al. (2014) noted in their study with trans youth that "although engaging in conversational self-theorizing about one's own gender with trans-affirming friends, family, or counselors was reported as a support to resilience . . . self-theorizing one's own gender in isolation was not found to be supportive of resilience" (p. 212). This suggests that using one's own agency is not always a solely individual endeavor but one that is completed by the recognition and respect of that agency by others. Further describing the importance of agency to resilience, Singh et al. (2014) defined the practice of *proactive agency*, which requires "recognizing areas where self-advocacy could be effective and creating contingency plans where self-advocacy could not fully address needs" (p. 212). Proactive agency was also utilized as a resilience practice by participants in Nicolazzo's (2017) study, in which students practiced resilience by "avoiding places and spaces where they met resistance" (p. 89). In other words, both resilience and proactive agency can be practiced by assessing effectiveness and choosing alternative options when effectiveness is not likely.

Resilience practices are not always resilience-enhancing when practiced alone, as in the practice of self-defining gender previously noted. Thus, advisors must recognize the role they play in supporting the resilience practices of trans students. Such support does not prohibit or conflict with student agency; on the contrary, it is important for advisors to recognize that trans students "with a trans-affirming counselor, professor, or mentor described an increased sense of support and connectedness" (Singh et al., 2014, p. 212). Whether one is an academic advisor, career advisor, or serving in another advising capacity, providing support and affirmation can make a meaningful impact on trans students' resilience. For example, Inselman (2017) found that "trans students define a variety of [staff and faculty members] as part of their support network" (p. 102). Advisors should not underestimate the meaningful impact they can have by taking small actions to support their trans students.

Contributing to a trans student's interpersonal resilience can easily be part of the advising process because supporting a student's recognition and use of their own agency should be intrinsic to advising. While some academic advisors are pressured to prioritize efficiency and transactional tasks like course scheduling, operating from a framework of resilience demands advisors look to students to define success for themselves. It then becomes the advisor's task to enable trans students to pursue that vision of success in the way *the student* would like. Although this may be a challenging undertaking for advisors, many, especially those in career development, have been able to work from a place of student agency rather than advisor control. Resilience becomes not about fitting into a box of predefined success, but rather about not needing to pay attention to the box at all. The beginning of this process can be built into the advising intake or other check-ins. For example, psychologist Panter-Brick stated, "The first thing I would do to identify resilience is to talk with people and listen to what their goals are" (Southwick et al., 2014, p. 10). Beginning an advising appointment by checking in with students about their long- and short-term goals can help make clear to the student their definitions of success and meaning are what matter most. With this understanding of the meaningful impact advisors can have, we suggest several methods advisors can employ as starting points for supporting resilience in trans students.

Implications

Adopting resilience as an organizing framework for understanding trans students and their experiences has important implications for practice and research. We explore these implications in the final sections of this chapter and offer suggestions for advisors and advising administrators who wish to better enable resilience in their trans students. Fully advocating for trans students may require embracing a social justice praxis (Burton et al., 2017). Some may struggle with the politically charged nature of such advocacy in higher education, but we argue that doing so can be a valuable tool for advisors to meet our obligations to the trans students we advise. This is especially necessary for cis advisors who can leverage their privilege without incurring the risks their more marginalized colleagues and students might face. The framework of resilience is just one dimension of a social justice approach, but one that will help move advisors away from deficit approaches when thinking about and working with trans students.

Implications for Practice

First, we must reiterate that a simple list of best practices is insufficient when advising trans students. Therefore, we encourage the deeper and more impactful work of transforming how advisors approach their practice. One way advisors can shift their thinking from the trans-as-tragic trope and move toward resilience-focused work with trans students is by adopting the *transgender look* as part of their educational practice (Nicolazzo, 2014). Similar to the male or female gazes in film, the *transgender gaze* or *transgender look* "allows [the viewer] to look *with* the transgender character instead of *at* him" (Halberstam, 2005, p. 78). Looking *with* the trans individual is to see the world through their eyes, and this practice can be taken out of the cinematic realm and applied to educational practice. An exercise in adopting the transgender look could be taking time to examine the structures that contribute to institutional cisgenderism on one's own campus and reflecting on what the experience of navigating those structures would be like for a trans student. This shift in perspective is not only a useful exercise in empathy, but also a tool that allows advisors and other student affairs professionals the ability to go beyond best practice checklists when creating change that disrupts gender normativity (Dries & Inselman, 2018).

In addition to the transgender look, advisors can adopt practices that support resilience-building for the students they advise. Singh et al. (2011) offered suggestions for counselors that can also apply to advisors, including asking students how they identify instead of making assumptions based on appearance or on records, working with students to identify and challenge both negative internal thoughts and societal messages, and connecting students to trans resources on campus and in the community. While a campus LGBTQA+ resource center can centralize resource referral, being aware of and recommending a few different options for trans students can help students find a meaningful sense of belonging, as not all trans students will feel a sense of belonging in the same spaces (Barr et al., 2016).

To contribute to structural supports of trans student resilience, advisors can identify and examine barriers that may make it difficult for students to practice proactive agency. In their department or at higher levels within the institution, advisors committed to becoming resilience allies for trans students can use their position to advocate for a campus environment conducive to supporting student agency and enhancing student resilience. Changes to the campus environment begin within the advising office—from intake forms and student records to marketing materials and office policies, advisors must assess where institutional cisgenderism contributes to barriers for trans students. Beyond one's own office, advisors may seek to make an impact through a variety of methods. A go-to solution may be to join a committee, but advisors can also contribute to transformative change by attending student actions and protests, voicing support for trans-inclusive practices on campus via social media or emails to administrators, and by speaking up in campus-wide forums. These actions eschew a neutral political stance but have important potential for enabling trans student resilience across campus.

Overall, for advisors to center resilience in their practice, they will need to listen to trans students and maintain humility around evolving terminology and issues in the trans community. This also requires that advisors understand the burden trans people, like other marginalized people, face when regularly asked to educate others or be a spokesperson for their identity.

There is no endpoint of competency at which one can arrive (Pope et al., 2019). Supporting trans students in their resilience and collegiate success is an ongoing process.

Implications for Research

Trans students are noticeably absent from research literature on academic advising, but there is evidence of research into career advising/counseling with trans students (e.g., Scott et al., 2011). Trans advisors are also absent, although we exist (both authors of this chapter are trans-identified). Methodologically, trans students are often excluded by a lack of gender-inclusive options for demographic questions in survey research; implementing recommendations regarding demographic questions on gender and sex is an essential step for quantitative researchers (Conron et al., 2014). However, even if trans-inclusive options are added, researchers must be willing to contend with the challenges of a small *n* and make analytical decisions that afford agency to the trans people who participate in surveys.

In a qualitative mode, participatory action research (PAR) holds important possibilities for addressing institutional cisgenderism. PAR is a form of critical inquiry that "focuses upon the political empowerment of people through group participation in the search for and acquisition of knowledge and subsequent action to change the status quo" (Merriam, 2002, p. 10). Such critical inquiry can create an opportunity for advisor-researchers to explore the experiences and needs of trans students on their own campuses with an orientation toward working alongside trans students to improve local conditions rather than uncovering generalizable knowledge (see Case et al., 2012, for an example of a faculty-student partnership through PAR).

Conclusion

Trans students are present on every campus, seeking guidance from advisors of all kinds. Every advisor has a responsibility to contribute to an inclusive environment for all students (Farr & Cunningham, 2017). Resilience offers a framework for advising trans students that encourages agency and drives advisors to take action for equity. To enable resilience, advisors must proactively support student agency; they must look beyond their offices to the barriers trans students identify and work to change these barriers to better allow trans students to achieve their goals. Leading change efforts or championing trans causes may not be on the agenda for every trans student, even when such efforts are needed. Understanding trans students as practicing resilience—and sometimes needing your efforts working for, with, and on behalf of them in order to do so effectively—is one way of countering the trans-as-tragic trope in higher education.

Above all, you should remain humble toward trans issues and take seriously your responsibility toward your trans students as you advise them. Terminology around gender can change rapidly, as can the legal frameworks that apply to trans students and nondiscrimination. Many states continue to pursue antitrans legislation, in addition to the Trump administration's revocation of Title IX nondiscrimination guidance for trans students (Battle & Wheeler, 2017). In this social climate, your approach in working with trans students can empower them, boost their agency, and lead to increased confidence and success in both their academics and their lives after college. By adopting a resilience-based framework, you can make a meaningful difference in the lives of your trans students.

Vignettes

Scenario 1

Iris, a computer science major, makes an appointment with you, her advisor, to discuss plans to search for an internship. You review her record closely and notice her legal name is a conventionally male name. Iris expresses concern about approaching one of the computer science faculty members to serve as a reference during the internship search: "He loved my projects and told me I was a talented student when I took his class last year. I just don't want him to use the wrong name. Maybe they'll think they called the wrong person, or that he doesn't really know me and I tried to set up a fake reference! I'll never get an internship if that happens."

Scenario 2

Jay comes to see you, their advisor, during drop-in advising hours. Jay is a student you have met with before, who you know identifies as nonbinary and recently began using they/them pronouns. Jay has dyed their hair several vibrant colors, and they are wearing bright, androgynous clothes that are atypical on your campus. They express frustration about their Medieval Architecture course, complaining about dry lectures and the lack of tutors on campus for that specific course. You suggest Jay form a study group with their classmates, but they immediately respond, "I've tried! Nobody wants to study with me. They're so cliquish, I don't have a single friend in class." You assume this is because of Jay's nonbinary identity.

Questions for Consideration

1. What additional background information is necessary in each scenario, if any?
2. What assumptions do you make about each student in these scenarios?
3. For Iris, would your advising approach change if you noticed her legal name was conventionally female? Why or why not?
4. For Jay, would you make the same assumptions if you didn't know their gender identity or if they dressed in a more conventional way? Why or why not?
5. How might you support each student's resilience when discussing their situation?

References

Barr, S. M., Budge, S. L., & Adelson, J. L. (2016). Transgender community belongingness as a mediator between strength of transgender identity and well-being. *Journal of Counseling Psychology, 63*(1), 87–97. https://doi.org/10.1037/cou0000127

Battle, S., & Wheeler, T. E. (2017). *Dear colleague letter: Transgender students.* U.S. Department of Justice and U.S. Department of Education. https://www2.ed.gov/about/offices/list/ocr/letters/colleague-201702-title-ix.pdf

Bloom, J. L., Hutson, B. L., & He, Y. (2013). Appreciative advising. In J. K. Drake, P. Jordan, & M. A. Miller (Eds.), *Academic advising approaches: Strategies that teach students to make the most of college* (pp. 83–99). Jossey-Bass.

Burton, S. L., Puroway, D., & Stevens, S. E. (2017). *Academic advising and social justice: An advocacy approach.* NACADA pocket guide series PG21. NACADA: The Global Community for Academic Advising.

Case, K. A., Kanenberg, H., Erich, S., & Tittsworth, J. (2012). Transgender inclusion in university nondiscrimination statements: Challenging gender-conforming privilege through student activism. *Journal of Social Issues, 68*(1), 145–161. https://doi.org/10.1111/j.1540-4560.2011.01741.x

Chang, S. H., & Leets, C., Jr. (2018). Introduction. In J. C. Garvey, S. H. Chang, Z. Nicolazzo, & R. Jackson (Eds.), *Trans*policies & experiences in housing & residence life* (pp. 1–20). Stylus.

Conron, K., Lombardi, E., & Reisner, S. (2014). Identifying transgender and other gender minority respondents on population-based surveys: Approaches. In J. L. Herman (Ed.), *Best practices for asking questions to identify transgender and other gender minority respondents on population-based surveys* (pp. 9–18). The Williams Institute. https://williamsinstitute.law.ucla.edu/wp-content/uploads/Survey-Measures-Trans-GenIUSS-Sep-2014.pdf

Crenshaw, K. (1989). Demarginalizing the intersection of race and sex: A Black feminist critique of antidiscrimination doctrine, feminist theory and antiracist politics. *University of Chicago Legal Forum, 1989*(1), 139–167. https://chicagounbound.uchicago.edu/uclf/vol1989/iss1/8

Dries, K., & Inselman, K. (2018, May 1). Disrupting gender in career services & recruiting. *NACE Journal, 78*(4), 24–32. https://www.naceweb.org/career-development/special-populations/disrupting-gender-in-career-services-recruiting/

Dugan, J. P., Kusel, M. L., & Simounet, D. M. (2012). Transgender college students: An exploratory study of perceptions, engagement, and educational outcomes. *Journal of College Student Development, 53*(5), 719–736. https://doi.org/10.1353/csd.2012.0067

Farr, T., & Cunningham, L. (Eds.). (2017). *Academic advising core competencies guide.* NACADA pocket guide series PG23. NACADA: The Global Community for Academic Advising.

Goldberg, A. E., Beemyn, G., & Smith, J. Z. (2018). What is needed, what is valued: Trans students' perspectives on trans-inclusive policies and practices in higher education. *Journal of Educational and Psychological Consultation, 29*(1), 27–67. https://doi.org/10.1080/10474412.2018.1480376

Goldberg, A. E., Kuvalanka, K. A., Budge, S. L., Benz, M. B., & Smith, J. Z. (2019). Health care experiences of transgender binary and nonbinary university students. *The Counseling Psychologist, 47*(1), 59–97. https://doi.org/10.1177/0011000019827568

Grant, J. M., Mottet, L. A., Tanis, J., Harrison, J., Herman, J. L., & Keisling, M. (2011). *Injustice at every turn: A report of the national transgender discrimination survey.* National Center for Transgender Equality and National Gay and Lesbian Task Force. https://www.transequality.org/sites/default/files/docs/resources/NTDS_Report.pdf

Gray, A., Crandall, R. E., & Tongsri, J. (2018). Transgender student-athletes and their inclusion in intercollegiate athletics. *New Directions for Student Services, 2018*(163), 43–53. https://doi.org/10.1002/ss.20269

Halberstam, J. (2005). *In a queer time and place: Transgender bodies, subcultural lives.* New York University Press.

Harding, B. (2008). Students with specific advising needs. In V. N. Gordon, W. R. Habley, T. J. Grites, & Associates, *Academic advising: A comprehensive handbook* (2nd ed.; pp. 189–203). Jossey-Bass.

Inselman, K. (2017). *Differences in use of campus resources for gender transition and support by trans college students: A mixed-methods study* (UMI No. 10606854) [Master's thesis, University of Utah]. ProQuest Dissertations and Theses.

Irving, D. (2008). Normalized transgressions: Legitimizing the transsexual body as productive. *Radical History Review, 2008*(100), 38–59. https://doi.org/10.1215/01636545-2007-021

Jaekel, K. S., & Catalano, D. C. J. (2019). More than pronouns: Problematizing best practices of trans* inclusion. In P. M. Magolda, M. B. Baxter Magolda, & R. Carducci (Eds.), *Contested issues in troubled times: Student affairs dialogues on equity, civility, and safety* (pp. 145–155). Stylus.

James, S. E., Herman, J. L., Rankin, S., Keisling, M., Mottet, L., & Anafi, M. (2016). *The report of the 2015 U.S. transgender survey.* National Center for Transgender Equality. https://transequality.org/sites/default/files/docs/usts/USTS-Full-Report-Dec17.pdf

Joslin, J. (2007). Lesbian, gay, bisexual, transgender, and queer students. In L. Huff, & P. Jordan (Eds.), *Advising special student populations: Adult learners, community college students, LGBTQ students, multicultural students, students on probation, undecided students* (Monograph No. 17; pp. 87–95). National Academic Advising Association.

McFadden, C. & Crowley-Henry, M. (2016). A systematic literature review on trans* careers and workplace experiences. In T. Köllen (Ed.), *Sexual orientation and transgender issues in organizations: Global perspectives on LGBT workforce diversity* (pp. 63–82). Springer.

Merriam, S. B. (2002). Introduction to qualitative research. In S. B. Merriam and Associates, *Qualitative research in practice: Examples for discussion and analysis* (pp. 3–17). Jossey-Bass.

Nicolazzo, Z. (2014). Celluloid marginalization: Pedagogical strategies for increasing students' critical thought through the multiple (re)readings of trans* subjectivities in film. *Journal of LGBT Youth, 11*(1), 20–39. https://doi.org/10.1080/19361653.2014.840762

Nicolazzo, Z. (2016). "It's a hard line to walk": Black non-binary trans* collegians' perspectives on passing, realness, and trans*-normativity. *International Journal of Qualitative Studies in Education, 29*(9), 1173–1188. https://doi.org/10.1080/09518398.2016.1201612

Nicolazzo, Z. (2017). *Trans* in college: Transgender students' strategies for navigating campus life and the institutional politics of inclusion.* Stylus.

Pope, R. L., Reynolds, A. L., & Mueller, J. A. (2014). *Creating multicultural change on campus.* Jossey-Bass.

Pope, R. L., Reynolds, A. L., & Mueller, J. A. (2019). *Multicultural competence in student affairs: Advancing social justice and inclusion* (2nd ed.). Jossey-Bass.

Pryor, J. T. (2015). Out in the classroom: Transgender student experiences at a large public university. *Journal of College Student Development, 56*(5), 440–455. https://doi.org/10.1353/csd.2015.0044

Pryor, J. T., Ta, D., & Hart, J. (2016). Searching for home: Transgender students and experiences with residential housing. *College Student Affairs Journal, 34*(2), 43–60. https://doi.org/10.1353/csj.2016.0011

Schulenberg, J. K. (2013). Academic advising informed by self-authorship theory. In J. K. Drake, P. Jordan, & M. A. Miller (Eds.), *Academic advising approaches: Strategies that teach students to make the most of college* (pp. 121–136). Jossey-Bass.

Scott, D. A., Belke, S. L., & Barfield, H. G. (2011). Career development with transgender college students: Implications for career and employment counselors. *Journal of Employment Counseling, 48*(3), 105–113. https://doi.org/10.1002/j.2161-1920.2011.tb01116.x

Seelman, K. L. (2014). Recommendations of transgender students, staff, and faculty in the USA for improving college campuses. *Gender and Education, 26*(6), 618–635. https://doi.org/10.1080/09540253.2014.935300

Seelman, K. L., Walls, N. E., Costello, K., Steffens, K., Inselman, K., Montague-Asp, H., & Colorado Trans on Campus Coalition. (2012). *Invisibilities, uncertainties, and unexpected surprises: The experiences of transgender and gender non-conforming students, staff, and faculty at colleges and universities in Colorado.* Colorado Trans on Campus Coalition. http://portfolio.du.edu/downloadItem/221246

Serano, J. (2007). *Whipping girl: A transsexual woman on sexism and the scapegoating of femininity.* Seal Press.

Singh, A. A. (2018). *The queer and transgender resilience workbook: Skills for navigating sexual orientation and gender expression.* New Harbinger Publications.

Singh, A. A., Hays, D. G., & Watson, L. S. (2011). Strength in the face of adversity: Resilience strategies of transgender individuals. *Journal of Counseling & Development, 89*(1), 20–27. https://doi.org/10.1002/j.1556-6678.2011.tb00057.x

Singh, A. A., Meng, S. E., & Hansen, A. W. (2014). "I am my own gender": Resilience strategies of trans youth. *Journal of Counseling & Development, 92*(2), 208–218. https://doi.org/10.1002/j.1556-6676.2014.00150.x

Southwick, S. M., Bonanno, G. A., Masten, A. S., Panter-Brick, C. & Yehuda, R. (2014). Resilience definitions, theory, and challenges: Interdisciplinary perspectives. *European Journal of Psychotraumatology, 5*(1), 1–14. https://doi.org/10.3402/ejpt.v5.25338

Steinmetz, K. (2018, April 3). *The Oxford English Dictionary* added 'trans*.' Here's what the label means. *Time.* https://time.com/5211799/what-does-trans-asterisk-star-mean-dictionary/

14

ADVISING LGBTQA+ INTERNATIONAL STUDENTS

Leonor L. Wangensteen

International lesbian, gay, bisexual, transgender, queer/questioning, and asexual (LGBTQA+) students' unique experiences in U.S. higher education and campus support systems present a nuanced and emerging area of study. Research on the internationalization of U.S. education includes the experiences of international students, the impacts of campus climates, the value of globalized learning environments and curricula, and opportunities for building transcultural awareness, exchange, and skills (Green, 2005). Scholarship on the experiences of international LGBTQA+ student populations are found within counseling and psychology (Bontempo & D'Augelli, 2002; Oba & Pope, 2013), foreign student affairs (Valosik, 2015; West, 2019), and international education publications (Fuks et al., 2018; Katz, 2008).

International LGBTQA+ students' psychological well-being and educational outcomes are at risk in hostile campus environments, as these students face higher rates of absenteeism, dropouts, feelings of isolation, depression, and suicidal ideation and attempts, substance use, and risky sexual behaviors (Kosciw et al., 2012; Kosciw et al., 2018; Oba & Pope, 2013; Rankin, 2003; Watson & Miller, 2012). Oba and Pope (2013) explored four main challenges these international LGBT students encounter, including "issues around their own sexual identity, relationship challenges, health issues, and returning to their home countries" (p. 186). International LGBTQA+ students face compounded psychological distress due to a range of variables including cultural differences, language barriers, academic differences in preparation and college readiness, financial issues, access to health insurance and health care, and isolation, marginalization, and discrimination.

Students' experiences are further complicated by educators' biases regarding international and minority students, educators' lack of cultural awareness, and systemic disenfranchisement and lack of equity. By paying careful attention to this unique student population, academic advisors and other student support specialists have an opportunity to make a positive impact on international LGBTQA+ students' experiences.

Educators with student-facing roles take on a large part of the institution's responsibility to cultivate and sustain welcoming, unbiased, and inclusive spaces that respect and honor the diversity of all individuals in the community. All students should be able to access campus opportunities and pursue their academic goals without having to confront a hostile environment due to their race, nationality or ethnic group, religious faith, gender, socioeconomic class, immigration status, sexual orientation, or other identities. Advisors can encourage student success by building affirming spaces for international LGBTQA+ students; the first step in this process is becoming familiar with current research, institutional practices and policies, and federal, state, local, and institutional political climates relevant to the intersections of these identities. Therefore, this chapter aims to synthesize some of the supporting theories and considerations presented across recent scholarship regarding the experiences of international LGBTQA+ students enrolled in U.S. higher education institutions and apply this knowledge toward academic advising praxis. The chapter will discuss the unique challenges LGBTQA+ international students experience, best practices for advising, and recommendations for institutions to build more inclusive campuses.

Contexts of LGBTQA+ International Students

Diversity in U.S. higher education is rapidly growing, and campus student support systems are working to cultivate and sustain welcoming, unbiased, and inclusive spaces that respect and honor the diversity of all individuals in the community. A recent report by the American Council on Education indicates that as the United States becomes more racially and ethnically diverse and more educated overall, the undergraduate population of students of color increases; indeed, the number of undergraduate students of color in U.S. institutions of higher education increased from 29.6% in 1996 to 45.2% in 2016 (Espinosa et al., 2019). International students include a vast range of intersecting identities, significantly impacting the number of underrepresented minority populations on many campuses. Moreover, the number of international college students coming to study in the United States has increased 61.3% from 2008–2009 to 2018–2019, or from 671,000 students to 1,095,000 (Open Doors, 2019). Public and private institutions of higher education will face significant challenges if they continue to increase recruitment of international students without allocating sufficient funding and human resources to successfully support these students. Gopal and Streitwieser (2016) argued:

> While international students are often welcomed for the tuition dollars they contribute and the cultural diversity they bring to a campus, institutions vary widely in their capacity to provide international arrivals with the support structures they need to successfully navigate immigration issues, deal with cultural challenges, and succeed academically. (para. 2)

It is difficult to know the exact numbers of LGBTQA+ domestic or international populations in U.S. colleges due to the confidential nature of these identity indicators. However, the growth of specialized student support units on campus addressing LGBTQA+ communities, including over 150 campuses across the United States with an LGBTQA+ dedicated office or center, suggests an increase in consideration and honoring of LGBTQA+ students' unique needs (Consortium of Higher Education LGBT Resource Professionals, 2019). While the exact demographics are unclear, it stands to reason that an increasing number of LGBTQA+ students exist within the overall expansion of international students in the United States.

Numerous studies (e.g., Bontempo & D'Augelli, 2002; King et al., 2008; Kosciw et al., 2012) have suggested a significant number of LGBTQA+ youth experience feelings of shame, guilt, isolation, depression, and higher risks of suicide ideation and attempts than their heterosexual and cisgender peers. LGBTQA+ international students face additional barriers related to "acculturative stress as manifested by uncertainty, anxiety, and depression" that lies "at the core of concerns for the health and well-being of individuals engaged in the acculturation process" (Berry, 2017, p. 20). Berry suggested that regardless of how people choose to acculturate to a new environment, acculturative stress and behavioral changes are always part of the eventual adaptation to intercultural encounters.

International students in the United States are coming from a wide range of environments that influence their exposure to and understanding of LGBTQA+ identities, as well as the relative freedom or victimization associated with these identities. Depending on their familiarity and comfort with the traditions and customs of the United States and, more specifically, their local and campus cultures, LGBTQA+ international students will encounter different intensities of culture shock or disorientation in their new setting and possible reverse-culture shock upon their return home. While some students come from areas with anti-LGBTQA+ laws, censorship, denial of family rights and recognition, and widespread discrimination and violence, others may be traveling from exceptionally LGBTQA+-inclusive locations that continue to push toward liberation through policies and practices. Country-specific policies regarding same-sex marriages, civil unions, and partnerships are one indicator of LGBTQA+-inclusivity. The Human Rights Watch (2021) section on LGBT Rights has created a clickable map with this data. As of this writing, the United States is only one of 28 countries worldwide with marriage equality, with an additional 14 countries currently honoring same-sex civil unions or registered partnerships. For state-to-state policies in the United States, the Movement Advancement Project (MAP; 2021) has aggregated the number of laws and policies related to sexual orientation and gender identity that help drive LGBTQA+ equality.

Some international LGBTQA+ students come from environments where they received inaccurate, stigmatized, or deficient information about sexual orientation and/or gender identity. Access to sexual education and health support is vital to a holistic model of student support. Oba and Pope (2013) contended, "LGBT international students may not have had an opportunity in their home countries to learn about sexual risks, the practice of safe sex, preventing sexually transmitted diseases, and the location of and how to access health systems" (p. 188). Misinformation and cultural stigmas surrounding mental health needs, including myths of reparative or conversion therapy or perceptions of counseling sessions as "mind control" may prevent international students from seeking care altogether. While international students may be coming from countries where conversion therapy is illegal, they may find themselves studying in locations in the United States where it is legal or normalized. For example, the Pan American Health Organization (2012) recognized evidence in several countries in the Americas of therapies that aim to "cure" nonheterosexual orientations; the organization subsequently denounced homophobic ideologies "resulting from blind fanaticism as well as pseudoscientific views that regard non-heterosexual and non-procreative sexual behavior as 'deviation' or the result of a 'developmental defect'" (p. 1). International LGBTQA+ students may experience a range of psychological and behavioral effects, from cultural shock and distress to a sense of liberation and exploration, as they confront radical shifts in regional ideologies and civil rights.

A 2020 Human Rights Watch (HRW) report, "*My Teacher Said I Had a Disease": Barriers to the Right to Education for LGBT Youth in Vietnam*, documented the "stigma and discrimination" LGBTQA+ youth in Vietnam face "at home and at school," including discrimination based on the false belief that "same-sex attraction is a diagnosable, treatable, and curable mental health condition" (HRW, 2020, p. 1). The report exemplifies that within societies wrought with anti-LGBTQA+ discrimination, prejudiced educators further perpetuate widespread myths and taboos, causing distrust among youth reporting peer-to-peer bullying and harassment. In general, international LGBTQA+ students have varying levels of exposure in school and at home to discussions of sexual orientation and gender identity. They may not possess basic facts regarding gender and sexuality or the ability to explore their own identity. Oba and Pope (2013) considered the diverse range of identity formation behaviors and comfort levels of disclosure students face as they transition to and from the United States and their home countries. Oba and Pope explained that while "some students do face forthrightly their sexual orientation or gender identity (development) in the context of their social networks of friends in the United States and in their home countries as well as with their families," other individuals "stay in the closet, feel isolated, and hopeless . . . [and] seem resistant to change their sexual identity" (p. 187).

International students may also face harassment and discrimination upon returning to their home countries if they fully or partially disclose their identities, and they may weigh these risks against the rewards of openly exploring their identities while in the United States. Many LGBTQA+ international students hope to form relationships that honor and liberate their full selves, even if this privilege proves to be impermanent. Valosik (2015) shared an example of an undergraduate student mitigating the rewards and risks of coming out in the United States. Saksham Rai, a Nepalese student, was able to more freely and safely express his gay identity at the University of Minnesota than he could at home. Rai expressed a potential loss of identity and feeling stuck in an "ultimatum" if he returned to his home country where he would have to "throw [his] identity out the window" while living with family or choose to "live on [his] own to reduce [his] relationship with [his] family" (Valosik, 2015, p. 51). In essence, Rai's newly found sexual identity would be under threat if he returned to his home country. He further anticipated he would encounter reverse-culture shock in his home country after living in a more liberated space in the United States for several years.

Additionally, international students have unique needs when it comes to their legal rights and immigration-related safety measures. Constant changes in U.S. government policies, some backed by anti-immigration sentiments, have complicated international travel to the United States in recent years. The Trump administration has issued numerous executive orders to ban international travel to the United States from majority-Muslim countries, reduced the number of visa and green card approvals, and increased border security and internal immigration enforcement (Appleby, 2020; Pierce & Meissner, 2017). Although some international LGBTQA+ students apply for asylum when the prospects of returning home are unsafe, seeking asylum in the United States as a sexual minority, transgender individual, and/or LGBTQA+ individual with HIV status is a complex process that can be (re)traumatizing and detrimental to students' safety (Nakamura & Skinta, 2016).

Recommendations for Advising Practice

Educators should be conscious of the serious concerns facing international LGBTQA+ students and be ready to discuss possible outcomes, resources, and coping skills students might use when considering the challenges of a return home (Oba & Pope, 2013). Educators who work to create welcoming and LGBTQA+-inclusive campus cultures and resources should remain aware that a different reality exists beyond the borders of their campus, as international students encounter different political circumstances and belief systems as they move within and across nations.

Certain critical theories and frameworks can be utilized to better understand international LGBTQA+ students' experiences and their transitions from their home countries to the United States. Berry (2017) used theories of acculturation to study intercultural relations and the processes by which people adjust or adapt to contact with a culture other than their own. Berry's (2017) model identifies four types of acculturation strategies—integration, assimilation, separation, and marginalization—people use when adapting or integrating into new environments. He cautioned that when people try to assimilate,

> there are obvious constraints on whether individuals can "pass" into, and become accepted as a member of, another ethnocultural group. People's characteristics, such as accent, dress, and physical appearance, will signal their existing group membership, and if these features are not acceptable to members of the other group, they will impede (even prevent) successful assimilation . . . [and] may induce acculturative stress. (Berry, 2017, p. 23)

Separation and marginalization between culturally distinct identities is not recommended. Integration strategies, which allow individuals to remain rooted in their own culture and community while reaching out to be involved in larger society, have the most positive adaptive value psychologically, socio-culturally, and interculturally. Berry's (2017) recommendations to ensure positive acculturation experiences for people moving into new environments can be easily adapted to the context of higher education and academic advising. He affirmed the following:

> Do not deny the cultural rights and identities of others; Do not exclude others from full participation in the life of the society; and Do not limit their power to live as they wish within the evolving legal and civic framework of the larger society. (Berry, 2017, p. 26)

Queer theory and Butler's theories of performativity (see chapter 4) may also be considered when analyzing international LGBTQA+ students' cultural transitions to the United States. International students who are not familiar with mainstream Western expressions of sexuality and gender and/or those who come from LGBTQA+-intolerant and repressed societies may be surprised to witness nuanced forms of communication, mannerisms, dress, and other visible cues being passed among domestic LGBTQA+ peers and allies on campus. When students begin to engage in multicultural campus settings, they may discover their understanding and self-expression of gender and sexuality differ from those of their peers. A closer examination of international LGBTQA+ student experiences through Butler's theory of performativity may identify the psychological effects of cultural dissonance, feeling misunderstood, or not fitting into the performance of culturally based and idealized norms of gender and sexuality.

Practicing cultural competency is equally essential when working with international LGBTQA+ students. Best practices related to skill-building and effective applications of cultural competency have been well documented in the fields of pedagogy (Paris & Alim, 2017), student affairs administration (American College Personnel Association [ACPA] & National Association of Student Personnel Administrators [NASPA], 2015), international education (NAFSA, 2015), and academic advising (Farr & Cunningham, 2017). Culturally inclusive best practices across all these disciplines condemn deficit approaches to student relationship-building that ignore and criticize internal and external cultural differences (e.g., see Hall's [1976] cultural iceberg model that provides an analogy of the complex layers of culture). Supporting students from a culturally responsive lens is guided by internal reflection of one's own biases and assumptions; learning about individual student's circumstances, backgrounds, and needs; and honoring and respecting students' full selves.

While learning about cultures from around the world is always help-ful to improve cultural competence, advisors should not feel disparaged if they know little or nothing about an international student's specific cultural background. Social workers Eible and Lewis (2019) described cultural com-petence as a "journey, not a destination" since "there is never a point at which one, despite training, experience, or interest, can achieve full competency in another person's culture" (para. 5). They characterized culturally competent social workers as continuous learners who intentionally integrate cultural humility and empathy while building relationships with clients. Through cultural humility, advisors, like social workers, must be open to learning from and honoring international LGBTQA+ students' perspectives of culture and experience while suspending personal biases, generalizations, and impulses to dominate as the expert in the room. A culturally empathetic advisor attempts to understand students' experiences through acknowledgment, emotional resonance, and human connection.

Crenshaw's (1989) theory of intersectionality and Yosso's (2005) model of community cultural wealth add a critical race theory (CRT) lens to the development of advisor cultural competency, which may prove especially helpful in working with international LGBTQA+ students. Intersectionality theory (see chapter 5) can be used to study the effects of systemic racism and discrimination in the United States on international LGBTQA+ students with multiple marginalized identities. A CRT lens explicitly centers the expe-riences of international students of color and shifts away from the traditional Western notions of white, middle-class culture and privilege. For example, Yosso's model recognizes that every individual has a unique set of aspira-tional, navigational, social, linguistic, familial, and resistant capital they acquire through their community and life experiences. Yosso's model can support a culturally-inclusive academic advising approach that views inter-national students' backgrounds and cultures as remarkable banks of talent and capacity. More specifically, this model can encourage advisors to help international students translate their unique skills and assets to a new college environment, empowering them to navigate with their own capital.

Faculty members and primary-role advisors across the university range in expertise and experience depending on the types of students they advise. LGBTQA+ international students may find themselves seeking answers to questions from multiple units on campus or in the local community, includ-ing international student scholar services, multicultural student services, LGBTQA+ and gender relations centers, student legal services, affin-ity student groups, faith-based centers, and more. Siloed student support services can cause disruptions to the continuity of student care and unrec-ognized gaps in student needs. Matthews's (2019) personal experiences as a

Black queer transfer student at Elon University provide a glimpse into the need for developing expertise in support of special student populations on campuses. Matthews explained that despite his university going

> out of its way to make black students welcome with [their] Multicultural Center, now the Center for Race, Ethnicity & Diversity Education . . . [and an] LGBTQ+ student organization at the time . . . [he] still did not believe there was someone on campus to confide in about [his] experiences. (2019, para. 1)

Matthews (2019) encouraged advisors to take specific actions to improve LGBTQA+ student experiences. He emphasized that advisors should make the effort to reach out and collaborate across campus and with national organizations such as Campus Pride, practice nurtured advising (e.g., Glenn et al., 2008) to provide students with a sense of security and belonging, and educate themselves about intersectional minority identities, including the Black queer and gender nonconforming (BQGN) population.

Furthermore, LGBTQA+ international students may find it frustrating and ineffective to build trust and connect with advisors if they must share private information and their personal story multiple times. Colleges with large international student populations should consider hiring a specialized advisor in one of these offices or providing professional development for existing advisors to act as a point person for LGBTQA+ students. If a dedicated mentor is not possible, advisors across all relevant units should receive professional development on making personalized referrals for international LGBTQA+ students. When making a referral, advisors should carefully listen to the student's request, respectfully make the student aware of the advisor's limitations, share the name of a specific person who may be able to better support the student, and ask the student what type of information they are comfortable sharing on referral documentation. In some circumstances, advisors may be able to locate information for an international LGBTQA+ student while keeping their name and sensitive information anonymous.

Advisors should never offer legal advice or pretend to know the intricacies of legal matters. Instead, advisors can be of great support to students by initiating a connection to campus or local experts. Only those with the relevant expertise should provide international LGBTQA+ students with information related to visas, travel, legal matters, foreign consulate services, and U.S. Citizen and Immigration Services (NAFSA, 2015). If direct legal support is not offered on campus, institutions should consider helping students mitigate the costs of off-campus support and/or help students access pro-bono or low-cost solutions.

That being said, advisors do not have to be experts on LGBTQA+ and international student issues to support students. Valosik (2015) suggested the following basic advising skills and resources to increase advisor awareness: create safe spaces, use gender-neutral language, avoid assumptions, incorporate LGBTQA+ issues into discussions of current events, attend professional development sessions, learn the vocabulary, establish a relationship with LGBT groups and international student services on campus, display affirming literature and visual cues, and encourage campus-wide changes. Valosik (2015) reminded advisors of the importance of meeting students where they are, noting that

> people are going through their own struggles and people have their own identities . . . It's not for us U.S. student affairs professionals or as college advisors to judge a student's experience . . . It's to support them through their journey. (p. 50)

When students disclose vulnerable aspects of their identities, they are trusting advisors to listen, acknowledge, and provide appropriate support and referrals.

Advisors must also ensure international students have access to information and health insurance coverage needed to lead healthy lives, make informed decisions, and protect themselves and others from harmful behaviors. Educators should consider best practices for providing LGBTQA+-inclusive health support and education to the international student community, connections to local LGBTQA+-friendly doctors and clinics, and easy access to information on safe sex and LGBTQA+ health-related topics. Campuses should provide or promote readily accessible suicide prevention education and local and state emergency numbers and crisis hotlines. All this information can be easily added to international student orientations and onboarding information sessions on campus addressing new international staff and faculty members. One helpful resource is The Trevor Project. The nationally recognized organization's TrevorLifeline is a national 24-hour, toll-free confidential suicide hotline that connects LGBTQA+ youth with experienced counselors in a safe and judgment-free space. Additionally, the associated website TrevorSpace provides social networking opportunities for LGBTQA+ youth, friends, and allies.

Building Inclusive Campuses

U.S. institutions of higher education must apply a social justice lens to their mission statements when expressing the importance of globally-informed and liberal spaces that foster intellectual exchange of diverse talent and perspectives. Institutional goals created using a social justice lens affirm equity and dignity amongst the academic community of students, teachers, and scholars, all of whom contribute and share in knowledge for the common good. Many international LGBTQA+ students are vulnerable to systemic discrimination and marginalization in the U.S. higher education system. Educators and advisors have the responsibility to protect all students' basic human rights and freedom of expression.

According to the Universal Declaration of Human Rights, Article 3, all people worldwide have the "right to life, liberty and the security of person" (United Nations Human Rights, 2019, paras. 1, 2). The 2019 United Nations Human Rights publication, *Born Free and Equal: Sexual Orientation and Gender Identity in International Human Rights Law*, affirms that "ending violence and discrimination against individuals on the basis of their sexual orientation and gender identity is a great human rights challenge" (p. 7). While a social justice lens and international standards help educators understand *why* they aspire to reach institutional equity and justice, it is imperative to consider the conditions and constraints LGBTQA+ students may face in their home countries. The Pan American Health Organization (2012) suggested several practices to improve a sense of belonging and well-being for LGBTQA+ campus communities worldwide: (a) forming support groups among faculty members and students; (b) forming sexual diversity alliances to reduce isolation and promote solidarity and respect; and (c) creating zero tolerance policies for homophobic harassment or maltreatment, including unethical health practices (Pan American Health Organization [PAHO], 2012). Informed by the World Health Organization's and the Human Rights Committee's recommended practices and sanctions, PAHO advised academic institutions to provide health professionals with professional development that "include[s] courses on human sexuality and sexual health in their curricula, with a particular focus on respect for diversity and the elimination of attitudes of pathologization, rejection, and hate toward non-heterosexual persons" (2012, p. 3).

U.S. campuses that express and intentionally work toward a welcoming, LGBTQA+-friendly, safe, and richly-diverse environment will attract international LGBTQA+ students. Increased global access to online information and international student outreach efforts have made it easier for prospective LGBTQA+ students from around the world to search for colleges that align with their educational goals, financial limitations, and personal preferences. Some nonprofit organizations, such as the Campus Pride Index (Campus Pride, 2020), have taken the lead on establishing best practices and LGBTQA+-inclusive benchmarks for campus policies and programs.

College-going international students can make use of these free online searchable databases of LGBTQA+-friendly campuses. Another easy-to-access resource is the Consortium of Higher Education LGBT Resource Professionals' map of LGBTQA+ Campus Centers. For international students looking into LGBTQA+-based curricular options, Younger (2020) is charting the growing number of academic programs in the United States and Canada that support the LGBTQA+ community.

It may also be helpful for student support specialists to take the time to examine the onboarding processes international students navigate using an LGBTQA+-inclusive lens. These many initial student touchpoints, which take place online and in person, have the potential to set a positive tone of inclusion and belonging. Consider ways to normalize LGBTQA+ identities, rights, and needs; reduce stigma; and increase visibility and representation on campus and in the community. Renn (2017) recommended administrators "ensure that non-discrimination policies include admissions, employment, educational programs, athletics, student health insurance, gender-inclusive facilities (e.g., locker rooms, restrooms, residence hall rooms) and prohibition of harassment" (para. 12). Institutions can enhance international student orientation and prestudy abroad programming by making use of current expertise across their campuses in relation to cultural competence, contemporary political and legal issues, and LGBTQA+-related information. Equity resources on college campuses, including Title IX professional development, bystander intervention programs, and anonymous reporting systems, should include scenarios and solutions specific to international and LGBTQA+ campus populations. When displaying visible symbols of support on campus, consider those that are most globally recognized, such as the gay pride rainbow.

Campus departments and student-facing units often work in silos, focusing on specific dimensions of a student's journey through college. In line with Berry's (2017) acculturative integration strategies, campuses should be mindful to maintain cultural integrity and to value LGBTQA+ and international students' participation as integral to the greater campus society. Developing a working group that taps into the existing campus expertise on international and LGBTQA+ students and which includes student representation can help bridge silos and amplify student voices. The working group may invite guest speakers, host conferences and workshops, petition for administrative buy-in and policy changes, and seek financial support from development offices and donors. Student feedback gathered through needs assessments, campus climate surveys, and focus groups can also inform a sustainable international LGBTQA+ student support system. Student support staff members and advisors can learn directly from students by taking a more active role in campus, community, and classroom events. An inclusive campus culture welcomes student activities that honor diversity and empower students to express their many cultures and LGBTQA+ pride in and outside the classroom. Institutions seeking to provide on-campus LGBTQA+ awareness events can look to The Safe Zone Project's (2020) self-guided online courses and 2-hour ally training workshop curriculum, which include in-depth train-the-trainer resources and activities.

International LGBTQA+ students may experience unique complexity in building casual and intimate relationships and navigating between spaces of belonging and resistance in U.S. campus communities. Student clubs, affinity groups, and faith organizations may be inclusive spaces, but they have the potential to leave international students feeling the need to prioritize one identity over their full selves. Berry's acculturation studies (2017) illustrate that international LGBTQA+ students may benefit from more inclusive integration rather than segregation of their identities on college campuses. More work can be done to develop academic, leadership, civic engagement, and social programming where individuals' multiplicities of identities are recognized and respected. Mentorship, buddy, and host family opportunities may also help bridge international and multicultural communities across campus and surrounding areas.

Conclusion

This chapter provided a glimpse into the contemporary challenges impacting international LGBTQA+ student populations attending U.S. institutions of higher education, and it should serve as a call for scholar-practitioners to pay distinct attention to this underrecognized and underserved demographic. Other related areas of interest that must be cross-examined include immigrant, undocumented, and DACA-recipient LGBTQA+ student experiences; nuances in the experiences of undergraduate versus graduate students; finding LGBTQA+-inclusive postgraduate research and work opportunities in the United States; experiences in short-term student programs, such as study abroad and cultural exchange; and experiences of U.S. domestic LGBTQA+ students who research, study, and work abroad. More research and data collection from campus climate surveys, student experience surveys, sexual assault and harassment reporting, and student needs assessments, as well as overall campus awareness of these issues, can bring to light areas in need of response and cross-campus collaboration. Institutions that take the necessary steps to understand and meet the needs of LGBTQA+ international students and improve campus climate and inclusivity of all diverse students show commitment toward human justice, dignity, and sensibility for the common good. All students deserve to experience a safe and affirming learning environment.

References

American College Personnel Association & National Association of Student Personnel Administrators. (2015). *Professional competency areas for student affairs educators.* https://www.naspa.org/files/dmfile/ACPA_NASPA_Professional_Competencies_1.pdf

Appleby, K. (2020, April 23). *President Trump issues executive order temporarily halting the issuance of green cards.* Center for Immigration Studies. https://cmsny.org/president-trump-covid-executive-order/

Berry, J. W. (2017). Theories and models of acculturation. In S. J. Schwartz & J. B. Unger (Eds.), *The Oxford handbook of acculturation and health* (pp. 15–27). Oxford University Press. https://www.oxfordhandbooks.com/view/10.1093/oxfordhb/9780190215217.001.0001/oxfordhb-9780190215217

Bontempo, D. E., & D'Augelli, A. R. (2002). Effects of at-school victimization and sexual orientation on lesbian, gay, or bisexual youths' health risk behavior. *Journal of Adolescent Health, 30*(5), 364–374. https://doi.org/10.1016/s1054-139x(01)00415-3

Campus Pride. (2020). *LGBTQ-friendly campus search.* Campus pride index: National Listing of LGBTQ-Friendly Colleges and Universities. https://www.campusprideindex.org/search/index

Consortium of Higher Education LGBT Resource Professionals. (2019). *Find an LGBTQ center.* LGBT Campus. https://www.lgbtcampus.org/find-an-lgbtq-campus-center

Crenshaw, K. (1989). Demarginalizing the intersection of race and sex: A black feminist critique of antidiscrimination doctrine, feminist theory and antiracist politics. *University of Chicago Legal Forum, 1989*(1).

Eible, L. M., & Lewis, J. B. (2019). Cultural humility and empathy—Steps on the journey of cultural competence. *Social Work Today.* https://www.socialworktoday.com/news/pp_031519.shtml

Espinosa, L. L., Turk, J. M., Taylor, M., & Chessman, H. M. (2019). *Race and ethnicity in higher education: A status report.* American Council of Education. https://1xfsu31b52d33idlp13twtos-wpengine.netdna-ssl.com/wp-content/uploads/2019/02/Race-and-Ethnicity-in-Higher-Education.pdf

Farr, T., & Cunningham, L. (Eds.). (2017). *Academic advising core competencies guide.* NACADA pocket guide series PG23. NACADA: The Global Community for Academic Advising.

Fuks, N., Smith, N. G., Peláez, S., De Stefano, J., & Brown, T. L. (2018). Acculturation experiences among lesbian, gay, bisexual, and transgender immigrants in Canada. *International Forum, 46*(3) 296–332. https://www.apa.org/education/ce/acculturation-process.pdf

Glenn, P. W., Wider, F., & Williams, I. L. (2008, March 1). Nurtured advising: An essential approach to advising students at historically black college and universities. *Academic Advising Today, 31*(1). https://www.nacada.ksu.edu/Resources/Academic-Advising-Today/View-Articles/Nurtured-Advising-An-Essential-Approach-to-Advising-Students-at-Historically-Black-College-and-Universities.aspx

Gopal, A., & Streitwieser, B. (2016, January 3). International students, support structures and the equity question. *Inside Higher Ed.* https://www.insidehighered.com/blogs/world-view/international-students-support-structures-and-equity-question

Green, M. F. (2005). *Internationalization in U.S. higher education: The student perspective.* American Council on Education. https://www.acenet.edu/Documents/Intlz-In-US-Higher-Ed-Student-Perspective.pdf

Hall, E. T. (1976). *Beyond culture.* Anchor Books.

Human Rights Watch. (2020). *"My teacher said I had a disease": Barriers to the right to education for LGBT youth in Vietnam.* https://www.hrw.org/sites/default/files/report_pdf/vietnam0220_web.pdf

Human Rights Watch. (2021). *LGBT rights.* www.hrw.org/topic/lgbt-rights

Katz, E. (2008). Working with LGBT international students. *International Educator, 17*(6), 56–61.

King, M., Semlyen, J., Tai, S. S., Killaspy, H., Osborn, D., Popelyuk, D., & Nazareth, I. (2008). A systematic review of mental disorder, suicide, and deliberate self-harm in lesbian, gay and bisexual people. *BMC Psychiatry, 8*(70). https://doi.org/10.1186/1471-244X-8-70

Kosciw, J. G., Greytak, E. A., Zongrone, A. D., Clark, C. M., & Truong, N. L. (2018). *The 2017 national school climate survey: The experiences of lesbian, gay, bisexual, transgender, and queer youth in our nation's schools.* GLSEN. https://www.glsen.org/sites/default/files/2019-12/Full_NSCS_Report_English_2017.pdf

Kosciw, J. G., Palmer, N. A., Kull, R. M., & Greytak, E. A. (2012). The effect of negative school climate on academic outcomes for LGBT youth and the role of in school supports. *Journal of School Violence, 12*(1), 45–63. https://doi.org/10.1080/15388220.2012.732546

Matthews, M. (2019, May 17). Approaches for advising and supporting black queer and gender nonconforming students. *Academic Advising Today, 42*(2). https://nacada.ksu.edu/Resources/Academic-Advising-Today/View-Articles/Approaches-for-Advising-and-Supporting-Black-Queer-and-Gender-Nonconforming-Students.aspx

Movement Advancement Project. (2021). *Home page.* https://www.lgbtmap.org/

NAFSA: Association of International Educators. (2015). *NAFSA international education professional competencies.* https://www.nafsa.org/professional-resources/career-center/international-education-professional-competencies

Nakamura, N., & Skinta, M. (2016). *LGBTQ asylum seekers: How clinicians can help.* American Psychological Association. www.apa.org/pi/lgbt/resources/lgbtq-asylum-seekers.pdf

Oba, Y., & Pope, M. (2013). Counseling and advocacy with LGBT international students. *Journal of LGBT Issues in Counseling, 7*(2), 185–193. https://doi.org/10.1080/15538605.2013.785468

Open Doors. (2019). *International student data from the 2019 Open Doors report* (2001/02–2012/13). [Data set]. Institute of International Education. https://opendoorsdata.org/data/international-students/enrollment-trends/

Pan American Health Organization. (2012). *"Cures" for an illness that does not exist: Purported therapies aimed at changing sexual orientation lack medical justification and are ethically unacceptable.* https://www.paho.org/hq/dmdocuments/2012/Conversion-Therapies-EN.pdf

Paris, D., & Alim, H. S. (Eds.). (2017). *Culturally sustaining pedagogies: Teaching and learning for justice in a changing world.* Teachers College Press.

Pierce, S., & Meissner, D. (2017). *Trump executive order on refugees and travel ban: A brief review.* Migration Policy Institute. https://www.migrationpolicy.org/research/trump-executive-order-refugees-and-travel-ban-brief-review

Rankin, S. R. (2003). Campus climate for lesbian, gay, bisexual and transgender people. *The Diversity Factor, 12*(1), 18–23.

Renn, K. (2017, April 10). *LGBTQ students on campus: Issues and opportunities for higher education leaders. Higher Education Today.* https://www.higheredtoday.org/2017/04/10/lgbtq-students-higher-education/

Safe Zone Project. (2020). *Safe Zone Training Facilitator Guide.* https://thesafezoneproject.com

The Trevor Project. (2021). *Home page.* https://www.thetrevorproject.org/

United Nations Human Rights (2019). *Born free and equal: Sexual orientation, gender identity and sex characteristics in international human rights law* (2nd ed.). United Nations. https://www.ohchr.org/Documents/Publications/Born_Free_and_Equal_WEB.pdf

Valosik, V. (2015). Supporting LGBT international students. *International Educator, 24* (2), 48–51. https://www.nafsa.org/professional-resources/publications/supporting-lgbt-international-students

Watson, S., & Miller, T. (2012). LGBT oppression. *Multicultural Education, 19*(4), 2–7. https://files.eric.ed.gov/fulltext/EJ1014937.pdf

West, C. (2019, January 1). Navigating the U.S. cultural climate. *International Educator.* https://www.nafsa.org/ie-magazine/2019/1/1/navigating-us-cultural-climate

Yosso, T. J. (2005). Whose culture has capital? A critical race theory discussion of community cultural wealth. *Race Ethnicity and Education, 8*(1), 69–91. https://www.tandfonline.com/doi/abs/10.1080/1361332052000341006

Younger, J. G. (2020, January 18). *University LGBT/queer programs: Lesbian, gay, bisexual, transgender, transsexual, & queer studies in the USA and Canada.* http://www.people.ku.edu/~jyounger/lgbtqprogs.html

15

ADVISING QUEER AND TRANS STUDENTS OF COLOR

Fabiola Mora and Mary Ann Lucero

Positionality Statement

We, as coauthors, represent a diversity of social identities (Latinx, queer, cisgender women) that informs how we approach and situate ourselves within this work. We have worked in various academic advising roles and other functional areas centered on students of color. We also want to name and acknowledge our cisgender privilege and recognize how our identities influence our point of view on this topic.

Advising Queer and Trans Students of Color

The intersectional experiences of queer and queer trans student(s) of color (QTSOC) are often invisibilized and silenced within higher education contexts, causing students to feel that they must choose one identity, race or sexuality, over another (Garvey et al., 2019). Understanding the complexities of QTSOC, as well as the oppressions they face on our campuses, is critical to supporting these students through academic advising praxis. QTSOC face many challenges regarding race, gender, and sexuality as they navigate different institutional environments, including academic advising. We will discuss five topics that we hope will enable academic advisors to better understand the unique situations of QTSOC while also equipping advisors to do equitable, just work on their campuses: queer of color critique, challenges of QTSOC, White supremacy and heteronormativity, QTSOC visibility in advising contexts, and implications for future work.

Theoretical Framework

Intersectionality (Crenshaw, 1991; Hill Collins & Bilge, 2016), critical race theory (CRT) (Delgado & Stefancic, 2017), queer theory (Denton, 2019), queer of color critique (Duran, 2019c), validation theory (Rendón, 1994), community cultural wealth (Yosso, 2005), and multiple dimensions of identity theory (Abes et al., 2007) all offer critical frameworks for examining the experiences of QTSOC in academic advising. These frameworks allow for the deconstruction of existing dominant narratives about QTSOC that are rooted in Whiteness while validating and affirming their stories and experiences. Some of these theoretical frameworks have been explored in this book and will be covered in more depth in this chapter as they relate to the academic advising experiences of QTSOC (see chapter 4 for queer theory and chapter 5 for intersectionality).

For the purpose of creating visibility within the QTSOC communities, we will be referencing quare theory. Rooted in queer of color critique, quare theory focuses on the experiences of QTSOC by "placing race at the center of its analysis, illuminating how matters of identity, resistance, and survival function differently" (Duran, 2019c, p. 395). Paired with intersectionality, quare theory provides a lens for reframing the ways race, gender, and sexuality shape a student's experience. Rather than placing emphasis on individual identities, we will explore the interconnections among race, sexuality, and gender identity, illustrating how we individually uphold structures of oppressions by engaging in systemic practices that create environments detrimental to the QTSOC community. Within quare theory, José Muñoz introduced the term *dissatisfaction*, acknowledging how QTSOC "have managed to survive in a White supremacist society by working on and against oppressive institutional structures" (Duran, 2019c, p. 395).

Challenges of Queer and Trans Students of Color

It is difficult to analyze homophobia and transphobia at the intersection of race due to the various cultural and political contexts of communities of color. There exist many nuances among queer, trans, and racial student identities. As this chapter is a broad analysis of QTSOC challenges, it should not be used as a generalization of the entire QTSOC population (BrckaLorenz & Clark, 2017). However different, LGBTQA+ students do share similarities in experiences due to homophobia, transphobia, heterosexism, and cisgenderism on college campuses (Garvey et al., 2015). Higher education is deeply rooted in Whiteness, which perpetuates and sustains the systems of power, privilege, and oppression negatively impacting QTSOC. The academic advising field is no exception. Racial demographics of academic advisors at predominantly White institutions (PWIs) fit the classification by consisting primarily of White advisors (Lee, 2018). This disproportionate representation of White advisors in the academic advising field can, intentionally or unintentionally, perpetuate systems of oppression for QTSOC. Ongoing examination and disruption of Whiteness is needed to address the challenges of QTSOC (Tyson, 2007). This examination and disruption is particularly important for a predominantly White field such as academic advising. We will discuss four factors illustrating what QTSOC face or must consider on college campuses: campus climate and mental health, racism, homophobia and transphobia, and identity disclosure.

Campus Climate and Mental Health

The climate of a campus directly impacts the mental health of its students. Campus climate refers to "the overall ethos or atmosphere of a college campus mediated by the extent individuals feel a sense of safety, belonging, engagement within the environment, and value as members of a community" (Renn & Patton, 2010, p. 248). QTSOC face emotionally, physically, and psychologically violent campus climates through multiple systems of oppression, which leads to QTSOC experiencing significantly poorer mental health than their non-QTSOC counterparts (Sutter & Perrin, 2016). In the Campus Pride report *2010 State of Higher Education for Lesbian, Gay, Bisexual, & Transgender People;* lesbian, gay, bisexual, and queer students of color identified sexual identity as "the primary risk factor for harassment," while trans students "were more likely than Men and Women of Color to experience harassment" (Rankin et al., 2010, p. 11). In addition, sexual and gender identity discrimination and harassment were found to predict a higher rate of suicide ideation for students of color (Sutter & Perrin, 2016). Sutter and Perrin (2016) were the first "to address the intersectionality of these identities, and the resulting additive effects of multiple forms of discrimination on mental health and suicidal ideation of LGBTQ POC" (p. 102). The discrimination and harassment QTSOC face is compounded by their multiple oppressed identities.

The academic campus climate is another element that impacts student mental health. QTSOC report that unwelcoming academic departments negatively impact their college experiences (Rankin et al., 2010). It is important to note that the academic success of QTSOC hinges on and is directly tied to campus climate and mental health. Siegel (2019) claimed that "trans people's experiences are nested within classrooms, departments, and finally institutions, where, on the one hand, administrative efforts can transform someone's experience," and on the other hand, "department [culture] can undercut virtually any college wide initiative" (p. 2). As on-ground advocates, academic advisors face an urgent call to action because they tend to interact with many students on campuses who may not be participating in other student support services or programs. We challenge academic advisors to examine the ways academic departments and the field itself reinforce these negative climates in order to create change and promote safety for QTSOC.

Racism

In addition to campus climate, racism greatly impacts QTSOC on college campuses. Racism creates unwelcoming and violent environments and climates for QTSOC. QTSOC not only have to negotiate their sexuality and gender identities but also their hypervisible racialization, the phenomenon that occurs when "queer and trans students of color are . . . forced to contend with racist acts and other forms of intolerance that derive from their White queer and trans peers" (Garvey et al., 2019, p. 171). In fact, QTSOC indicated higher rates of racial profiling experiences than their White peers (Rankin et al., 2010). Racism within queer and trans communities leaves QTSOC searching for a sense of belonging within heterosexual, racialized environments where they face homophobia and transphobia (Strayhorn, 2013). Unfortunately, trans student discourse focuses mostly on White trans students and leaves trans students of color not reflected in these issues, so addressing issues of racism within the trans community is difficult (Nicolazzo, 2016b). However, "the racial composition of an institution also impacts trans people's experiences" (Siegel, 2019, p. 8). Therefore, homophobia and transphobia within communities of color, as well as racism within White queer and trans communities, leave QTSOC searching for places that embrace and validate their queerness *and* race (Duran, 2019b).

Homophobia and Transphobia

In addition to facing racism within White queer and trans communities, QTSOC experience homophobia and transphobia within the spaces of communities of color (BrckaLorenz & Clark, 2017). In single-identity spaces within higher education, where students of color may feel welcomed and affirmed, queer students of color face harassment due to their sexuality or gender identity (Means & Jaeger, 2013). This is not only evident at minority-serving institutions, but also at PWIs (Duran, 2019b). Moreover, internalized transphobia and cisgender privilege within queer communities of color creates an added layer of oppression for trans students who face antitrans oppression in these communities (Siegel, 2019). Even though literature examining transphobia within queer communities of color is limited, we know that "queer community both contributed to and detracted from [trans students'] comfort on campus" (Duran & Nicolazzo, 2017, p. 538). If trans students do not feel like they belong in queer spaces and if QTSOC do not feel supported in single-identity racial groups, they often begin searching for communities where they can be their full, authentic selves (Siegel, 2019).

Identity Disclosure

Negative campus climates, racism, and homophobia and transphobia all have an impact on QTSOC identity disclosure. Additionally, queer and trans identity salience and disclosure are heavily influenced by varying familial, societal, cultural, and social contexts (Samuels, 2003). Continued experiences of oppression, emphasized by poor campus climates and internalized homophobia and transphobia, make gender and identity disclosure a complex issue. Furthermore, identity disclosure of a QTSOC level of "outness" varies across race, and not all QTSOC want to disclose their sexual and gender identities (Garvey et al., 2019). Gender identity also influences decisions about identity disclosure, and this process is quite complex for trans students. "Trans students of color choose to 'pass' within the gender binary to circumvent" (Garvey et al., 2019 p. 168) and "eliminate any sign of deviation from gender and sexual norms that are dominant in a heteronormative society" (Bailey, 2013, p. 58). Trans students' intentional, preventative decisions to disclose to close friends can have impacts on misgendering (Nicolazzo, 2016a). Misgendering is when students are referred to with pronouns that do not match their gender identities. Misgendering has a detrimental impact on trans students and sends messages that their identities are not valid (Siegel, 2019). There are many ways institutions, faculty members, and staff members out and misgender QTSOC, including using incorrect pronouns, not offering chosen name options in class or on institutional records, and releasing information in the housing assignment process and other institutional reporting processes (Siegel, 2019). Overall, QTSOC face consequences as a result of identity disclosure, including compromising their safety, which makes this a complex process (Garvey et al., 2019).

We encourage advising professionals to examine campus climate and mental health, racism, homophobia and transphobia, and the identity disclosure processes in their departments and institutions by exploring the following questions:

- Does your institution conduct a campus climate survey? If so, how have you used that data to shift culture in your area? If not, how do you assess your departmental culture and make changes?

- Do you disaggregate student data on surveys or other assessments to learn about the experiences of QTSOC in your area/institution? If not, how might you do this?
- What types of intentional conversations do you have with students about mental health? How do the resources you share with students explicitly name QTSOC identities?
- What types of antiracism work do your institution's staff and faculty members engage in? What actions have you taken to actively examine racism in your policies and practices?
- How do you currently work with identity-based spaces at the intersections of race, sexuality, and gender? What types of services and programs does your area specifically provide for queer and trans students of color?
- What work do you personally engage in that would help QTSOC know they could disclose to you if desired? Is your office/department safe? How do you know this? If not, how do you make this change?

Disrupting White Supremacy and Heteronormativity

As one of the first offices a student engages with, academic advising is central to influencing a student's perception of campus climate and level of belonging. Acknowledging how a student's race, sexuality, and gender identity can implicate and exacerbate a student's sense of belonging and ability to embrace their intersecting identities is paramount. Results from a study on the identity disclosure of QTSOC and college context revealed a positive relationship between the identity disclosure of QTSOC and the perception of campus climate (Garvey et al., 2019). These results indicate that the more welcoming a college climate, the more likely QTSOC are to disclose their true identities. Inherent in each of us is a microcosm of identities, including race, sexuality, and gender, which are all shaped by group memberships and the position of power within each membership (Misawa, 2010). It is important to remember that advising approaches are influenced by our positionalities and created within the contexts of institutional structures that intentionally and/or unintentionally perpetuate oppression (e.g., racism, homophobia, transphobia).

While remaining grounded in CRT, quare theory, and community cultural wealth, we offer three strategies for disrupting White supremacy and hegemonic structures within academic advising settings: examining racial contexts, disrupting heteronormative views, and recognizing assets.

Examining Racial Contexts

Race is deeply embedded in the fabric of social, institutional, and political structures (Patton et al., 2007). Through the lens of CRT and intersectionality, academic advising can be examined within a historical and contemporary racial context, allowing us to critically assess how academic advising practices continue to uphold systemic forms of racism and White supremacy. It is essential to question the ways the cultural experiences of students of color have been removed from the advising context. It is also important to consider whether we are adjusting our advising practices based on the current racial context.

Race is one of the most visible and discriminated identities for marginalized people, but our understanding of race is often based on preconceived notions that have been predetermined by dominant narratives (Misawa, 2010). In a recent study of 255 articles on how "researchers explain, discuss, and theorize about racial differences in student achievement" (Harper, 2012, p. 11), two themes emerged when explaining racial phenomena in the context of academic achievement: scholars (a) rarely named racism as a plausible reason for reduced achievement of students of Color, and (b) rarely engaged racism as an explanation for negative experiences reported by minoritized students (Harper, 2012). Greater emphasis must be placed on the structures that uphold systemic forms of racism within the education context. Examining advising practices, including student success initiatives, within a historical and contemporary racial context, provides a vehicle for assessing how institutions uphold systemic forms of racism and White supremacy.

Too often, we student affairs practitioners perpetuate the status quo by failing to examine and critically critique the role of race in our practices (Patton et al., 2007). By critically examining our daily practices and decisions related to academic advising approaches through a CRT perspective, advisors are choosing to dismantle racism and White supremacy while forging a new path toward equity.

Disrupting Heteronormative Views

Examining racial contexts is the first step to disrupting White supremacy and hegemonic structures; disrupting heteronormative views is the next. Much work needs to be done in this area. Study findings from six national surveys conducted by four postsecondary research centers highlighted higher education's failure to provide queer and trans students with an equitable learning environment. Specifically, the study revealed that queer and trans students experience a significant decrease in feelings of belonging and safety during their first year compared to their heterosexual and cisgender peers (Greathouse et al., 2018). It is evident that queer and trans students experience an increase in harassment, discrimination, and other forms of mistreatment compared to their heterosexual counterparts. There are immeasurable ways advisors can create an inclusive space that disrupts heteronormative views within their sphere of influence. Advisors must first critically assess decisions and practices through an inclusive lens. On a practical level, advisors can encourage the use of chosen names and pronouns within their departments, ensure that local resources and services extended to students are queer- and trans-inclusive, refrain from using binary language, and use images to create an inclusive academic advising space.

Recognizing Assets

Academic advisors can create inclusive spaces for QTSOC who have experienced trauma from White supremacy and heteronormativity by utilizing CRT's examination of community cultural wealth (Yosso, 2005). Yosso's (2005) model recognized the assets students of color bring into educational spaces. Generally the dialogue around QTSOC centers on the deficits, but Yosso's (2005) model can help us to explore the assets of QTSOC instead. Duran (2019a) achieved this by exploring the resiliency of queer students of color within higher education contexts. While students shared their challenges in finding affirming, inclusive spaces, they *also* shared details about the communities where they felt emotionally, personally, and academically supported (Duran, 2019a). By approaching QTSOC support through asset-based paradigms, advisors can actively resist racism, homophobia, and transphobia and create counter spaces for QTSOC to experience joy, connection, and healing.

QTSOC Visibility in the Advising Context

In a recent literature review of the experiences of QTSOC, four themes revealed the complexities students navigate at the center of race, sexuality, and gender (Duran, 2019c).

1. Identity disclosure and finding a source of support: QTSOC are less likely to come out publicly and/or engage within the queer community.
2. Navigating singular identity spaces: QTSOC contend with finding communities that simultaneously center around race, sexuality, and gender. This leaves the student vulnerable to experiencing racism, homophobia, or transphobia.

3. Complex individuality: Student affairs practitioners must refute the idea that shared racial, sexual, and/or gender identity is a uniform experience.
4. Lack of resources and representation: QTSOC are challenged with finding individuals with similar identities. Additionally, many institutions have limited or no resources centered on race, sexuality, and gender identity.

By acknowledging the complexities students experience while navigating institutional systems, advisors are acknowledging the needs within the QTSOC community. Keeping in context the four themes in the previous list, we offer four strategies for dismantling oppressive systems while creating a space where the humanity of QTSOC is not questioned: validation, maintaining student privacy, acknowledging the academic advising climate, and knowing your resources.

Validation

The first thing advisors can do to create a safe space for QTSOC is to use validation techniques that shift the mindset of academic advising from passive to active while giving attention to the emotional and social experiences of students (Rendón, 1994). A recent study examining the sense of belonging of QTSOC revealed QTSOC experience a greater sense of belonging when their intersecting identities are validated (Duran, 2019c). Interpersonal validation occurs when in- and out-of-class agents take action to foster students' personal development and social adjustment (Rendón, 1994). This can take the form of building a relationship with a student by asking thoughtful questions while remaining sensitive to the risk and vulnerability a QTSOC might feel. It is important not to assume all QTSOC experiences are the same, and it is important to affirm the racism, homophobia, and/or transphobia they have experienced as a result of being a QTSOC.

Maintain Student Privacy

Another step advisors can take to create a safe, inclusive space is to maintain student privacy. The coming-out process for QTSOC is selective and private. As a result, QTSOC are left to navigate the pressures of society alone while also balancing safety as it relates to racism, homophobia, and transphobia. Disclosing sexual and/or gender identity requires vulnerability on the student's part and is shaped by the rapport developed between the advisor and student (Garvey et al., 2019). Maintaining student privacy as it relates to a student's sexuality and/or gender identity is essential for supporting QTSOC and providing an inclusive climate that fosters identity safety and human dignity. Disclosing a student's sexual and/or gender identity without permission from the student can further isolate QTSOC while also hindering their safety.

Acknowledge the Academic Advising Climate

If we do not acknowledge our own biases and/or department cultures, we are more likely to maintain racial and heteronormative judgment that perpetuate racism, homophobia, and transphobia (see chapter 16 on becoming an ally and advocate). Therefore, it is important that advisors acknowledge the academic advising climate in which they operate. A recent study revealed that queer and trans students experienced more harassment and/or discrimination when compared to their heterosexual and cisgender peers (Greathouse et al., 2018). It is not enough that we reduce the harm being done; we must create an affirming space for QTSOC to make meaning of their racial and queer identities. Some steps advisors can take to reduce harm include refraining from making assumptions related to a student's sexuality or gender identity, asking students their chosen pronouns and/or name and then addressing them as such, and not assuming a student has disclosed their sexuality and/or gender identity to others.

Know Your Resources

Lastly, it is important for advisors to be very familiar with available resources. Queer and trans students experience higher rates of disengagement due to depression, anxiety, and stress than their heterosexual and cisgender counterparts (Greathouse et al., 2018). Thus, it is critical for academic advisors to recognize disengagement patterns related to QTSOC and to increase their knowledge of local and campus resources (Greathouse et al., 2018). Resources can include mental health professionals who are experienced in supporting queer and trans communities (see, e.g., chapter 8), affinity groups and/or resource centers that support racial and queer identities, and building a network of folks who are knowledgeable about and/or share similar identities as QTSOC. Advisors and the academic advising field hold power to create change on campuses for QTSOC students. Many institutions claim to value equity, diversity, inclusion, and social justice via mission, vision, and values statements. As employees of these institutions, whether these statements align with our own personal values or not, we have a role in creating inclusive spaces for QTSOC. The following vignette provides advisors with an opportunity to think about how to support QTSOC experiencing homophobia and transphobia in the classroom while considering how to advocate for change.

Vignette

Over the last year, your institution has been working toward a new policy that will allow students to identify their chosen name and pronouns. As addressed earlier in this chapter, providing students with the opportunity to communicate their chosen names and pronouns is critical to the support and success of QTSOC. While the policy is near implementation, it has not yet been finalized. You have also heard from your supervisor that institutional leadership has concerns regarding the drafted policy and does not understand its purpose.

During open office advising hours, a student walks in; they are upset and want to drop a course. They share an experience they just had in one of their general education classes. You are familiar with the instructor and the numerous concerns students, specifically Latinx students, have submitted regarding their practices. The student explains that the professor insists on referring to the student by their legal name, which is listed on the attendance sheet, even after the student expressed their desire to be called by their chosen name and pronouns.

Questions to Consider

1. What issues or patterns are emerging in this vignette?
2. Do you believe the institution should implement the chosen name and pronouns policy? Within your capacity and agency, how do you advocate?
3. What implications do you foresee for other queer and trans students at the institution? If you do not foresee any implications, how do you support future students who share similar identities and may enroll in the class discussed in this vignette?
4. Given the complaints you have received regarding the instructor, how do you respond?
5. Acknowledging the patterns you have tracked with the instructor, how do you support the student?

Implications for Practice and Research

In general, QTSOC are not feeling supported or welcomed on our college campuses (Renn & Patton, 2010). In fact, queer students of color report less satisfaction with their collegiate experience due to institutional barriers, lack of support, and negative interactions with advisors, all of which impact student success and retention (BrckaLorenz & Clark, 2017). Strayhorn (2014) stated:

Facing rejection, whether perceived or real, from both major identity groups, students are left with few options for establishing meaningful relationships, finding peers who affirm their experiences, or connecting with others who share aspects of their identity, which are the fundamental ingredients of college students' sense of belonging. (p. 592)

Addressing the challenges of QTSOC and creating welcoming, inclusive environments through critical academic advising frameworks is imperative. It is evident that there is a disproportionate negative impact on QTSOC through institutional practices, policies, and procedures. Academic advising units need to examine "overt and covert institutional practices and traditions that exist and function with racism, genderism, transphobia, and homophobia" in order to create systemic change (Garvey et al., 2019, p. 170). We must work against the "toxic environments" where transphobia and queerphobia are present so QTSOC can embrace their identities (Garvey et al., 2019, p. 165). Our inability to do this critical work creates inconsistencies in policies using an intersectional paradigm, which can undermine the intentions of a policy and strategic plans, creating unwelcoming and unsafe spaces for QTSOC. Inclusive policies and programs can drastically change the experiences of QTSOC and make bold statements about a department's or institution's commitment to equity and support for this student population (Rankin et al., 2010). By creating systemic change, academic advisors can help foster positive campus climates and educational outcomes for QTSOC (Rankin et al., 2010).

There is scant research on this topic within the academic advising literature. Additional research on academic advising of QTSOC is needed to further explore the multiple marginalized experiences and oppressions of this student population. Furthermore, research about transphobia within communities of color is lacking and needed in regard to advising this student population. We must be able to identify issues facing this community in order to combat them and create a more inclusive space.

Conclusion

Our inability to address the lack of diversity and examine power structures within academic advising keeps the voices of marginalized persons at the margins. However, this should not prohibit the field from moving forward in advocating for these student populations. Because the academic advising field is made up of predominantly White professionals, the professional and cultural competence development of advising staff members is important to adequately support QTSOC. Advising staff members and leaders need to develop a critical consciousness toward race, sexuality, and gender identity in order to provide holistic support of QTSOC populations. This includes doing the hard work of examining our own "preconceived notions, stereotypes, and prejudices" about QTSOC (Smith, 2006, para. 1). Additionally, we must be able to understand intersectionality beyond race, gender, and sexuality to help students make meaning of their experiences. Advisors must work across identity and in partnership with multicultural and LGBTQA+ student support offices whose missions are to create inclusive campus environments for QTSOC populations (Greathouse et al., 2018). However, the sole responsibility of supporting QTSOC in ways that are affirming and valuing should not lay solely on LGBTQA+ resource centers—this further perpetuates systems of inequity. If we look at academic advising as a tool for equity and justice, we possess the potential to transform the experiences of QTSOC on our campuses.

References

Abes, E. S., Jones, S. R., & McEwen, M. K. (2007). Reconceptualizing the model of multiple dimensions of identity: The role of meaning-making capacity in the construction of multiple identities. *Journal of College Student Development 48*(1), 1–22. https://doi.org/10.1353/csd.2007.0000

Bailey, M. M. (2013). *Butch queens up in pumps*. University of Michigan Press.

BrckaLorenz, A., & Clark, J. (2017). *Marginalization at the crossroads: Exploring the experiences of queer students of color* [Conference presentation]. 2017 Association for the Study of Higher Education Conference, Houston, TX, United States. http://cpr.indiana.edu/uploads/ASHE_2017_BrckaLorenz_Clark_slides.pdf

Crenshaw, K. (1991). Mapping the margins: Intersectionality, identity politics, and violence against women of color. *Stanford Law Review, 43*(6), 1241–1299. https://doi.org/10.2307/1229039

Delgado, R., & Stefancic, J. (2017). *Critical race theory: An introduction* (3rd ed.). New York University Press.

Denton, J. M. (2019). Queer theory: Deconstructing sexual and gender identity, norms, and developmental assumptions. In E. S. Abes, S. R. Jones, & D.-L. Stewart (Eds.), *Rethinking college student development theory using critical frameworks* (pp. 55–63). Stylus.

Duran, A. (2019a). "Outsiders in a niche group": Using intersectionality to examine resilience for queer students of color. *Journal of Diversity in Higher Education.* Advance online publication. https://doi.org/10.1037/dhe0000144

Duran, A. (2019b). A photovoice phenomenological study exploring campus belonging for queer students of color. *Journal of Student Affairs Research and Practice, 56*(2), 153–167. https://doi.org/10.1080/19496591.2018.1490308

Duran, A. (2019c). Queer and of color: A systematic literature review on queer students of color in higher education scholarship. *Journal of Diversity in Higher Education, 12*(4), 390–400. https://doi.org/10.1037/dhe0000084

Duran, A., & Nicolazzo, Z. (2017). Exploring the ways trans* collegians navigate academic, romantic, and social relationships. *Journal of College Student Development 58*(4), 526–544. https://doi.org/10.1353/csd.2017.0041

Garvey, J. C., Mobley, S. D., Jr., Summerville, K. S., & Moore, G. T. (2019). Queer and trans* students of color: Navigating identity disclosure and college contexts. *The Journal of Higher Education, 90*(1), 150–178. https://doi.org/10.1080/0022 1546.2018.1449081

Garvey, J. C., Taylor, J. L., & Rankin, S. (2015). An examination of campus climate for LGBTQ community college students. *Community College Journal of Research and Practice, 39*(6), 527–541. https://doi.org/10.1080/10668926.2013.861374

Greathouse, M., BrckaLorenz, A., Hoban, M., Huesman, R., Rankin, S., Stolzenberg, E., & Bara, E. (2018). *Queer-spectrum and trans-spectrum student experiences in American higher education: The analyses of national survey findings.* Rutgers Tyler Clementi Center. https://doi.org/10.7282/t3-44fh-3b16

Harper, S. R. (2012). Race without racism: How higher education researchers minimize racist institutional norms. *The Review of Higher Education, 36*(1), 9–29. https://doi.org/10.1353/rhe.2012.0047

Hill Collins, P., & Bilge, S. (2016). *Intersectionality.* Polity Press.

Lee, J. A. (2018). Affirmation, support, and advocacy: Critical race theory and academic advising. *NACADA Journal, 38*(1), 77–87. https://doi.org/10.12930/ NACADA-17-028

Means, D. R., & Jaeger, A. J. (2013). Black in the rainbow: "Quaring" the Black gay male student experience at historically Black universities. *Journal of African American Males in Education, 4*(2), 124–140. https://jaamejournal.scholasticahq. com/article/18442-black-in-the-rainbow-quaring-the-black-gay-male-student-experience-at-historically-black-universities

Misawa, M. (2010). Queer race pedagogy for educators in higher education: Dealing with power dynamics and positionality of LGBTQ students of color. *The International Journal of Critical Pedagogy, 3*(1), 26–35. http://libjournal.uncg.edu/ijcp/ article/view/68/53

Nicolazzo, Z. (2016a). "It's a hard line to walk": Black non-binary trans* collegians' perspectives on passing, realness, and trans*-normativity. *International Journal of Qualitative Studies in Education, 29*(9), 1173–1188. https://doi.org/10.1080/09 518398.2016.1201612

Nicolazzo, Z. (2016b). *Trans* in college: Transgender students' strategies for navigating campus life and the institutional politics of inclusion.* Stylus.

Patton, L. D., McEwen, M., Rendón, L., & Howard-Hamilton, M. F. (2007). Critical race perspectives on theory in student affairs. *New Directions for Student Services, 2007*(120). https://doi.org/10.1002/ss.256

Rankin, S., Weber, G., Blumenfeld, W. J., & Frazer, S. (2010). *2010 state of higher education for lesbian, gay, bisexual & transgender people.* Campus Pride. https:// www.campuspride.org/wp-content/uploads/campuspride2010lgbtreportssum-mary.pdf

Rendón, L. I. (1994). Validating culturally diverse students: Toward a new model of learning and student development. *Innovative Higher Education, 19*(1), 33–51. https://doi.org/10.1007/BF01191156

Renn, K. A., & Patton, L. D. (2010). Campus ecology and environments. In J. H. Schuh, S. R. Jones, & S. R. Harper (Eds.), *Student services: A handbook for the profession* (5th ed.; pp. 242–256). Jossey-Bass.

Samuels, E. J. (2003). My body, my closet: Invisible disability and the limits of coming-out discourse. *GLQ: A Journal of Lesbian and Gay Studies, 9*(1–2), 233–255. https://doi.org/10.1215/10642684-9-1-2-233

Siegel, D. P. (2019). Transgender experiences and transphobia in higher education. *Sociology Compass, 13*(10), 1–13. https://doi.org/10.1111/soc4.12734

Smith, B. (2006). *Working more effectively in advising: Understanding multicultural dimensions of gay, lesbian, bisexual, and transgender identities.* NACADA: The Global Community for Academic Advising. https://nacada.ksu.edu/Resources/Clearinghouse/View-Articles/Advising-LGBTQ-students.aspx

Steele, C. M., & Aronson, J. (1995). Stereotype threat and the intellectual test performance of African Americans. *Journal of Personality and Social Psychology, 69*(5), 797–811. https://doi.org/10.1037/0022-3514.69.5.797

Strayhorn, T. L. (2013). And their own received them not: Black gay male undergraduates' experiences with White racism, Black homophobia. In M. C. Brown, II, T. E. Dancy II, & J. E. Davis (Eds.), *Educating African American males: Contexts for consideration, possibilities for practice* (pp. 105–120). Peter Lang.

Strayhorn, T. L. (2014). Beyond the model minority myth: Interrogating the lived experiences of Korean American gay men in college. *Journal of College Student Development, 55*(6), 586–594. https://doi.org/10.1353/csd.2014.0059

Sutter, M., & Perrin, P. B. (2016). Discrimination, mental health, and suicidal ideation among LGBTQ people of color. *Journal of Counseling Psychology, 63*(1), 98–105. https://doi.org/10.1037/cou0000126

Tyson, S. Y. (2007). Can cultural competence be achieved without attending to racism? *Issues in Mental Health Nursing, 28*(12), 1341–1344. https://doi.org/10.1080/01612840701686518

Yosso, T. J. (2005). Whose culture has capital? A critical race theory discussion of community cultural wealth. *Race, Ethnicity and Education, 8*(1), 69–91. https://doi.org/10.1080/1361332052000341006

Voices From the Field

Approaches for Advising and Supporting Black Queer and Gender Nonconforming Students

Maximillian Matthews

As a transfer student at Elon University, I only met with my academic advisor when I needed an approval for something. Being a Black, queer young man, I was already accustomed to not having safe spaces. The interactions with my academic advisor indicated nothing would change during my time at Elon. While she may not have been culturally insensitive or could have even had a rainbow flag on her office door indicating LGBTQ+ allyship, spaces specifically designed for someone with my identity intersections were unheard of. Elon went out of its way to make Black students welcome with our Multicultural Center, now the Center for Race, Ethnicity, & Diversity Education. The university even had a LGBTQA+ student organization at the time, but I still did not believe there was someone on campus to confide in about my experiences.

The experiences I had at Elon reaffirmed my ideas on the nonexistence of safe spaces available to me as a Black queer young man. Taking classes as a freshman at North Carolina A&T State University the year before, I received the same messages and felt invisible in navigating college on my own. Although I graduated from Elon with a solid GPA and went on to graduate school, this does not mean my invisibility could not have been avoided. Academic advisors cannot forget about Black queer and gender nonconforming (BQGN) students who may feel similar invisibility.

While there is lack of research on the experiences of BQGN students, current research on Black gay male college students primarily focuses on how they tackle challenges regarding lack of support, being a double minority at PWIs, and their personal and psychological struggles (Means, 2014). Patton and Simmons' (2008) research on the experiences of Black lesbian students at an HBCU found these students encountered numerous challenges including feeling their identities were in conflict and not being accepted due to their sexuality. Existing research suggests higher levels of gender nonconformity increase the likelihood of adversity across both peer and family domains (Martin-Storey & August, 2016).

William A. Smith comprised the term *racial battle fatigue* in his research on how microaggressions affects Black students at PWIs. The RBF framework explains the physiological, psychological, and behavioral burdens imposed on racially marginalized and stigmatized groups and the amount of energy expended while coping with and fighting against systemic racism (Smith et al., 2016). These systems are found in higher education as Black students must navigate institutions that favor Whiteness (Chesler et al., 2005). Such experiences are not only what BQGN students carry when we advise them, but also to their classes.

Rather than serving as institutions of learning and scholarship, colleges and universities can be places of antagonism for Black students. There have been increasing reports of Black students experiencing racial trauma from their universities. Professors using racial epithets, White students calling the police on their Black peers using common areas, university employees calling the police on Black students attempting to use the library, and nooses appearing on campus after a Black student body president getting elected are only a few of the numerous cases seen in recent years. When Blackness, queerness, and nonconformity intersect, the burdens can be more profound as many studies have shown a connection among queerness and discrimination, harassment, and victimization on U.S. college campuses (Rankin, 2003; Rankin et al., 2010; Yost & Gilmore, 2011). Academic advisors cannot underestimate how these incidents impact the lives and academics of BQGN students. To best serve these students, there are methods that can be utilized.

Partner with the LGBTQ+ resource center on campus, if applicable. LGBTQ+ resource centers collaborate with faculty, staff, and students to develop programs and increase awareness on LGBTQ+ student issues. They usually host workshops and activities, oversee LGBTQ+ student organizations, and manage LGBTQ+ resource materials. There is a wealth of information that advisors can learn from working with their LGBTQ+ resource centers. Reach out and set up a meeting with the center staff, schedule a tour of the center, inquire about potential collaborations, and/or attend their sponsored events.

Explore and utilize the resources offered by Campus Pride. Campus Pride is a nonprofit organization that serves LGBTQ students, campus organizations, and allies in leadership development, support programs, and services to create safer and more inclusive LGBTQ friendly institutions (Campus Pride, n.d.). They provide several resources in the areas of leadership, organization, event planning, activism, and advocacy for queer and transgender students of color. Campus Pride also runs an Advisor Academy for professional staff and faculty members seeking to increase LGBTQ inclusivity and safety on their campuses.

Practice nurtured advising. Williams et al. (2008) describe nurtured advising as a specialized form of advising that simulates a concerned family member. They argue the nurturing advisor is a caring adult who shows they have the student's best interest at heart by communicating expectations and extending the core values of advising into teachable moments. As BQGN students are in need of safe spaces, the presence of a nurturing advisor can provide security and a sense of belonging to their institution.

Learn about the various facets of the BQGN community. Although far more research is needed on BQGN college students, advisors can still educate themselves on this population. Thanks to platforms such as Black Youth Project, Native Son Now, and *Out Magazine*, more BQGN stories are being told. With BQGN authors including Audre Lorde, bell hooks, Janet Mock, Patrisse Khan-Cullors, James Baldwin, Essex Hemphill, Clay Cane, and Darnell L. Moore to name a few, there are various books available for those who are interested in the BQGN experience. There is no better way to learn about the BQGN community than from our own perspectives.

BQGN students will notice when advisors are invested in their lives. Advisors should strive for these students to feel empowered and equipped after using their services. This can be verified through utilizing assessments where students can give feedback on the work advisors do. Through being intentional with BQGN students, advisors can ease concerns and make a notable difference. The success of BQGN students is certainly worth the effort.

Editors' Note

The text of this section was originally published in the June 2019 issue of NACADA's *Academic Advising Today*. Permission was graciously granted by both NACADA and the author to reprint in this book. While the content of the manuscript remains the same as the original publication, formatting has been updated to conform to the APA Publication Manual (7th edition) guidelines.

References

Campus Pride. (n.d.). *Mission, vision & values*. https://www.campuspride.org/about/mission/

Chesler, M. A., Lewis, A., & Crowfoot, J. (2005). *Challenging racism in higher education: Promoting justice*. Rowman & Littlefield.

Martin-Storey, A., & August, E. G. (2016). Harassment due to gender nonconformity mediates the association between sexual minority identity and depressive symptoms. *Journal of Sex Research, 53*(1), 85–97. https://doi.org/10.1080/0022 4499.2014.980497

Means, D. R. (2014). Demonized no more: The spiritual journeys and spaces of black gay male college students at predominantly white institutions (1720060413; ED557552). ERIC. https://search.proquest.com/dissertations-theses/demonized-no-more-spiritual-journeys-spaces-black/docview/1720060413/se-2?accountid=10639

Patton, L. D., & Simmons, S. L. (2008). Exploring complexities of multiple identities of lesbians in a black college environment. *Negro Educational Review, 59*(3–4), 197–215. http://citeseerx.ist.psu.edu/viewdoc/download?doi=10.1.1.706.7671&rep=rep1&type=pdf

Rankin, S., Weber, G., Blumenfeld, W., & Frazer, S. (2010). *2010 state of higher education for lesbian, gay, bisexual & transgender people*. Campus Pride.

Rankin, S. R. (2006). LGBTQA students on campus: Is higher education making the grade. *Journal of Gay & Lesbian Issues in Education 3*(2–3), 111–117. https://doi.org/10.1300/J367v03n02_11

Smith, W. A., Mustaffa, J. B., Jones, C. M., Curry, T. J., & Allen, W. R. (2016). "You make me wanna holler and throw up both my hands!": Campus culture, Black misandric microaggressions, and racial battle fatigue. *International Journal of Qualitative Studies in Education 29*(9), 1189–1209. https://doi.org/10.1080/0 9518398.2016.1214296

Williams, I. L., Glenn, P. W., & Wider, F. (2008, March 1). Nurtured advising: An essential approach to advising students at historically black college and universities. *Academic Advising Today, 31*(1). https://www.nacada.ksu.edu/Resources/Academic-Advising-Today/View-Articles/Nurtured-Advising-An-Essential-Approach-to-Advising-Students-at-Historically-Black-College-and-Universities.aspx

Yost, M. R., & Gilmore, S. (2011). Assessing LGBTQ campus climate and creating change. *Journal of Homosexuality, 58*(9), 1330–1354. https://doi.org/10.1080/0 0918369.2011.605744

Ally Narrative

Wendy Kay Schindler

Even as a queer woman, my journey as an ally took quite some time. I grew up an Evangelical Christian, believing being gay is a sin. I didn't have language beyond the word *gay* (and maybe lesbian/bisexual), and the concepts of being transgender or gender nonconforming were nowhere on my radar. I am fortunate to have wonderfully hospitable parents, so I never felt any animosity toward any LGBTQA+ identities. However, I unintentionally formed deeply held internal biases that any diversity in sexuality and gender identity was wrong and would lead a person to eternal damnation in Hell; I also believed it was my job to save people. Can you imagine the internal struggle I experienced to reckon with my own queer identity, let alone acting as an ally to others?

During my undergraduate years, many of my friends identified in some way under the LGBTQA+ umbrella. As a homesick college freshman, my new friends became my home-away-from-home and (unknowingly) made all the difference in the world when it came to my own identity and eventual work as an ally. I finally identified myself as bisexual in my early 20s and officially left Christianity (which left me feeling lost, but I eventually found peace in my identity as a spiritual humanist). At the time, had you asked me outright, I would have said, "I am an ally," but my actions wouldn't have reflected it. I was too focused on my own identities to truly perform the active work of an ally.

As I completed my graduate degree and started working as an academic advisor, I began to understand how to educate myself beyond the classroom. Because I had a greater sense of my own queer identity, I wanted to be an ally for my students. However, I certainly could not do so without becoming much more informed about the marginalization of LGBTQA+ populations. I attended my first NACADA Annual Conference and found the LGBTQA+ Advising and Advocacy Community. Attending their business meeting was a springboard for my journey, connecting me with resources and inciting my passion for allyhood.

My early focus was very student-driven. I started an LGBTQA+ student organization on my small campus and hoped students could recognize me as a safe person. Others took notice and began referring students to me, sometimes going so far as to drop a student off at my office without warning. I began to feel like the "token queer" and wished my colleagues would realize they can also do the work of an ally, no matter their identity. I realized I needed to take the next step in my journey: educating others about allyhood and advocating for larger systemic change on campus.

I now regularly present on LGBTQA+ topics and how they relate to students, addressing topics from basic terminology to Safe Zone training. I've advocated for all-gender restrooms with proper signage, college web pages dedicated to LGBTQA+ student resources, and institutional policies for using a student's chosen name. Additionally, I take opportunities for conversation on an individual level. When I hear something problematic, I look for ways to gently correct and educate. (Note: I take into account my physical safety and the safety of those around me in situations with strangers. Discretion is key.)

This journey has not been easy. I've learned to sit with discomfort when my worldview is challenged. I've been called out for problematic behavior and had to apologize, making a commitment to do better. As we all do, I make mistakes, but I've done my best to learn from them. Continual learning is important, but equally important is unlearning the urge to act on the internal biases I was socialized to accept from a young age. None of that feels good; it's all out of my comfort zone. However, I understand the value in discomfort. Discomfort drives me to make change.

I understand religion and allyhood can be a complex discussion. Ultimately, the work of an ally is to lift others up. If your beliefs are holding you back, you have extra work to do in order to be an effective ally. Dive deeper into the teachings of your religion. You may be surprised to find the tenets of your faith may react neutrally (or even positively) to diverse sexualities and genders. If you find you cannot reconcile your faith with allyhood, find neutral ways to assist and avoid harm. For example, knowing campus LGBTQA+ resources and making referrals can get a student the support they need without you feeling as though you've compromised yourself. If you feel this indirect method of assistance still compromises your religious beliefs, consider whether working with students is a good fit when you cannot fully commit yourself to the work of an ally.

In summary, my advice is to educate yourself. There is so much information available. Keep in mind it is not the responsibility of any queer person to teach you; you must take time to seek information on your own.

Contact people with whom you've developed a trusting relationship and ask if they would be willing to have a nuanced conversation about what you've learned. Use your newfound knowledge to support and advocate for your students. Prepare to be uncomfortable; it's inevitable but ultimately leads to good. Share what you've learned with others. Finally, realize you're on a journey. The work of an ally is ongoing and active. Ultimately, it is everyone's responsibility.

PART FOUR

CREATING INCLUSIVE SPACES

16

BECOMING ALLIES AND ADVOCATES

Craig M. McGill and Wendy Kay Schindler

With contributions from Debra A. Dotterer, Mark Duslak,
Mark S. Nelson, Dana Parcher, Andrew W. Puroway,
Kyle W. Ross, Amy Sannes, and Roxane Timon

Although academic advisors who identify as lesbian, gay, bisexual, trans, queer/questioning, asexual (LGBTQA+) have a vested interest in fighting against the marginalization of their community, it is crucial to enlist the support of dominant social group members as allies because they have more societal power. But what is an ally? Is it someone who is heterosexual or cisgender who is simply tolerant of LGBTQA+ people? What are the roles and responsibilities that come along with being an ally? Is it enough to simply identify as one?

An ally "works to end oppression in his or her personal and professional life through the support of, and as an advocate with and for, the oppressed population" (Washington & Evans, 1991, p. 195). There are many intrinsic benefits of being an ally, including a greater ability to relate to and work with all members of society, broader interpersonal relationships, a stronger sense of self-efficacy, increased self-esteem, and congruence between one's values and actions (Katz, 1978; McIntosh, 1998; Washington & Evans, 1991). However, no one is an ally automatically, even by virtue of their own marginalized identities. Allyhood involves a period of learning to break the "cycle of socialization" (Harro, 2000) through which we discern our role in an unjust society.

The notion of allyhood is not new, and it is easy for an advisor to say they advocate for the equity of every LGBTQA+ student. However, different identities are marginalized in unique ways, and LGBTQA+ is an umbrella term encompassing many different identities. An advisor who identifies with one or more of the identities under the LGBTQA+ umbrella is not automatically an ally for all other LGBTQA+ identities. For example, a bisexual woman is not automatically an ally to transgender individuals even though her identity is included in LGBTQA+. Additionally, internalized homo/bi/transphobia or heterosex/cissex/cisgenderism can lead to self-marginalization (Hardiman & Jackson, 1997). Allyhood requires active work and continuous practice; simply retaining the name is not the final objective.

Academic advisors are on the front lines of student success and often work with students who are different from themselves, which can cause dissonance. In his study gauging the comfort of academic advisors working with LGBTQA+ students, McGill (2013) found that participants grappled with what it meant to be an ally while weighing the cost of advocating for LGBTQA+ students. Struggling to be an ally is not inherently wrong; we are socialized to keep the current power structures in place: "People from privileged groups are routinely denied information and opportunities to understand their role in an unjust social system as well as honest feedback from people in oppressed groups" (Torres et al., 2003, p. 25). For example, even the most well-meaning cisgender advisor may not realize they have harmed a transgender student by failing to use their chosen name over their legal name. The advisor has simply been socialized otherwise. Regardless, the student may feel uncomfortable correcting the advisor due to the power dynamics at play in an advising appointment. This is not to say marginalized populations are responsible for ending oppression. However, we should recognize that people with privilege are systematically made oblivious to marginalization and must work to break this cycle of socialization (Harro, 2000).

Although academic advising literature has explored some of the needs of and resources for LGBTQA+ students (Forest, 2006; Joslin, 2007; Lindenberg, 2012; Matthews, 2019; Moorhead, 2005; Self, 2007; Smith, 2006), little has been written about advisors' comfort level and developmental needs when working with and supporting this cohort (Harrison, 2019; McGill, 2013). At the time of publication, no peer-reviewed, full-length articles on advising LGBTQA+ students had appeared in advising literature for over a decade, and no empirical studies had ever been conducted in the field of academic advising.

To help bridge that gap, we introduce some helpful development models, discuss potential barriers to ally formation, and propose an LGBTQA+ ally development model for academic advisors. To complement these concepts, we invited several advising professionals to reflect on their journey as LGBTQA+ allies through individual discussions over Zoom. After providing each participant with the transcript from their Zoom discussion, we asked them to write a brief personal reflection, organizing their experiences around three areas: their evolution of becoming an ally, previous and/or ongoing struggles with enacting allyhood, and advice for other allies. Five of these narratives are published in full within this book, and the remaining eight are incorporated into this chapter. We are indebted to Debra "Deb" A. Dotterer, Mark Duslak, Mark S. Nelson, Dana Parcher, Andrew "Drew" W. Puroway, Kyle W. Ross, Amy Sannes, and Roxane Timon for their important contributions.

Ally Formation

Over the past 20 years, scholars have developed several ally development models, ranging from a general approach (Broido, 2000; DiStefano et al., 2000; Ji, 2007; Jordan, 2012; Waters, 2010) to models with specific contexts. Space precludes thoroughly discussing all of these models, but we encourage readers to explore the topics and articles in the following list:

- Motives for heterosexual allies to work toward equity (Russell, 2011)
- Roles of allies in the workplace (Brooks & Edwards, 2009)
- Ally formation for counselors and career counselors (Asta & Vacha-Haase, 2013; Lynch et al., 2013)
- The impact of privilege when working in helping fields (Middleton et al., 2009)

The following literature explores ally advocacy within higher education:

- The effect of ally training on campus climate (Ballard et al., 2008; Worthen, 2011)
- Narratives of faculty members and staff allies on college campuses (Ryan et al., 2013)

Although the discussion of ally development focuses on advocating for LGBTQA+ students, much of what is discussed in this chapter can be applied to better serving any marginalized student. In this section, we discuss two models that have proved to be useful in exploring ally formation for LGBTQA+ students. Chojnacki and Gelberg's (1995) model—although originally designed for a counseling setting—can be applied to an academic advising context. Harro's (2000) cycle of socialization is helpful for any social justice work, including being an ally for LGBTQA+ students.

Allies in Helping Professions

Chojnacki and Gelberg (1995) were the first to describe ally formation in helping professions. Replace "counselor" with "advisor" and this model becomes appropriate for advisors to use in assessing their allyhood. Drawing on foundational gay identity formation work (Cass, 1979), the model consists of six stages:

1. *Confusion* is the first stage, when an advisor is unaware of gay, lesbian, and bisexual (GLB) oppression.
2. *Comparison* is the second stage, when an advisor becomes aware of GLB students.
3. *Tolerance* is the third stage, when an advisor meets GLB students and experiences emotional dissonance over becoming an ally.
4. *Acceptance* is the fourth stage, when an advisor "comes out" as an ally.
5. *Pride* is the fifth stage, when an advisor's fears and anxiety turn to feelings of "increased self-esteem and efficacy" (Broido, 2000, p. 354).
6. *Integration* is the sixth stage, when "the values [advisors] espouse in their professional lives are continued in their personal lives" (Broido, 2000, p. 347).

Dana's evolution as an LGBTQA+ ally provides an illustration of the Cass (1979) model. As a child, in the *confusion* and *comparison* stages, Dana was vaguely aware of the differences between herself and her sister, but she was unaware of a specific and broader context for LGBTQA+ individuals:

> My sister was 9 years older than me and not interested in "playing Barbies," but I knew that was not the only reason for her lack of interest. Even as a kid, I knew the gender norms I learned to follow felt out of place for my sister and that her signed photo of Olivia Newton John signaled more than fandom. So, when she decided to attend an all-women's university, I knew her decision was more complex than my parents realized. My sister (who gave her permission for me to share this) did not come out to my family until she was in her 30s, which meant my conservative parents did not discuss the needs and experiences of LGBTQA+ individuals with my brother and I as kids. Still, my sister's unspoken identity certainly set the stage for my allyhood journey.

Dana moved into the *tolerance* and *acceptance* stages when she attended college. By participating in relevant trainings, Dana gained more awareness of LGBTQA+ oppression and was able to form relationships with more LGBTQA+ people. However, her actions were limited to safe environments:

As an undergraduate student at an institution in Texas not known at the time for its commitment to inclusiveness, I became involved as a mentor, helping incoming students, like myself, transition from small, rural towns to a large university. I attended my first Safe Zone training, and felt relieved by finally discovering vocabulary and stories that shed light on my childhood. The more involved I became, the more I learned about gender and the complexity of identity. As an upperclassman, I volunteered for the student-driven campus HelpLine, undergoing 60 hours of intense training and learning to apply active listening and collaborative problem-solving skills into conversation. While role-playing scenarios in training petrified me, they also changed me. They strengthened the skills I had begun to develop as a mentor. I needed those tools in order to talk openly about isolation, loneliness, and thoughts of suicide—challenges LGBTQA+ individuals too often face.

In graduate school, I began building professional growth from the personal growth experienced during my undergraduate years. In the classroom, I spent time learning about gender and sexuality theory and applied that knowledge to my professional work, helping students overcome challenges. In my personal life, many of my friends identified as LGTBQA+. One of my closest friends was an openly gay man who taught me the value of being comfortable with discomfort and what it means to truly support something meaningful. I realized through my friendship with him that to call myself an ally was easy—of course I supported inclusive spaces for all individuals. But, creating those spaces requires more than just support; it requires action.

As she continued her journey into her career, Dana transitioned into the *pride* stage and then to the *integration* stage. She overcame her feelings of discomfort and found greater self-esteem in her support of LGBTQA+ rights. While working to create equity for her students on campus, Dana's personal and professional lives were integrated as she became an advocate in the community. She experienced greater efficacy in her work, recognizing the need to continue to learn and grow in her allyhood:

In 2015, I was working at a university in Alabama when same-sex marriage had become legal in the state. However, the probate judge of the county I lived in no longer offered office weddings. Immediately, I utilized the power of the internet to become ordained and joined a group of people who were arranging weddings in the city park. We organized volunteer officiants, photographers, florists, bakers, and musicians to gather in the park to help all individuals celebrate their love and make a choice I believe all individuals should have. "Wedding week"—as it was known—taught me that even in a state typically known for its narrow views on same-sex marriage, individuals can make change. The opportunity to create change is the reason I have volunteered at various crisis hotlines, become a victim's advocate, participated in protests, and used my voice to support the needs of others.

Only 5 months after wedding week, a student of mine, transitioning from female to male, died by suicide. In my career, I had lost count of the number of students who had trusted me enough to come out, who had shared the difficulties they faced with their family, or with trying to get their preferred name to be used by faculty. However, the struggles of all my students could not have prepared me for the death of this student, which also served as a reminder to me of the work that remains. As an ally, I believe in creating a more equitable, safe, and supportive community for all individuals. And, as an advocate, I am committed to strengthening my skills in working with college students, staying current on emerging LGBTQA+ challenges, and developing campus policy that creates more inclusive spaces and processes for students. I continue to evolve, but I have come a long way from a time when I had no words to communicate with my sister about her identity. I continue to use my voice to advocate for others and for a world in which everyone feels like they belong.

Overall, Chojnacki and Gelberg's (1995) model provides academic advisors with a helpful framework for LGBTQA+ ally development. Although this model is presented as linear, consistent progress is not guaranteed. LGBTQA+ is not a monolithic identity but an umbrella, encompassing many identities, so one may move through the stages of ally formation more quickly for certain identities. For example, an advisor may have more knowledge of and opportunities to support gay and lesbian students, so that advisor may move into the *pride* stage relatively quickly for students with commonly understood sexualities. However, that same advisor may have little experience and understanding of transgender students, causing them to remain in the *tolerance* stage longer for identities related to gender. Additionally, accepting a position at a more conservative workplace or within a politically oppressive climate could lead an advisor to regress from *pride* or *acceptance* for the sake of personal preservation. Allyhood requires continual and intentional action along with reflecting on the socialization that has shaped our thoughts and biases.

Cycle of Socialization

Although advisors may have a desire to help students, they must first realize the system from which they have come and recognize how that system influenced the way they think about the world. People are born into various social identities over which they have no control (e.g., race, sex assigned at birth, socioeconomic standing, country of origin, ability status, etc.) and, as a result, are positioned to experience different levels of privilege and oppression. These systems are historic, and humans are born blamelessly into them: "There is no reason for any of us to feel guilty or responsible for the world into which we are born. We are innocents, falling into an already established system" (Harro, 2000, p. 16). Privileged identities create dominant agent groups (e.g., cisgender men, white, Christian, heterosexual, etc.) that lead to the oppression and creation of subordinated groups (e.g., women, historically disenfranchised races, non-Christian religions, LGBTQA+, etc.).

Observing this reality, Harro (2000) proposed a cyclical socialization model that begins at birth and cycles through multiple phases: *first socialization, institutional and cultural socialization, enforcements, results,* and *actions* (Harro, 2000).

Our *first socialization* comes from those we love and trust most: our caregivers. We learn social roles, norms, and rules from family and close friends that we must follow to "be" each of our social identities. As children, these are seen as unquestioned truths. Examples include: "girls are supposed to like boys," "boys don't cry," "homosexuality is a sin," and "girls play with dolls; boys play with trucks." These messages may be passed on consciously or unconsciously, but they are generally not questioned by the child.

We move into *institutional and cultural socialization* when external messengers strengthen our worldview. Governmental, religious, medical, media, and educational institutions bolster the learned norms about who should have power and who should not, thereby reinforcing biases and stereotypes. At this point, *enforcements* (i.e., rewarding the status quo and punishing anything else) begin. Punishment can be enforced against target and agent group members. For example, a transwoman may be beaten to death for using a woman's restroom and a heterosexual man marching in a pride parade may be accused of and harassed for being a closeted gay man.

The *result* is an oppressive society for target and agent groups. Target groups may experience high levels of stress, depression, anger, and learned hopelessness from their disempowerment. Agent groups may experience high levels of stress due to guilt over their unearned privilege, fear caused by a distorted reality, and dehumanization of target groups. At this point, we have the choice to take *action*, which is where allyhood begins. As oppression becomes apparent, individuals can choose to maintain the status quo or they can break the cycle by choosing to challenge the system. In order for societal change to occur, this cyclical cycle must be interrupted.

Breaking the cycle of socialization is difficult and uncomfortable, but it is necessary to dismantle oppression. Drew recognized and illustrated this feeling as a member of an agent group:

> My ally journey has been imperfect and messy. Like any unfolding and never-ending process of enlightenment, I wish to have been enlightened first and lived it second. In retrospect, I want to have seen people's humanity—to truly know what it means to see someone's humanity. I still want that more than ever. I want to have lived not hurting others because of my internalized homophobia and pressure to perform a toxic masculinity that conflates sex, sexuality, and gender. In my journey, I have been blessed with so many gracious, patient, and forgiving friends along the way.

When we break the cycle, we may experience strong emotions, but it is important to keep those potentially strong emotions from pushing oneself away from allyhood.

Barriers to Becoming an Ally

In addition to our own painful awareness, there are many barriers to becoming an ally. For example, allies in higher education might be perceived as being too liberal or radical, especially by senior administrators at institutions with conservative boards or locales. As academic advisors are generally not protected by tenure and have limited power compared to upper administration (Pryor, 2020), job security is a legitimate concern when advocating for potentially controversial campus policies. Mark D. described his struggle as follows:

> One challenge I faced in becoming an ally was balancing advocacy versus safety and security. My job is fairly visible and taking strong stances, especially when they are in opposition to the beliefs of executive leaders, is dangerous. I feel guilty that I have not done enough to advocate for the LGBTQA+ community, and I wrestle with the risks of putting my employment (and future employment) in jeopardy. I have not found a satisfactory way to resolve this tension yet but continue to reflect upon it.

In addition to the fear of societal backlash, a potential ally may lack confidence in their ability to make a difference. They may fear saying or doing the "wrong thing" and therefore, choose inaction. Roxane shared:

> One of my challenges in allyhood is the fear of inadvertently offending someone. When I walk into a room to greet a group of people and say

something like, "Hey *guys*," I'm mad at myself for not thinking before I speak. I try to be more mindful of the words I use and continue to get in the habit of using correct and inclusive language.

Amy, in contrast, noted that being afraid of making a mistake should not lead to inaction:

> Don't shy away from being an ally just because you fear offending someone with an incorrect usage of a term or a pronoun. I have found individuals are willing to help with your understanding if you are willing to ask and make an effort to educate yourself.

Drew added that complacency can be the enemy of action:

> There have been times in which I rested on my laurels. I fear the more my career in advising administration takes on in terms of duties, the less space there is for listening to student voices and needs. There is a culture on campus that still must change and at times, I lose sight of my responsibility in changing it. I think of where we were when I started, and the progress that has been made—I feel okay. Our leadership is more open to inclusion than when I began at my institution 14 years ago, which gives some comfort, but we were not in a good place having had major controversies months before I arrived at the institution. However, we are not yet a society transformed. Getting comfortable can be a bad sign for an ally.

Additionally, allies may lack the self-awareness to realize their privilege and participation in an oppressive society. Mark D. described his initial ignorance around the concept of being gender nonconforming by saying:

> Gender fluidity is a concept I didn't grow up with or immediately understand fully. So, my initial thoughts about it were ignorant and uninformed. I had a moment of realization when I attended a conference and spent some time with someone who was gender nonbinary. It humanized this concept for me, and I immediately realized when something is new to me, I have a tendency to draw more assumptions and conclusions about it than I should. This experience taught me that I must be skeptical of my first impressions, and that it's important to learn from the source, not others' opinions and biases.

Working toward dismantling a system of power cannot be effective if one denies or ignores their contribution to that system—regardless of whether that contribution is passive or active. Nor can one effect change without knowing the marginalized people at the heart of the struggle. Drew advised:

> Being an ally is an always/constant sense of becoming. I hope that as I grow and age, I continue to see everyone's humanity more deeply in ways that enrich my own humanity. Allyhood runs aground when you are not connecting with communities of oppressed people. My advice is that it takes intention to stay connected with the community on your campus of both students, faculty, and staff. It may get more and more difficult the further you advance in your career. Listen. Act. You will fuck it up, it is messy, but keep showing up.

Perhaps most importantly, an ally must be patient with themselves. Amy noted, "Be sure to give yourself a break. It is important to be knowledgeable, but information is constantly changing. As long as you are committed to supporting and advocating to end oppression, you can do the work of an ally." Stepping into the role of an ally is often and necessarily uncomfortable. But overcoming these barriers is critical to allyhood and the creation of a more just society.

A Model for Academic Advisor LGBTQA+ Ally Development

According to Ji (2007), "in a homo[/bi/trans]phobic society, it is not enough to accept passively LGBT persons; allies need to express openly their support so everyone can be free to either say they are LGBT or that they know someone who is" (p. 179). Advisors who become active allies can play a crucial role in a student's coming out process and, thereby, contribute to that student's college success (Self, 2007). However, ally development is not incumbent solely upon those who identify as heterosexual and/or cisgender. A gay or lesbian person can still perpetuate biphobia and transphobia.

Introspection is a key part in an advisor's ally development process. All advisors, including LGBTQA+ advisors, must reflect upon their sexual and gender identity development and ally development to become more effective allies (Broido, 2000; Chojnacki & Gelberg, 1995; Gelberg & Chojnacki, 1995; Ji, 2007; Waters, 2010). Heterosexual and/or cisgender individuals may never have needed to think about their development in the same way as most LGBTQA+ individuals because they are members of a privileged social group (Mohr, 2002). For those interested in debunking the perception that heterosexuality is the "default" sexual orientation, it may be useful to read literature concerning heterosexual identity development (Jordan, 2012; Mohr, 2002; Worthington et al., 2002). Regardless of sexual or gender identity, all helping professionals can better aid clients if they engage in reflection (Young, 2016).

From our review of current literature, we have developed a five-tenet model for ally development:

- Become informed about LGBTQA+ affairs and concerns
- Advocate for LGBTQA+ students
- Embrace discomfort
- Educate others
- Keep learning

Tenet 1: Become Informed About LGBTQA+ Affairs and Concerns

Becoming an ally requires learning LGBTQA+ terms, definitions, symbols, and culture. Roxane suggests, "exploring novels, films, articles, and podcasts that tackle LGBTQA+ issues . . . and build connections with other allies—this will all give you a better understanding of what this community needs." Advisors can participate in Safe Zone training on campuses where it is available. If it is not available, advisors can contact local institutions that would allow them to join their trainings. Although in-person training is preferable because of the chance to discuss and process with others, there are online Safe Zone resources, if an in-person option is not available. Advisors can also grow and learn by attending conference sessions that focus on working with LGBTQA+ students. If travel funding is limited at an institution, advisors can participate in webinars. Webinars provide a way for multiple advisors to participate. For example, NACADA has multiple webinars available online (e.g., McGill et al., 2014). Kyle suggested:

> There are also many other opportunities beyond formal education with which you can engage. For me, art in all its forms can be powerfully disruptive of my unconscious biases grounded in heteronormativity. Find the opportunities that resonate with you and help you learn and unlearn.

Furthermore, asking campus colleagues and students questions is a powerful way to learn and show concern for students. Advisors can also observe colleagues who share their identity and are experienced, effective allies to learn how to be a better ally (Harrison, 2019). However, advisors should exercise caution and good judgement; it is not the job of LGBTQA+ people to educate those wanting to be allies, especially considering that so much information is readily available. It may be better to save more nuanced questions for trusted relationships.

Tenet 2: Advocate for LGBTQA+ Students

Being an ally demands more than simply declaring it. Allyhood requires action and commitment. This involves recognizing heteronormative bias (see chapter 2) and seeking to overcome it. Using inclusive language will help LGBTQA+ students feel more comfortable and will help non-LGBTQA+ students become aware of their privilege. For example, advisors could use terms like *partner* or *significant other* instead of assuming gender with terms like *boyfriend* or *girlfriend.* Identifying your gender pronouns when meeting with students and in email signatures helps raise awareness that pronouns should not be assumed. In the quest for inclusivity, advisors should be prepared to support students who have experienced anti-LGBTQA+ incidents.

Mark N. suggested it is important to "learn, know, and understand when to sit and when to stand," saying:

> When allies sit, we are providing our LGBTQA+ students, peers, colleagues, and friends the opportunity to express their voice through storytelling and teaching. We provide our allies a platform to exercise their voice. We provide a space to speak clearly and confidently. But there comes a time when the ally must stand. Maybe it's when our LGBTQA+ students, peers, colleagues, and friends are unavailable or not in the room. Maybe it's when they are unable to speak or lack the right words for the moment. Maybe it's when you know their rights and civil liberties have been violated, thus meaning our LGBTQA+ students, peers, colleagues, and friends need the . . . ally to assist in setting up a strategy to move forward. It starts with listening and asking questions.

Mark D. echoed the importance of action, but claimed that one must engage in action that brings about societal change:

> Make a distinction between activities that actually lead to social change and activities that are "political hobbyism" (Hersh, 2020). There's a huge difference in effect between liking a tweet and canvassing for a local politician who is championing LGBTQA+ causes. It may feel like certain actions should be making a huge impact (because your Instagram post reached 1,000 followers), but, in reality, that does not amount to much change. Often, it is the error of acting too globally and missing out on the local ways to change communities. So, my recommendation is to reflect upon the impact of your allyhood. I continue to ask myself, "What has my work actually done?" At the most basic level, my plan is to continue to communicate and provide a safe space for LGBTQA+ students. Additionally, I will continue to identify and advocate for substantive changes at the college and my community to build a more equitable and supportive environment for LGBTQA+ individuals.

Advisors should be aware of resources for LGBTQA+ students both on and off campus, and they should advocate for all-inclusive policies. Further, it is essential to use a student-centered approach when addressing their needs: "Allies *ask* how to help instead of *assuming they know* how to help" (Harrison, 2019, para. 5).

If campus culture is less-than-welcoming or even outright hostile for LGBTQA+ students, advisors should create an inviting office space. Displaying LGBTQA+-friendly symbols, such as a rainbow flag or a Safe Zone symbol, allows students to easily identify the space as inclusive. Deb described finding ways to show inclusivity at a NACADA conference after the state where the conference took place passed discriminatory legislation against LGBTQA+ individuals:

> The NACADA Executive Office worked with the conference commit-tee to address ways we could provide a welcoming environment to our attendees. As a team, the committee identified gay-friendly restaurants and businesses to highlight for attendees. We designed buttons that read "Love All, Advise All" to sell during the conference with proceeds sup-porting a local organization supporting LGBTQA+ youth. Attendees overwhelmingly responded and wore the buttons proudly throughout their time at the conference. They frequented the inclusive businesses we provided and turned a negative action into an opportunity to demon-strate their support for the LBGTQA+ community. Before the end of the conference, the conference facility staff met with the conference commit-tee to praise our response to the situation and ask if they could share our actions with other properties throughout the state. I was never prouder of our team and of the organization.

Additionally, allyhood can be considered a retention tool: "Advisors who are available and affirming to students who share important milestones of romantic interest, cultural festivities, and group identification, demonstrate support that may lead to increased institutional retention and students bet-ter integrating their intellectual and social identities" (McCleaf, 2007, p. 5). Roxane said:

> Assuming that someone else will stand up for LGBTQA+ students is not enough. You don't need to have formal experience to be involved in allyhood nor do you need to identify as LGBTQA+ to be an ally—these are common misconceptions that potential allies may have.

Anyone can act as a refuge for LGBTQA+ students and aid in their college success.

Tenet 3: Embrace Discomfort

Being an ally can be uncomfortable. This discomfort can come from internal and external sources. However, exposure to LGBTQA+ oppression can help allies understand the systemic nature of oppression in a heteronormative society. Mark N. noted:

> The first challenge to allyhood is a willingness to learn and listen and confront your biases. Learning to listen and listening to learn empowers oppressed people while building rapport and trust. To do so, I must confront my prejudices and my Christian privilege before I can learn and listen freely. My aim is to learn and listen without casting judgment, without making preconceived assumptions, and without drawing false conclusions. Allies must refrain from growing numb to the feelings of the oppressed. We must allow our LGBTQA+ friends an honest ear built on trust.

When an advisor engages in introspection, it is important to assess their implicit biases, which can lead to some unexpected results. No matter how enlightened a person may believe themselves to be, everyone has experienced a lifetime of messaging that subconsciously shapes their internal thought process (Harro, 2000). To move forward, one must recognize these biases and seek to reduce them. There are helpful tools to help you get started. For instance, the Gay Affirmative Practice Scale (GAP) asks 30 questions to gauge a counselor's competency and comfort level working with gay and lesbian clients (Crisp, 2006). Similarly, the Implicit Association Tests (IAT) developed by researchers at Harvard, "measures the strength of associations between concepts (e.g., Black people, gay people) and evaluations (e.g., good, bad) or stereotypes (e.g., athletic, clumsy)" (Project Implicit, 2011).

An advisor may experience external discomfort when considering how others may perceive their actions. Advocacy may lead others to assume the advisor identifies as LGBTQA+ and, thus, the advisor may be subjugated to the marginalization LGBTQA+ individuals experience. This is a real fear. However, an advisor could be experiencing internal discomfort as they project this fear onto colleagues who are not passing judgment. In either case, advisors should remind themselves why being an ally is vital. Amy related to this experience, noting:

> I was divorced after 27 years of marriage, and, as my personal life changed, I found I began to struggle with my identity, something I had previously not questioned for years. Cycling back through my own identity redevelopment, I found it harder to be an ally for other groups. This was disturbing to me at first as I started to wonder if my ally work had been convenient

or "fake." In the face of my singlehood, I was too afraid to be labeled as gay and, therefore, the reason I was single (an off-handed comment I overheard). As I reflect on this time, I realize I was even more aware of how it felt to be a straight woman who was now "labeled" something she isn't and how uncomfortable that is, but more importantly, how fragile our identities can be and how hard it is to not allow what others think of us to affect our actions.

Deb also described her discomfort:

I see myself as an ally, but I would like to move toward being more of an advocate. I wish I had the strength to better support LGBTQA+ students as an ally in public settings. This is not my natural, comfortable response to things. I have never protested, but I feel I could be more outspoken, and I do find I am moving in that direction when conversations take a discriminatory or exclusive turn. I will advocate for students, but it is as a result of a one-on-one experience, I still hesitate in a large group to take the lead. Often power differentiation stifles my ability to speak up in the moment. I then beat myself up for not saying something. Fundamentally, we need to stop beating ourselves up in these situations. We must forgive ourselves and put that negative energy into speaking up the next time an opportunity rises.

Allyhood is about showing support to others and dismantling an oppressive system. It is a powerful stance to take and the right thing to do. Mark N. shared his experience:

In my late 20s, a friend of mine, who identifies as a gay, queer man, shared with me how his clients made derogatory and suggestive comments about his sexuality. My friend felt he did not have support nor anyone he could turn to in his office and left his job because of "irreconcilable differences" between the office philosophy and his own beliefs. Not only did my friend report feeling alone and voiceless, he was not provided the opportunity to defend himself. I supported him as a living, breathing, eating, educated man who needed to earn a living just like me. Despite our identity differences, we all deserve fair treatment. From that day forward, I committed to becoming an LGBTQA+ ally. But at times, I have struggled with allyhood and advocacy. Becoming a better ally comes with time, experience, mistakes, forgiveness, learning, love, understanding, and growth. Interpreting and navigating my allyhood came with the charge to confront my Christian privilege. Confronting that privilege meant heartfelt, honest apologies, admission of my own wrongdoing, and seeking forgiveness.

Embracing the discomfort of allyhood is crucial because equity for those who identify as LGBTQA+ (as well as other marginalized populations) leads to liberation for us all.

Tenet 4: Educate Others

As an advisor becomes a stronger ally, educating colleagues becomes increasingly important. The more informed others become, the more likely campus culture will unravel heteronormative assumptions in day-to-day practice. Kyle considered this notion, saying, "Right now, I am committed to educating others on privilege and concepts of social justice, but I have not found what action looks like for me yet beyond informing others." Educating others can take on many forms—from one-on-one conversations to conference presentations to formal research projects.

One-on-one conversations can be casual but rich in content, leading all parties to learn more about being an ally. Advisors should seek out these conversations often to educate others and keep themselves immersed in learning. In some instances, a conversation may become uncomfortable, particularly if it is in response to an anti-LGBTQA+ incident. When possible, it is best to confront problematic behaviors immediately to make the most impact. Not only does confrontation address the actions of the person responsible, it also benefits others in the vicinity who can learn from the situation. At times, you may only learn about incidents after the fact. For example, an advisor may need to address a colleague after learning the colleague is not using a transgender student's correct pronouns. A direct conversation may be best, but if that colleague is violating a campus policy, an advisor should also report the incident to human resources.

Conducting and presenting research on campus or at conferences can reach a broader audience beyond immediate colleagues. The more informed advisors are about being an ally and about issues such as heteronormativity and homophobia, the more students will be supported to achieve success. In light of the minimal literature regarding academic advisors as allies for LGBTQA+ students, formal research projects are always a needed addition to higher education.

Tenet 5: Keep Learning

Becoming informed, advocating for students, embracing discomfort, educating others, and other steps toward being an ally should not be viewed as one-time activities. Rather, they are iterative and ongoing, keeping abreast of new and ever-changing information. Being an ally for LGBTQA+ students is a journey, not a destination. Deb articulates this idea:

Being an ally is a continual journey without an end. You consistently need to deal with your own biases as you engage with others. I have a long way to go but understand that we are all human beings who I believe ultimately try to do our best every day. Always keep an open mind and listen to individuals' stories. It is through listening we allow the voices of those who have been silenced to be heard.

Kyle noted:

> The process of learning and unlearning never stops. There will always be a counternarrative you are not aware of that sheds light on the systemic oppression of LGBTQA+ people. There will always be an unconscious bias you may not be aware of because of its link to other aspects of your identity in relationship to gender and sexuality. There will always be opportunities to educate yourself. Continue to read books written by LGBTQA+ people on social justice and engage in professional development opportunities that deepen your learning and advocacy skills.

In addition to self-reflection, engaging in current literature is also important because research is paramount to acting with authority. Without the backing of quality research, we can only hope to make a positive difference, potentially doing harm without recognizing it. We must always look forward and track our results—even in informal ways. From there, we can adjust our methods as we receive new information. The goal of an ally should always be progress, not perfection. For Roxane, part of learning is to practice patience with herself:

> It may take some trial and error to know exactly what to say or how to react to situations. Ultimately, the most important question that allies should ask themselves is how they can contribute to a more equitable, respectful, and safer environment for the LGBTQA+ community.

Beyond advising literature, advisors can also learn valuable information about working with LGBTQA+ students from other disciplines. For instance, what does career counseling literature say about life outside of academia for LGBTQA+ students? Graduation is a scary prospect for many LBGTQA+ students who may consider their campus to be safer than the outside world. What are the legal issues for LGBTQA+ persons in your area? What does K–12 literature say about LGBTQA+ students before they enter college? Literature on LGBTQA+ issues in adult education (Eichler, 2010) and career counseling (Gelberg & Chojnacki, 1995) can be a helpful tool in advisor ally development (see chapter 7).

Self and Group Reflection

Becoming comfortable with the roles and responsibilities of being an ally takes time. Advisors will make mistakes but can persistently learn to do and be better. As Ji (2007) reminds us, "Allies are not born; they are trained" (p. 183). Becoming an ally is a continual journey. It is unrealistic to expect an academic advisor to understand and accept allyhood overnight. However, academic advisors can be better allies by becoming informed about LGBTQA+ affairs and concerns, advocating for LGBTQA+ students, embracing discomfort, educating others, and maintaining a commitment to continual learning. Creating a more just and equitable society for LGBTQA+ individuals creates a better world for everyone. It is worth the work. The daunting process of being an ally must be acknowledged, appreciated, and commended.

Throughout this chapter, we have demonstrated the importance of introspection into an advisor's social identity development and the biases they learned through the cycle of socialization. In concluding this chapter and reflecting on the other five ally narratives in this book, we ask that you consider the following self-reflection questions to start interrogating your privilege (or lack thereof) within an oppressive society:

- When did you first become aware of diverse sexualities?
- When did you first become aware of diverse gender identities?
- What did you first learn about the dominant view toward sexuality and gender?
- How were these views about societal roles and norms strengthened and by whom (e.g., parents, friends, school, television, religion, etc.)?
- Have your views changed over time? How so? Has any of that change come from advising students?
- In what ways do you benefit from societal privilege? In what ways are you marginalized? How does this information help or hinder your work with advisees?
- What are some things you are unlearning in order to break the cycle of socialization? How does this make you a better advisor for your students?

To gain even more perspective on allyhood within an oppressive society, we recommend using this activity in graduate classrooms and professional development group activities. For instance, the group could read this chapter in advance, partner up to consider responses to the material and these questions, and, finally, hold a discussion with the full group. Additional questions to consider with others could include:

- How do your answers differ from your partner's?
- What can you learn from each other?
- Is the full group more diverse than you realized?
- Whose experiences are similar to your own and whose are different?
- Have you encountered any surprises?
- What can you take away from reflecting with this group?

An important note for activity facilitators: Group members should only be asked to share at their comfort level. Those with marginalized identities should not be expected to carry additional emotional labor or relive trauma in a group setting simply for the sake of sharing.

References

Asta, E. L., & Vacha-Haase, T. (2013). Heterosexual ally development in counseling psychologists experiences, training, and advocacy. *The Counseling Psychologist, 41*(4), 493–529. https://doi.org/10.1177%2F0011000012453174

Ballard, S. L., Bartle, E., & Masequesmay, G. (2008). *Finding queer allies: The impact of ally training and Safe Zone stickers on campus climate.* https://files.eric.ed.gov/fulltext/ED517219.pdf

Broido, E. M. (2000). Ways of being an ally to lesbian, gay, and bisexual students. In V. A. Wall, & N. J. Evans (Eds.), *Toward acceptance: Sexual orientation issues on campus* (pp. 345–370). University Press of America.

Brooks, A. K., & Edwards, K. (2009). Allies in the workplace: Including LGBT in HRD. *Advances in Developing Human Resources, 11*(1), 136–149. https://doi.org/10.1177%2F1523422308328500

Cass, V. C. (1979). Homosexual identity formation: A theoretical model. *Journal of Homosexuality, 4*(3), 219–235. https://doi.org/10.1300/J082v04n03_01

Chojnacki, J. T. & Gelberg, S. (1995). The facilitation of a gay/lesbian/bisexual support-therapy group by heterosexual counselors. *Journal of Counseling & Development, 73*(3), 352–354. https://doi.org/10.1002/j.1556-6676.1995.tb01763.x

Crisp, C. (2006). The gay affirmative practice scale (GAP): A new measure for assessing cultural competence with gay and lesbian clients. *Social Work, 51*(2), 115–126. https://doi.org/10.1093/sw/51.2.115

DiStefano, T. M., Croteau, J. M., Anderson, M. Z., Kampa-Kokesch, S., & Bullard, M. A. (2000). Experiences of being heterosexual allies to lesbian, gay, and bisexual people: A qualitative exploration. *Journal of College Counseling, 3*, 131–141. https://doi.org/10.1002/j.2161-1882.2000.tb00173.x

Eichler, M. A. (2010). Joining the family: Experiences of being and becoming ally activists of LGBTQ people. *Journal of Transformative Education, 8*(2), 89–102. https://doi.org/10.1177%2F1541344611406904

Forest, L. (2006, December 1). Advising gay, lesbian, bisexual, and transgender students. *Academic Advising Today, 29*(4). https://nacada.ksu.edu/Resources/Academic-Advising-Today/View-Articles/Advising-Gay-Lesbian-Bisexual-and-Transgender-Students.aspx

Gelberg, S., & Chojnacki, J. T. (1995). Developmental transitions of gay/lesbian/bisexual-affirmative, heterosexual career counselors. *Career Development Quarterly, 43*(3), 267–273. https://doi.org/10.1002/j.2161-0045.1995.tb00867.x

Hardiman, R., & Jackson, B. W. (1997). Conceptual foundations for social justice courses. In M. Adams, L. A. Bell, & P. Griffin (Eds.), *Teaching for diversity and social justice* (pp. 16–29). Routledge.

Harrison, C. (2019, November 18). Why allyship matters in advising. *Academic Advising Today, 42*(4). https://nacada.ksu.edu/Resources/Academic-Advising-Today/View-Articles/Why-Allyship-Matters-In-Advising.aspx

Harro, B. (2000). The cycle of socialization. In M. Adams, W. J. Blumenfeld, R. Castañeda, H. W. Hackman, M. L. Peters, & X. Zuñiga (Eds.), *Readings for diversity and social justice: An anthology on racism, antisemitism, sexism, heterosexism, ableism, and classism* (pp. 15–21). Routledge.

Hersh, E. (2020). *Politics is for power: How to move beyond political hobbyism, take action, and make real change.* Scribner.

Ji, P. (2007). Being a heterosexual ally to the lesbian, gay, bisexual, and transgendered community: Reflections and development. *Journal of Gay & Lesbian Psychotherapy, 11*(3–4), 173–185. https://doi.org/10.1300/J236v11n03_10

Jordan, M. L. (2012). Heterosexual ally identity development: A conceptual model. *Journal of the Indiana University Student Personnel Association,* 67–78. https://scholarworks.iu.edu/journals/index.php/jiuspa/article/view/1342/1947

Joslin, J. (2007). Working with lesbian, gay, bisexual, transgender, and queer students. In P. Jordan & L. Huff (Eds.), *Advising special populations* (pp. 87–95). NACADA.

Katz, J. H. (1978). *White awareness: Handbook for antiracism training.* University of Oklahoma Press.

Lindenberg, M. (2012). *Transgender students: Seven recommendations for academic advisors.* NACADA Clearinghouse of Academic Advising Resources. http://www.nacada.ksu.edu/Resources/Clearinghouse/View-Articles/Advising-issues-for-transgender-students.aspx

Lynch, S. L., Bruhn, R. A., & Henriksen, R. C. (2013). Influences of training and personal experiences on counselor trainees' GLBT ally development: A case study. *The Qualitative Report, 18*(4), 1–20. https://nsuworks.nova.edu/cgi/viewcontent.cgi?article=1561&context=tqr

Matthews, M. (2019, May 17). Approaches for advising and supporting black queer and gender nonconforming students. *Academic Advising Today, 42*(2). https://nacada.ksu.edu/Resources/Academic-Advising-Today/View-Articles/Approaches-for-Advising-and-Supporting-Black-Queer-and-Gender-Nonconforming-Students.aspx

McCleaf, K. (2007, June 1). Sexual minority students: An academic advisor's thoughts. *Academic Advising Today, 30*(2). https://nacada.ksu.edu/Resources/Academic-Advising-Today/View-Articles/Sexual-Minority-Students-An-Academic-Advisors-Thoughts.aspx

McGill, C. M. (2013, November 11). LGBTQA allyhood: Academic advisors reflect. *Academic Advising Today 36*(4). https://www.nacada.ksu.edu/Resources/Academic-Advising-Today/View-Articles/LGBTQA-Allyhood-Academic-Advisors-Reflect.aspx

McGill, C. M., Metzger, A., Carlson, C., & Vickers, N. (2014, January 30). *LGBTQA ally development and advocacy empowerment for academic advisors* [Webinar]. NACADA Webinar Series. http://www.nacada.ksu.edu/Resources/Product-Details/ID/REC054CD.aspx

McIntosh, P. (1998). *White privilege and male privilege: A personal account of coming to see correspondences through work in women's studies.* Wellesley College Center for Research on Women.

Middleton, V. A., Anderson, S. K., & Banning, J. H. (2009). The journey to understanding privilege: A meta-narrative approach. *Journal of Transformative Education, 7*(4), 294–311. https://doi.org/10.1177%2F1541344610386868

Mohr, J. J. (2002). Heterosexual identity and the heterosexual therapist: Using identity as a framework for understanding sexual orientation issues in psychotherapy. *The Counseling Psychologist, 30*(4), 532–566. https://doi.org/10.1177%2F00100002030004003

Moorhead, C. (2005). *Advising lesbian, gay, bisexual, and transgender students in higher education.* NACADA Clearinghouse of Academic Advising Resources. https://nacada.ksu.edu/Resources/Clearinghouse/View-Articles/Advising-Lesbian-Gay-Bisexual-and-Transgender-Students-in-Higher-Education.aspx

Project Implicit. (2011). *Education overview.* https://implicit.harvard.edu/implicit/education.html

Pryor, J. T. (2020). Queer advocacy leadership: A queer leadership model for higher education. *Journal of Leadership Education, 19*(1), 69–83. https://journalofleadershiped.org/wp-content/uploads/2020/01/19_1_Pryor.pdf

Russell, G. M. (2011). Motives of heterosexual allies in collective action for equality. *Journal of Social Issues, 67*(2), 376–393. https://doi.org/10.1111/j.1540-4560.2011.01703.x

Ryan, M., Broad, K. L., Walsh, C. F., & Nutter, K. L. (2013). Professional allies: The storying of allies to LGBTQ students on a college campus. *Journal of Homosexuality, 60*(1), 83–104. https://doi.org/10.1080/00918369.2013.735942

Self, C. (2007). Advising lesbian, gay, bisexual, and transgender first-year students. In M. S. Hunter, B. McCalla-Wriggins, & E. R. White (Eds.), *Academic advising: New insights for teaching and learning in the first year* (pp. 213–221). National Resource Center for the First-Year Experience and Students in Transition.

Smith, B. (2006). *Working more effectively in advising: Understanding multicultural dimensions of gay, lesbian, bisexual, and transgender identities.* NACADA Clearinghouse of Academic Advising Resources. http://www.nacada.ksu.edu/Resources/Clearinghouse/View-Articles/Advising-LGBTQ-students.aspx

Torres, V., Howard-Hamilton, M. F., & Cooper, D. L. (2003). Identity development of diverse populations: Implications for teaching and administration in higher education. *ASHE-ERIC Higher Education Report, 29*(6), 1–141. https://files.eric.ed.gov/fulltext/ED479151.pdf

Washington, J., & Evans, N. J. (1991). Becoming an ally. In N. J. Evans & V. A. Wall (Eds.), *Beyond tolerance: Gays, lesbians and bisexuals on campus* (pp. 195–204). American Association for Counseling and Development.

Waters, R. (2010). Understanding allyhood as a developmental process. *About Campus, 15*(5), 2–8. https://doi.org/10.1002/abc.20035

Worthen, M. G. (2011). College student experiences with an LGBTQ ally training program: A mixed methods study at a university in the southern United States. *Journal of LGBT Youth, 8*(4), 332–377. https://doi.org/10.1080/19361653.2011.608024

Worthington, R. L., Savoy, H. B., Dillon, F. R., & Vernaglia, E. R. (2002). Heterosexual identity development: A multidimensional model of individual and social identity. *The Counseling Psychologist, 30*(4), 496–531. https://doi.org/10.1177%2F0011000002030004002

Young, M. E. (2016). *Learning the art of helping.* Pearson.

17

CREATING AN LGBTQA+-INCLUSIVE CAMPUS

Casey Self and Natalie Oliner

A s LGBTQA+ students select, matriculate, persist, and graduate from colleges and universities, it is critical for institutions and academic advisors to create an inclusive environment that allows LGBTQA+ students to feel a sense of belonging on campus. LGBTQA+ students investigating college possibilities can easily conduct online searches for information related to campus climate and services. This can include websites that rank the most gay-friendly campuses, such as the Campus Pride Index, as well as web pages identifying campus or community LGBTQA+ resources. Some institutions are more open than others when providing these online resources, but the availability of local and international LGBTQA+ resources is only a click away for most students. Academic advisors and other campus professionals should conduct their own online searches for their institution and local community to be aware of the information visible and available to LGBTQA+ students and their families. Conducting such searches provides an opportunity to address gaps in resources or messages the institution wishes to promote.

Some students entering college campuses today are self-aware and not hesitant to hide their sexual or gender identity, and these students likely expect campuses to provide LGBTQA+-specific services. These services allow the campus community to reach out to students in a similar manner to other underrepresented student groups to promote relevant resources. Family members also have expectations regarding campus support services for LGBTQA+ students. Therefore, academic advisors should be prepared to answer student and family questions about campus- and community-specific LGBTQA+ resources, or at least know where to find resources to share with students and family members. Furthermore, while many students are arriving on campus "out and proud," it is critical for higher education professionals to not assume most students are self-aware and "out" LGBTQA+ community members. The college years remain a critical time for students to explore their sexual and/or gender identities. As LGBTQA+ students are exposed to a variety of perspectives and opinions related to sexual and gender identity, they will need support in navigating and coping with the range of emotions they and their non-LGBTQA+ peers will experience.

While advisors should be aware of the circumstances and issues unique to LGBTQA+ students, advisors should not assume these students only need guidance regarding LGBTQA+ issues. General college concerns and resources for all students are still critically important regardless of the student's sexual or gender identity. Matters such as appropriate major selection, career goals, financial aid and scholarship support, and housing arrangements are all examples of concerns LGBTQA+ students might have. As student diversity increases on college campuses, it is important to consider students' intersecting identities and subsequent needs, including age, ethnic and racial identity, socioeconomic status, religious affiliation, nationality, and more. Since many campuses are now offering online academic programs, advisors and other academic professionals should also be familiar with issues and resources related to supporting online LGBTQA+ students as they work to complete their education remotely from the traditional campus setting.

In the following section, we provide examples of ways institutions can create inclusive environments for LGBTQA+ students through campus functional areas, policies, practices, professional development opportunities, curriculum, cocurricular activities, marketing, and student resources. We conclude with a discussion of specific methods academic advisors can use to support LGBTQA+ students and contribute to an inclusive environment, including a list of LGBTQA+ resources for students, advisors, and other higher education professionals.

Action Items for Creating an Inclusive Campus

Colleges and universities should take proactive measures to promote a strong LGBTQA+ community and make campus services available to students. The following examples demonstrate actions institutions can take to create an LGBTQA+-inclusive campus.

Recruiting/Admissions

Colleges and universities participate in numerous recruiting events, marketing their academic programs and campus life through printed materials, social media, and online resources. Inclusion of the LGBTQA+ campus community in recruiting events and marketing materials helps new students and families identify the campus as welcoming and inclusive. Examples may include photographs of students attending community events that display visible LGBTQA+ symbols, such as rainbow buttons, pink or lavender triangle stickers, and transgender-inclusive symbols. Some institutions have updated admissions applications to allow students to self-identify as members of the LGBTQA+ community, which helps institutions identify and communicate with students who may be interested in LGBTQA+ support services and community activities. Institutions should also be aware of how online campus rating systems (e.g., Campus Pride Index) present their campus. An online search of "gay-friendly" or "LGTBQA+-friendly" campuses will provide details on how rating agencies include, evaluate, and perceive the institution. Campuses wishing to improve their overall marketing and advertising approaches to LGBTQA+ students and families can review the Human Rights Campaign's (n.d.b) "LGBTQ Marketing and Advertising: Best Practices" resource.

Campus Policies and Procedures

Institutions should routinely review policies and procedures to ensure all faculty members, staff members, and students have access to benefits and campus resources that are inclusive of LGBTQA+ individuals and their families. These policies and procedures can include protection against discrimination, health-care benefits, partner and family benefits, and identification cards. We also recommend reviewing the Campus Pride's (n.d.) "LGBTQ Policy Inclusion" list within any institution's profile page to examine specific areas the Campus Pride Index uses to evaluate LGBTQA+-friendly campuses. When publishing and promoting information about policies and procedures, institutions should use inclusive language that accurately reflects the campus' practices.

Campus Mission and Diversity Statements

Acknowledging and directly stating campus support of LGBTQA+ students can make students feel welcomed and included and may influence the campus climate and community perceptions toward LGBTQA+ individuals (Gackowski, 2017). Having this exposure to pro-LGBTQA+ messaging can also influence students and campus professions to have less biased attitudes toward diverse gender and sexual orientation identities (Chonody et al., 2013). Many institutions publish diversity, equity, and inclusion statements on their websites and in other documents while also linking to programs, policies, and resources for diverse populations. Specifically mentioning LGBTQA+ issues, sexual orientation, and/or gender identity in these statements (e.g., Ithaca College's [n.d.] and Tufts University's [n.d.] diversity and inclusion statements) or highlighting LGBTQA+ resources on the institution's mission and diversity statement web pages (e.g., Murray State University Office of Institutional Diversity, Equity and Access [n.d.] and Emory University [n.d.]) is paramount to establishing a campus climate supportive of LGBTQA+ students, faculty members, and staff members.

Student Records Changes

Universities and colleges should allow students to update campus records to reflect their appropriate names, gender pronouns, and gender identity indicators. Examples of items which could reflect this personal information include class rosters, email addresses, campus directories, and student identification cards. As one example, Arizona State University Student and Cultural Engagement (n.d.) provides a Web resource for students who wish to change the displayed name on their records, make legal name and gender marker changes, and/or notify instructors about their name and pronouns through an email template.

Institution Web Pages

Individuals and offices responsible for campus web page search features should regularly evaluate which, if any, campus LGBTQA+ services and community indicators appear when conducting a general search of the institution's website. Students and family members must be able to easily navigate and locate appropriate LGBTQA+ resources; therefore, Web designers should strategically and prominently place each resource on the website or specific web page. Formatting issues on different devices (e.g., phones, tablets) may cause certain information to disappear or be relocated. For example, if a web page includes a rainbow logo at the top of the computer screen, the logo may not automatically format correctly on the mobile version. Therefore, Web designers should carefully review each platform to ensure consistent LGBTQA+ visibility and inclusiveness.

First-Year Student Orientation and Welcome Week Activities

First impressions are critical. When first-year students visit campus in the early stages of their college journey, the institution should make the LGBTQA+ community visible and available. New student orientation programs and welcome week activities are valuable contexts in which to demonstrate the institution's LGBTQA+ support resources, clubs, and organizations. Orientation and welcome week marketing materials should highlight LGBTQA+ resources and events as prominently as other support services and events, making them immediately visible to all new students and family members. Specific LGBTQA+ welcome events that highlight resources and promote LGBTQA+ community opportunities can include an open house or meet and greet at the LGBTQA+ center or social parties and celebrations hosted by LGBTQA+ organizations on campus.

Social and Academic Clubs and Organizations

Campus promotion of LGBTQA+ social and academic groups on any published or online resources referencing campus clubs and organizations should be standard practice. This can help students easily identify opportunities to become involved and assist faculty and staff members in locating resources for students when making referrals. In addition to providing community for the LGBTQA+ student population as well as its subgroups (e.g., specific organizations for transgender, asexual, bisexual/pansexual students, etc.), institutions should also offer LGBTQA+ student clubs/organizations that support students' intersecting identities and academic disciplines. The University of Michigan's Student Life (n.d.), for example, offers student groups for Jewish LGBTQA+ students, queer students of color, and specific subpopulations within the LGBTQA+ community, including political activists and students who are studying science, technology, engineering, and mathematics (STEM); business; dentistry; law; medicine; public policy; social work; and so on.

Additional LGBTQA+ Student Programming

Dedicated LGBTQA+ programming can provide academic and social opportunities for students of all sexual orientations, gender identities, and other backgrounds to interact and meaningfully engage with one another, which can create a more welcoming campus environment and possibly improve campus perceptions of LGBTQA+ individuals. Mere exposure to or contact with LGBTQA+ individuals has been cited as a predictor of positive attitudes toward the LGBTQA+ community (Goldstein & Davis, 2010). This holds true even within athletic and Greek life communities, which have historically been perceived as less welcoming to LGBTQA+ individuals (Worthen, 2014). Common student programming can include awareness initiatives such as LGBTQA+ Pride Month, Day of Silence, and Trans Inclusion as well as formal professional development on topics including allyship, LGBTQA+

101 (also sometimes called Queer 101), pronouns, social justice, and more. We recommend reviewing the University of Nebraska-Lincoln LGBTQA+ Center's (n.d.) presentation and workshops for some examples.

Gender-Inclusive Restrooms Maps

One of higher education's common and most immediately recognizable examples of binary gender practices is restrooms. When possible, institutions should create gender-inclusive (or "gender-neutral") restrooms on campus. Creating and providing a map identifying locations of gender-inclusive restrooms across campus will assist students in feeling safer and more comfortable as they visit different campus buildings. Some transgender, nonbinary, and gender nonconforming students as well as other individuals in the LGBTQA+ community, may be more comfortable using single-stall, gender-inclusive restrooms rather than larger, public options to avoid harassment or violence. If gender-inclusive restrooms are not an option, providing signage such as "transgender-friendly restroom" can be helpful to LGBTQA+ students. However, campus professionals should be mindful that simply including a sign on a restroom that accommodates multiple people still poses a risk for LGBTQA+ students, as harassment can occur despite the institution's stated support.

Safe Zone Programs

A common strategy to promote an LGBTQA+-friendly campus is to create a Safe Zone workshop in which interested campus community members can learn more about the LGBTQA+ community and resources to support LGBTQA+ individuals. Many such programs offer a small sign or symbol to display on backpacks, apparel, or in offices to indicate the owner's support of LGBTQA+ students. Safe Zone participation could be a common expectation outlined in academic advisor professional development activities. Educational materials for those looking to create programs or use in place of formal campus professional development sessions are available through the Gay, Lesbian and Straight Education Network (GLSEN) (n.d.) and The Safe Zone Project (n.d.).

Peer and Faculty/Staff Member Mentor Programs

Some higher education institutions have created LGBTQA+ student mentoring programs to offer one-on-one support from peers, faculty members, and/or staff members. Program mentors should participate in inclusivity professional development opportunities, including LGBTQA+-focused sessions or Safe

Zone instructional sessions. The University of Southern California LGBT Resource Center (n.d.) created an exemplary peer mentoring program in which LGBTQA+ mentors can guide, challenge, and support students who are exploring their identity and/or seeking community in a confidential space.

LGBTQA+-Friendly Curriculum

All students should have access to curriculum and class options inclusive of LGBTQA+ information. Faculty members and instructors should review course materials and strive to be inclusive of LGBTQA+ materials and information, as they should for any other underrepresented group. Institutions may also wish to provide a list of courses taught which are inclusive of or focused on LGBTQA+ content across all academic programs. Many institutions have developed majors, minors, and certificates related to LGBTQA+ studies. The University of Louisville LGBT Center (n.d.), for example, offers an LGBT Health Certificate that requires medical students to complete modules and simulations to create or improve inclusive practices with LGBTQA+ patients. Regardless of the specific course or program of study, institutions should promote and support LGBTQA+ curriculum along with other academic programs focused on underrepresented or marginalized populations.

Inclusive Residence Hall Living Options

LGBTQA+ students living on campus may experience challenges related to their specific circumstances. Campus housing offices are increasingly offering gender-inclusive living arrangements and resources to better support LGBTQA+ students. For example, the University of California San Diego LGBT Resource Center (n.d.), offers housing for transgender, genderqueer, and gender nonconforming students (i.e., gender-inclusive housing) as well as LGBTQIA+ themed housing. Institutions such as UC San Diego also mandate extensive professional development for residence life staff, which is critical because LGBTQA+ students may need assistance with roommate and floor community issues or with navigating other aspects of their identity while in campus housing. Residence life instructional materials should include such guidance on assisting LGBTQA+ students. Lastly, institutions should consider providing emergency housing for LGBTQA+ students and other students who may be homeless due to family rejection or other adversities.

Financial Aid and Scholarship Services

LGBTQA+ community organizations and donors often make scholarships available specifically to LGBTQA+ students. Organizations such as the

Human Rights Campaign (n.d.c) and Best Colleges (n.d.) have comprehensive resources for national LGBTQA+ student scholarships; however, it is also helpful to incorporate these resources on institutions' websites, especially the web pages of LGBTQA+ centers, financial aid offices, and other locations where scholarship opportunities are advertised or discussed. Institutions may offer campus financial awards and scholarships that honor former or present LGBTQA+ faculty members, staff members, students, or community activists who made meaningful contributions to the college or university. Additionally, institutions should consider financial contingency plans and support for students whose family support, housing, or financial situations may change as they progress through the coming-out process.

Campus Health Resources

LGBTQA+ students, like all college students, use campus health services. Campus health centers can create an environment where LGBTQA+ students feel their identities and health concerns are safe and understood by requiring health-care staff members and medical practitioners to learn about LGBTQA+ students and their unique needs. Health center web pages should also include campus, community, and nationwide information on counseling, medical services, insurance, health wellness, and confidentiality for LGBTQA+ students as well as specific health resources and services for transgender students.

International Students

North American campuses continue to attract large numbers of students from around the world. Some students arrive on campus with a thorough understanding of LGBTQA+ community needs, while others arrive with no previous exposure to LGBTQA+ issues. Campus international student support services should consider providing educational opportunities for students from other countries to learn about the LGBTQA+ community in the United States and promote the value of inclusivity of all students at the institution. The University of Wisconsin-Madison International Student Services (n.d.), for example, offers information on LGBTQA+ culture, visas, and other resources as well as the opportunity to connect with an LGBTQA+-identified individual or community ally.

Graduation Ceremonies

Some campuses offer separate graduation or convocation ceremonies to recognize and congratulate students from diverse populations. The

LGBTQA+ ceremony is commonly known as the Lavender Ceremony. Developed at the University of Michigan, the Lavender Ceremony celebrates the accomplishments, contributions, and culture of LGBTQA+ students. An extensive list of institutions that offer Lavender graduation celebrations can be found on the Human Rights Campaign (n.d.a) website.

Promote National and Local LGBTQA+ Resources

Institutions that are unable to provide many of the services previously mentioned should consider making local and national resources available on campus for students if possible. Smaller campuses and institutions located in rural areas may not have the benefit of providing LGBTQA+ students the support and resources needed on campus. However, educating students about other local, state, national, or international resources can indicate a caring, supportive environment. A list of recommended resources is provided at the end of this chapter.

There are numerous other options for creating an LGBTQA+-friendly campus to meet an institution's needs. To better ensure those needs are addressed, institutions should seek input from the LGBTQA+ community on campus to help identify necessary improvements to policy, practice, and overall campus climate for LGBTQA+ students.

Academic Advisors' Role

Academic advisors provide an opportunity for students to develop a meaningful and supportive relationship with a staff or faculty member on campus. On an interpersonal level, advisors can create a sense of "safety, trust, and confidentiality" with students by building rapport (Vespone, 2016, p. 221). Advisors can also integrate inclusive practices by incorporating their own pronouns in email signatures, displaying LGBTQA+ resources or Safe Zone stickers, or completing other actions that clearly denote to students that the advisor is welcoming of all identities. Demonstrating inclusivity can encourage students to share their aspirations, achievements, challenges, or personal concerns with an advisor. Disclosing their identity to an advisor or someone in an environment they perceive to be safe can lead to positive outcomes such as stress reduction for LGBTQA+ students (Legate et al., 2012). This then provides an opportunity for the advisor to validate the student's identity and experiences and offer relevant support. However, LGBTQA+ students may hesitate to disclose their identity if they do not perceive the relationship or environment to be safe.

To create a welcoming relationship and environment, academic advisors should participate in ongoing professional development to learn about diverse student needs. Specific education regarding LGBTQA+ resources and services on campus and in the local community is also helpful in guiding and supporting students. For example, as LGBTQA+ students seek social connections or ways to get involved on campus, advisors can refer them to LGBTQA+ clubs and organizations. Additionally, organizations that are not specifically focused on LGBTQA+ identity but are openly supportive, such as Greek life or religiously affiliated organizations that welcome LGBTQA+ students, are valuable resources to share with advisees. Partnering with campus offices that provide LGBTQA+ resources, support, programming, and events can ensure advisors remain updated on upcoming opportunities.

Advisors may also have opportunities to create welcoming spaces and visible support by personally becoming involved in LGBTQA+ organizations and attending LGBTQA+ events. If an advisor works with student groups (e.g., student organizations, peer mentors, student leaders, etc.) in an advising or mentoring capacity, for example, they can help the student group advocate for a physical safe space (if desired) and develop intentional professional development and programming to incorporate LGBTQA+ identities and experiences for all students, which might encourage other students to be visible allies as well (Rockenbach & Crandall, 2016; Rockenbach et al., 2016).

Furthermore, advisors can review policies and practices within their unit to assess inclusivity and determine if there are any policies or procedures that might disadvantage LGBTQA+ students. For example, if a student wants to change their name, pronouns, or gender identity on their record, is there a process for advisors to ensure the student's personal records are broadly updated on a master list, curriculum sheet, and so on? Advisors might also consider surveying students about their perceptions of the campus climate or their experiences with advising at the institution. While campus-wide climate surveys are important, they usually produce findings outside the scope of advising. Therefore, after considering where advisors have authority and can make changes to practices or the environment, using student feedback might improve student experiences and/or give advisors an idea of how students perceive advising. Depending on the feedback received from students, advisors may need to adopt an advocacy role.

When working with campus-wide committees or engaging with leadership, academic advisors can advocate for LGBTQA+ student needs by recommending changes to policies and practices. While an advisor may not have the authority to change a particular policy or practice, having concrete evidence from one-on-one relationships with students can be powerful when advocating for a more welcoming and inclusive environment. Advisors can be instrumental in implementing these changes within advising units and other areas of student support and success. Advisors should also encourage administrators to push a similar message, which can have a robust and far-reaching impact (Rockenbach & Crandall, 2016).

The reality of the many developmental issues college students may experience only enhances the need to educate academic advisors and the campus community about resources and ways to support LGBTQA+ students as they navigate their campus environment. As administrators take steps to actively include LGBTQA+ students in policies, practices, curricula, and programming, and as advisors educate themselves on LGBTQA+ identities, experiences, and resources to better support and advocate for LGBTQA+ students, higher education institutions can create more welcoming and inclusive campuses.

LGBTQA+ Resources

- The Asexual Visibility & Education Network: https://www.asexuality.org/
- Bisexual Resource Center: http://biresource.org
- Campus Pride Index: http://www.campusprideindex.org
- Consortium of Higher Education LGBT Campus Professionals: https://www.lgbtcampus.org/
- Gay & Lesbian Alliance Against Defamation: https://www.glaad.org
- Gay, Lesbian & Straight Education Network: https://www.glsen.org
- Human Rights Campaign*: http://www.hrc.org
  (*Note: While this organization has helpful indexes, databases, and resources for the LGBTQA+ community and educational institutions, we recognize and condemn the organization's problematic and harmful history of transphobia.)
- Lavender Graduation Ceremonies: https://www.hrc.org/resources/lavender-graduation
- LGBTQA+ College Scholarships Guides:
  - Best Colleges: https://www.bestcolleges.com/financial-aid/lgbtq-scholarships/
  - Fast Web: https://www.fastweb.com/college-scholarships/articles/lgbtq-community-scholarships-internships
- LGBTQA+ Student Resources & Support: https://www.accreditedschoolsonline.org/resources/lgbtq-student-support/
- LGBTQA+ Symbols: https://algbtical.org/2A%20SYMBOLS.htm

- National Center for Transgender Equality: https://transequality.org
- The Safe Zone Project: https://thesafezoneproject.com/
- The Trevor Project: https://www.thetrevorproject.org

References

Arizona State University Student and Cultural Engagement (n.d.). *Trans specific resources.* https://eoss.asu.edu/student-andcultural-engagement/out-at-asu/transgender-resources

Best Colleges. (n.d.). *College scholarships for LGBTQ+ students.* https://www.bestcolleges.com/financial-aid/lgbtq-scholarships/

Campus Pride. (n.d.). *Campus Pride Index.* https://www.campusprideindex.org/search/index

Chonody, J., Woodford, M. R., Smith, S., & Silverschanz, P. (2013). Christian social work students' attitudes toward lesbians and gay men: Religious teachings, religiosity, and contact. *Journal of Religion & Spirituality in Social Work: Social Thought, 32*(3), 211–226. https://psycnet.apa.org/doi/10.1080/15426432.2013.801730

Emory University. (n.d.). *Diversity.* https://www.emory.edu/home/life/diversity.html

Gackowski, I. (2017). *Perceptions of campus climate for lesbian, gay, and bisexual students at a religious college* (UMI No. 10616822) [Doctoral dissertation, Roosevelt University]. ProQuest Dissertations and Theses.

Gay, Lesbian & Straight Education Network. (n.d.). *Programs: GLSEN safe space kit.* https://www.glsen.org/activity/glsen-safe-space-kit-be-ally-lgbtq-youth

Goldstein, S. B., & Davis, D. S. (2010). Heterosexual allies: A descriptive profile. *Equity & Excellence in Education, 43*(4), 478-494. https://doi.org/10.1080/10665684.2010.505464

Human Rights Campaign. (n.d.a). *Lavender graduation.* https://www.hrc.org/resources/lavender-graduation

Human Rights Campaign. (n.d.b). *LGBTQ marketing and advertising: Best practices.* https://www.hrc.org/resources/lgbt-marketing-and-advertising-best-practices

Human Rights Campaign. (n.d.c). *LGBTQ student scholarship database.* https://www.hrc.org/resources/scholarship-database

Ithaca College. (n.d.). *Diversity statement and goals.* https://www.ithaca.edu/diversity/statement/

Legate, N., Ryan, R. M., & Weinstein, N. (2012). Is coming out always a "good thing"? Exploring the relations of autonomy support, outness, and wellness for lesbian, gay, and bisexual individuals. *Social Psychological and Personality Science, 3*(2), 145–152. https://doi.org/10.1177/1948550611411929

LGBT Resource Center. (n.d.). *LGBT peer mentoring program.* University of Southern California. https://lgbtrc.usc.edu/mentoring/

Murray State University Office of Institutional Diversity, Equity and Access. (n.d.). *Our office.* https://www.murraystate.edu/headermenu/administration/OfficeOfInstitutionalDiversityEquityandAccess/index.aspx

Rockenbach, A. N., & Crandall, R. E. (2016). Faith and LGBTQ inclusion: Navigating the complexities of the campus spiritual climate in Christian higher education. *Christian Higher Education, 15*(1–2), 62–71. https://doi.org/10.1080 /15363759.2015.1106355

Rockenbach, A. N., Lo, M. A., & Mayhew, M. J. (2016). How LGBT college students perceive and engage the campus religious and spiritual climate. *Journal of Homosexuality, 64*(4), 488–508. https://doi.org/10.1080/00918369.2016.1191239

The Safe Zone Project. (n.d.). *Curriculum.* https://thesafezoneproject.com/curriculum/

Self, C. (2007). Advising lesbian, gay, bisexual and transgender first-year students. In M. S. Hunter, B. McCalla-Wriggins, & E. R. White (Eds.), *Academic advising: New insights for teaching and learning in the first year* (pp. 213–221). National Resource Center for the First-Year Experience and Students in Transition.

Student and Cultural Engagement (n.d.). *Trans specific resources.* Arizona State University. https://eoss.asu.edu/student-and-cultural-engagement/out-at-asu/transgender-resources

Tufts University. (n.d.). *Diversity and inclusion.* https://www.tufts.edu/strategic-themes/diversity-and-inclusion

University of California-San Diego LGBT Resource Center. (n.d.). *On campus housing.* https://lgbt.ucsd.edu/resources/on-campus-housing.html

University of Louisville LGBT Center. (n.d.). *LGBTQ+ affirming healthcare series.* https://louisville.edu/lgbt/hsc/lgbtq_affirming_healthcare_series

University of Michigan Student Life (n.d.). *LGBTQ student groups at U-M.* University of Michigan. https://studentlife.umich.edu/article/lgbtq-student-groups-u-m

University of Nebraska-Lincoln LGBTQA+ Center. (n.d.). *Resources: Presentations & workshops.* https://lgbtqa.unl.edu/presentations-and-workshops

University of Wisconsin-Madison International Student Services. (n.d.). *LGBTQ.* https://iss.wisc.edu/resources/lgbtq/

Vespone, B. M. (2016). Integrating identities: Facilitating a support group for LGBTQ students on a Christian college campus. *Christian Higher Education, 15*(4), 215-229. https://doi.org/10.1080/15363759.2016.1186250

Worthen, M. G. F. (2014). Blaming the jocks and the greeks? Exploring collegiate athletes' and fraternity/sorority members' attitudes toward LGBT individuals. *Journal of College Student Development, 55*(2), 168–195. https://doi.org/10.1353/ csd.2014.0020

EDITORS AND CONTRIBUTORS

Editors

Craig M. McGill (he/him/his) is an assistant professor for the Department of Special Education, Counseling and Student Affairs at Kansas State University. Prior to completing a 2-year post-doctoral research fellowship at the University of South Dakota, he was an academic advisor at the University of Nebraska-Lincoln and Florida International University. He holds masters degrees in both music theory from the University of Nebraska-Lincoln and academic advising from Kansas State University; he also holds a doctorate from Florida International University in adult education and human resource development. Dr. McGill serves on the editorial boards for the *NACADA Journal, Journal of the First-Year Experience & Students in Transition, New Horizons in Adult Education and Human Resource Development*, and *Journal of Women and Gender in Higher Education*. Dr. McGill is a qualitative researcher with an emphasis on identity (personal, professional, and organizational). His research agenda is focused on social justice and the professionalization of academic advising, and he has also published articles within the fields of musical theatre studies and queer studies. He has given almost 60 advising-related presentations at NACADA state, regional, annual, and international conferences. His publication record consists of two coedited books and over 20 peer-reviewed articles.

Jennifer E. Joslin (she/her/hers/their/theirs) works at Drury University as associate vice president for Academic Affairs and director of the Robert and Mary Cox Compass Center. She is a former NACADA president and current NACADA consultant. She is coeditor of the academic advising edition of *New Directions in Higher Education* with Wendy G. Troxel (Wiley, 2018); *The New Advisor Guidebook* with Pat Folsom and Frank Yoder (Jossey-Bass, 2015); and *Academic Advising Administration* with Nancy L. Markee (NACADA, 2011), among other publications. Dr. Joslin helped envision and globally implement the NACADA eTutorial modules for professional development of advisors and administrators with George Steele and Elisa Shafer. Dr. Joslin has been an out lesbian since earning her undergraduate degree at

Occidental College. She is a former chair of the NACADA LGBTQ Advising and Advocacy Advising Community and a former chair of The University of Iowa LGBTQ Staff and Faculty Association (where she earned her masters and doctorate). She is wife to Kathy Davis, mom to Melissa, Anthony, and Truman, and a proud member of the Jane Austen Society of North America. She lives on land belonging to Kickapoo, Osage, and Sioux peoples.

Contributors

Christy Carlson (she/her/hers) is an academic advisor/team lead at Trent University's Peterborough campus in Peterborough, Ontario. She holds a bachelors degree in English (Toronto), a masters degree in English (McMaster), and a masters degree in Academic Advising (Kansas State). Carlson's primary areas of interest are theory, philosophy, history of advising, social justice, and advisor training and development. She has served as a long-standing member of the steering committee for the NACADA Theory, Philosophy, and History of Advising Community and has presented on topics related to queer theory and feminist philosophy. Her previous publications include a book chapter on the cultural politics of queer online fan production (O'Riordan & Phillips, 2007).

Editors' Note: We are deeply saddened that Christy, our friend and colleague, passed away during the final stages of this book. We are grateful for her friendship and her rich contribution to this volume. We honor her legacy to the practice and scholarship of academic advising.

erin-donahoe-rankin (she/her/hers) is currently the director of advising for the College of Visual Arts and Design at the University of North Texas. She was previously the director of students for the Utah State University-Tooele Regional Campus. She discovered her passion for academic advising during her undergraduate studies as a nontraditional, single parent student at Utah Valley University. There she earned degrees in Interdisciplinary Studies-History and Religious Studies and Philosophy. While advising across multiple departments and programs at UVU, donahoe-rankin completed her masters degree in Academic Advising from Kansas State University in 2012. She coordinated internships for many programs, including advising internships, and taught philosophy (ethics). A member of NACADA since 2007, donahoe-rankin has served as a Region 10 Conference cochair, Liberal Arts Advising Community chair, and Steering Committee representative in the

Advising Communities Division. She is an ELP mentor and Region 7 representative on the Membership Recruitment and Retention Committee.

Heather Doyle (she/her/hers) holds a bachelors degree in Psychology from University of Prince Edward Island and masters degree in Counselling Psychology from Memorial University. She serves as director of Assessment and Special Projects at Dalhousie University. She also works as a sessional lecturer at Florida Atlantic University and University of Manitoba, teaching the online Appreciative Advising course, Advising Essentials, and Assessment in Advising courses respectively. Doyle has presented and published in Canada, the United States, and Africa in the areas of academic advising, career advising, appreciative advising, social justice in advising, advising assessment, and student success.

Ryan Fette (he/him/his) is the Education and Outreach coordinator in the Office of Institutional Equity and Compliance at the University of Nebraska–Lincoln. Fette has earned a bachelors degree in International Studies and a masters degree in Educational Administration. Before working in education and outreach, he worked as a Title IX investigator and as an assistant director for student conduct. Fette served as a program coordinator for student conduct at the University of Arizona. His research interest has been campus climate for LGBTQA+ students, and he coauthored *Perceptions of Campus Climate by Sexual Minorities* with Pat A. Tetreault, Peter C. Meidlinger, and Debra A. Hope (*Journal of Homosexuality*, 2013). His areas of professional expertise are student conduct and sexual misconduct on college campuses. He served on the boards of the LGBTQ+ Alliance Fund of the Community Foundation for Southern Arizona in Tucson, AZ, and Out Nebraska (formerly OutLinc), in Lincoln, NE.

Josh Fletcher (he/him/his) is the director of advising, outreach, and math placement for the Department of Mathematics, Statistics, and Computer Science at the University of Illinois at Chicago. In the position, he academically advises students, oversees the math placement process, and coordinates outreach initiatives for the department. Previously, he held positions at the University of Georgia as the senior coordinator of the LGBT Resource Center and at the University of Louisville as an honors academic advisor. He holds an MS in Student Affairs in Higher Education (SAHE) from Miami University and a BS in Communication from the University of Evansville. His past experiences as a Division I springboard diver helped to solidify his interest in researching and creating spaces of support for marginalized subcommunities. In addition to his work in higher education, he also owns and operates JFDA Choreography in Chicago, IL.

Jennifer M. Gess (she/her/hers), PhD, LMHC, LCPC, is clinical training director for the Family Institute at Northwestern University. Dr. Gess is currently pursuing her certification in sex education and sex therapy through the American Association of Sexuality Educators, Counselors, and Therapists. As a licensed counselor in Washington State and Idaho, Dr. Gess has worked as an affirmative counselor with queer, trans, and gender expansive young people for the past 10 years. She has several publications and dozens of local, regional, and national presentations on topics related to social and sexual justice with and on behalf of queer, trans, and gender expansive people. Additionally, Dr. Gess started the Idaho Association of LGBT Issues in Counseling in 2015. She lives with her wife and two dogs in the Pacific Northwest.

Ashley Glenn (she/her/hers) is a first-generation, queer advisor who serves as director of Outreach and Orientation within the Academic Advising Center at the University of Utah. In this role, she works with exploring students in identifying pathways for academic exploration and navigating their personal journey of learning. She was awarded the NACADA Outstanding New Advisor Award in 2017, and she is the current chair of the Liberal Arts Advising Community. Glenn earned her undergraduate degree in English and history from Charleston Southern University before completing her masters degree in history, with an emphasis in colonialism and imperialism, from the University of Utah. Her research on the deep-rooted impacts of colonialism has informed her work across higher education—coordinating programs in a LGBTQA+ Resource Center, teaching career exploration and first-year seminar courses, advising for study abroad and international education, and now working with early college and undecided/exploratory student populations.

Cody Harrison (he/him) is the director of Academic Support at the Knoxville location of Lincoln Memorial University's DeBusk College of Osteopathic Medicine. Harrison earned a masters in College Student Personnel Administration from James Madison University. He served on the NACADA Steering Committee for the LGBTQA Advising and Advocacy Community from 2018 to 2020 and was published in *Academic Advising Today*'s December 2019 issue.

Jessica L. Henault (she/her/hers) serves as Kansas State University's first-ever sexual and relationship violence prevention specialist. She holds a bachelors degree in Cultural Anthropology, a masters degree in Counseling and

Student Development, as well as an Academic Advising Graduate Certificate and is a certified victim advocate. Prior to serving as the prevention specialist, she worked as a graduate research assistant for the NACADA: The Global Community for Academic Advising's Executive Office, and for the Academic Achievement Center at K-State. Henault's previous publications include a case study titled, "Complications with FERPA" in *Maybe I Should . . . Case Studies on Ethics for Student Affairs Professionals* (University Press of America, 2019), and a scholarly article titled, "The Thriving Culture of Trans* Oppression Across College Campuses" in the *National Association of Student Personnel Administrators Knowledge Community Annual Publication* (NASPA, 2019). Her areas of expertise focus on how students' positionality, interaction with their physical and sociocultural environments, and power dynamics influence the levels and lasting impacts of oppression and victimization on college campuses.

Kyle Inselman (he/him/his) is an assistant director of Career and Professional Development and an instructor at the University of Denver. He is also a writer and speaker focusing on trans inclusion and gender in work and higher education, with over 10 years of experience in facilitating trainings to a variety of student and professional audiences. He is the 2021–2022 president of the Collegiate Career Services Association of Colorado and Wyoming, and he is the cochair of the Committee on Diversity Initiatives and Cultural Inclusion for the National Career Development Association. He holds an MEd in Educational Leadership and Policy from the University of Utah, a BA in Linguistics, a BFA in Film Studies, and a certificate in LGBT Studies from the University of Colorado Boulder.

Michael M. Kocet (he/him/his) is professor and department chair of the Counselor Education Department at The Chicago School of Professional Psychology. He earned his PhD in Counselor Education from the University of Arkansas. He is a licensed mental health counselor, Board Certified Counselor, Approved Clinical Supervisor, and Fellow of the American Counseling Association. He is editor of *Counseling Gay Men, Adolescents, and Boys: A Guide for Helping Professionals and Educators* (Routledge, 2014). He is past president of the Society for Sexual, Affectional, Intersex, and Gender Expansive Identities (SAIGE). His professional interests include ethical and legal issues in counseling; LGBTQA+ issues; grief counseling; and culinary therapy. Dr. Kocet provides pro bono counseling at the Center on Halsted, an LGBTQ community center in Chicago. Dr. Kocet's work on culinary therapy, which uses cooking as a therapeutic tool, has been featured on CNN, *The Washington Post, Eating Well Magazine*, and other publications.

kristen a. langellier, (she/her/hers) PhD, NCC, is an assistant professor of Counseling at the University of South Dakota. She is a dedicated counselor and educator who seeks to further social justice efforts within counselor education through scholarship and activism. Her research interests revolve around the intersections of counseling and feminism, social justice, racial justice, fat studies, classism, and advocacy. dr. langellier has been a passionate advocate for the rights of LGBTQA+ individuals since her teens and is proud to contribute a chapter to this book. A native Illinoisan and a lifelong learner, dr. langellier has moved around the country to pursue education and be of service to the counseling profession. When not on campus, dr. langellier can be found restoring old furniture, spending time with her partner and children, and riding her bicycle.

Mary Ann Lucero (she/her/hers) is the associate director for the Academic Advancement Center at Colorado State University. Prior to her current position, she spent over a decade supporting student success initiatives. Lucero is a practitioner whose focus is on addressing the underpinnings of racism in education, deconstructing and reimaging student success, and examining the invisible influences and underlying assumptions of minoritized communities within education. She earned her masters degree in educational leadership and policy studies from University of Northern Colorado, and she is currently a doctoral student at Colorado State University, in the School of Education, Higher Education Leadership program.

Maximillian Matthews (all gender pronouns respectfully) is based in Durham, North Carolina, and has been working in higher education for over 10 years. Previous roles have been in academic advising, enrollment management, learning support, and recruitment. Matthews is a graduate of Elon University and North Carolina State University. Matthews's writings have been featured on platforms such as Black Youth Project and Rethinking Schools. A firm believer in abolition, Matthews envisions a world without white supremacy, patriarchy, misogyny, capitalism, imperialism, ableism, and every -ism that results in oppression of any kind.

Carolyn Meeker (she/her/hers) is an assistant director for Career and Talent Development at Florida International University (FIU) in Miami. She also serves as the 2020–2022 chair for the NASPA Student Career Development Knowledge Community and as the CARAS mentoring program director for the Community-Academic Consortium for Research on Alternative Sexualities. Prior to FIU, Dr. Meeker worked as a resident director at the University of California, Riverside, and at Binghamton University (SUNY).

Dr. Meeker has an AA in Humanities from College of the Canyons; a BA in Spanish; an MEd in Counseling in Student Affairs from the University of California, Los Angeles; and an EdD in Adult Education and Human Resource Development from FIU. Her work and research interests include career and professional development; identity, feminism, and BDSM; and allyship and (in)civility in the workplace.

Donna J. Menke (she/her/hers) is currently the area director of advising at Mid-Plains Community College. Menke earned a doctorate in Counseling and Student Development through Kansas State University. She has published articles in the *NACADA Journal* and the *Journal for the Study of Sports and Athletes in Education* among others. She is the author of *College Athletes and Their Transition Out of Sport* (Peter Lang, 2020).

Fabiola Mora (she/her/hers) serves as the director of the Academic Advancement Center at Colorado State University. She is currently pursuing a doctorate degree in Higher Education Leadership through Colorado State University. For the last 10 years, she has worked with and advocated for students who are minoritized by race, class, ability, citizenship, and first-generation status in higher education at the local, state, and national level. Mora has served in a myriad of functional areas including financial aid, multicultural services, advising, access and retention, TRIO, and first-year experience programs. She approaches her work through a critical, intersectional lens toward the goals of equity, justice, and liberation. Her interests include examining systems of power, privilege, and oppression that perpetuate violence on students who have been historically marginalized in higher education. Throughout her career, she has conducted research, presented at national conferences, and served as a keynote speaker on topics related to equity and social justice. Lastly, Mora's liberatory work is and will remain deeply rooted in amor.

Natalie Oliner (she/her/hers) is the assistant director of Retention and Assessment in the Office of Student Success at the University of Louisville J. B. Speed School of Engineering, where she has also been an academic counselor since 2014. She earned her bachelors degree in Religious Studies and Sociology from Indiana University, masters degree in Higher Education from the University of Michigan, and is currently working toward her doctorate in Counseling and Personnel Services with a concentration in college student personnel from the University of Louisville. Her current research focuses on underrepresented students' sense of belonging, identity navigation, persistence, resilience, and success in curricular and cocurricular science, technology, engineering, and mathematics (STEM) environments. Other research interests include students with disabilities, religiosity, deviance, and access and equity in higher education.

Meghan Pfeiffer (she/her/hers) is the director of quality enhancement planning, academic coaching, and support services at the University of Memphis. In addition to her work as director, she is an affiliate faculty member in the College of Education and Kemmon's Wilson School of Hospitality and Resort Management. She teaches undergraduate and graduate classes in the Sport and Leisure Management department, including computer applications, athletic administration, and research methods. Dr. Pfeiffer received a bachelors degree in Business Administration from the University of Missouri in 2009, a masters degree in Sport Commerce in 2012, and a doctorate in Higher and Adult Education in 2018, both from the University of Memphis. Her research area concentrates on exploring lesbian, gay, bisexual, transgender, and queer student-athletes' academic and athletic experiences in higher education and creating inclusive environments in college settings.

Kristen Renn is professor of Higher, Adult, and Lifelong Education at Michigan State University and serves as associate dean of Undergraduate Studies for Student Success Research. With a background in student affairs administration, including inaugurating the role of LGBTQ resource provider at Brown University, she has for the last 20 years focused her research on the identities, experiences, and development of minoritized students in higher education. She is co-PI of the National Study of LGBTQ Student Success, a two-phase study of LGBTQ college students comprising a mixed-methods survey/interview phase and a 4-year longitudinal interview study conducted with LGBTQ students.

Wendy Kay Schindler (she/her/hers) has 15+ years of experience as an academic advising and first-year experience professional and is currently the coordinator for TRIO Student Support Services at Northern Kentucky University. She earned her masters degree in Higher Education Administration from Saint Louis University in 2005. Schindler serves on the NACADA Council as an advising communities division representative (2020–2022) and is a former chairperson of the NACADA LGBTQA Advising and Advocacy Community (2014–2016). She is an experienced conference presenter, speaking on topics such as LGBTQA+ allyhood, intersectionality, and fat liberation from her position as a white, cisgender woman who is fat, queer, able-bodied, middle-class, U.S. citizen by birth, and brain tumor survivor. Schindler and her husband live in northern Kentucky (across the river from Cincinnati) with their rescue cats. She is a knitter and crafter, punk/goth enthusiast, gamer (video, board, and card), singer, cheese lover, and social justice warrior.

Casey Self (he/his/him) is the senior director of academic advising for The College of Liberal Arts and Sciences at Arizona State University. Self became a NACADA member in 1996. In 2000, he was elected LGBTA Concerns Commission chair. Casey was elected to the NACADA Board of Directors for the 2006–2009 term, and while on the board, served as vice president for 2007–2008, and NACADA President for 2008–2009. Current NACADA involvement includes the Consultant and Speaker Service and a fellow for the Excellence in Academic Advising program. Self was given The Bobbie Flaherty Service to NACADA Award in 2019 and the NACADA Leading Light Award in 2011. He earned his bachelors degree in Speech Communication at the University of Northern Colorado in 1986 and completed his masters degree in College Student Personnel Administration at Western Illinois University in 1990. Self is an ASU sports fan and enjoys traveling with his husband Doug.

Richard A. Sprott (he/him/his) received his PhD in Developmental Psychology from UC Berkeley in 1994. As a researcher, he has examined the relationship between professional identity development and the development of professional ethics in medical doctors, ministers, and teachers, as well as professional identity development in emerging fields of work. He is president-elect of the Society for the Psychology of Sexual Orientation and Gender Diversity (APA Division 44). All these efforts highlight the ways in which stigma, prejudice, minority dynamics, health, language, identity development, and community development all intersect and affect each other.

Sarah E. Stevens (she/her/hers) is the director of the Honors Program and Living Learning Communities at the University of Southern Indiana, where she was previously a director of advising. She is also a faculty member in gender studies. Stevens has a doctorate in Chinese from Indiana University, Bloomington. Stevens loves cats, chocolate, and coffee, and spends her free time making chain maille jewelry, painting, playing board games, and writing fantasy and science fiction. Check out the first book of her series, *Dark Moon Wolf* (The Wild Rose Press, 2017), if you like feminist werewolves. She's a geek, a social justice warrior, and a special snowflake.

Pat Tetreault (she/any), PhD, is director of the LGBTQA+ and Women's Centers at UNL. Tetreault is a member of ACPA and the Consortium for

LGBT Resource Professionals in Higher Education, serves on numerous committees, and is a representative on the Chancellor's Commissions for the Status of Women and Gender & Sexual Identities. Tetreault has received numerous awards over the years, including ACPA's Research Recognition Award, the Commitment to Social Justice Education Award (LGBTQA+ Center), the LGBT Public Service Award, the Chancellor's Fulfilling the Dream Award, Contributions to the Status of Women, and Outstanding Contributions to the GLBT Community. Recent publications include *Perceptions of Campus Climate* (*Journal of Homosexuality, 2013*); the Nebraska section in *Proud Heritage: People, Issues, and Documents of the LGBT Experience* (ABC-CLIO, 2014, Vol. 3); and is coauthor of a chapter on Religious Freedom Restoration Acts in *LGBT Americans at Risk* (Praeger, 2018). Tetreault is a social justice advocate, a consultant, and has presented at regional, national, and international conferences.

Ashley A. Thomas (she/her/hers) has served as a primary-role advisor since 2008 beginning at Allen Community College in Iola, KS, and transitioning to the College of Business at Kansas State University. During this time, she was highly involved in both college and university-level work, including spending 3 years as the cochair of the Faculty Senate Professional Staff Affairs Committee. Following an 11-year advising career, Thomas joined the NACADA executive office team in May 2019 as assistant director of Resources and managing editor for scholarly publications. She holds a bachelors degree in Agriculture: Animal Science from Kansas State University, a masters degree in Community Counseling from Fort Hays State University and is pursuing a doctorate in Counseling and Student Development through the College of Education at Kansas State University. Wife to Willie Thomas, a 10-year combat veteran, and mother to two amazing children, Bailey (15) and Dante (5), Thomas enjoys spending quality time with her family, traveling, and exercising.

Janie Valdés (she/her/hers) is assistant vice president for Enrollment Management and Services (EMS) at Florida International University (FIU). In this role, Dr. Valdés develops strategies to improve the transfer student experience, end-to-end. This highly collaborative work has resulted in significant improvements in AA transfer-in rates, retention and completion rates, and percentage of transfer students graduating without excess credits. Together with her dedicated team, Dr. Valdés implemented best practices around course equivalencies and student engagement. She has also evolved Connect4Success, a nationally recognized transfer pathway for state/community college students. Her lifelong career in higher education blends her passion for students with her experience in organizational development to meet one overarching goal: to positively impact student access and success. Dr. Valdés received a BA in Psychology from FIU, an MS in Industrial/Organizational Psychology from FIU, and an EdD in Human and Organizational Learning from The George Washington University.

Aurélio Manuel Valente (he/him/él) has 25 years of experience in student affairs and currently serves as the vice president for student affairs and dean of students at National Louis University. Supporting LGBTQA+ students has been a consistent thread of his work in student affairs. He has served as a student organization advisor, advanced LGBTQA+ inclusive policies and practices, and given presentations focusing on LGBTQA+ student services. Dr. Valente's research interests are at the nexus of academic and student affairs, with a focus on institutional efforts to promote student engagement and academic success. He has published articles in the *Journal of College and Character* and served as a contributing chapter author for three editions of *The Handbook of Student Affairs Administration* (Jossey-Bass, 2009, 2016, anticipated 2023). Most recently, Valente has led multiple grants addressing equity gaps in student success and is currently working on initiatives to address student poverty as a barrier to degree attainment.

Gisela P. Vega (she/her/they/them) serves as the director for the LGBTQ Student Center at the University of Miami. Previously she served as the inaugural LGBTQ professional at Florida International University (FIU) for their LGBTQIA Initiatives Program, the first of its kind in any South Florida college or university. At FIU she also served as an adjunct professor with the Center for Women's and Gender studies, assisting in the establishment of the Queer Studies Certificate program. Her research areas include: gender, sexuality, social justice and global human rights issues, sexual minorities in higher education, and mentoring marginalized populations. In 2019, the National LGBTQ Task Force's prestigious Eddy McIntyre Community Service Award was bestowed upon her. She holds her doctorate in Higher Education Leadership from Florida International University, a masters degree in Education Instructional Leadership, a bachelors of fine arts in Art Education as well as a bachelor of fine arts in Graphic Design from the University of Illinois at Chicago. She has worked in higher education for more than 28 years.

C. J. (CJ) Venable (they/them/their) is a candidate for the PhD in Cultural Foundations at Kent State University. Living on land belonging to Indigenous Sioux and Pawnee peoples, Venable's research and writing falls into three key areas: critical whiteness studies, cultural politics of emotion, and trans people in higher education. Their work is informed by their position as a fat, white-settler, U.S. American, mostly-abled, middle class, queer, and gender-queer scholar-practitioner. They also serve as the training and professional development specialist for University Advising at the University of Nebraska-Lincoln. They earned their MA in College Student Personnel from Bowling Green State University and BAs in Mathematics and Secondary Education from Webster University. Venable currently chairs the NACADA Theory, History, and Philosophy of Advising Community (2019–2021). Outside of higher education, they can be found cooking or baking, playing late-90s video games, or learning Baroque music for the alto recorder.

Leonor L. Wangensteen (she/her/ella) has been an academic advisor at the University of Notre Dame and a member of NACADA since 2013. She earned a BA in Spanish Literature and Fine Arts and an MA in Iberian and Latin American Studies from Notre Dame. In addition to advising first-year students, she has played a lead role in establishing institutionalized support and campus awareness for the undocumented and DACA recipient student community. Her research and praxis in undocumented student advising has led to national leadership opportunities, including ongoing building of the NACADA Clearinghouse resources site called Working with Undocumented, Dreamer, and Immigrant Students. Her NACADA 2017 article "Building Undocumented Student Support in Higher Education through a Culturally-Responsive Lens" served as the anchor reading for a spring 2018 NACADA Reads. She has given numerous presentations and workshops in NACADA conferences and helped develop and teach NACADA UndocuAdvising etu-torials. She is currently coauthoring a book chapter focused on intercultural competence advisor training which will be published in the upcoming book, *Comprehensive Advisor Training & Development: Practices That Deliver, 3rd Edition* (Stylus and NACADA, anticipated release 2022).

204–210; mentors, 205–213;
organizations, 207–210, 213;
professional development,
209–210; questions to ask,
213–214; reflective practice,
210, 214; role models, 205–213;
stereotype threats, 199–200,
204–208, 213; support for,
199–214; vignette, 202–204
Stonewall Riots, 1
storytelling, 26–27, 96–117,
193–194, 280–285
stress: disorders, 118, 124–126;
mental health, 118–137;
minority stress, 33, 95–99,
103, 118–126, 160–164;
post-traumatic stress disorder,
124–126
Strong Interest Inventory, 98, 100
student orientation, 294–295
student records changes, 294
student-athletes: advising, 183–198;
athletic identity, 184, 188–195;
campus climates, 183–198;
campus policies, 191–194;
intersectional considerations,
188–195; research, 194–196;
support for, 183–198; vignette,
188–191

terminology, 5–6, 34, 47–50, 73,
172, 222–224, 265. *See also*
pronoun usage
theoretical foundations, 4, 6–7,
11–76
theory of performativity, 49–58, 235
trans students: advising, 215–228,
245–262; of color, 245–262;
completion narratives, 79–88;
graduation rates, 80–84;

resilience support, 215–228;
retention narratives, 79–88;
success for, 84–85; support for,
40–41, 199–228; umbrella of,
216, 264, 269–270, 274. *See also*
LGBTQA+
TransAthlete, 192
Trevor Project, 238
TrevorLifeline, 238
TRIO programs, 99
tropes: resilience support, 215–228;
resisting, 215–228; structural
barriers, 217–218, 222–223;
trans-as-tragic trope, 217–224
Trump administration, 224, 233

undifferentiated gender, 18
United Nations, 2, 239
Universal Declaration of Human
Rights, 239
U.S. Citizen and Immigration
Services, 237
U.S. Supreme Court, 89, 92,
142–143

validation theory, 246, 253

Ward v. Polite, 142
white supremacy, 62, 68, 218,
245–246, 250–253
Women's Sports Foundation, 192
work environments, 90–93,
98–104, 112, 116
workplace discrimination, 89–92,
96–104, 170
workplace relationships, 90–92,
100–101
World Health Organization, 239

You Can Play Project, 192

Trans* Policies & Experiences in Housing & Residence Life

Edited by Jason C. Garvey, Stephanie H. Chang, Z Nicolazzo, and Rex Jackson

Foreword by Kathleen G. Kerr

"As a resource for practitioners, educators, and students, this book does important work in examining the pervasiveness of binaried gender norms in higher education, and the ways those norms shape institutions and policies. Its aim is not to serve as a guide for enacting trans*-supportive policies but, instead, as a collection of moments when such policies came to be, and a consideration of why those policies mattered to the institutions and *all* of their students. The chapters' emphases on context and personal reflection reinforce that such policies are ongoing and essential, and that ever-shifting understandings of gender demand equally dynamic and responsive efforts to support trans* students."—*Teachers College Record*

Men & Masculinities

Theoretical Foundations and Promising Practices for Supporting College Men's Development

Edited by Daniel Tillapaugh and Brian L. McGowan

Foreword by Ryan P. Barone

Afterword by Tracy Davis

"Tillapaugh and McGowan have compiled an essential resource for everyone who works with college men, from the newest faculty member or student affairs professional to the experienced veteran. Starting with a history of masculinities studies within college student development, they introduce new voices that challenge us to examine our assumptions with an intersectional lens. Perhaps most useful is their practical advice for creating campus coalitions and taking our work into the future."—*Jan Deeds, PhD, Director, University of Nebraska-Lincoln Women's Center*

Also available from Stylus

Trans*in College

Transgender Students' Strategies for Navigating Campus Life and the Institutional Politics of Inclusion

Z Nicolazzo

Foreword by Kristen A. Renn

Afterword by Stephen John Quaye

"Dr. Z Nicolazzo's first book, *Trans*in College* is a beautifully written, rigorous, and masterful insight into the lives of nine trans* collegians at City University [a pseudonym] and how postsecondary educators can do better to support the education, resilience practices, and life chances for trans* collegians. Through the use of critical theoretical frameworks and methodologies that begin from the experiences and needs of the participants, Nicolazzo also demonstrates new possibilities for both the doing and reporting of research in higher education. As a scholar, I look forward to sharing this book with future graduate students as an example of how we can proliferate possibilities through and for scholarship. As a trans* parent of a trans* child, I am unspeakably grateful to the nine trans* collegians who have collaborated with Nicolazzo to create together this beautiful reflection of us."—**D-L Stewart**, *Professor, School of Education and Cocoordinator, Student Affairs in Higher Education Unit, Colorado State University*

22883 Quicksilver Drive
Sterling, VA 20166-2102

Subscribe to our alerts: www.Styluspub.com

NACADA The Global Association for Academic Advising

NACADA is a global association of professional advisors, counselors, faculty, administrators, and students working to enhance the educational development of students.

NACADA promotes and supports quality academic advising in higher education institutions to enhance the educational development of students. NACADA provides a forum for discussion, debate, and the exchange of ideas pertaining to academic advising through numerous activities and publications. NACADA also serves as an advocate for effective academic advising by providing a Consulting and Speaker Service, an Awards Program, and funding for Research related to academic advising.

NACADA evolved from the first National Conference on Academic Advising in 1977 and has over 12,000 members in over 30 countries around the world. Members represent higher education institutions across the spectrum of Carnegie classifications and include professional advisors/counselors, faculty, administrators, and peer advisors whose responsibilities include academic advising.

NACADA functions with volunteer leadership with support from the NACADA Executive Office and the Executive Director. Members have full voting rights and elect the global Board of Directors as well as other leadership positions within the association. NACADA is designated by the IRS as a 501(c)3 non-profit educational association incorporated in Kansas.

Diversity

NACADA: The Global Community for Academic Advising values and promotes inclusive practices within the association and the advising profession. NACADA provides opportunities for professional development, networking, and leadership for our diverse membership and fosters involvement and engagement across identity groups, geographic regions, and professional levels. NACADA promotes the principle of equity and respects the diversity of academic advising professionals across the vast array of intersections of identity, which includes but is not limited to age cohort, institutional type, employment role, location, nationality, socioeconomic status, faith, religion, ethnicity, ability/disability, gender identity, gender expression, and/or sexual orientation.

nacada.ksu.edu

NACADA: The Global Community for Academic Advising
2323 Anderson Avenue, Suite 225
Manhattan, KS 66502
Phone: 785-532-5717